Rowan
University

The
Domosh
Collection

A Gift

JUBAL EARLY'S
RAID ON WASHINGTON
1864

JUBAL EARLY'S
RAID ON WASHINGTON
1864

by

Benjamin Franklin Cooling

The Nautical & Aviation Publishing Company of America
Baltimore, Maryland

Published by The Nautical & Aviation Publishing Company of America, Inc., 101 W. Read Street, Suite 314, Baltimore, Maryland 21201.

Library of Congress Catalog Card Number: 89-60483

ISBN: 0-933852-86-X

Printed in the United States of America

Dustjacket photograph: Courtesy of The National Park Service

Library of Congress Cataloging In Publication Data

Cooling, B. Franklin.
    Jubal Early's raid on Washington in 1864.

    Includes bibliographical references.
    1. Fort Stevens (Washington, D.C.)—History—
19th century.   2. Maryland Campaign, 1864 (June-August)
3. Washington (D.C.)—History—Civil War, 1861-1865—
Campaigns.   4. Early, Jubal Anderson, 1816-1894.
5. United States—History—Civil War, 1861-1865—
Campaigns.   I. Title.
E476.66.C85   1989   973.7.37   89-60483
ISBN: 0-933852-86-X

To the memory of my parents who raised me within view of the Civil War forts of Washington and to Paul Sedgwick, Chairman of the District of Columbia Civil War Centennial Commission, 1961–1965, who provided me with my first job in Civil War history.

Contents

✕

Acknowledgments

I T is never easy to thank all of the kind people who assist in a project of this type. Colonel Thomas A. Ware (USA Ret.) of Alexandria, Virginia, and Peter Seaborg, proprietor of the Rock Creek Bookshop in Washington, D.C., took time to read and comment on the text. Walton Owen of Alexandria, and my co-author for *Mr. Lincoln's Forts*, helped with photographic support. Ron Van Sickle graciously permitted xeroxing at his well-appointed Gaithersburg, Maryland bookstore. David Smith, National Park Service interpreter at Fort Stevens, provided materials from his files, as did private individuals such as Lieutenant Colonel Joseph Whitehorne (USA Ret.), Kim Holien, and Kevin Ruffner. Dr. Richard Sauers of Harrisburg, Pennsylvania, led me to the wonderful *National Tribune* veterans' material at the U.S. Army Military History Institute, Carlisle Barracks, Pennsylvania. Staff members there, such as Louisa Arnold, John Klonaker, Dennis Vetock, David Keough, Michael Winey, and Randy Hackenburg, as well as Dr. Richard J. Sommers, provided their customary courteous and helpful service. Special gratitude must be extended to retired Texas A&M University president and Civil War/ Southern scholar, Dr. Frank Vandiver who provided a copy of the Lucius C. Chittenden manuscript mentioned in this volume. Finally, I would be remiss if I did not mention the patience and help of my wife Mary Anne, who not only suffered through my countless manuscript revisions, self-doubts, and tramps to the historic sites, but also mastered the word-processing and typing chores on various occasions.

Preface

THE subject of this book is Jubal Early's campaign against Washington — the last Confederate invasion in 1864. The war was in its fourth summer. Victory for the United States was by no means assured against its rebellious southern states. The administration of President Abraham Lincoln stood perilously close to losing the scheduled autumn elections. Rebel armies still ranged unvanquished across the South.

General Robert E. Lee's Army of Northern Virginia seemed as invincible as ever, while its counterpart, the Army of Tennessee under General Joseph E. Johnston, feinted and dodged its way back through north Georgia, attempting to shield the invaluable railroad center of Atlanta. Other Confederate forces in the Mississippi Valley, and beyond, fought on tenaciously in near isolation against the ever-strengthening forces of the army and the navy of the United States. Above all, a sense of stagnation pervaded the war — fairly begging for some bold stroke by one side or the other to break the stalemate.

At this moment the Confederacy launched perhaps its boldest move of the war. An army of approximately 20,000 men moved to threaten or capture the national capital of Washington, D.C. Commanded by the colorful, unpredictable, and dangerous Jubal Anderson Early, the gray-clad Confederates came closer to taking the city and scattering the Lincoln government than at any other time during the war. Even the president himself was threatened with possible death or capture when the tall, stark figure of the chief executive actually came under fire at Fort Stevens in Washington, D.C.

Yet the tale of Old Jube's raid has other fascinating themes. The two sharp battles of Monocacy and Fort Stevens highlighted the campaign. True, they did not result in the huge casualty lists of Antietam, Gettysburg, or Shiloh. However, they arguably overshadowed those bloody battles in terms of political-military significance. They alone could have led directly to the capture of the nation's capital — in this critical year of the war. It was during the hot summer of 1864 that war-weariness threatened to sap the willpower of the northern people, disrupt the nation's financial markets, and cause the citizenry to demand a negotiated peace with their rebellious countrymen. Capture of Washington would have tipped the scales of war in that direction.

The story centers on a crusty, bachelor general bearing the unlikely name of Jubal, and his band of daring rebels who scared the blue blazes out of soldiers and government officials alike in Washington. It is a saga of the eleventh hour reprieve by reinforcements drawn from General Grant's veteran armies deployed one hundred miles to the south before the Confederate capital at Richmond. It is a spectacle of the only battle ever fought within the limits of the District of Columbia. And it excites the imagination as to the many possible consequences of a southern victory.

How close a thing it truly proved to be: Confederates who were a scant five miles from the capitol dome, thwarted as much by climactic conditions as any Yankee forces; Abraham Lincoln, who escaped death or injury from sharpshooters' bullets by a few feet or inches; and a botched Confederate scheme to free thousands of their comrades held prisoner at a Union prison compound on the lower Potomac, all these lent additional suspense to the story. This same raiding force brushed the suburbs of an equally terrorized Baltimore City, but stopped to enjoy the delicacies of a captured ice cream wagon in the simmering July heat. Then, too, there was the Horatian epic stand of Lew Wallace (later the author of the famous novel, *Ben Hur*) holding the Monocacy bridges to delay the onrushing Confederates a full day, and so helping the Federals win the race to save or capture the capital.

Early's invasion north of the Potomac has been traditionally viewed as the preliminary event leading to the more exotic autumn campaign in the Shenandoah Valley—the first phase of military operations which ended all hope of Confederate possession of that scenic granary. But conversely the battles between Early and Philip H. Sheridan in September and October may also be viewed as the culmination of a four-year struggle to capture or protect Washington. Monocacy and Fort Stevens effectively ended the Confederacy's last hope for winning that prize and thus quite possibly the war.

As always in history, the story must ultimately remain one of humanity. Profane and talented Jubal Early, tragically cast to don the mantle of the noble, but fallen, Stonewall Jackson, led the Army of the Valley in its last great action. Even in defeat, Early shined in contrast to the middling Union generals sent to bring him to bay. Of course, Early was the chosen instrument of a strategic gamble by his leader Robert E. Lee. They stand silhouetted against the laggard and nearly fatal Union response of General Ulysses S. Grant. Other military and political figures enter and leave the stage at will, and we see more pivotal participation in the events of the time by unknowns. These characters include railroad president John W. Garrett, the politically influential Blair family, and even the commander-in-chief of the army and navy, Abraham Lincoln. Along the way, common folk flesh out the chronicle whether they were civilians or men in blue and gray. A Free Black woman, Elizabeth "Aunt Betty" Thomas, added to the legend of a president under enemy fire by claiming that indeed she had shouted "get down, you fool" to Lincoln that day at Fort Stevens.

Naturally, historical events become vivid only when we can link them to our own life and times. Monocacy, Fort Stevens, and the cemeteries which hold their dead are only meaningful when we visit them as national shrines. They were preserved through the patriotic efforts of postwar veterans and public-spirited citizens. In a sense, the presence of Washington as we know it today is tribute enough to the rows of graves marking Battleground National Cemetery in D.C. or Mount Olivet Cemetery in Frederick, Maryland.

Publication of this volume completes my trilogy on the defense of Washington during the Civil War. *Symbol, Sword, and Shield: Defending Washington During the Civil War*, published in 1975, addressed the history of protecting the city as reflected in overall policy and operations in the eastern theater. *Mr. Lincoln's Forts: A Guide to the Civil War Defenses of Washington*, co-authored with Walton B. Owen in 1988, provided a more intimate study of individual forts and their role in the formal defense system. The present work focuses on the principal military threat to the city during the war, best remembered as Early's Raid in July 1864. Research materials for all three volumes have been gathered in one public repository—the Library of the Fort Ward Museum and Historic Site, administered by the city of Alexandria, Virginia. Many of the fort sites and portions of Monocacy and Fort Stevens battlefields are open to the public, as are the cemeteries holding remains of the participants in these actions. Hopefully, when enjoyed together, these volumes, on-site visitation, and reflection upon the historical events, will provide a better understanding of Washington's defense during the Civil War.

B. Franklin Cooling
Washington, D.C.
July 11–12, 1989

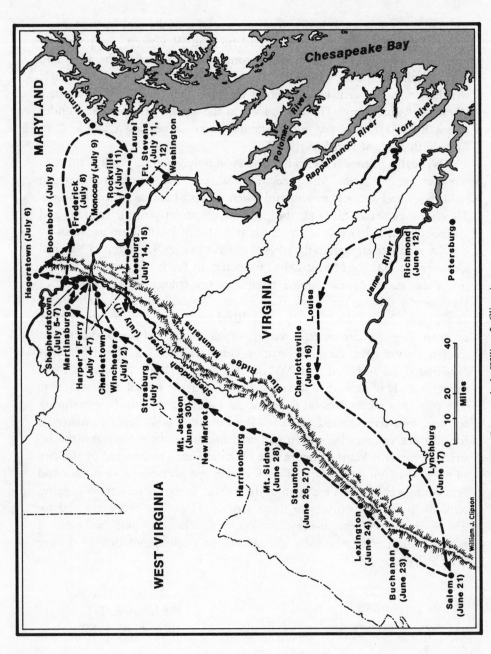

Jubal Early's Raid, June 12–July 18, 1864. (Cartography by William J. Clipson)

Chapter One

⚹

TAKING RISKS IN VIRGINIA

THE Army of the Potomac began to file out of its Cold Harbor, Virginia lines after dark on June 12, 1864, turning south for the James River. The men in blue had received a terrible blow only the week before. Seven thousand had fallen dead or wounded before Confederate lines at Cold Harbor. It was an assault which Lieutenant General Ulysses S. Grant would regret the rest of his life. All told, some 54,000 of his men had been lost in eastern battles since the onset of the campaign in May. The Wilderness, Spotsylvania, and Cold Harbor were names etched in blood; they sent shudders across the north for their huge casualty lists and meager return. Young Edgar S. Dudley, a lieutenant with the 2d United States Artillery, later noted that about this time he had traveled to Washington on a boat with its cabins and decks piled high with wounded and "not a bit of space that could be occupied was vacant." People wondered where it would all end.[1]

"Butcher" Grant (as he was now called) knew precisely where he intended it to end. If it took large casualties to achieve the destruction of the Confederacy, then so be it. To defeat Robert E. Lee's vaunted Army of Northern Virginia and to capture Richmond had been the twin goals of other leaders before Grant. But this mild-mannered yet tenacious Midwesterner was bent on victory this time. So, that soft June night, the veteran soldiers of the Army of the Potomac once more moved out to accomplish the elusive

1

goal. Earlier skepticism about their commander dissipated as they marched ever closer to the Confederate capital. "Butcher" Grant, they thought, was not a man to retreat.

Major Eugene Blackford of the 5th Alabama, Confederate States Army, wrote to his sister after Spotsylvania expressing this same sentiment. "Grant is the most obstinate fighter we have ever met," he noted. Grant was resolved to lose every man rather than retreat, for retreat "is equivalent to our independence." The Alabamian claimed that the Federal commander gave his men whiskey before every fight and sent them out to meet their death "in a furious state of intoxification" and with $50 bounty money in their pockets to engage "in one of their reckless charges on our works." Can you conceive of the "avarice of a people who will receive money to undertake such work in such a cause," Blackford questioned. Avarice or not, Grant certainly resolved not to return to the banks of the Potomac without total victory. Every mile closer to Richmond meant even greater hardships for his adversary. Union losses might actually exceed Lee's total available fighting strength, but the dogged Grant was determined to plod onward. Worse still for the shrinking Confederacy, blue-clad armies ranged widely all the way from Virginia to Georgia and beyond the Mississippi River.[2]

"Sam" Grant (as he had been known before the war) had come east in March 1864 to accept President Abraham Lincoln's invitation to command all the armies of the Union. Moving with Major General George Gordon Meade's Army of the Potomac (to avoid Washington's political intrigues), Grant as general-in-chief already had a grand strategic plan in mind. Writing to Meade from Culpeper Court House, Virginia, on April 9, Grant said that insofar as possible, he wanted all Union armies to move together and toward one common center. The bulk of the western armies under Major General William Tecumseh Sherman were to aim at General Joseph E. Johnston's Confederate Army of Tennessee protecting Atlanta and the heart of Georgia. Elsewhere, Massachusetts politician-soldier, Major General Nathaniel Banks was to relinquish his movements in the trans-Mississippi sector in favor of a campaign toward Mobile, Alabama, which would support Sherman's attempt to "secure the line from Chattanooga to Mobile." Closer to Meade in the east, however, lay an equally ripe target, and one essential to Lee's operations around Richmond—the beautiful and agriculturally rich Shenandoah Valley. It had eluded Union occupation for most of the war, and Grant wanted it taken. So troops under marginally competent major generals like Franz Sigel and David Hunter received that assignment. As for Meade's Army of the Potomac, Grant stated bluntly: "Lee's Army will be your objective point. Wherever Lee goes there you will go also."[3]

There were other Union command missions, but they were always in support of this grand design. Naturally, problems arose in implementing the design. As Grant told Major General Benjamin F. Butler (that other arch-politician in uniform), who commanded on the Virginia and North Carolina coast at this time, the necessity for covering Washington with the Army of the Potomac and of "covering your department with your army," made it impossible to unite the two for concerted action against Richmond. This would come later. However, here at the very outset of the campaign, Grant seemed to grasp the central issue for fighting a war in the east. Protection of Washington—"Mr. Lincoln's City," the national capital and symbol of Union, as well as logistical hub for eastern forces—had to take precedence. Yet how to circumvent this issue and better focus his offensive against Lee while protecting Lincoln's Achilles' heel, plagued Grant all the way to Richmond that spring and summer.[4]

Grant simply shelved the problem in his mind at first. After all, the logic behind his scheme for using the Army of the Potomac offensively lay in its power to counter Lee's own ability to move north and threaten Washington. Lincoln and official Washington had heard all this before. Protection of the city had been uppermost in the President's mind since before his inauguration in 1861. He had watched patiently as a succession of Union commanders marched off to conquer Richmond only to suffer catastrophic defeats—thereby leaving Washington vulnerable. He had listened to their promises to leave sufficient protective forces only to find Lee's adroit maneuvers had drawn those reserves away in the heat of battle. First and Second Bull Run (Manassas), Antietam and Gettysburg had all displayed an unswerving Confederate theme—frighten the Lincoln government by threatening the capital, and thwart the Union's plans in the east. Consequently, Grant and Meade had much to prove that spring and summer. Even Grant's predecessor, now his chief-of-staff, Major General Henry W. Halleck, doubted the soundness of the strategy of the 1864 overland campaign. All these factors increased pressure upon the new general-in-chief.[5]

Of course, the value of Washington had changed during the course of the war. No longer merely the political symbol of the Union as it had been in 1861, the city was now a bustling military base and staging area. Located on the malarial banks of the Potomac River, with muddy streets in winter and dusty thoroughfares in summer, it was never imposing as a capital city; in fact, its wilderness look had earned it the appropriate title of "city of magnificent distances." Major public buildings such as the Capitol, the Executive Mansion or White House, the Supreme Court, Patent Office, Navy Yard, and Smithsonian Institution had changed little during the war. Equestrian

The unfinished National Capitol at Washington in 1861. Although reflective of the unfinished character of the still emerging nation, the Capitol was a primary monument in a city torn by civil war but still a symbol of the Union. (National Archives)

statues of presidents George Washington and Andrew Jackson beckoned wartime tourists—the soldiers and hucksters in town. More evident were changes in population swollen from the 1860 census figure of 75,115 (including 3,185 slaves) to more than 200,000 at various times during the war. Both the physical and human dimensions of the city took on a transient, even ramshackle cast. Temporary frame barracks, hospitals, warehouses, and repair facilities stood alongside permanent public buildings. Teamsters, hackers, prostitutes, and charlatans competed with soldiers, politicians, and old-line residents for a place on the still wretched public ways. White tent cities and wagon parks clung to the outskirts and reflected the military capital at its best. Farther out, a vast system of interlocking fortifications and military roads attested to Washington as the assembly point for the full application of military power of a nation determined to suppress rebellion and to protect its capital in the process. In the spring of 1864, Ulysses S. Grant, the new general, may simply not have grasped all of this when he visited the city en route to his new assignment.

Grant, who was determined not to remain at a desk job as general-in-chief but rather to travel with the eastern army, frankly thought that Washington could fend for itself. He knew, even if he had not physically visited the ring of fortifications surrounding the city, that nearly $1 million had been lavished on that construction project. Halleck knew more details. Through engineer briefings, he realized that over 800 field, siege, and seacoast cannon ostensibly bristled from more than 100 earthen forts and batteries, with miles of intervening interconnecting trenches for infantry support. Upwards of 45,000 infantry, artillery, and cavalry were spread out, covering the whole capital region, to deter rebel attack on the capital. As Assistant Adjutant General James Hardie of the Department of Washington reported on March 8, 1864: "The general impression of my mind, produced by observations of the last seven days, is that the city is provided against attack with a system of fortifications calculated to inspire confidence as to the result."[6] This was surely the message that Halleck conveyed to Grant when the Army of the Potomac moved southward from its winter encampments that spring.

The situation changed drastically only upon receipt of Meade's staggering battle casualty figures as the campaign progressed. Where could replacements be found for those casualties? Casting about, the Union high command discovered the flush Washington garrisons. The 2d Pennsylvania Heavy Artillery, numbering 1,800 men, served as an example. Grant had quickly added that unit to the Army of the Potomac in March. Other units of this type promised a likely replacement pool for the eastern army.[7]

Regimental Officers of the 2d Pennsylvania Heavy Artillery at Fort Lincoln, Military Defenses of Washington. In July 1864, these heavy artillerists were sent to the field armies leaving Washington, D.C. virtually defenseless. (Library of Congress)

Major General Henry Wager Halleck, chief of staff to the general-in-chief of all Union Armies, was most directly involved with planning and coordinating efforts to contain Jubal Early's 1864 raid. (U.S. Army Military History Institute)

The flood gates opened from that point on. As the War Department enjoined northern governors to raise more recruits, Washington's garrisons supplied the immediate reinforcements for Meade's army. Many of the troops were being wasted anyway as road and bridge guards, messengers, or roving patrols. Partisan chieftain, Lieutenant Colonel John Mosby, seemed to be the sole Confederate disturbing the peace near the capital. So, by June 7, Halleck could report that he had stripped 48,265 replacements from the Department of Washington rolls and shipped them to the Army of the Potomac. Major General Ambrose E. Burnside's venerable IX corps was rebuilt largely from such replacements. It seemed a simple task to draw down Washington's protective screen to about 33,000 men by the time of Cold Harbor. No matter that engineers like Major General John Gross Barnard (who had designed the fort system early in the war) protested that barely one-third that number actually manned the earthworks. Government officials, such as Halleck and Secretary of War Edwin M. Stanton, thought limited duty Veteran Reserve Corps, convalescents, and 100-day limited service volunteers (raised by northern governors), might work the heavy ordnance and stand guard until Grant and Meade could dispatch a relief column from the Army of the Potomac in time of need.[8]

Grant knew the risk. He had wired Halleck in April that he intended no wholesale withdrawal of garrisons from around Washington. He agreed that even Major General Lew Wallace at Baltimore might retain heavy artillerists for forts guarding that city. Yet the nature of attritional warfare in Virginia became insidious. Grant needed more men and guns; it was Halleck's job to find them. At times, "Old Brains," as Halleck was called, could deliver olympian views on the subject of Washington's protection, and he often advanced the notion that the least threatened sector east of the Anacostia River might be abandoned entirely. The eleven forts in this part of the line could supply men for Grant and Meade. Yet they were not given up, for those forts shielded the Navy Yard and Capitol Hill against imagined rebel thrusts from southern Maryland. So, Halleck and the War Department sought replacements at random from all over the defenses, thereby weakening the whole rather than a particular sector.[9]

Hence, Washington appeared safe and Grant got more men. Even President Lincoln allowed the military to go their own way on the matter. He was tired of haggling over the city's safety. Grant, Halleck, and Meade seemed to be a capable team, and larger issues and other problems loomed in an election year. By late May and early June, with Lee pressed back close to his own capital, surely Grant and Meade could make better use of the men in

the garrisons; Lincoln did not badger them on the issue. It may have been
at this point that the two generals lost sight of that nagging question of
Washington's safety. In fact, they may have had little choice but to proceed
with the bloody offensives. Fighting it out on this line if it took all summer
was a key part of Grant's thinking. Ironically, it was at that precise point that
Grant's wily opponent plotted some risk-taking of his own. Lee's risks involved the Union's traditional point of weakness in the east—Washington.

General Robert Edward Lee—scion of one of Virginia's first families,
southern gentleman and professional soldier—was considered a traitor by the
Lincoln government because he had resigned his commission in the United
States Army to side with his state in her secession. He was not a man to
permit the enemy to seize and hold the initiative against him. He had directed
the course of events in the east for two years. Now, in 1864, he chafed
inwardly that fate had awarded Grant the upper hand. Lee searched for a way
to regain the initiative. If Federal losses were huge, the Confederacy's own
casualties were even costlier to Lee's frontline strength. Replacements were
as difficult to find in the south as in the north. Dwindling food supplies,
shortages in clothing, medicine, and equipment, and the threat to Lee's breadbasket in the Shenandoah Valley all weighed heavily on him. President Jefferson Davis and the chief executive's principal advisor, General Braxton Bragg,
sought answers from Lee while the Virginian pondered his own limitations.
Gone were the days when the Army of Northern Virginia could make those
brilliant forays north of the Potomac. And yet, some bold counterstroke was
needed to save the valley from Yankee invasion and provide relief from Grant's
relentless strangle-hold on Richmond. As Lee explained to President Davis
on June 11: "I acknowledge the advantage of expelling [the] enemy from the
Valley," but "the only difficulty with me is the means." If hazarding the
defense of Richmond by withdrawal of an army corps seemed the only way
to accomplish these tasks, then Lee was willing to try it. The other alternative
of a direct assault on the Army of the Potomac was too dangerous.[10]

Lee needed some bold move to reverse the Union tide in Virginia. A
plan had been on his mind for some months. His able First Corps commander, Lieutenant General James Longstreet, had written in January from a
detached assignment in East Tennessee, suggesting that, if mounted on
mules, his own troops might team up with Lee's cavalry and make a dash on
Washington. Lee also entertained a proposal by Marylander Bradley T.
Johnson that the latter might rush into the capital with his cavalry and
abduct President Lincoln and then carry him captive to Richmond at the
same time a diversion was created by more rebel cavalry riding on to Canada.

Lieutenant General Jubal Anderson Early, C.S.A. Attempting to capture Washington, D.C., Early led the Second Corps of Stonewall Jackson and the Army of the Valley District on the South's final invasion of the North in July 1864. (U.S. Army Military History Institute)

As whimsical as these notions surely sounded to Lee and the Confederate government, a flicker of appeal could be seen in Lee's own replies to Longstreet and to President Jefferson Davis. Writing to the president from Orange Court House, Virginia, in early February, the army commander thought: "If I could draw Longstreet secretly and rapidly to me I might succeed in forcing Gen. Meade back to Washington, an exciting sufficient apprehension, at least for their own position, to weaken any movement against our [capital]." But nothing came of any of these schemes even after Longstreet returned to the main army that spring. Grant's build-up in central Virginia simply precluded any action. Lee considered a victory on the Rappahannock River line might disrupt Grant's agenda and force a recall to Washington. But Grant kept sideslipping ever closer to Richmond. Now, with his army depleted by battle, only a detached column offered hope by mid-June. Lee looked to newly minted Lieutenant General Jubal Early and his Second Corps for help.[11]

Lee had great confidence in Early. He wrote Davis modestly on June 14: "If the movement of Early meets with your approval, I am sure it is the best that can be made," although he admitted the limited extent of his own knowledge "to perceive what is best." But, "Old Jube," as many called Early, commanded units once led by the redoubtable Thomas Jonathan "Stonewall" Jackson, and more recently by Richard Stoddert Ewell, and they would be returning to scenes of earlier triumph in their beloved Shenandoah Valley. Jackson's Valley Army had spread havoc among its foes there in 1862, and its survivors still spoiled for a fight with the Yankees to protect that sacred spot. Early was a West Pointer, with service in the Seminole and Mexican wars before turning to civilian life as a back-country Virginia lawyer. He had been a unionist before Virginia's secession called him back into uniform—as a Confederate officer. He rose progressively through regimental and division command by hard work and proven pluck on the battlefield.[12]

Old Jube was the very antithesis of a southern gentleman. This forty-seven-year-old, grizzled, and profane bachelor represented yet another south-land at war. Early represented the common folk who also had a stake in the conflict. Like them, Early was independent by nature, pungent and acerbic in tongue, and often irascible under the yoke of military discipline. Some of his people noted his protrusive ears and referred derisively to him as "old lop ear," according to George Mooney of Company H, 5th Virginia. His falsetto country drawl constantly irritated more gentrified staffers like Major Henry Kyd Douglas. Early was no Jackson, though similar to his mentor from up-country. Stonewall had once stated that Early might one day lead 20,000 men comfortably. Yet questions existed about Early's ability to handle independent command, even though Lee really had nobody else to assign to redeem the valley. Both Ewell and Longstreet were temporarily lost to wounds or ill-health. Jubal Anderson Early was selected to threaten and perhaps even capture Washington.[13]

Lee gave Early verbal orders on June 12. First, he was to march to Lynchburg and help Major General John C. Breckinridge ward off a Federal thrust at that valuable rail and manufacturing center. Major General David Hunter's army had been at work destroying war production facilities, storehouses and even civilian property in the Shenandoah. They had torched the famed Virginia Military Institute and Governor John Letcher's home in Lexington. Such blatant violations of the code of civilized warfare inflamed southern hearts. Lee wanted to punish, even destroy, Hunter. Early's force was to be the instrument of that destruction. But Lee's orders contained a second mission. If Grant suddenly became threatening before Richmond and

Petersburg, then Early would have to return to the main army. Lee hoped if circumstances permitted Early to move northward, then he was to cross the Potomac and threaten Maryland and Washington. It had all worked so well before, especially when Jackson lived. It might work again now that Old Jack's pupil commanded the small strike force. Mere destruction of Hunter alone would not cause Grant and Meade to retreat. A definite threat to the nation's capital just might have that effect.[14]

Early accomplished the first phase of his mission within a week. Departing camp before dawn on June 13, he led his nearly 9,000 infantry and artillery westward on hot, dusty roads toward the piedmont. Lieutenant Leonidus Lafayette Polk of the 43d North Carolina wrote his wife that he had personally thought "like Grant, like the whole Yankee nation, and like everybody else I suppose except Genl' Lee and a few others," that the army was destined for a long stay in the Petersburg trenches. He quickly added that to the surprise of everyone they left their camps quietly at 2:00 a.m. that Monday. Secrecy was vital, he said, and so he could not tell his wife their ultimate destination lest Yankee interception of the letter give the army's mission away. General Lee, in fact, had gone to the president to try to muzzle the southern press about Early's expedition, although some mention was made in a Mobile, Alabama paper long after the army had gone north. Still, it was hard to hide a force the size of Early's corps even if one of his staffers claimed, "it was not any army, it was a disorganized rabble." He claimed that divisions were commanded by colonels, brigades by majors, regiments by captains, and companies by sergeants, with many officers actually carrying muskets in the ranks. Strictly speaking this was not true. Still, only one brigadier (Cullen Battle of Alabama) remained in command of the same troops he had left with from the Rapidan six weeks before, and the Second Corps was decidedly a skeleton of its former self as it marched away that June morning.[15]

The force closed on Charlottesville by June 16, and Early immediately set to work organizing transportation to take his men and their equipment to Lynchburg. While awaiting the arrival of rickety rail cars from the Virginia Central Railroad, the general chanced upon some old friends who invited him for a drink at a nearby hotel. Ordnance Chief, Colonel William Allan, later found his commander a bit tipsy but together with other staffers managed to take him to a local professor's house for tea. Early was back at work by nightfall, as sober as ever. He had already wired Breckinridge that his first objective was to destroy Hunter, "and the next it is not prudent to trust to telegraph." He wanted the handsome Kentuckian and former Vice President of the United States to hold out until relief could reach him. Then, threatening to lynch any railroad official who dared impede the army, Early raced his men by train and wagon road to reach the city ahead of Hunter's oncoming legions. By mid-morning of June 17, the Confederates stepped on to the Lynchburg depot and marched out to the feeble earthworks south and west of Lynchburg where they found 11,000 defenders preparing to meet the enemy. Early rode to the lines just as the first blue-clad columns came in sight on the Salem road from the southwest. The feisty Early yelled at a motley group of rebel cavalrymen nonchalantly retiring before the Federals near a Quaker meeting house: "No buttermilk rangers after you now, damn you!"[16]

Old Jube's words, plus the timely arrival of Major General Stephen D. Ramseur's division at that point, blunted the initial Yankee attack. Both sides settled in to wait while their leaders made plans. The next morning dawned and the wait continued, broken intermittently with skirmishing. Hunter later claimed that sounds of troop trains arriving in the city during the night had

Major General David Hunter, U.S.A., friend of Ulysses S. Grant and veteran of many campaigns, whose conduct of war against civilians in the Shenandoah Valley earned him the undying hatred of southerners, including Jubal Early, who was determined to exact retribution. (U.S. Army Military History Institute)

caused his hesitation. The pause cost him the initiative and certainly the battle. Early had no such uncertainty. By noon, he had ordered a sharp assault on the enemy center at the Bedford turnpike. The battle surged back and forth until about 2:00 p.m. Then, noted Hunter, Early proceeded to devote the afternoon "to refreshment and repose, expecting to strike a decisive blow on the following morning." Hunter did not wait. He ordered a retreat under cover of darkness, claiming lack of ammunition. Subordinates like Chief of Artillery, Captain Henry A. DuPont, protested bitterly. Most of the men in the ranks would have welcomed a battle. Days of heavy marching, destroying private property and enjoying the beautiful scenery had taken the edge off their fighting proficiency, but they certainly wanted action. Hunter, however, stole off at night, leaving Early and Breckinridge in possession of the field. The Federals gained some measure of solace, according to one chaplain, for the rebels had hoped to "bag" the whole Yankee army within a few miles of Lynchburg. Instead, he said, "the bird had flown."[17]

Hunter's retreat actually proved more important than his defeat at Lynchburg. Fearing Early's pursuers might block off the valley route, the Federal commander retreated into the West Virginia mountains. Cut off from his supply base on the Potomac, he chose a route through Salem (June 21), Lewisburg (June 26), Charleston (June 30), and thence by river and rail to Parkersburg on the Ohio River. Early's men caught up with the retreating column near Salem, wrecking several batteries of artillery and destroying eight Yankee guns. Early broke off active pursuit when the enemy took to the mountains, leaving one North Carolinian to declare, "they outran any Yankees I ever traveled after." Guerrillas, hunger, fatigue, and demoralization overtook Hunter's men. Chaplain William Walker of the 18th Connecticut called the march one of the most "difficult and dangerous retreats of the war," and recounted marching twenty miles a day under a broiling sun, and "in the face of appalling dangers from starvation and death, for days in succession." Hunter tried to put the disaster in a better light. He wired Washington from Gauley, West Virginia, on June 28, claiming that his expedition had been "extremely successful, inflicting great injury upon the enemy," and suggesting that his army had been victorious in every engagement. Patently untrue, Hunter still proclaimed that his command was in "excellent heart and health," and, with rest, would be ready for further orders.[18]

Hunter was partially correct. His actions prior to Lynchburg had been successful. He had seriously, if not permanently, damaged parts of the Confederacy's breadbasket. He had taken a risk after Lynchburg, one calculated to bring his army back alive rather than risk the chance of its possible destruction in a fighting retreat down the valley. Lee and Early were clearly disappointed that Hunter had escaped. They feared later trouble from him. Yet, as things developed, the Federal line of retreat proved as effective to Confederate plans as if Hunter had been wiped out in battle. Lee wrote the Federal commander after the war that he had been most gratified at the time "that you preferred the route through the mountains to the Ohio," for it had left the Shenandoah Valley open for Early's advance into Maryland. But, writing to President Davis on June 26, 1864, the southern general had been much less confident. "I fear he has not been much punished," Lee noted, "except by the demoralization of his troops and the loss of some artillery." Although he did not realize it, Lee was most assuredly winning the game of risk in Virginia at the time.[19]

Early began his campaign against Washington following the Lynchburg victory. Lee was momentarily paralyzed by Federal pressure at Petersburg culminating in the July 18 offensive which failed to capture that southside town, but effectively immobilized Lee's maneuverability. Thus, Lee had wired Early on June 18 to strike Hunter as quickly as possible so that he could either return to help at Richmond, or carry out the original plan. A week later, a much calmer Lee sent additional orders that since circumstances had changed, Early should press forward with "execution of the first plan." Early was already ahead of Lee, for three days before he had wired his chief stating that since Hunter had taken himself out of the war, even temporarily, he would now proceed "in accordance with original instructions." Still nervous, Lee sent word to Davis asking for his approval even though everyone knew the plan had already been set in motion.[20]

Early's army swung jauntily down the Valley pike, heading north to adventure and victory. They deplored the ruined houses and barns which provided testimony to Hunter's earlier passage. The cavalry kept to back roads so as to avoid congestion on the main highway, and the men began to capture the tone of where they might be headed, and what they hoped to accomplish. As early as June 16, Lieutenant Polk had told his wife that she should not be surprised to hear that they were anywhere from Pennsylvania, Maryland, Ohio "or anywhere else," and suggested that Early's force was on a "sort of independent wild goose chase," with no telling where it might all end. He could say no more, he claimed, for fear his letter might be intercepted by the enemy. Coming to sylvan Botetourt Springs on June 22, Early determined to stop and rest his army at this prewar spa for the rich and famous in the Old Dominion. While his men flirted with local belles at a girl's seminary nearby, Early and his commanders pondered the next move. When

Confederate soldiers endured days of hard marching. Here they are shown marching down Patrick Street in Frederick, Maryland, in September 1862. Two years later, survivors from this battle-worn contingent marched down the same street en route to battles at Monocacy and Fort Stevens. (Frederick Historical Society)

the army left refreshed the next day, his senior officers, at least, knew that the Potomac was their destination. By nightfall of the 23d, the army had crossed the James River, single file over a burned out bridge at Buchanan. Spirits were high, the weather fine, and the countryside exquisite, noted ordnance chief William Allan in his journal. The army of Stonewall Jackson seemed reborn, flush with excitement, anxious to advance once more against the foe. Local cherry orchards along the highway received special attention at the hands of the jubilant and ever hungry young Confederates.[21]

However, before long some of Early's men may have begun to voice doubts. The hot and dusty miles, the blistered feet, and the relentlessly hard highway sapped the spirit. After encamping at Buffalo Springs south of Lexington, Ramseur led a portion of the army off to see one of the state's legendary landmarks, the Natural Bridge. A regimental band serenaded the southerners as they cavorted beneath the archway. Some of Early's young staff rode ahead to visit one of their number's mother's place in Lexington. Sandie Pendleton's boyhood home soon filled with chatter and even Major General

John B. Gordon stopped in to feast on cold ham, lettuce, rice, and fresh raspberries—quite a change from army rations. Mrs. Pendleton told lurid tales of Yankee insults and depredations during Hunter's recent visit.[22]

The main body of Early's army reached Lexington the following day. Officers and men filed slowly past the flower-covered grave of the fallen Jackson, with muskets reversed, in an emotion-charged ceremony. "What hallowed memories the moment evoked for everyone," noted John Worsham of the 21st Virginia. "Many a tear was seen trickling down the cheeks of the veterans," he wrote, for here lay "*the* greatest Christian patriot and soldier . . . the veritable unsurpassed warrior of this age," suggested Tar Heel Brigadier William G. Lewis in a note to his sister. "You have no idea what feelings passed over me," he continued, as he contemplated how the hated Yankees had desecrated the grave several weeks before. Captain H. W. Wingfield of the 58th Virginia echoed that sentiment as he recounted how the Federals had taken the head and foot boards from Jackson's grave. He wondered how the enemy mustered such courage to disturb the general's remains "who while living was such a terror to the Yankee nation."[23]

The soldiers were soon staring sullenly at the ruins of the Virginia Military Institute and Letcher's home. They vowed revenge. Local citizens fueled their animosities by lurid accounts of Federals breaking into private homes, with insults to women, children, and the elderly. Residents soon turned out with food and drink to help the hot and tired soldiers. G. W. Nichols of the 61st Georgia proclaimed Lexington to be one of the prettiest towns in Virginia, noted for good women and pretty girls. "I never saw prettier girls," he recalled, "how I did want a nice suit of clean clothes and permission to stop with them a week or two." Tales of Yankee cruelty mixed with images of good food and fair damsels as the rebel troops moved on from Lexington the following day.[24]

Another day of hard marching brought the army to Staunton, where Early stopped to take stock of his forces. They had experienced what Ramseur termed the hardest marching of the war. Still, he assured his wife that they hoped to relieve Richmond and make "Yankeedom smart in a sore place." Early knew that he needed to rest his footsore soldiers and cull out the spent horses, broken-down wagons, and marginal artillery batteries. The army had covered about two hundred miles in fourteen days. Many of the men had fallen out of ranks from lack of shoes. Their tattered uniforms and sunburned faces told the story every morning at roll call. Sickness dogged their footsteps resulting from marginal diets and rugged campaigning since leaving winter quarters. The army had to stop. It could not embark upon a major offensive without restoring men and equipment.[25]

Early set to work quickly correcting the problems even as his troops filed into campsites around the town. While the soldiers rested, strayed off to visit local relatives or friends, or foraged in the flush orchards and fields, the army commander consulted with key staff members. He learned from his quartermaster, Major John Harmon, and commissary chief, Major Wells J. Hawks, that while army resupply lagged badly, some stores had arrived from Richmond and other eastern distribution points. Local crop production pointed to abundant food supplies for fall and winter, although lack of farm labor would handicap the harvest. A rain shower on June 27 raised everyone's spirits for no moisture had fallen on the area since the third of the month. Still, Early knew that he had to make some changes before pressing on.[26]

Old Jube planned to leave worn-out material at Staunton; he wanted his army to travel with minimal incumbrances. His aide, Sandie Pendleton, drew up an order stripping the wagon train to the barest numbers. One six-horse wagon was allotted corps headquarters, a single four-horse wagon went to each division and brigade headquarters (to include quartermaster and commissary of subsistence), and one four-horse team was permitted every 500 officers and men for their cooking utensils. Otherwise, "regimental and company officers must carry for themselves such under-clothing as they need for the present expedition," Early ordered. Additional gear went into the regimental baggage wagons which would stay in a safe place at Staunton.[27]

Many of Early's officers grumbled about the strict order. Captain Robert E. Park of the 12th Alabama hated to leave behind prized diaries, entrusting them to the keeping "of an unknown and perhaps careless quartermaster and teamster." But Early was adamant and adhered rigidly to his own requirement. When Father James Sheeran of the 14th Louisiana protested "the manner in which you have treated me" several days later at Winchester, Early chuckled and with customary bluntness told the chaplain, ". . . [I] brought with me but one pair of drawers and had to do without them whilst they were being washed." A cumbersome wagon train was the last thing Old Jube wanted on his march northward.[28]

Early also reorganized his army. What should he do about Breckinridge? The forty-three-year-old officer, veteran of Confederate battles both east and west, had accompanied Early's army with his own force from Lynchburg, even after Hunter ceased to be a threat. But he wasn't really assigned a place in the army's structure. Early was unsure just how to best use the Kentuckian's services. Forthwith, Early created a corps command, gave it to Breckinridge and regarded him as second-in-command. When Breckinridge's invalid division commander, Major General Arnold Elzey, proved unable to keep up

Major General John Cabell Breckinridge, C.S.A. This former Vice President of the United States from Kentucky defended the Shenandoah Valley before Early's arrival in 1864 and became deputy commander of the Army of the Valley District during the July campaign. (U.S. Army Military History Institute)

Brigadier General John Echols, C.S.A. Able but uninspiring, this West Virginian rose from regimental command to lead a division during the Washington campaign. (U.S. Army Military History Institute)

with the rigors of the march and asked to be relieved, Early regretfully obliged. Elzey still suffered from an old wound although he was only forty-eight years old. He would return to local defense chores at Richmond, and forty-one-year-old John Echols (another Lynchburg native and valley veteran) would replace him. Indeed, all the troops in this division called the montain region home and had to be closely watched. Sometimes their patriotic ardor lessened once the Confederate army moved beyond their local area of interest.[29]

There was another facet to Breckinridge's assignment. The corps arrangement allowed him to supervise the particularly disruptive troops of Major General John B. Gordon's division. Only a thin veneer of civility hid the almost daily friction between Early and the forty-two-year-old Georgian. Gordon was a fire-eating fighter who disdained many of the qualities of the unpolished Virginian. Moreover, within Gordon's ranks were men like the spirited Louisiana "Tigers" of Harry Hays, Leroy Stafford, and Zebulon York. Early hoped that the steady, even patrician hand of Breckinridge might steady this lot.[30]

Early's other two divisions promised to give less trouble. Handsome Robert Emmett Rodes, aged thirty-five and another VMI and Lynchburg

Major General John Brown Gordon, C.S.A. This brilliant division commander from Georgia successfully broke the back of Union resistance at Monocacy despite heavy losses. Early placed him under Breckinridge during the Washington campaign. (U.S. Army Military History Institute)

Major General Robert Emmett Rodes, C.S.A. This Lynchburg native commanded a division during the Washington campaign and proved to be one of the south's finest soldiers before his death at Third Winchester in September 1864. (U.S. Army Military History Institute)

Major General Stephen Dodson Ramseur, C.S.A. This North Carolinian ably commanded a division under Early until his death at Cedar Creek in October 1864. (North Carolina Department of History and Archives)

son, led one of them. North Carolinian Stephen Dodson Ramseur commanded the other. Ramseur was only twenty-seven, newly married, and expecting news of a first-born. Equally solid was Early's artillery chief, the able thirty-nine-year-old Brigadier General Armistead Long. His nine batteries, organized in two battalions, numbered forty guns (mostly 12-pounder Napoleon smoothbores). They would provide fire support for Early's infantry—backbone of his army. Early's cavalry was another matter. They had performed only marginally earlier in the valley, and Early never understood or trusted their abilities. The mistrust was mutual. As Andrew Hunter of the 17th Virginia Cavalry put it, Early was quite unfit to command a separate army by virtue of his personal habits, "even had he possessed the qualifications." Still, it is important to bear in mind that the mounted arm was composed of free-wheeling souls, their equipment was marginal, and their discipline was still worse. Robert Ransom, a thirty-six-year-old North Carolinian, was entrusted with their assignments. In turn, Ransom's brigade commanders were a mixed and unpredictable group, including Marylander Bradley T. Johnson and Virginians W. L. "Mudwall" Jackson, John D. Imboden, and

Brigadier General Armistead Lindsay Long, C.S.A. Robert E. Lee's military secretary, Long was an authorized postwar biographer who served Early as artillery commander of Second Corps. During the Washington campaign, he was overshadowed by the tactical artillery leadership of Lieutenant Colonel J. Floyd King. (U.S. Army Military History Institute)

Major General Robert Ransom, Jr., C.S.A. Basically an infantry general in Virginia, this North Carolinian was placed in charge of Early's cavalry to give it better organization and leadership but proved to be timid and uninspiring during the Washington campaign. (U.S. Army Military History Institute)

John McCausland. A three-battery horse artillery battalion (some ten to fifteen guns) accompanied the cavalry arm under the leadership of Lieutenant Colonel J. Floyd King.[31]

In one bold and somewhat controversial decision, Early disbanded all reserve units in the Valley District. Secretary of War James Seddon protested to Lee and Davis about the general's exceeding his authority in the matter. However, Early felt that these men could better serve the cause at home, harvesting crops so that civilian and military alike might eat the following winter. Nonetheless, the move left Lynchburg and other towns virtually unprotected except for invalids and other marginal home guard contingents. With Hunter out of the way, Early felt confident that few Yankees would be returning to the Shenandoah very soon.[32]

Early's resurrected "Army of the Valley" (even evoking the name as well as the spirit of Stonewall Jackson's 1862 force), marched smartly from its camps near Staunton shortly before 3:00 a.m. on June 28. Precise strength figures will always remain elusive. Early may have had as many as 20,000 men or more, fifty or fifty-five cannon, and sixty or more wagons all rolling north on the Valley turnpike. Others later claimed he may have had less than that.* At any rate, local farmers and their families rushed to the roadside, shouting encouragement, offering food and drink as the sun rose higher in the sky, and generally welcomed the Confederates once more to the area. Most of all, the civilians rejoiced that their men were carrying the war north to the enemy's country for a change.[33]

The army's pace was slow at first. Too many distractions on the first day out of Staunton restricted the distance covered to a mere eight or nine miles. The fertile fields, the scenic Blue Ridge lifting itself peak above peak to the east, and the Alleghenies reclining against the sky, led the observant J. Kelly Bennette to think "the eye never wearies with looking at such a country." Crossing the south fork of the Shenandoah River Early's force encamped that night at Mount Crawford. They marched on through Harrisonburg on the 29th, scooping up a few stragglers from Hunter's army on the way. These prisoners were sent to the rear by stagecoach, raising derisive comment by footsore rebel infantry as they passed. Here, on their old turf, the Valley Army breathed deeply and lengthened its stride in covering twenty-four miles on July 29. Rumors swirled about going north once more to Pennsylvania or even to take President Lincoln and Washington. These veterans were now passing scenes of earlier victories—Port Republic and Cross Keys, and countless tiny skirmishes emblazoned in their memories of Jackson and happier times; "classic ground" was the way Louisiana brigadier Zebulon York phrased it. Early began to wonder when they might encounter Federal outposts of the garrisons closer to the Potomac. However, they marched on past New Market, where six weeks before the Virginia Military Institute cadets and Breckinridge's scratch force had bested the Yankees, and still no enemy was seen.[34]

---

*Early's own strength estimates were rendered long after the fact, and suggested a total force of 12,000–13,000 men. He claimed to have departed Lee's army on June 13 with only 9,000 effectives. Various computations by Colonel W. H. Taylor (Lee's chief of staff) and Colonel William Allan (Early's ordnance chief) suggested a low of 9,570 infantry alone to a total force of 13,000–14,000, including cavalry and artillery at the time of Lynchburg. Composite figures integrating those above with new evidence on Breckinridge's units alone at the time of Lynchburg, suggest 16,943–17,830 as more plausible figures. One recent count places Early's total force at Lynchburg at 20,423 (including the Virginia Military Institute cadets and 1,900 home guardsmen) and further suggests that on June 28, his strength figures included 13,561 infantry, 4,250 cavalry, and 990 artillerists for a total of 18,801. Possibly more exaggerated were Federal figures like those of Major General John G. Barnard, Grant's chief engineer and architect of the capital's fortification system, who claimed Early had 22,420 officers and men in front of Washington. We will probably never know the exact strength figures of Early's forces, for it may well have been that Early himself had no precise knowledge of his numbers at the time of his advance on Washington. (See note 33.)

The valley began to show the strains of war by the time the army reached Strasburg. Standing on Fisher's Hill, just south of that town, medical corpsman J. Kelly Bennette noted: "You have as pretty a landscape spread out before you as poet or painter ever exulted over." The Shenandoah River made as perfect "an hyperbole as could be described by the most exact mathematical rule," he exclaimed, "with hedgerows as though they had been planted and dressed by the hand of art." The silvery green leaves of those rows contrasted with the richer combinations of elms and sycamores under the slanting sunbeams until he admitted that this really wasn't war until one also noticed the destroyed fences and stone walls, the damaged buildings and but two old cows which "command your pity from their very looks forlorn." Bennette had an appreciation for beauty scenic and feminine, and his diary fairly sings with praises of valley girls and hamlets resplendent with carefully planted shade trees. War seemed a distant thing to his young mind until duty brought him back to its harsh edges.[35]

An obviously cheered Early fired off a dispatch to Lee telling about the "fine condition and spirits" of his men, the crop situation in the valley, and the fact that telegraph wires had been repaired from Lynchburg to Salem thus reopening communications with southwestern Virginia. Early advised Lee that "if you can continue to threaten Grant I hope to be able to do something for your relief and the success of our cause shortly." Above all, Early promised to hurry.[36]

A contingent of Confederate scouts under Captain George W. Booth, adjutant in Colonel Bradley Johnson's Maryland cavalry, found the first Federal opposition near Winchester. Whatever their own sympathies, some of the local populace now became guarded in helping the rebels for fear of reprisal. Yet when the army passed through Winchester on July 2 and 3, Alabamian Captain Park found "the good people of W. received us very kindly and enthusiastically." As the army fanned out to Charlestown, Leetown, and Smithfield, other sympathetic citizens emerged. Young Lucy Buck noted in her diary that some of the local boys brought in news that Early was marching upon Martinsburg and recorded she was "so enraptured to hear it." The 43d North Carolina especially recalled that John Brown had been tried and hung in Charlestown while others cited citizenry rushing out to feed the hungry Confederates. Every household seemed more than willing to give the hungry men milk, butter, bread, as well as food not normally found in the army's diet.[37]

Additional orders from Lee reached Early at Winchester. Lee told his subordinate to remain in the lower valley "until everything was in readiness to cross the Potomac." He particularly wanted the Baltimore and Ohio Railroad destroyed as it cut westward from Harpers Ferry into West Virginia. Early later claimed in his memoirs (unverifiable since the original document appears lost) that Lee's dispatch confirmed his previous set of options. It was not possible, recorded Early, to advance through Loudon county directly against Washington from the Virginia side of the Potomac. Provisions were nearly exhausted, and he would have had to stop, thresh wheat, and have it milled, "as neither bread nor flour could otherwise be obtained." All of this would have occasioned more delay than using a more circuitous route across the Potomac, seizing "provisions from the enemy" and then moving through Maryland to the capital. Admirable hindsight or contemporary reality notwithstanding, Early's use of friendly civilian suppliers and captured enemy supplies resolved his dilemma. Still, Old Jube lost valuable time in the lower valley in early July. This would have to be recovered once they were across the river.[38]

The army's mission was clear as it approached the Potomac: capture the Federal reserve division which guarded the railroad and supply dumps, then destroy the means by which Hunter might return from the Ohio to threaten Early's rear. Rumors in the rebel ranks held that old foes like Generals John Pope and Franz Sigel commanded the rear echelon railroad and supply guards. The graycoats scoffed that neither general could withstand an onslaught of Jackson's veterans. In reality, Pope had long since departed for Indian pacification duties on the western frontier. However, Sigel did indeed command some 5,000–6,000 troops protecting Martinsburg and the Baltimore and Ohio (B&O) Railroad. His four regiments of infantry were supplemented by both mounted and dismounted cavalrymen, and Brigadier General Max Weber had another 580 cavalry and infantry shielding Harpers Ferry. Sigel's headquarters had received a warning from Major J. L. Yellott, Provost Marshall at Frederick, Maryland, as early as July 1, that a lady in his town had received information that her husband would be part of a rebel army that would attack the railroad center on Saturday, July 3. Further word of the Confederates' advance reached Sigel the next day. Neither Sigel nor Weber wanted combat for they were too weak, and as both scout and refugee reports noted the rebel advance, both generals tried to evacuate their positions and supplies to escape disaster. A flurry of activity took place principally at Martinsburg as Sigel rushed to have the supply warehouses emptied and the goods shipped to safety. B&O president John Garrett and other company officials worked with the army to accomplish this task, undismayed by periodic forays of partisan rangers under John Mosby and William McNeill against the rail line.[39]

If possible, Early certainly intended to bag both garrisons. The curtain for this drama rose early on the warm morning of July 3—a year to the day after Lee mounted his final abortive assault against George Gordon Meade's Army of the Potomac at the little Pennsylvania town of Gettysburg. Now, in 1864, on a stage some eighty miles in length from east to west, and stretching from the Shenandoah to Patterson's Creek beyond the mountains, the Confederates once more stood poised to redeem the lost opportunities of the past. McNeill's Rangers rushed forward on the western side of this stage to capture the Patterson's Creek railroad bridge before pushing on against an equally guarded crossing on the North Branch of the Potomac. Another cavalry force under Imboden operated against the railroad bridge over the South Branch before turning eastward against more crossings over St. John's Run and Big Capon Creek. Still a third mounted force under McCausland aimed at the Back Creek bridge, after which it would continue eastward on the railroad and cut Sigel's line of retreat at Hainesville on the main Martinsburg-Hagerstown road. McCausland would then join Bradley Johnson advancing from Middleway and Leetown to Kearneysville on the B&O, and thence to Hainesville to complete entrapment of Sigel's force. Rodes and Ramseur would follow Johnson with their infantry. Breckinridge's men would push forward into Martinsburg directly via the Winchester pike, screened by Major Harry Gilmor's Maryland cavalry. The scheme had the earmarks of a Jackson-like stroke.[40]

The plan misfired. Johnson experienced stiffer resistance than anticipated from Colonel James Mulligan's cavalry in the Leetown sector and had to summon Ramseur for assistance. Gilmor also had his hands full with Union cavalry under Brigadier General Julius Stahel. The combat raged from breakfast until mid-afternoon as Mulligan staged a fighting withdrawal. Sigel claimed this action gave him time to complete evacuation of the Martinsburg stores, so his Ohio militiamen could retreat to Shepherdstown while being protected by the rear guard valor of a hard-pressed 23d Illinois infantry. As Sigel's assistant adjutant general, Major A. T. Meysenberg, noted in his diary, by 11:30 a.m.: "Trains are out of Martinsburg. Everything except some forage reported loaded and sent off." The Confederates later claimed that Sigel had fled in panic, and even U.S. Attorney General Edward Bates wrote disgustedly in his diary that Sigel had "incontinently" run away because some guerrillas had made a show of force on the railroad with superior numbers. More realistically, Sigel drew off in good order, saved his command and large amounts of the government property entrusted to his care. He eventually consolidated his own force with Weber's men on Maryland Heights across the Potomac from Harpers Ferry. Sigel lost perhaps sixty men in combat as compared to approximately half that number of Confederates. Railroad cars and wagons alike had been saved from sack by the rebels, and Early's timetable had been somewhat upset.[41]

Early was disappointed that Rodes and Ramseur arrived at Leetown only after dark and too late to help destroy Sigel. They were too exhausted after a twenty-four mile march, he decided. He issued an order at 8:00 p.m. from Leetown which directed Breckinridge to secure all public and private property in Martinsburg which might be useful to the army, and "to take the most efficient measures to prevent all plundering or private appropriation of these goods or any other captures." However, the Kentuckian proved powerless to prevent looting. Gordon reached Martinsburg about 3:30 p.m. and camped in the suburbs to guard approach routes according to his report. However, soon his men fell to plunder and drinking. Father Sheeran of the 14th Louisiana blamed "our thieving quartermasters," who enforced Early's orders rather than give the captured supplies to the men in the ranks. Nevertheless, the men got plenty. Surgeon and Medical Inspector R. G. Coleman told his wife that few of the supplies that would have been so valuable to the Confederacy were "saved for their legitimate uses." He complained that the soldiers "in their unbridled license destroyed fifty times as much as they consumed." He blamed John B. Gordon for hooliganism, and declared that it was deplorable that an officer of such magnificent military qualities as Gordon ("almost an inspired man on a field of battle" said Coleman), should be so devoid of the great military virtue of discipline. Breckinridge seemed to be the only model of propriety in the sack of Martinsburg, according to Coleman.[42]

It was the same at Harpers Ferry the next day. Unrestrained by their officers, regiments of Gordon's and Ramseur's commands went berserk and feasted as well as feted the Fourth of July. "A universal pillaging of United States Government property, especially commissary stores, was carried on all night," noted Captain Park. T. E. Morrow of the 8th Louisiana wrote his father that "our boys got the 4th of July dinner" of the Yankees, including all kinds of fruit, preserves, sardines, oysters, wines, liquors, and meat. They enjoyed the "delicacies as well as the substantials," he added. Private Henry Robinson Berkeley, a Virginia artilleryman, told of securing "quite a lot of sugar, coffee, hardtack, molasses, etc.," literally under hostile gunfire from Maryland Heights. Over at Charlestown that day, the 43d North Carolina was "half demoralized" by all the food and drink lavished upon it by local secessionists, and some of the officers got so drunk that Rodes had to establish a guard against rioting and pillaging, and he arrested many tipsy soldiers

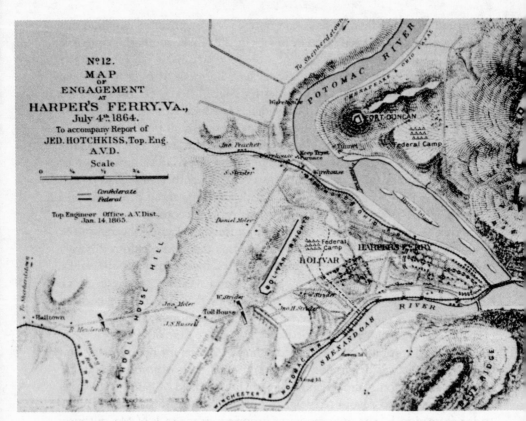

Capture of Harpers Ferry, July 4, 1864. The Federal garrison evacuated this strategic point at Early's approach, effectively eluding capture and destroying the Potomac bridge crossings at this point. (Official Records Atlas, Plate LXXXII)

who were absent from their units. J. Kelly Bennette admitted to tending a number of accidentally injured celebrants at Sharpsburg, Maryland, soon thereafter.[43]

Memories of the feast lasted into the postwar years. George H. Lester of the Tom Cobb Infantry (Company E, 38th Georgia) recalled as late as 1879 what he styled the "Dutch General's Barbecue." Blending events at Martinsburg and Harpers Ferry together, perhaps, Lester cited "a table spread about 200 yards long, loaded with all the good things that could be imagined." He admitted to the ill-mannered trick "our boys" had played on the enemy as they unavoidably fell "aboard of those delicious viands, barbecued meats and everything in profusion, which they discussed to the fullest extent, while the Yankees on the other side of the river, watched us with mouths watering and eyes filled with tears." Besides, Lester decided, Sigel and his "Dutch" really had no right to eat this fine spread on Virginia soil in the first place. The Confederates might well celebrate their good fortunes. They had marched nearly two hundred miles since leaving Richmond, and they had beaten Hunter back from Lynchburg. They had chased the Federals from the Valley, and now they had captured quantities of desperately needed supplies. Booth's scouts brought in reports of cooperation from local partisan bands for an advance into northern territory, and a wildly enthusiastic populace swelled the southerner's pride. How pleased Early and Lee would both have been if they had been privy to a telegram sent by Grant from his City Point headquarters at 5:00 p.m. on July 3. In it, Grant proclaimed boldly to Halleck that "Early's corps is now here. There are no troops that can now be threatening Hunter's department, except the remnant of the force W. E. Jones had, and possibly Breckinridge." The ghost of Stonewall Jackson once more stalked the Shenandoah Valley. The fog of war was completely baffling Federal commanders in 1864 as it had two years before.[44]

Chapter Two

DELAYS ON THE ROAD
TO THE CAPITAL

ULYSSES S. GRANT followed developments in the Shenandoah Valley from afar. He could hardly have done otherwise, for one hundred miles separated him from both the valley and Washington, respectively. Linked with his field commanders such as Major Generals David Hunter and Franz Sigel by the fragile wires of the telegraph, the Union's senior general had to relay ideas and orders through War Department intermediaries. This system of command was destined to cause problems at the time, so long as Grant distanced himself from Washington headquarters by moving personally with Major General George Gordon Meade's Army of the Potomac. The wartime confusion, time-lag in message traffic, and Grant's apparent disregard for the capital city's safety all fell in upon the northern military effort in late June and early July. Severe problems surfaced as the Federal government tried to find, fix, and fight Jubal Early's Confederates.

Much of the trouble lay with communications. The telegraph was itself barely twenty years old. Complex technology and often incompetent telegraphers made it an unreliable tool for war. Weather, enemy guerrillas, and the time required to transmit, receive and decode enciphered messages caused delay and frustration. Organizationally, Secretary of War Edwin Stanton jealously guarded his control of this activity in Washington, and even Grant, the army leader, had no direct access to the secret ciphers used to send messages. Only the president enjoyed ready access to the telegraph corner in the War Department at Seventeenth Street and Pennsylvania Avenue N.W. in the city. Beyond Washington, the wires ran beside the railroad to Baltimore, then to places like Harpers Ferry and the west, or northward to the rest of the Union. Army Signal Corps stations provided supplemental contact with the armies in the field. However, to reach Grant at City Point, for instance, a more circuitous route was needed. Telegrams had to go north to Wilmington, Delaware, then down the eastern shore of Chesapeake Bay to Cherrystone Inlet, across a twenty-mile stretch of the bay underwater, overland via Fort Monroe to Williamsburg on the peninsula, southward to the James River, again underwater to Fort Powhatan, and then above ground to City Point. It was an overall trip of four hundred miles to cover a straight distance between Washington and City Point that was half that figure. The aim was secure transmittal, away from possible interception or interruption by roving rebels. Still, "the telegraph wires were frequently broken between the capital and City Point," admitted Colonel Adam Badeau of Grant's staff. The general himself complained about such breakdowns during Early's movements in Maryland. Delays of up to twenty-four and even thirty-six hours were not uncommon. These factors certainly affected how the United States government responded to Early's escapades that summer.[1]

Command and control issues compounded the problems of communication. If Lincoln increasingly kept his hands off military operations as the war wore on, Stanton and Major General Henry Halleck tried to preside over matters during Grant's absence in the field. Halleck, in fact, had preceded Grant as general-in-chief, and he naturally chafed at being subordinated now to one of his own former field commanders. He saw his function as a sort of "chief-of-staff" and "military adviser to the Secretary of War and the President." He was supposed to implement Grant's orders "to keep things from getting into a snarl." Of course, he claimed, "I must obey and carry out what they decide upon whether I concur in their decisions or not." Some in the cabinet like Secretary of the Treasury Salmon P. Chase and Secretary of the Navy Gideon Welles thought Halleck incapable of making a decision. He was certainly prejudiced against foreigners like Sigel and Major General Lew Wallace, the War Democrat in uniform, who commanded the Middle Department—VIII corps at Baltimore. Just how well Halleck would function during a budding crisis such as that posed by Early's movement remained a central question.[2]

The War Department kept Grant informed about Hunter's failure before Lynchburg despite its own relative lack of information concerning the Shenandoah Valley. It was up to Grant how he planned to use such information. News that Confederate troops had passed through Gordonsville and Charlottesville en route to relieve Lynchburg reached Grant shortly after Hunter had bungled his chance to capture that city. Grant's reaction was disinterest, unless Hunter was running short of ammunition. The senior leader was more upset that Hunter and Major General Philip Sheridan's cavalry had failed to connect, and that "another diversion may become necessary" for Hunter's protection. The fact that his sixty-two-year-old subordinate had proven totally incompetent before Lynchburg did not seem to bother Grant. Grant's instructions to Meade on June 21 merely noted: "The only word I would send Hunter would be verbal and simply to let him know where we are and tell him to save his army in the way he thinks best." Here was a commander concentrating only upon the most immediate task at hand—the defeat of Robert E. Lee and capture of Richmond. Everything else in the east was secondary. Grant assumed Hunter would either retreat back down the valley or make a wide sweep southward to join the main armies facing Richmond-Petersburg. Either way, Grant said little to properly guide Hunter's subsequent course of action. The Shenandoah situation remained muddled and potentially dangerous for everyone.[3]

Halleck also informed Grant about Brigadier General Julius Stahel's scheme to resupply Hunter with ammunition from the Martinsburg, West Virginia, supply depot, but Grant dismissed this idea as sheer folly. He told Halleck on June 28 to "put Gen. Hunter in a good place to rest" and as soon as possible start him for Charlottesville "to destroy the Rail Road there effectively," before turning on the Kanawha Canal in similar fashion west of Richmond. Obviously out of touch with what was unfolding west of the mountains, Grant had not the slightest clue of Jubal Early's intentions. Various dispatches from the Department of West Virginia mentioned increased cavalry activity but nothing notable. Only a telegram from a prominent Maryland businessman with commercial interests involving the upper Potomac turned heads in Washington when it reached the War Department at 1:00 a.m. on June 29. In it, John Garrett, president of the B&O Railroad (which transited the lower Shenandoah Valley west of Harpers Ferry, West Virginia), alerted Federal authorities about Confederate incursions in that sector. His closing remarks cited Breckinridge and Ewell (the old corps commander whom he mistook for Early) as moving toward the Potomac crossings with major numbers of men and weapons. "I am satisfied," he declared, "the operations and designs of the enemy in the Valley demand the greatest vigilance and attention."[4]

Nonetheless, Union authorities reacted slowly to Garrett's information. Halleck wired Grant at 1:30 p.m. on July 1, repeating Garrett's words while advising: "It certainly would be good policy for the Confederates to destroy the rail line and make a raid in Maryland and Pennsylvania" while Hunter remained in the mountains to the west. He thought Sigel poorly supplied with troops besides militia, and by sending additional artillery requested by Grant, "we shall have nothing left here with which to reinforce Sigel." Grant replied quickly that Hunter should now get back on the railroad line for "operating from there he will have the enemy in front of him." Everybody expected much from Hunter, who at that point (unbeknown to either Washington or City Point) was crossing rugged country hundreds of miles out of position to deal effectively with Early in the Shenandoah. Halleck dutifully conveyed Grant's thoughts to the West Virginia commander by wire at 10:30 a.m. on July 2, and indicated that nobody as yet realized that a sizable enemy force had almost reached the crossings over the Potomac.[5]

Franz Sigel's so-called Reserve Division at Martinsburg suddenly took on great importance. Sigel, at least, realized that help from Hunter could not be forthcoming. By the evening of July 2, this German emigré had sent two frantic dispatches to the capital recounting severe cavalry fighting that day at Winchester and calling attention to refugee reports: "Early with three divisions was moving toward Strasburg [below Winchester] last night." Sigel would feel the full force of those divisions the next day, at the very moment in fact that Halleck was forwarding his messages to Grant. The General-in-Chief brushed aside such news from the Valley in a 5:00 p.m. wire on July 3, telling Halleck that he not Grant could better direct Sigel, and that Meade's intelligence sources at Petersburg indicated that Early was still in the trenches there. Grant still believed that the next day when Early's army busily savoured its own version of an Independence Day feast. "Except from dispatches forwarded from Washington in the last two days," claimed Grant, "I have learned nothing which indicated an intention on the part of the rebels to attempt any northern movement." He dismissed rumors that Early was in the lower valley or across the river from Washington. Grant did allow Halleck to retain every possible unit already posted at Washington, Baltimore, Harpers Ferry, or even Cumberland in western Maryland, so as to concentrate more rapidly should real danger develop upriver. "If Genl. Hunter is in striking distance there ought to be veteran force enough to meeting [sic] anything the enemy have [sic] and if once put to flight he ought to be followed as long as possible," concluded an obviously determined Grant.[6]

Major General Franz Sigel, U.S.A. Although Sigel performed poorly at New Market and was censured for failing to blunt Early's invasion of the north, his retirement to Maryland Heights effectively stymied Early's most direct route across the mountains to Washington and Baltimore, thus delaying the Confederates' advance. (U.S. Army Military History Institute)

If Grant seemed to possess somewhat skimpy information about the unfolding drama, more news began to trickle into the War Department. Much of it came from civilians like John Garrett, so much so in fact that an obviously vexed Secretary of War Stanton shot back a statement at 4:40 p.m. on July 3 that measures had been taken "as far as within my power" to meet the emergency. The great difficulty, he admitted to the B&O president, "is to know the exact truth, and to avoid being misled by stampede and groundless clamor, or being surprised by real danger." He icily instructed Garrett that if he had "any source of truthful information you had better resort to it." Garrett replied by laying out all the data he had at hand, which was based on a variety of sources, he claimed, principally his company employees and telegraphers out on the rail line west. Early, Breckinridge, and Imboden had passed through Winchester with between "15,000 and 30,000 men" according to the refugees. A battle had taken place at Leetown, near Winchester that very afternoon. One-half of the government stores in Martinsburg "have

John W. Garrett, president of the Baltimore and Ohio Railroad. Always conscious of Confederate raids on his railroad line (a vital transportation link for the Union), he was the first official to recognize the seriousness of Early's threat and pressured Washington to take action. (With permission of the Maryland Historical Society)

been abandoned to the enemy," with the telegraph and railroad destroyed. Hunter seemed days away from helping, and the Harpers Ferry garrison was too small to stop the enemy thrust. The departmental commander in Garrett's region (railroad headquarters was also at Baltimore), Major General Lew Wallace, "has no advices whatever from General Sigel, nor can we obtain any knowledge of his position or movements since 10:35 this morning," noted Garrett. He concluded that while the enemy's numbers were doubtless exaggerated, it was scarcely credible that Sigel would abandon such an important post as Martinsburg "unless he had reliably ascertained that the enemy was in decidedly superior numbers."[7]

Disbelief still swept over Washington. Aging military adviser, Major General Ethan Allen Hitchcock, found little sympathy for his warnings about the danger as Stanton and Halleck turned away, and President Lincoln only indulgently listened to the old man's forebodings that "an enterprising general could take the city." Stanton wired Garrett tersely that Hunter "has been under orders three days ago to move forces up to the threatened points," and that Brigadier General J. C. Sullivan's cavalry should "have already been up before now." The fact was that they were not up, and Halleck's own pessimism showed clearly in a 4:00 p.m. wire to Grant on July 3. "The three principal officers on the line of the road are Sigel, Stahel, and Max Weber," he told his chief, so Grant could "judge what probability there is of a good defense if the enemy should attack the line in force." There still seemed to be sufficient manpower out there to contain a threat. Hunter's department numbered 28,000 men and thirty-four heavy as well as forty-four light cannon. Sigel's division comprised two brigades and various miscellaneous contingents. Wallace's department boasted 7,000 men, with another 1,100 in Major General Darius Couch's Department of the Susquehanna in central Pennsylvania. Close-in protection for the nation's capital rested with 33,288 officers and men as noted on June strength reports with thirty-nine field and nine hundred and fifty heavy cannon in the fortifications of Major General Christopher C. Augur's Department of Washington. Several mounted artillery companies from Augur's force had gone forward to supplement Weber's numbers at Harpers Ferry. In sum, however, the War Department thought perhaps 75,000 men might be arrayed from West Virginia to the northeast as protection for the capital region. Hardly half that number actually existed in fact for any immediate concentration against a Confederate invasion.[8]

Sigel and Weber did what they could to slow Early's passage of the upper Potomac. Halleck told Weber at 12:30 p.m., July 4, that "everything should be prepared for a defense of your works and the first man who proposes a surrender or retreat should be hung." Weber, of course, never received this message until some twenty-four hours later, with his men, by that time, safely entrenched on Maryland Heights across from Harpers Ferry. Yet, ironically, Sigel and Weber presented a far more formidable obstacle to Early on Maryland Heights than if they had followed Halleck's original prescription to fight or die for Harpers Ferry. Despite disproportionate numbers, the Federals stood as a threat to Early's line of communications should he decide to bypass the Heights. If the Confederates chose to attack, the outnumbered combined force could seriously damage Early's army for the march farther east. The rebels crossed the river at Shepherdstown and Boteler's Ford on July 5 and 6, and began delicately probing the Sigel-Weber position. Gordon particularly deployed Brigadier General Clement A. Evans' brigade to drive in outposts on the main federal entrenchments. They soon discovered the earthworks to be too strong for direct assault—or so they said. The two German-American generals had effectively neutralized Early's direct access to the Baltimore and

Washington highways via the line of the railroad. Neither Stanton nor Halleck ever realized how his evacuation of Martiinsburg and Harpers Ferry was inadvertently helpful. Halleck was still unsure just what he needed to defend Washington, having sent forward Brigadier General Albion Howe with 2,800 extra artillerymen to Harpers Ferry, and having told Grant on July 4 that all he really needed was more dismounted cavalry from the Petersburg lines, which he promised to return fully remounted almost immediately.[9]

Impatience mounted hourly in Washington by July 5. The lack of hard information about the enemy was frustrating. Even Lincoln wired his friend Garrett: "You say telegraphic communications re-established with Sandy Hook [near Harpers Ferry]. Well what does Sandy Hook say about the operations of the enemy—of Sigel doing today?" Sandy Hook operators said very little, for their preoccupation lay with rebel raiders on the rail line, and a bungled military attempt to destroy the railroad bridge into Harpers Ferry. Communicating anything about Early's main army, or even government opposition in that quarter lay beyond both their capacity and their concern for the moment. Confusion continued to stand between Washington and the upper Potomac as the city and its residents simmered in typical summer heat and humidity.[10]

Suddenly, almost simultaneously, Lincoln, Stanton, Halleck, and even Grant, began to have misgivings about the situation. Shortly after noon on July 5, the general-in-chief sent a revealing telegram. "If the enemy cross into Maryland, or Pennsylvania I can send an army corps from here to meet them or cut off their return South." He suggested that Quartermaster Montgomery C. Meigs make arrangements for water transport appropriate to the task. He bluntly told Halleck: "We want now to crush out and destroy any force the enemy dares send north." At the same moment, Grant ordered Meade to "send in one good Division of your troops and all the dismounted Cavalry to be forwarded at once." Then, contrary to what he had just wired Halleck, he told Meade: "I will not send an army corps until more is learned." The Army of the Potomac commander had already read the latest intelligence gleaned from Confederate deserters that Early and Breckinridge were invading Maryland "with a view of capturing Washington supposed to be defenseless." He readily complied with Grant's order by directing Brigadier General James Ricketts' Third Division, VI corps, and all dismounted troopers from the cavalry corps' Second Division to be sent to City Point. Unit commanders could soon be seen scurrying around bivouacs. When all was in place, Ricketts mounted his horse and directed, "let the column move." The sleepy veterans trudged off through a heavy, scented July evening in ankle deep dust toward embarkation points on the James River. Here, at last, was the first visible sign that Grant finally realized what was going on far to the north. It now became a race as to which side could place its forces before the United States capital before the other.[11]

Jubal Early soon proved that he was no equal to Stonewall Jackson in the foot-race department. If Washington's capture was truly the Confederate objective, then Early and his men dallied far too long on the upper Potomac. He had hesitated in bagging Sigel and Weber, permitted his army to get out of hand on the Fourth of July, and now had to make up lost time in order to cooperate in a scheme for a Confederate naval raider, Colonel-Commander John Taylor Wood, to free Confederate prisoners at the Point Lookout, Maryland compound. Sometime during the afternoon of July 6, young Captain Robert E. Lee had ridden into Early's headquarters near Sharpsburg bearing a message from his father about the mission. Everything was a bit vague (despite, it turns out, the elder Lee's being privy to the details through discussions with President Jefferson Davis since June 26). In general, the idea was for Early to dispatch the newly-minted Maryland brigadier, Bradley T. Johnson, and his cavalry brigade on a circuitous raid between Baltimore and Washington. They would help with the rescue mission deep in southern Maryland where the Potomac River emptied into the Chesapeake Bay. An estimated 15,000–20,000 Confederates were incarcerated in the Yankee prison—simply inviting release and a return to reconstitute Lee's fighting ranks before Petersburg. It was up to Early to integrate this new mission with his original orders to threaten or possibly capture the nation's capital.[12]

After 125 years, it remains unclear precisely what Lee told Early about the Point Lookout scheme. That Lee understood the prison camp to be poorly guarded by U.S. Colored Troops was evident. The army leader also knew that the naval part of the expedition expected success. "By throwing them suddenly on the beach with some concert of action among the prisoners," Lee had told Davis upon initial discussions, "I think the guard might be overpowered, the prisoners liberated and organized, and marched immediately on the route to Washington." Lee thought that Bradley Johnson, being a Marylander, could move easily through secessionist-sympathizing southern Maryland, living off the country and returning the escapees safely for a juncture with Early, who would be besieging the capital by this time. But just how much of this was contained in the dispatch carried to Early by Lee's son is unknown. Old Jube probably uttered a renowned oath, and perhaps despaired of the plan's success. He deferred to his leader's orders, yet said nothing immediately of the mission to Johnson. Certainly, Early's own memoirs are sparing in comment on the whole business.[13]

The weather was hot and dry, and the jaded Confederates of 1864 needed more rest stops than their predecessors under Jackson two years before. Early did not immediately push his men as they crossed into Maryland. Local boys from Bott's Grays of the 2d Virginia Infantry were allowed to wander off to visit families and re-outfit themselves. Loyal staffer and Maryland Confederate, Major Henry Kyd Douglas, persuaded Early, Breckinridge, Gordon, and Ramseur to briefly dine at the Douglas home at Shepherdstown on the way to Sharpsburg.

Some soldiers encountered ghosts of an earlier battle as they passed across Antietam Creek. Captain Robert E. Park of the 12th Alabama noted that "memories of scores of army comrades and childhood's friends, slain on the banks of this stream came before my mind, and kept away sleep for a long while." Memories would dog the footsteps of this army every step of the campaign, showing they had all been at war too long. Regimental bands once more played "Maryland, My Maryland" at the Potomac crossing, but gone were the smiles of citizens, and the only thing men like John Worsham of the 21st Virginia recorded about the return to the Old Line State were very sharp stones in the river bed which "stuck in my feet at every step." Tearfully, Worsham plunged on, but "never in as much torture for the same length of time."[14]

Temporary restovers after crossing the Potomac permitted Early to rethink his position and what he intended to do about Sigel and Weber. He determined to take the longer route through South Mountain passes at Fox's, Turner's, and Crampton's Gaps en route to Frederick and the highways southeastward. First, he needed to gather up stragglers, as many convalescents and weaker men still streamed in from the valley below Winchester. John Cassler of the 33d Virginia recalled later that he had been too "played out" after his illness earlier that summer, and "did not like the idea of marching on after the army such a long distance." Early sent a Louisiana officer and his men back to Winchester to collect late arrivals until after the army had returned from Maryland. He also dispatched five companies (like Company E or the "Tom Cobb Infantry," of the 38th Georgia) back to guard the captured stores at Harpers Ferry and Martinsburg. George H. Lester of Company H of the Georgians remembered fifteen years later that they had enjoyed a splendid time on such duty. Major General Stephen Ramseur might write home to his bride that she should not worry about the army, all was well, "but we have plenty of hard work to do." That work would have to be done by greatly diminished contingents, however. Company D, 43d North Carolina, for example, could report barely two dozen men present for duty out of seventy-one on the rolls when a head count was taken soon after entering Maryland. The rest were carried as sick, wounded, under arrest, absent without leave, or simply "deserted"—a sad commentary upon the condition of the Valley Army by 1864. Still, hardly any regiment on either side counted more than 300-400 men compared to the one thousand prescribed by Army Regulations by this time in the war.[15]

Early was also concerned that his army's discipline seemed to be breaking down. Deploring the "accounts of plundering and confusion" at Martinsburg and Harpers Ferry after their capture, the general issued stern orders that "strictest discipline must be preserved, and all straggling, marauding, and appropriation of property by unauthorized parties must be prevented." He wanted no harm done to Maryland citizens (once again the Old Line State was thought to be ready to embrace the Confederate cause), and food and forage would be secured only in exchange for Confederate money or government certificates redeemable at the end of the war. Arrest and stiff punishment would be meted out to offenders, he said. Early particularly frowned on the liquor consumption by his army. He felt that too much alcoholic punch had been consumed on the Fourth of July, and he wanted his men back in fighting trim quickly. Army cartographer Jedediah Hotchkiss noted in his diary that lemon punch had caused "quite a row in camp on the 7th," and drinking and looting continued virtually unabated for the duration of the invasion. Despite all the captured supplies in Yankee warehouses on the upper Potomac, the Confederate army constantly foraged on the civilian economy all along the way to Washington and back. This too was part of Early's mission.[16]

Decaying efficiency among the troops surfaced when John Imboden's cavalry failed to completely disable the railroad at Martinsburg as the army passed through town. Gordon's infantry did better in damaging the Chesapeake and Ohio canal on the north bank of the Potomac, and particularly in wrecking the aqueduct over Antietam Creek and burning numerous canal boats (thus earning the enmity of Washington, D.C. area businessmen and boat owners downstream). If Early intended a peaceful message to Marylanders, his actions at Hagerstown hardly augered well. He sent John McCausland's troopers into that valley town with orders to extract $200,000 from the burghers. A Federal quartermaster fled northward to the barracks town of Carlisle, Pennsylvania, at the Confederates' approach, leaving bulging warehouses behind him. McCausland bungled his assignment by failing to note the proper decimal point in the requested sum, and ended up asking for one-tenth the required amount. He demanded the money in three hours, as well as delivery of all government stockpiles and civilian clothing from local stores, including 1,500 suits, 1,500 pairs of shoes or boots, 1,500 shirts, 1,500 pairs of socks, and 1,900 pairs of underdrawers.[17]

The Hagerstown Council convened and decided to try and comply with the Confederate demands, while McCausland stationed a regiment in front of the courthouse to intimidate the locals. The Hagerstown Bank, First National Bank, and Williamsport Branch Bank put up most of the cash, but the requisite amount of clothing was not forthcoming, despite McCausland's cold-blooded threat to burn the town down. Members of his own staff interceded on behalf of Hagerstown inhabitants to take the $20,000 in cash and whatever clothing had been brought forth (which amounted to about twenty per cent of what McCausland wanted). The Confederates then pilfered stores for shoes and milliners for headwear. Some 830 new hats left Hagerstown on rebel heads; meanwhile similar thievery took place at Williamsport, Sharpsburg, and Shepherdstown with druggists hardest hit—perhaps due to all the lemon punch drunk by Early's riders. Stores, some private dwellings, and barns were all entered with impunity in this region, claimed local Unionists, with the rebels carrying off "whatever suited their purpose." Wagons, horses and livestock all became fair game as Early's army moved across western Maryland. They also destroyed the print shop of the *Odd-Fellow* newspaper in Boonsboro. After McCausland's cavalry, bands of roving guerrillas came and Hagerstown once more found an additional $500 in cash and offered a $100,000 bond stipulating that grain belonging to the United States government would be burned. Just before the guerrillas left town they demanded ten pairs of boots—the citizenry gladly complied just to be rid of this menace.[18]

Early desperately wanted to repeat Stonewall Jackson's feat of capturing the Harpers Ferry garrison in 1862, but simply could not crack the Federal positions on Maryland Heights. As a result, by the evening of July 7 the dusty Confederates had moved on. A supply of shoes had now arrived (Federal warehouses having none of this invaluable commodity, apparently), and Breckinridge and Ramseur reached Rohrersville in Pleasant Valley, between the South and Catoctin mountain ranges, with Ramseur's troops still behind around Sharpsburg. Confederate outriders began to encounter inhospitable farmers whose shotgun blasts proclaimed that they did not wish to yield cattle and horses to the invaders. A part of Cole's Independent Maryland

Volunteer Cavalry tangled with advance elements of Brigadier General W. L. "Mudwall" Jackson's horsemen near Keedysville, sending the troopers reeling back upon their infantry supports still crossing Antietam Creek. Major Harry Gilmor's portion of Bradley Johnson's force experienced even stiffer Yankee resistance just east of Middletown (another Maryland hamlet ransomed by Early's men—but for only $1,500 of the requested $5,000). Here, some hard-bitten veterans of the 8th Illinois Cavalry under Lieutenant Colonel David R. Clendenin (fresh from besting partisans of John Mosby's band on the lower Potomac) fought the Confederates' eastward progress.[19]

Clendenin's 250 men, plus other local cavalry squadrons from the Frederick post, all moved across the mountains west of the city to scout the rebels. The Illinois contingent had been sent from Washington to clean out Mosby's band, and from Point of Rocks had turned northward into Pleasant Valley west of Frederick. News from these cavalrymen eventually enabled not only Washington officials, but also Middle Department commander Lew Wallace,

Lieutenant Colonal David R. Clendenin, U.S.A., 8th Illinois Cavalry. Clendenin and several companies of his midwesterners successfully harried and shadowed Early's invasion force as it moved from the mountains west of Frederick toward Washington, informing Federal authorities of their actions. (U.S. Army Military History Institute)

to determine the extent of Early's invasion. In fact, as Wallace moved to help B&O president Garrett with protection of the Monocacy railroad bridge, he and Clendenin cooperated closely, knowing full well the long odds they faced in trying to block the onrushing Confederates. Indeed, the Illinois horsemen proved to be a real problem to Early's legions as they came closer to Frederick. Engaging Early's cavalry, Clendenin's people successfully pricked the grayclad screen in front of the main army. Supported by two 3-inch rifles from Captain Frederick Alexander's Baltimore Battery, the Union horsemen stubbornly engaged elements of Bradley Johnson's 1,000-man Confederate cavalry division just outside Middletown in Pleasant Valley. Overwhelmed by superior numbers, the Illinois troopers nonetheless bloodied their opponents and then conducted a fighting retreat back toward Frederick. Meanwhile, Middletown burgess William J. Irving further thwarted Early's plans by cleverly negotiating downward his town's tribute to the rebels. Johnson yearned to make a dash across the Catoctin Mountain and down into his native Frederick. But Early's cavalry chief, Brigadier General Robert Ransom, timidly demurred, preferring to await arrival of Early's infantry. Soon it was too late. Wallace had come out from Baltimore with his small force by the afternoon of July 7. He dispatched an advance blocking force under Colonel Charles Gilpin to join Clendenin's men just west of Frederick. Federal forces now sat squarely athwart the main roads coming from the mountain into Frederick City.[20]

Despite their inferior numbers, Gilpin and Clendenin (supervised by Brigadier General Erastus B. Tyler) took a stand on elevated ground amid the lush farmland on the edge of Frederick. Available troops included Gilpin's own 3d Maryland Potomac Home Brigade, as well as Clendenin's 300 troopers, 150 men of the 159th Ohio Mounted Infantry, and an irregular group styled the Independent Loudon County Rangers. Three of Alexander's guns provided fire support. The Union force numbered possibly 1,200 men. Sometime around 4:00 p.m. that afternoon, the Confederates came in sight on both the Harpers Ferry and Hagerstown roads, planted their own Baltimore Light Artillery on "Hogan's Hills" and the "Red Hills" with cavalry in between, and opened the engagement with Wallace's troops. Captain Alexander's guns, situated at the head of Patrick Street with two companies of the 1st Maryland Potomac Home Brigade in support, suppressed the Confederate artillery. According to the unit historian, the guns were manned by duck hunters from the Havre de Grace section on the lower Susquehanna north of Baltimore, and their calmness and sharp aim was just what was needed in this fight. Rebel cannoneers managed to send some shells into Frederick proper, and reportedly damaged the altar of the Presbyterian church, but

Gilpin's infantry kept gray-clad troopers out of Rizer's field on the Hagerstown road and despite running short of ammunition, the Union line held. Skirmishing continued until dark as roads east and south of the town became crowded with residents seeking to get away both from the battle and the invading Confederates. Ransom and his cavalry decided to await arrival of Early's infantry, and an elated Wallace sent word from the junction: "You have behaved nobly. Compliment Lieutenant Colonel Clendenin and Captain Alexander for me. Endeavor to hold your ground. At 1 p.m. tonight 8,000 veterans will be here." To his chief of staff back in Baltimore, who was hurrying reinforcements forward by rail, the Hoosier warrior trumpeted: "Think I have had the best little battle of the war. Our men did not retreat, but held their own. The enemy were repulsed three times." He might have added that the fighting had reputedly cut down as many as 140 Confederates at a cost to the Federals of only two killed and eighteen wounded.[21]

Wallace's militia force had held. That night, Tyler dispatched a young volunteer aide, Lieutenant E. Y. Goldsborough (a Frederick native who had recently retired from active service with the 8th Maryland to serve as state's attorney in that city), to determine Gilpin's state of affairs. Goldsborough's reply was that reinforcements were needed. So, early the next morning, three companies of the 144th and seven companies of the 149th Ohio National Guard regiments marched from Monocacy Junction up the east bank of the river, across the ancient stone or jug bridge east of town on the National Pike, and through the streets out to Gilpin's battle line at the head of Patrick Street. Some of Wallace's anticipated reinforcements from the Army of the Potomac now arrived by train from Baltimore. Colonel William W. Henry's 10th Vermont veteran volunteers were the vanguard, and Wallace immediately accompanied this contingent on the train into the Frederick station. They took their places on the battle line, and soon delighted in a bit of deception, marching round and round the same little hill west of the town in order to make the rebels on the mountainside think large bodies of fresh Yankee troops were arriving to reinforce the defense. Veterans of the 10th Vermont told that tale for years afterward at postwar regimental reunions. Wallace's other troops feigned retreat several times and briefly succeeded in luring Johnson's men down from the heights. Meanwhile, Clendenin's own horsemen made additional forays up the mountain on the Hagerstown and Harpers Ferry roads (some accounts said the Mountain or Shookstown road also), and in one sharp bout near secessionist-owned Hagers' tavern, stampeded the rebels. One of Alexander's cannon accompanied part of the column, and some of Clendenin's men actually galloped into Johnson's rear area and wrought havoc behind his headquarters until Gilmor's Marylanders arrived to "clean them out." Cavalry medic J. Kelly Bennette of the 8th Virginia clinically described the bloody action, and how one Yankee shell had struck a gray-clad rider at the shoulder then passed out of his body at the hip "nearly severing his body in twain, thence through his saddle it finished its commission by killing his horse."[22]

Early's infantry now closed rapidly after heavy marching through Jefferson, Shookstown, and other hamlets on the Hagerstown and Harpers Ferry roads. Ramseur's men passed Boonsboro with Gordon and Breckinridge moving through Middletown. Rodes traversed Crampton's Gap in South Mountain to reach Jefferson. Brief rest stops at places like Rohrersville helped the tired marchers. Early set up temporary headquarters at the western foot of these heights while Gordon took some of the headquarter's staff to tour the site of the battle fought two years previously during the Antietam campaign. The fighting men were left to trudge on in what Captain Robert Park of the 12th Alabama styled "very uncomfortable heat." Still, the young men in the ranks appreciated the beautiful countryside, unspoiled by war, so neat and tidy in the eyes of Park and Bennette. Ranks thinned as the rebels fell out to steal cattle and horses with abandon and to strip orchards and berry patches. North Carolinians like Billy Beavans and George Wills of the 43d Infantry, and Sergeant Major John G. Young of the 4th North Carolina State Troops, later boasted that they had lived handsomely eating cherries, apple butter, milk, and "the fat of the country." Army quartermasters claimed the stolen livestock which numbered 1,000 horses and cattle were secured in one day's activity alone. Little did anyone realize how burdensome all this booty would become for the army. By the time that Early's men eventually got into Frederick on July 9, Young himself calculated that the army's wagon train alone now stretched for nine miles along the highway.[23]

The Federals on the outskirts of Frederick began to worry as they saw mounting signs of the Confederate advance by late afternoon on July 8. Wallace had heard rumors about the size of the raiders—some said only cavalry, others estimated as many as 30,000 veterans. "In the hope of evolving something definite out of the confusion of news," he had strengthened Gilpin's force with more of Brigadier General Erastus B. Tyler's division, including the 14th New Jersey and the 149th Ohio National Guard (a 100-day outfit). Someone spotted Johnson's cavalry edging toward the Federals' left flank in the direction of Buckeystown Road south of the city, which suggested the rebels' real interest lay with the route to Washington, not Baltimore. This was precisely what Wallace had been waiting for. The move might threaten

*Early's Cavalry Driving Off Cattle and Plunder during the Invasion of Maryland, 1864. Civil War sketch artist Edwin Forbes portrays one of Early's missions—providing supplies for Lee's army. Such depredations hampered the Confederates' main mission against Washington and created harsh feelings among border-state citizens. (*The Soldier in Our Civil War, *II, 302–303)*

his rear at Monocacy Junction, but it surely indicated something definite which he could pass along to his superiors.[24]

Wallace withdrew through Frederick after dark. New Jersey veterans remembered later how Lieutenant William Craig of Company D, 14th New Jersey, effected the delicate task of extricating his skirmishers using whispers. One particular picket became separated from his comrades only to encounter a figure dressed in gray, reputedly some sort of Maryland militiaman. The pair discharged several shots at the oncoming rebels and made good their escape to Union lines. Meanwhile, hundreds of staunch Unionists in Frederick sensed they were to be left to the tender mercies of the enemy. Wallace sympathized with them for many had come out that afternoon to cheer the blue-clad soldiery while themselves experiencing Confederate shot and shell. In the evening, they placed standing barrels of drinking water on every corner for the hot and tired government troops. Still, Wallace had no choice but to retire south of town. He had accomplished his task of uncovering the size and intent of the enemy, as he wrote in his colorful autobiographical account after the war: "There could no longer be room for doubt; what I saw were

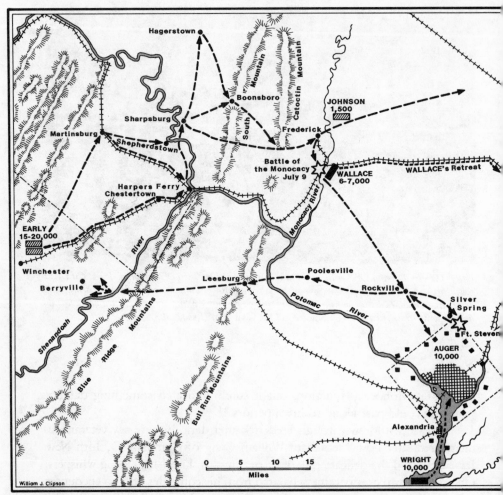

Early's Operations, Capital Region, July 4–18, 1864. (Cartography by William J. Clipson.)

columns of infantry, with trains of artillery. Good strong columns they were too, of thousands and thousands."[25]

Wallace broke his self-imposed silence at 8:00 p.m. by telegraphing Washington: "Breckinridge, with a strong column moving down the Washington pike towards Urbana, is within six miles of that place. I shall withdraw immediately from Frederick City and put myself in position on the road to cover Washington, if necessary." Wallace had feared Henry Halleck's displeasure if he had known the Hoosier general had left Baltimore without permission, and was now about to bring on a major confrontation. Discretion now thrust aside, Wallace could see that Jubal Early and a large Confederate force had marched from the highlands. Frederick lay at his mercy as Unionists made ready to flee the town, and quartermasters tried desperately to remove supplies from government warehouses at the last minute. Wallace knew his duty. He would try to further impede the enemy in order to give Washington extra hours to gather reinforcements for that city's defense.[26]

Heavy rains spoiled overnight bivouacs for the Confederates atop Catoctin Mountain, according to some Confederate accounts. Bradley Johnson felt especially miserable and chafed at his inability to free his hometown from the hated Yankees. At some point during the evening, he was called to Early's headquarters just south of Middletown to receive instructions about the Point Lookout mission. Meanwhile, the rest of the army passed a restless night awaiting the dawn of another hot day. Wet blanket rolls rested heavy on the men's shoulders as they set out early on the morning of July 9. Confederate skirmishers, led by Major Henry Kyd Douglas of Early's staff, moved down into Frederick by sunrise. A very handsome town, noted Sergeant Major Young, and thought it contained any quantity of pretty girls "most of them I believe *secesh* [sic]." Virginian J. Kelly Bennette saw the spires of Frederick "rising far above the hills glitter like silver and gold in the burning sun." From his position atop the mountain it seemed as if the whole countryside was so thickly populated that it all looked like an immense city. Friends of the invaders soon alerted Early to Wallace's evacuation, then cheered wildly as the Confederates moved into town. Father James Sheeran, the Louisiana padre, lost control of his horse in the clamor, and some secessionists like Peter Bahm gave a pair of handsome spurs to Douglas as thanks for deliverance from the enemy. Alabama Captain Park recalled happily that he neither saw nor heard anything of the "mythical Barbara Frietchie," of flag-waving fame when Jackson had marched through town two years before, and of "whom the abolition poet, Whittier, wrote in such an untruthful and silly strain."[27]

Frederick soon showed a sterner, Unionist spirit, too. The town had been in a flutter for days with rumors, and like so many Maryland communities was split politically by the Civil War. Old marketplace and county seat from colonial frontier days, Frederick had a population of 8,054 people (including 443 slaves), according to the 1860 census. It numbered among earlier first citizens Bradley Johnson's ancestor, Judge Thomas Johnson, Revolutionary patriot and first governor of the state. Francis Scott Key, author of "The Star Spangled Banner," called Frederick home, as did Chief Justice Rodger Brooke Taney of the famous Dred Scott antebellum slave case.

Out beyond town lay the rich farmland of the Monocacy River Valley, and eastward stretched hamlets like New Market, Ridgeville, and Ellicott City on the great National Road to Baltimore. Down the turnpike to the south, and across the Monocacy could be found similar towns named Urbana, Hyattstown, and Gaithersburg. The land was lovely, in a manner not unlike the Valley of Virginia, and its people, while hospitable, had no desire to see their land split by warfare.

Yet war had passed Frederick's way. City voters in 1860 had voted for southern Unionist party candidate John Bell for president although the state had voted for southern States Rights Democratic John Breckinridge). A dramatic county vote for union or secession that December had witnessed 341 voters passing through the east courthouse gate (signifying their love of the Union), while 117 of their fellow townsmen marched through the south gate (thus voting for secession). Many of Early's men had kinsmen and friends in the area, and the Maryland legislature had briefly met in Kemp Hall (later a Yankee supply depot) in Frederick, when turbulence and violence grew too heavy in Baltimore and Annapolis in 1861. Later, the city's streets, which had felt the heavy wheels of westward-bound Conestoga wagon trains during the early national period, echoed to the tramp of marching thousands bound for the killing grounds at Antietam and Gettysburg. But miraculously, Frederick itself had escaped untouched—until now. As wary Frederick residents closed their shutters and blinds to the invaders on July 8 and 9, Jubal Early and his men made their way into town. Old Jube was welcomed by slaveholder and southern sympathizer, Dr. Richard Hammond, and immediately set up temporary headquarters in the physician's home at Second and Market Streets.[28]

Early did not think Frederick held the rich treasure trove that had been found in Martinsburg and Harpers Ferry. His informers swore that Federal authorities had acted so quickly and efficiently that government warehouses had been emptied before midnight the night before. The banks had also made their own arrangements to secure their property, and the Internal Revenue collector had sent $70,000 in funds to Washington for safekeeping. Railroad officials had withdrawn all locomotives and train cars out of harm's way east of the Monocacy. Nearly all the civilians' horses had been sent away and much other personal wealth with them. Wallace's two days of delaying tactics, plus Early's slow pace eastward, had permitted Unionists time to avoid confiscation of their treasure. Nevertheless, Early was determined to ransom this city and he dispatched members of his logistical staff to give Frederick's town father an ultimatum. Early's hard-boiled instructions were to meet with them and impose a financial levy, or else burn the city down.

He intended to have his border-state community feel the invader's wrath, "in retaliation for similar acts by the Federal forces within our borders," he told his officers.[29]

Lieutenant Colonel William Allan, ordnance chief; Major W. J. Hawks, commissary chief; Major John A. Harmon, quartermaster; and Dr. Hunter McGuire as chief surgeon, all presented the demand for $200,000 "in current money for the use of the army," or $50,000 in material goods at current prices for each of their respective departments. The officers also demanded 500 barrels of flour, 6,000 pounds of sugar, 3,000 pounds of coffee, 3,000 pounds of salt, and 20,000 pounds of bacon. A strong guard of Confederate soldiers stood by during the negotiations, ready to burn the city if the mayor and council failed to comply with the demands. As friendly citizens entertained the passsing army and Early made ready to battle Wallace south of the city, the supply officers and Frederick officials haggled over these terms.[30]

Allan and his cohorts negotiated long and hard with Mayor William G. Cole's group. Allan claimed later that the civilians tried to stall "until the issue of the battle with Wallace should be ascertained." Indeed, Cole and members of the city corporation argued bitterly against the harsh demands. The city had barely 8,000 residents, they claimed, with an annual corporate tax revenue of only $8,000. Citing Hagerstown's tribute as merely one-tenth of that demanded of them (for news had ostensibly been received of the demands made on their sister city), Cole's group asked that Early reconsider the figure. He would not, responded Allan and the other officers. (If he had been given Cole's request, Early might have intervened personally at this point.) Finally, by early afternoon, the fearful civilians gave in to the Confederate demands. Local bankers from the Farmers and Mechanics, Franklin Savings, Frederick County, and Central banks as well as the Fredericktown Savings Institute, put up the requisite cash as a "loan to the city." Major J. R. Braithwaite, the only bonded quartermaster officer in Early's whole army, received the cash and reputedly hauled it away in baskets like some medieval robber baron receiving payment from his serfs. The city would labor until October 1, 1951 to liquidate this public debt which eventually totaled $600,000 including interest.[31]

When the negotiations had ended, Early's twenty-four-year-old aide Lieutenant Colonel Alexander (Sandie) Pendleton happened to ride in from the battlefield to see how the ransom demands were going. Together with the other officers, he found a friendly restaurateur who plied the happy group with a victory meal including champagne and ice cream. Confederate fighting men, who happened to be facing death and disfigurement at that very moment, later took a rather prosaic view of the whole affair. North Carolinian John Young confided in his journal: "The inhabitants of the place gave Genl. Early $200,000 in greenbacks . . . if he would not impress anything," and permitted him to buy anything needed by the army at government prices. The actual facts might differ from Young's interpretation. Many rebel cavalrymen, in particular, simply walked into Frederick stores and helped themselves to what lay on the shelves, leaving at best rather worthless Confederate script in payment. No wonder local storekeeper Jacob Englebrecht wrote in his diary: "These are awful times, one day we are as usual and the next day in the hands of the enemy." But, whatever the final outcome, he decided, "come weal or woe—come life or death, we go for the Union of the States forever,—one and Inseparable."[32]

It proved ironic that the Confederates soon discovered that the government warehouses were still full of Union quartermaster supplies. Some 380,872 cubic feet of space in seven locations plus ten or twelve hospital buildings all contained at least $262,500 worth of government stores on the morning Early exacted his tribute. The rebels uncovered this fact only after execution of the agreement with town officials, and payment had been made to them. Officers felt duty-bound by the honor of that agreement to apply protection to those supplies—which were soon recaptured by the Federals once Early had moved on toward Washington. Rebel scavengers undoubtedly made off with some of the goods. However, plaintiffs in the case to recover civil damages on behalf of Frederick citizens nearly a generation later noted wryly: "It is apparent that the Government of the United States received the benefit of this ransom in the saving of its stores." Frederick, they noted, was the only town in the nation in which government property was saved by payment of such a ransom. In 1864, Frederick residents were probably much too pleased at simply being spared southern torches and did not take much notice.[33]

Chapter Three

✕

BUYING TIME
ON THE MONOCACY

T HE turnpike to Washington and the Baltimore and Ohio Railroad both crossed the Monocacy River within a quarter-mile of one another just south of Frederick, Maryland. Here, on July 9, 1864, Major General Lew Wallace decided to make a stand against the oncoming army of Jubal Early. Wallace had not been directly involved with the campaign until this point. His curiosity, more than concern, had been aroused when railroad president John W. Garrett burst into his Baltimore headquarters on July 2, demanding that the army do something to protect the road. The Indiana general demurred, suggesting that events to the west lay beyond his jurisdiction, but he agreed to guard the iron railroad bridge across the Monocacy at the western boundary of his department.* Thinking that Garrett might be over-

---

*A serious question may be raised about Wallace's judgment. Wallace, for whatever reasons (whether a desire to aid Garrett, a desire for combat, or a plan to retrieve lost glories and his reputation through a victory), may well have consciously exceeded his authority and pushed some thirty actual miles beyond his official departmental jurisdiction. According to reorganization orders published in March and June, Wallace's boundary came nowhere near the Monocacy. General Order 97, Adjutant General's Office, March 12, 1864, established the Middle Department as ". . . the eastern shore of Maryland, and Cecil, Harford, Baltimore, and Anne Arundel counties in Maryland." General Order 214, Adjutant General's Office, June 21, 1864, prescribed

Major General Lewis "Lew" Wallace, U.S.A. Censured by the War Department for actions at the battle of Shiloh in 1862, this midwestern commander of the Middle Department-VIII Corps partially redeemed himself by blunting Early's army at the battle of Monocacy on July 9, 1864, thus "saving Washington." (U.S. Army Military History Institute)

reacting at this point, Wallace did not realize that he would soon be directly defending that bridge against the Confederates.[1]

Lew Wallace was no stranger to danger and battle. Veteran citizen-soldier of the Mexican War before embarking on a political career in his home state, he raised the crack 11th Indiana Zouave Regiment at the outbreak of the Civil War. He advanced to general officer rank, and saved the budding career

---

the Department of the Potomac "to consist of that part of the State of Maryland west of Baltimore and Anne Arundel counties, east of the Monocacy, and north of a line from the mouth of the Monocacy to Annapolis Junction. . . ." As of that same June date, the Department of Washington comprised "that part of Maryland south of a line from the mouth of the Monocacy to Annapolis Junction and west of the Patuxent River, the District of Columbia. . . ." See Raphael P. Thian (John M. Carroll, editor), *Notes Illustrating the Military Geography of the United States, 1813-1880* (Austin and London: University of Texas Press, 1979) pp. 91, 104.

of then-Brigadier General Ulysses S. Grant by blocking a rebel sortie from Tennessee's Fort Donelson in February 1862, which led to the surrender of that post the next day. This victory later catapulted Grant on the road to the command of all the Federal armies by 1864. Wallace advanced to division command in time for the Battle of Shiloh in April. Here, however, Wallace's own military career plummeted in the wake of a questionable and dilatory march to reinforce Grant's embattled army. Grant severely chastised his subordinate, and from then on Wallace seemed to labor under a cloud. Democrat in politics, volunteer officer in an army commanded by West Pointers, Lew Wallace was shunted off to administrative assignments at Cincinnati and Baltimore. He helped organize the defenses of the Ohio city during Braxton Bragg's Kentucky invasion in the fall of 1862, but he never commanded troops in the field again. By July 1864, mindful of War Department displeasure and his own idea that Major General Henry W. Halleck was out to sack him, Wallace needed a battlefield success to redeem his career.[2]

Mounting pressure from railroad officials, increased message traffic on the telegraph wires from the upper Potomac, and rumors of heightened tension in the Shenandoah—all alerted Baltimore headquarters. Still, little or no guidance emerged from Washington (only forty miles away); Wallace made his move to handle the disintegrating situation to the west. He surveyed his available resources—only 6,000–7,000 officers and men on paper, with about one-third that number actually deployable for battle. By July 3 and 4, Wallace could direct Brigadier General Erastus B. Tyler to take part of his First Separate Brigade by railroad west to Monrovia, about eight miles east of Monocacy Junction where the line crossed the river. Work parties would go forward to fortify that crossing. He dared not inform Halleck and the War Department that he planned to personally go forward to take charge of the defense preparations, so Wallace slipped out of Baltimore aboard a B&O locomotive shortly after midnight on July 5. Absence from his post without permission "might be turned to my serious disadvantage," he noted, for it was "enough that I knew [Halleck] to be lying in wait for me." Better that Wallace go forward quickly and clandestinely to help stop Early's invasion.[3]

Wallace's melodramatic memoirs portray the general's trip westward from Baltimore's Camden Street station. Racing through the hot July darkness inside the cab of the wood-burning engine, Wallace and a single aide reached Monocacy Junction without mishap. Stepping from the locomotive in predawn darkness, he and Major James R. Ross made their way to a nearby timber blockhouse, ate "a soldier's breakfast," and prepared to survey their situation at first light. The Hoosier general was immediately captivated by

Brigadier General Erastus Barnard Tyler, U.S.A. Veteran commander of war in the Maryland-Virginia area and commander of the Baltimore defenses prior to Wallace, Tyler commanded a brigade defending the Stone or Jug bridge over the Monocacy east of Frederick on July 9, 1864. (U.S. Army Military History Institute)

the sight of Frederick's spires in the distance, much as Confederate cavalryman J. Kelly Bennette recorded several days later. Wallace also admired the gently flowing river, farmland which he likened to a western prairie, and fields "actually golden with wheat just ready for the reaper." It was "so seemingly Acadian" that the thought of the place as a battleground simply shocked him. Nonetheless, he realized that the terrain provided certain advantages. Two miles upstream to the north lay the National Road, crossing an ancient stone bridge—known locally as "the Jug Bridge" for an antique decorative piece adorning the structure's end. High ridges on the river's eastern bank lay between that bridge and the railroad crossing and would provide coverage of various farm fords by a minimal number of men. A short distance downstream and to the west of the railroad crossing lay a ramshackle covered wooden bridge which carried the turnpike over the Monocacy and southward to Urbana and eventually to Washington. J. Gambrill's farm and mill lay in a depression where Bush Creek and the railroad both exited the ridges and reached the river. Rich, rolling farmland belonging to J. Best, C. K. Thomas, John T. Worthington, and D. Baker lay along both sides of the Monocacy downstream to the west, or left flank of the Union position. Farm fords in that direction were open to enemy exploitation (if discovered), but Wallace could do little about that problem with his inadequate strength. His limited manpower left few choices but to concentrate at the junction, the turnpike bridge to Washington, and to the north at the Jug Bridge on the National Road.[4]

The Federal commander spent the next three days preparing his defense, welcoming more troops from Baltimore, and scouting the mountains to the west for the enemy. Initially counting under 3,000 men, the general had quickly assessed their capability. In Colonel William S. Landstreet and his 11th Maryland, Wallace found "a good-looking, clean body of city men, but like their commander, green to a lamentable degree." The 3d Maryland Potomac Home Brigade was led by Colonel Charles P. Gilpin, a quiet man of "veteranish complexion," with iron-gray hair, who took evident pride in his regiment—a sort of "French-styled 'Father of the Regiment,'" in Wallace's view. Five companies of the 1st Maryland Potomac Home Brigade under Captain Charles Brown, three companies of the 144th Ohio National Guard, and seven companies of the 149th Ohio National Guard under Colonel Allison L. Brown, were also present. Available horsemen included Lieutenant Colonel David R. Clendenin's 8th Illinois Cavalry, Captain Edward Leib's 159th Ohio Mounted Infantry, and the Loudon Rangers under Major Charles Wells. The only artillery was provided by Captain Frederick W. Alexander's Baltimore Battery, boasting six 3-inch rifled guns, fine horses and equipment, and commanded by a "gentleman looking like a college professor." Wallace realized that his VIII Corps troops were basically militiamen, or "100-day" troops and hardly capable of coping with a veteran enemy. What he probably did not realize was that his artillerymen had recently re-enlisted at the expiration of their original three-year stint, "not so much from patriotic motives, as on account of the large bounty offered" (some $950 per man). Furthermore, as the unit historian bluntly declared later, coming out to fight with Wallace "ended the good time we had so near home, where we could go three or four times a week, and get a square meal, have a good bath and change clothes, go to the theatre and other amusements."[5]

Wallace's cavalrymen, local Unionists, and newspapers kept the Monocacy defenders abreast of the Confederates' progress. By July 6, telegrams from Franz Sigel and the railroad officials confirmed that a full enemy corps plus three divisions, and some 3,000 cavalry were descending upon Frederick. Wallace dispatched Gilpin with the 3d Potomac Home Brigade, the 159th Ohio Mounted Infantry, and one of Alexander's guns to join Clendenin's cavalry men. Meanwhile, from his headquarters in railroad agent Frank Mantz's house and office at the junction, Wallace deployed Companies C and K of Brown's 1st Maryland Potomac Home Brigade into the blockhouse, two companies of the Ohio guardsmen to picket duty at the bridges and fords along the two and one-half mile river front, and ordered Landstreet and Alexander's remaining artillerists to dig a small earthwork for a brass howitzer that had been previously mounted in the blockhouse. Most of Tyler's brigade remained at the Jug Bridge, which was really the principal road within Wallace's official jurisdiction in the Middle Department. He stubbornly refused to help stragglers coming in from Harpers Ferry because he regarded them as cowardly and unreliable. In any event, these men might have added marginally to Wallace's numbers. Wallace recalled after the war that he viewed his role distinctly, "to hold the enemy back until the reinforcements reached me," and then to fight behind the river holding the three bridges.[6]

Wallace learned on July 7 that reinforcements were on their way. The news did not come from the War Department or even from departmental headquarters, but rather from Garrett. The railroad executive wired at 3:40 p.m. saying that veteran troops from the Army of the Potomac had landed at Baltimore. Fast transports *Columbia, Thomas Powell, Jersey Blue,* and *Sylvan Shore* had carried some 5,000 veterans of Brigadier General James B. Ricketts' Third Division, VI Corps from City Point with orders to relieve Harpers Ferry via Point of Rocks. They had marched down from Petersburg through heat and ankle-deep dust the day before. Everyone looked "like the original man," said one commentator from Wayne County, New York, "if not made of the dust of the earth." The cool breezes off the Chesapeake, the chance to bathe themselves and their vermin-ridden clothing, the soul-restoring martial music of the 87th Pennsylvania Band, and just plain relaxation aboard the steamboats restored them. There were malcontents, of course. The 9th New York Heavy Artillery, now turned to infantry, complained that their transport's previous occupants had left their mark, for the ship "still bore unmistakable traces of the stable." Almost anything seemed better than the stench and heat of the trenches, as well as the sharpshooter bullets at Petersburg. Even ashore, the rail trip west to the Monocacy felt good to veterans like those of the 138th Pennsylvania. "Every house along the road displayed the national flag and waving handkerchiefs as old men and matrons, fair ladies and wondering children, farm-laborers and blacks watched, cheered, and wished the troop trains 'god-speed,'" recorded Osceola Lewis of that unit. One officer was consoled: "If a man was to be killed in such a country, he would at least receive decent Christian burial."[7]

There had been predictable delays for these reinforcements. Orders had kept everyone aboard ship until Ricketts' arrival. Finally, Garrett and Baltimore headquarters authorities convinced the War Department to order the men ashore and off to Harpers Ferry. Colonel William H. Henry's 10th Vermont reached Monocacy Junction first, arriving before dawn on July 8. An aide aroused a fitful but exultant Wallace to inform him of the train's appearance. At first, Henry simply requested permission to pass on to Harpers Ferry until Wallace informed him that only rebels could be found there now, and that duty lay with a stand on the Monocacy. Henry concurred, and after a quick breakfast the train took Wallace, Henry, and the Vermonters on to the day's activities west of Frederick. Lieutenant Colonel Lynde Catlin was left in charge at the junction.[8]

Wallace watched the delaying-action skirmish all afternoon, and then wired Washington that night: "I shall withdraw immediately from Frederick City and put myself in position on the road to cover Washington if necessary." He still hoped that Halleck and other War Department authorities would not suspect that he was personally supervising battle preparations on the Monocacy. Actually, Secretary of War Edwin M. Stanton had told Wallace the night before to disregard the legalities of departmental boundaries, and the Hoosier had gone on to contact Major General Darius Couch of the Department of the Susquehanna, who was then trying to muster enough troops to block any rebel moves into Pennsylvania. Keystone state residents along the border with Maryland fled when they learned the rebels were across the Potomac and into Chambersburg and Shippenburg. Carlisle merchants sent away their goods and valuables for safekeeping while Pennsylvania and neighboring Maryland farmers tried to hide livestock and food stores. Wallace could expect no aid from that quarter, and he still could not tell anyone that he had left Baltimore because he had not received the authority to do so. At midnight, a tired but resolute Federal commander arrived back at the junction to find that additional regiments from Colonel William Truex's first brigade of the VI Corps had arrived. Ricketts, it was said, would be there in the morning.[9]

Wallace tried to sleep on the floor of the threadbare command post. He worried that Ricketts would not reach him in time to help, and that his

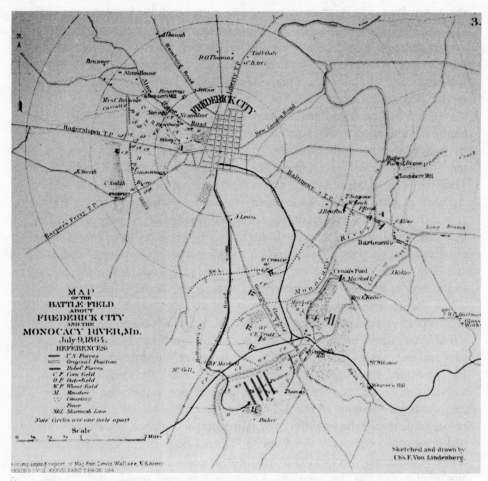

Map of the Monocacy battlefield by Charles F. Von Lindenberg, showing the action west of Frederick on July 7 and 8, 1864, as well as the main action of July 9. (Official Records Atlas, Plate XCIV)

totally outnumbered force was stretched too thin along the river. The midwesterner even fretted "to what extent did my right as commander go in the exposure of the men under me" to maiming and death in battle—thoughts that should have been erased years before in Mexico or at Donelson or Shiloh. Most of all, Wallace worried that night about Halleck's potential displeasure. Amidst this mental anguish, a train whistle sounded about 1:00 a.m.; it heralded Ricketts' arrival. Wallace greeted the old regular officer

enthusiastically. He portrayed Ricketts in his memoirs as slightly above average height, a bit portly, quick and bluff in manner and speech, "Celtic" in
feature and complexion, and eminently serious. The forty-seven-year-old division commander passed few pleasantries with Wallace, but got straight to the
point. Where was Early? How many men did Wallace have, and what were
his objectives, his mission, his plans? Wallace explained everything. Ricketts,
like Colonel Henry the previous night, merely grunted and requested orders.
"I put you across the Washington Pike because it is the post of honor,"
Wallace told him, and "there the enemy will do his best fighting." The pair
shook hands, and Major Ross escorted the brigadier off to deploy his men
at first light. Wallace returned to his pallet, "lay down and slept never more
soundly."[10]

Saturday, July 9, dawned cloudless after a passing overnight shower.
There was a cool freshness to the air. Local farmers and their workers went
out early to gather wheat despite the threat of battle. Black field hands John
Ephraim Tyler and Thomas Palm on John T. Worthington's "Clifton," or
"Riverside Farm," watched circling buzzards and assured one another that
trouble lay ahead. The harvesting stopped by 8:30 or 9:00 a.m. on Colonel
C. Keefer Thomas's adjacent "Araby" farm. Both Thomas and Worthington
told their hands to flee with the horses to nearby Sugarloaf Mountain.
Neither farmer wanted to lose precious livestock or crops to either army.
Despite precautions, sharp-eyed rebel cavalrymen eventually spotted the
mountain hiding places, with a resulting financial loss that Thomas nor
Worthington ever recovered. Actually, the colonel had only recently moved
back to his native Frederick County from Baltimore, purchasing Araby in
1860. The property's 1780 period house and two-hundred and forty acres
were his pride, and stood astride an ancient Indian trail which came north
from the Washington, D.C. area, passed Sugarloaf, and crossed the Monocacy
at the mouth of Bush Creek behind the Gambrill Mill. Sounds of blue and
gray picket fire now disturbed the peaceful farmland that July morning with
civilians soon scampering into cellars to wait out the anticipated fighting.[11]

By 11:00 a.m., when the battle sharply escalated, Mrs. James Gambrill
took her two sons to join Mrs. Frank Mantz and her four children from the
junction in the Araby cellar—already occupied by five members of the
Thomas family. James Gambrill chose to remain behind at the mill and sat
chatting with General Ricketts that morning on the porch of his house
nearby. They were joined at some point by three "deserters" who had quite
a tale to tell. It seemed that Julius H. Anderson and Hugh M. Gatchell of
Baltimore had spent the Fourth of July celebrating with Anderson's attractive

fiancee, Alice Thomas and her friend Mamie Taylor, as well as Samuel S. Thomas at Araby. A squad from Landstreet's 11th Maryland had passed by the next day and "impressed" the three young men into that unit's ranks "by order of General Wallace." Armed and equipped, but still in civilian dress, the trio had participated in the skirmishing west of Frederick until one sympathetic Union officer noted that their clothing might get them killed as spies or rebels. He suggested that they simply slip away from the army. They did so, ending up on the Gambrill porch, and later retreated to the mill as the battle began to swirl around them.[12]

The smell of campfires and brewing coffee wafted across the hills and fields along the Monocacy that morning, as both sides prepared for battle. Wallace and Ricketts rode over the ground inspecting the troops, and Wallace was naturally impressed by the veterans from the Army of the Potomac. He posted his own VIII Corps men all the way north from the junction to beyond the Jug Bridge. Landstreet's Marylanders covered the interval between the railroad and Jug Bridge; Tyler's brigade covered the latter and beyond to Hughes Ford. In fact, Landstreet's men spent the day marching forward and back in the heat, making a false impression of a larger army, but got more tired in that way than through any fighting. However, the critical point on the Union line was to the south of all this action. Here, Major Ross had guided Ricketts' division into place from the Washington Turnpike to the Thomas farm beyond. Farther to the left, Clendenin's troopers covered the army's flank on the farm fords all the way downriver to the Buckeystown crossing. A detachment of the 1st Maryland Potomac Home Guard went across the covered bridge to act as skirmishers back toward Frederick. The 24-pound howitzer nestled inside its earthen parapet near the blockhouse, while Alexander's six 3-inch Parrott rifles were dispersed equally between Tyler and Ricketts. Somewhere back on the railroad lay several additional VI Corps regiments, expected to arrive by 1:00 p.m., according to railroad officials. As it turned out, Wallace and Ricketts would await their arrival in vain. They got no farther than Monrovia, eight miles to the east, although nobody knew this until after the battle.[13]

The battle of Monocacy opened about 8:00 a.m. with skirmishing north of the river near Frederick itself. Robert D. Lilley's brigade of Rodes' division probed eastward on the National Road toward the Jug or stone bridge, running into Tyler's skirmishers. Within the hour, long-range artillery fire opened between Alexander and Confederate cannoneers positioned on high ground north of the Best farm near the turnpike to Washington. As the first rebel shells burst among still drowsy Federals near the railroad junction, a

B&O train suddenly pulled out, taking with it Wallace's telegrapher and other railroad men. For awhile, it was held just beyond the hills across the river to evacuate any wounded. Its final departure later that day would deprive Wallace of critical transportation and communication linkage with Baltimore headquarters. All the while, Old Jube's main force could be seen moving southward out of Frederick toward Wallace's principal line of defense astride the Washington road. Here, Stephen Ramseur's men had the mission of testing Yankee positions at the junction and turnpike bridge crossings. Wallace and Ricketts watched intently as the Confederates methodically deployed in the vicinity of the Best Farm. The 24-pound howitzer (directed by Captain William H. Wiegel of Tyler's staff) joined Alexander in bombarding the Confederate formations. First Lieutenant George E. Davis with Company D, 10th Vermont, and Captain A. S. Wood with Company M of the 9th New York Heavy Artillery, raced across the covered bridge to assist Captain Charles J. Brown's hard-pressed Marylanders in countering the advance of gray-clad skirmishers. Wood remembered later that he had marched up the pike toward Frederick that morning, "anticipating a pleasant day on picket." Not so, as sixteen bronze Napoleon guns soon added to the Confederate firepower in this sector, and rebel infantry edged ever closer to the river crossings. Still, Ramseur's people did not press their attack, but merely sought an opening. All morning, 300–500 Federal rifleman effectively delayed Brigadier General Robert D. Johnston's brigade of veteran North Carolina fighting men before the junction.[14]

The first Federal prisoners were taken between 7:00 and 8:00 that morning, and included Hospital Steward W. G. Duckett of the 9th New York "Heavies." Captured about midway between the junction and Frederick on the turnpike, the New Yorker appeared before Brigadier General John G. Echols. "Damn that 6th corps," swore the Virginian, "we meet them wherever we go." Unawed by general officers, the plucky Duckett responded that the rebel would soon find the whole corps there to welcome the general and his men "with bloody hands to hospitable graves." Duckett purposely deceived Echols, "and I believe they were more cautious than they would have been had they known our real strength, and we were saved from greater disaster," he claimed. At any rate, the desultory fighting continued during the morning on the Frederick side of the river.[15]

Early rode forward in person by late morning. Delayed possibly by the ransom haggling in town, he was anxious to find a way around the impasse on the Monocacy. Valuable time was passing, the July sun was moving higher in the sky, and Old Jube remained unsure of both the terrain and opposition across the river. If he could outflank the Union position at the bridges, then he might regain the Washington Road and be on his way before nightfall. Timing was critical. It was absolutely necessary to find a ford or some other crossing downstream. The fact that the whole army might have simply side-slipped down the Frederick-Buckeystown Road seems not to have occurred to any Confederate. Brigadier General Bradley T. Johnson's knowledge of his home neighborhood would have been helpful in that regard. The army could have simply crossed the Monocacy at Buckeystown against mere cavalry ve-dettes, and reached Wallace's rear at Urbana by early afternoon. Once again, Early may well have been poorly served by his cavalry. Johnson, of course, was off on his Point Lookout mission by this time. However, John McCaus-land had been ordered by Early to move to the right the day before, and "the next day" or July 9, to cut the telegraph and railroad between Maryland Heights and Washington and Baltimore, cross the Monocacy, and, "if possible occupy the railroad bridge over that stream, at the jun:tion near Frederick." McCausland narrowly adhered to his orders as the railroad bridge focused his attention. It is possible the rebels may have been too anxious to close with and rout their enemy, who they imagined were mere militia and capable of little opposition. Certainly the Confederates missed a superb opportunity to avoid a bloody confrontation, outmaneuver Wallace, and get back on schedule for the march to the capital. The Buckeystown route eluded Jubal Early as he watched his cavalry clatter up and begin to seek out a way across the river closer to the covered bridge and junction.[16]

McCausland's 900 to 1,000 motley-attired cavalrymen (the figure may have been higher since the record is unclear) quickly searched out an old farm ford just above the place where Ballenger Creek entered the river directly across from the Worthington farm. Clendenin had posted Lieutenant George W. Corbitt's Company B, 8th Illinois Cavalry to guard that crossing. McCaus-land's troopers overwhelmed that contingent, and the Confederates quickly splashed across the shallow Monocacy. Corbitt retired to the Baker Valley Road, nearer Araby, and for the moment, Clendenin's command was divided and separated by a hostile force. Tight places were familiar to the Illinois horsemen (they had battled Confederate artillery at close quarters the year before at the classic Battle of Brandy Station), and their leader knew how to reconstitute his command under adverse circumstances. Four of his com-panies had gone down the morning of July 9 to reinforce a fifth under Major John M. Waite near Buckeystown, and these men were now cut off from Wallace's main position. Clendenin led the rest of his command in sharp feints and hard overland riding back to a point where he could try to shield

Ricketts' left flank. Lieutenant Lemuel Abbott of the 10th Vermont—the left flank infantry unit in the line—noted: "Having little faith in our cavalry I feared a cavalry charge from the enemy down the pike to my left." However, McCausland soon had his hands full with Ricketts' infantrymen, and his success against Clendenin had a fleeting quality to it.[17]

The Confederate cavalry leader halted and dismounted his men near the Worthington house after clearing the river crossing. McCausland formed some 350 to 400 of his men into a battle line of sorts in the shadow of Brooks Hill, and made ready to assault what he assumed to be merely militiamen to his front. Horseholders led the command's mounts back across the river to safety behind a screen of thick foliage on the river bank. Meanwhile, a Federal messenger carried the unwelcome news of McCausland's crossing back to Wallace at his command post on high ground behind the howitzer position near the junction. Wallace's own elation at successfully delaying Early for about four hours gave way to concern as he realized he had lost his natural advantage of terrain and position. He quickly sent a courier to warn Ricketts to change brigade fronts to counter McCausland's threat. The veterans from Meade's army easily shifted position behind the wooden boundary fence separating the Thomas and Worthington properties.[18]

Ricketts, like Clendenin, was accustomed to tight places on a battlefield. He had started the war in command of a Union artillery battery which was overrun during the First Battle of Bull Run. Imprisoned, he was subsequently exchanged and led a division at Second Bull Run and Antietam, was twice wounded, and would eventually end up as commander of the whole VI Corps. However, at Monocacy his small third division of that corps would bear the brunt of the Confederate efforts commencing with McCausland's cavalry assault. Ricketts' men watched the dismounted enemy advance unsuspectingly through young, waist-high corn, their guidons waving in a light breeze, and the shrill "rebel yell" on their lips. The Confederates came within one hundred and twenty-five yards of the fence, before Ricketts' men rose to their feet and unleashed a blinding volley into their ranks. When the smoke cleared, the cornfield seemed to hide the rebel dead, dying, and a few survivors trying to crawl back to safety out of range. Even civilian John T. Worthington, watching the action from an upstairs window in his house, could not understand why McCausland's people had gone forward as if on parade. He could clearly see (thanks to his elevation above the field) that Ricketts was strongly posted behind the boundary fence. However, McCausland's command could not, and they understandably blamed their leader for

Brigadier General James Brewerton Ricketts, U.S.A. A highly respected commander of the Third Division, VI Corps at Monocacy, Ricketts fought Gordon's division of infantry and McCausland's cavalry in the Araby farm fields in a brutal stand-up confrontation typical of Civil War battles. (U.S. Army Military History Institute)

rashly leading them into an ambush. The Confederate cavalry realized too late that they faced veterans, not militia, on the Monocacy. Years later, Major General John B. Gordon, by that time a postwar senator from Georgia, admitted as much when questioned at a Washington soiree.[19]

It was now the noon hour. "Notwithstanding the attacks received, we were exactly as in the morning," noted Wallace, and counted six hours gained in the delay of the Confederate army. Indeed, the outnumbered Federals were acquitting themselves quite well. Munching on a lunch of sardines and crackers, the Hoosier counted himself lucky. Just then, the Confederates seemed to increase their pressure all across his front. The 11th Maryland's position on high ground at Crum's Ford between the railroad and stone bridges might have seemed too strong to the southern troops, but Rodes soon routed Tyler's skirmishers in a brisk attack. In turn, Tyler ordered Company B, 149th Ohio National Guard to restore the skirmish line on the Frederick side of the river, by bayonet point if necessary. The Buckeye militiamen failed in the task, but reinforcement from their sister unit, the 144th Ohio National Guard, stiffened their backbone and the position was recovered. Farther north at Hughes Ford, Captain Charles McGinnis with some of Leib's men and with men from the 149th Ohio successfully stopped outriders of Bradley Johnson's column of cavalry from crossing the stream. Both sides then dropped back into desultory skirmishing in this sector for the remainder of the afternoon. Witnessing all of this action was Lieutenant Colonel Theodore O'Hara, a Kentuckian serving with the 12th Alabama, who would later write the poignant poem seen today in every national cemetery: "The Bivouac of the Dead."[20]

Ramseur's pressure against the covered bridge position downstream also mounted at this time. Sharp fighting and heavy losses on the skirmish line of both contenders dominated this sector. The Union position slowly constricted back toward the river under the weight of superior Confederate numbers. Vermont Major Charles G. Chandler, the senior officer on this portion of the line, had unaccountably gone back across the river, leaving Maryland Captain Brown in charge. Brown became frustrated at his inability to recognize advancing rebels clad in captured Yankee garb and readily relinquished responsibility to Lieutenant Davis of the 10th Vermont. This Vermonter was temporarily taken aback by being thrust "into such a responsible position, where authority must be used, and great risk taken." Nonetheless, he caught hold, aligned his men with Ricketts' position across the river, and used the fire from Ricketts' men to avoid being outflanked and cut off from his line of retreat to the bridges. Other events took place about this time which compromised Wallace's ability to effectively contain Ramseur's slow but steady progress toward the bridge crossings.[21]

The sequence of events is not clear. At some point, Wiegel's howitzer was accidently spiked by its crew. Then, the special train, retained for evacuation of the morning's wounded (there being no field ambulance service available), steamed off to the east without warning when its engineer was spooked by the heavy incoming Confederate artillery fire. Wallace, already denied direct telegraphic communications between Monocacy Junction and his Baltimore headquarters, now lost his remaining link with the world beyond the battlefield. Still waiting for Ricketts' remaining 1,000 men (detained at Monrovia without the knowledge of either Wallace or Ricketts), this train could have returned with these missing troops. Instead, it was found after the battle, together with that command, idly waiting just beyond support range of the embattled army. Together, the spiking of the howitzer and the missing reinforcements reflected Wallace's difficult situation by early afternoon.[22]

It remains equally unclear when and why Lew Wallace directed the burning of the Washington Turnpike covered bridge. One observer from the 9th New York Heavy Artillery thought the order came from his regimental commander, Lieutenant Colonel William H. Seward, Jr. (son of the Secretary of State), at 12:30 p.m. Lieutenant Davis suggested later that word had arrived "in the early part of the noon attack" by the Confederates. Wallace himself declared that his decision was made in the neighborhood of 2:00 p.m. Whatever the precise time, the New Yorkers gathered wheat sheaves from a nearby field, placed them under the southeast corner of the shingled roof of the bridge, and Privates A. N. Sova, Samuel R. Mack, and Sergeant Albert L. Smith soon had a blazing fire going "which wrapped the roof in flames like magic." The New York contingent near the bridge withdrew quickly, and everybody assumed that the rest of the Federal skirmishers had done likewise. Wallace remembered these men at the last minute and sent an aide to rescue them, but the burning bridge forced him to turn back. Davis and his men, caught unaware by the burning bridge, continued to hold the enemy at bay all afternoon.[23]

What had been a lull in the action following McCausland's repulse in Ricketts' sector ended sometime in the afternoon. A refreshed, if chastened gray-clad cavalry (reinforced by some of the horseholders left on the other side of the river in the first attack), now attempted to advance again across the fields between the Worthington and Thomas places. To Lemuel Abbott of the 10th Vermont who stood watching the onrushing, yipping enemy, "if this was an average-sized brigade in Early's army then half the truth as to its numbers has not been told." Striking south of the Worthington house rather than to its north as in the first attack, McCausland's men moved in defilade and out of view of Ricketts' veterans until they nearly overlapped the already extended Federal battle line. Wallace spotted the danger from his elevated command post and sent a messenger to warn Ricketts. The VI Corps general wheeled his men around like true veterans and in plain sight of Ramseur's artillery across the river. Two of Alexander's Parrott guns similarly adjusted their fire to compensate for McCausland's renewed offensive. This time, the shrieking Confederates came forward in two battle lines, determined to avenge the loss of so many comrades earlier in the day.[24]

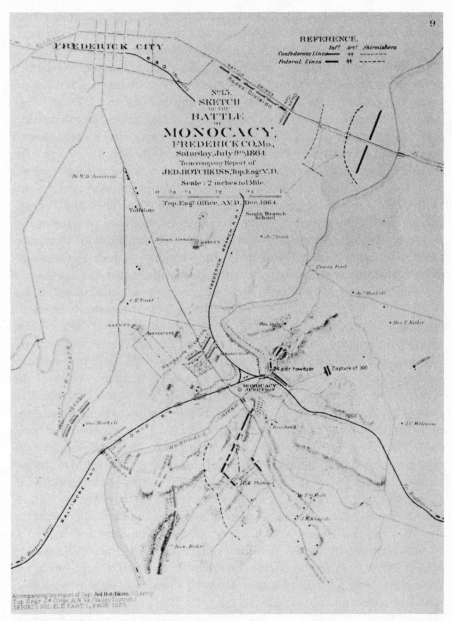

Map of the Battle of Monocacy by Confederate cartographer Jedediah Hotchkiss showing actions of July 9, 1864. (Official Records Atlas, Plate LXXXIII)

The axis of McCausland's attack now drove Ricketts' picket line back toward the Thomas house. Passing beyond the structure, the Federals reformed on their reserves behind the road embankment of the Washington Turnpike where it passed the Baker Valley Road. Heavy fighting took place in the fields around Araby, and McCausland's troops maintained hold of the house and outbuildings for at least twenty minutes between 2:25 and 2:45 p.m. However, wavering once again, the gray-clad cavalry began to drift rearward under the galling Yankee fire, at the very time that Wallace ordered Ricketts to counterattack with his reserves. The 14th New Jersey and 87th Pennsylvania surged up the tree-lined front lane of Araby and regained the dwelling and surrounding dooryard in heavy fighting. Subsequently joined by the 106th and 151st New York, the men from New Jersey and Pennsylvania, as well as those from the Empire state, were hardened veterans of two and three years of fighting in the eastern theater. Perhaps leavened by replacement manpower during that period, they handily pushed McCausland's thoroughly fatigued troopers back to the Worthington farm.[25]

Wallace and Early differed on the exact number of attacks by McCausland's men. The Federal commander seemed to imply two separate attacks in both his after-action and postwar accounts. (Chronicler of the battle, Judge Glenn Worthington did also, having witnessed the fighting as a boy.) Early, who gave the whole Battle of Monocacy relatively little space in his official report, noted only a single assault in his postwar memoirs. Whatever the number, the importance of McCausland's action lay in the vista which it opened for Early. Despite the general's opinion of his mounted arm, the twenty-nine-year-old Virginia cavalryman "solved the problem for me," claimed Early, for he had shown how to outflank the Federals who were strongly situated behind the river. No sooner had Early watched McCausland exploit the farm ford than he sent a courier to his second-in-command, John C. Breckinridge, to have Gordon's division advance via that crossing. Echols' less-experienced division could remain in reserve on the Frederick side of the river. Braxton and Nelson would support Gordon with their artillery.[26]

Gordon had moved his division earlier from the vicinity of Frederick's Mount Olivet Cemetery to the Buckeystown Road which diverged from the Washington Turnpike about a mile south of town, and posted them on a hillock overlooking the unfolding battlefield. "We made ourselves comfortable and lay down under the shelter provided," recalled Private John Worsham of the 21st Virginia. The troops welcomed a rare chance to just "*look* at a battle," rather than participate, and everyone cheered and shouted when the Confederate skirmishers and artillerists scored hits on their opponents. Some of the rebels wanted to cross over and join in the fun as McCausland battled Ricketts. Others, like Worsham, remained perfectly content to remain as bystanders. Then, when Breckinridge's orders to advance arrived at about 2:00 p.m., most of Gordon's people bridled at having to leave blankets, oilclothes, and "articles we had captured in some former battle" behind, but they dutifully formed ranks. Off they trudged in the heat, down the Buckeystown Road, across Ballenger Creek via the farm lane between the McGill and Markell houses to the McKinney-Worthington ford, which had been discovered by the cavalry.[27]

Brigadier General William Terry told his brigade of Virginians to remove their shoes and wade across the Monocacy; others claimed it was Gordon himself that gave that order. Once across, Terry reminded his men to replace their footware "and be in a hurry about it but take time to tie them well," recalled James A. Hutcheson of the 5th Virginia. Starting off toward the Yankee line at the double, Hutcheson distinctly heard Terry yell, "stop running and walk or you will break yourselves down and will not be able to fight the enemy when you get to the fence." I. G. Bradwell of the 31st Georgia heard similar commands from his brigade commander, Clement A. Evans. Riding behind his regiments, Evans urged the men to keep aligned, for after passing over Brooks' Hill they were to "fall on the enemy with the Rebel Yell as you did at the Wilderness and scatter them." Indeed, Ricketts' battle-tested men stood a scant seven hundred yards away across fields studded with "huge grain-stacks which the harvesters had recently piled," declared Gordon after the war. Every observant private in his command, said the Georgian, "must have known before we started" that the assault would become "tangled and confused" when it moved over those fields. Gordon and his staff had reconnoitered the scene, but somehow felt that the move would be undetected by the enemy. The formation of Gordon's battle line took a lot of time as he arrayed his own brigades: Zebulon York in the center, Clement Evans on the right, and Terry on the left, in reserve. The formation would move against Ricketts by echelon from the right. All of the preparation, however, was perfectly obvious to the waiting Federals, many of whom doubted their own ability to hold against what they perceived were overwhelming numbers. But they were determined to give it a try. In actual fact, both Ricketts' and Gordon's forces were of almost equal strength, (between 3,000 and 3,500 men).[28]

Lew Wallace had spotted several riders leisurely scouting Federal positions in Ricketts' sector about 2:00 p.m. It may have been Gordon and his staff; possibly it was Early, for Wallace supposedly had turned to his own aides and commented: "Yonder, I take it, is the man in chief command reconnoitering us." He had then warned that the skirmishing was over; the battle was about to begin. Wallace continued to monitor the situation, advising Ricketts to shift his own command further to left flank and wondering where the long-awaited reinforcements of the VI Corps had gotten to.* About mid-afternoon, Wallace consulted with both Ricketts and Tyler about a possible retreat. The trio agreed to await developments since every passing moment meant a further delay in Early's plans to move on toward Washington before dark. It would be the following noon before Early could get his artillery across the river, observed a profusely perspiring Ricketts. So they agreed to fight on, while Wallace directed Tyler to reinforce his covering force at the Jug Bridge and to hold Landstreet's Marylanders in readiness to form a rear guard once the retreat began via the National Road to Baltimore.[29] No reinforcements went forward, however, and Colonel Brown fought on with three companies of the 144th and seven companies of the 149th Ohio, as well as 100 of Leib's mounted infantrymen.

Wallace also summoned his aides, Majors Ross and Max Woodhull, and dictated dispatches that he wanted them to carry to Monrovia for eventual transmission by telegraph to Halleck and Grant. The crux of those messages (given the lapses of memory in postwar memoirs, Wallace may have erred in thinking that the two went off together) was that the Federals had been delaying Early's army since dawn; that the Confederate goal was clearly Washington, not Baltimore. They also warned that the enemy force numbered 18,000–20,000 men, reserves, and strong artillery. "If you have not already strengthened the defensive force at Washington," Wallace recalled advising Grant, "I respectfully suggest the necessity for doing it amply and immediately." Wallace also claimed later that he worded the message to Halleck "thinking to scare that general into action. He was, in my opinion, so constitutionally slow, if not timid."[30]

Wallace could see the distinct Confederate buildup along the line of woods on the Worthington farm by 4:00 p.m. "They are coming," the general shouted, and called to his aides for the horses, "we may have to ride." "See

---

*J. W. Garrett told Secretary of War Stanton sometime during July 9 that the westbound troop trains carrying what must have been the "lost" contingent had left "Plane No. 4" station stop (some thirteen miles east of the Monocacy) at 4:00 p.m. and had stopped to get rations for three days. At this point, "scouts" warned the troop commander not to proceed farther than Monrovia because Wallace's force was beaten and in retreat. Whether or not these were truly the missing reinforcements, remains unclear. Their non-arrival at the battlefield significantly contributed to the Union defeat. Certainly Ricketts saw to cashiering its commander for dereliction after the battle.

how long the line is," he noted to a listener, and suddenly realized that this particular rebel attack would overlap Ricketts' whole line. First came a thin line of skirmishers, then the solid ranks of Gordon's whole division "while out of it arose the inevitable "Yelp, yelp, yelp," remembered Wallace in his memoirs. Evans' Georgians headed toward the Thomas house and the five regiments of Truex's brigade. York's Louisianans advanced across the fields west of Araby against the 110th, 122d, and 126th Ohio of Colonel Matthew McClennan's second brigade, veterans of many bloody fights with the Army of the Potomac. Terry's Virginians clung to the river bank as they approached the 110th Ohio, 138th Pennsylvania, and relatively untried 9th New York Heavy Artillery (also belonging to McClennan). Gordon recalled after the war that it was one of the few times when he had seen enthusiasm among his men "which amounted almost to a martial delirium."[31]

Evan's brigade was the first to encounter the full fury of Ricketts' Federals. A bloody battle developed and continued for some forty minutes on the extreme left flank of the battlefield. Truex's brigade hotly contested the grounds around the Araby house and outbuildings. Evans went down with a nasty wound as a bullet hit a pocket sewing kit and spewed needles into his side. Colonel Edmund Atkinson of the 26th Georgia took over in command. Virtually every saddle was soon emptied of officers, leading I. G. Bradwell to decide years later that the fight was made by "private soldiers of our brigade without leadership." The 61st Georgia lost its young and popular Colonel John H. Lamar, as well as his second-in-command, David Van Valinburg, and ninety-eight of its 152 men engaged. Lieutenant Colonel John Baker of the 13th Georgia was wounded, and six consecutive flagbearers of the 12th Georgia Battalion were cut down. Thomas Nichols of the 61st Georgia sat down abruptly with a terrible head wound, proceeded to wipe his own brains from his forehead, and was heard to mutter incoherently that he would return forthwith to Virginia, find a horse to go home, and never cross the Potomac again. He clung to life for twelve more hours in great agony. It was the particularly accurate sharpshooting of the 14th New Jersey and 87th Pennsylvania which took the heavy toll of southern officers. The 10th Vermont also poured in a murderous crossfire from the Baker Valley Road against Evans' left flank opposite the Thomas house. McCausland's troopers were not screening that flank, apparently, as Colonel William Henry told his Vermonters to "wait, boys, don't fire until you see the C.S.A. on their waist belts and then give it to 'em." Evans' brigade was stopped cold and suffered as badly in this as in any of its battles during the war, declared observers. I. G. Bradwell was convinced that only 800–1,100 men in the brigade survived.[32]

The fighting proved equally tough elsewhere along the battle line. Forty-four-year-old Zebulon York, a transplanted Down-Easter from Maine who had gone south to amass a cotton fortune, brought Stafford's and Hay's consolidated Louisiana Brigade (hardly 250 men, said one rebel), into action just to the left of Evans. Able to work their way forward and deploy almost unnoticed by Truex's Federals thanks to ground configuration at this point, York's "Tigers" sprang forward to exploit the seam between Truex and McClennan. The grandiloquent York reported later that "my veterans marched under fire with the precision of automata [sic]," and that the "spirit of twenty victories burned in their bosoms and flashed along their faces," while "no eye quailed and no mind doubted." Once again, stubborn Yankee resistance cut down scores of southerners. But the bluecoats were also taking increasing casualties by this point. Three colorbearers of the 126th Ohio, and a like number from the 14th New Jersey fell in succession. Altogether, the New Jerseymen lost three officers and 140 men in this fighting. Araby house changed hands several times, while the basement fugitives huddled against the firestorm overhead. Major Peter Vredenburgh of the New Jersey regiment rushed into the house at one point, looking for the family which had befriended him several years earlier when the regiment finished its initial training for war at Monocacy Junction. Assured that the Thomas family survived, Vredenburgh took time to hide a basket of silver left lying on the dining room table and then carefully locked the outside doors before returning to the firefight. Later that afternoon, the Confederates managed to get at least one of King's artillery pieces across the river and placed it in the Worthington yard where its crew blasted away at Federal sharpshooters in Araby house. As York confessed to a Richmond friend after the battle, Monocacy was one of the "fiercest and bloodiest that my command has ever been engaged in, considering the numbers," and citing losses of "more than one-quarter of the number I took into the fight."[33]

Gordon now realized, like McCausland before him, that he faced Union veterans, not militia. He sent two couriers back to Breckinridge's command post at the Worthington house to request reinforcements. Echols' division still watched the battle from the McGill farm across the river. Gordon realized that delays would attend this request, so he sent word for Terry's brigade, made up of the remnants of fourteen Virginia regiments, to change front and assault that portion of Ricketts' line closest to the river. The Federals here occupied a long, high ridge on the Thomas Farm, directly adjacent to the covered turnpike bridge. Five of the Virginia units received the honor of exploiting the Worthington spring hollow to maneuver around McClennan's

flank and enfilade an old sunken road position that had been occupied by
the bluecoats. The rest of Terry's men were to re-cross the ground covered by
McCausland earlier. The whole maneuver would be accomplished under covering artillery fire from Confederate guns north of the river. As the Confederates marched into position, John Worsham of the 21st Virginia caught sight
of Gordon. "I shall recollect him to my dying day," remembered the enlisted
man. "He was sitting on his horse as quietly as if nothing was going on,
wearing his old red shirt, the sleeves pulled up a little, the only indication
that he was ready for the fight." The general cautioned the men to hurry but
to keep quiet, as he planned to take the Federals by surprise.[34]

Terry's attack held the key to the battle of Monocacy. This was the most
exciting fight he had ever witnessed, claimed young Worsham. Terry's men
went forward with a rush as "the men were perfectly wild when they came
in sight of the enemy's column," he wrote. Helped by enfilading artillery fire
from King's guns north of the Monocacy, Terry's command quickly dislodged
the 110th Ohio (veterans of two years of campaigns), and Seward's 9th New
York Heavy Artillery (whose officers and men, while recruited from the
Finger Lakes region of upstate New York back in 1862, had only two months
of actual field service before this battle, having spent the rest of their time in
Washington's fortifications). Back across the Thomas hill field and down to
the turnpike scrambled the disorganized Federals. They intended to make a
stand on a line running from the Baker Valley Road to the broad Bush Creek
Valley around Gambrill's Mill. But Alexander's guns began to run short of
ammunition, and their decreasing effect prompted infantryman Osceola
Lewis of the supporting 138th Pennsylvania to later record his disgust at the
absence of a good VI corps battery: "Every soldier present deplored their
absence." The staying power of Rickett's veterans now evaporated, and Wallace lost control of the battle.[35]

The Federals also began to lose valuable officers as their right flank
crumbled. Both Lieutenant Colonel Seward and his second-in-command,
Major Edward P. Taft, were shot down. Seward wore a private's uniform that
day, and he feigned death to escape capture. He later made his way from the
scene on a mule and rejoined his command after the battle. Taft was captured,
however, but later regained his freedom when a Union mounted patrol re-cap-
tured Frederick the next day and released all the wounded captives. The battle
on the Monocacy now became more fluid. As Gordon rode forward, even he
was unhorsed by hostile fire, although he escaped injury. The Georgian noted
the ferocity of the fighting in this quarter, recalling a small stream of water
("probably the one flowing across the Thomas lawn down toward Gambrill's

Mill and Bush Creek," according to a local authority on the battle, Judge Glenn H. Worthington), as running red with the blood of dead and wounded. "Nearly one half of my men and large numbers of the Federals fell there," said Gordon after the war. Now, the victorious Confederates surged over the Thomas farm, routing all further Federal resistance, as even the vaunted VI Corps' unit cohesion came apart under the fanatical rebel assault. Still, Georgia private I. G. Bradwell noted, "Our ranks were pretty thin—hardly a good skirmish line—but ranged along the higher ground we continued for a while to exchange shots at the heads of the enemy in the road below us."[36]

Ricketts tried to execute the most difficult military maneuver of extricating a command under fire, the order for which (recorded Wallace in his after-action report) was given by 4:00 p.m. At some point, Wallace also ordered the burning of the blockhouses. He swore: "The men of the Third Division were not whipped, but retired reluctantly, under my orders." Most of the participants saw it otherwise, with Confederates claiming complete rout and their Federal opponents admitting only confusion. Rebel private I. G. Bradwell recalled years later that the Federals fled "faster than did Ben Hur in that celebrated chariot race" in Wallace's famous book of that title. Whatever the appearance at the time, organized Union defense ceased, and the Confederates now engaged in merely mopping up isolated pockets of resistance. Everyone on the Federal side could think of but one thing—how to reach the country lanes leading upstream to the National Road to Baltimore. Henry's 10th Vermont, the far left unit on Ricketts' line, was almost cut off from the rest of its retiring brigade and division. The colonel had to double-time his men over rough terrain under heavy enemy fire to escape, and he left his severely wounded in enemy hands. Laboring over one of the ridges above Gambrill's Mill, both Vermont colorbearers fell exhausted from their labors. Corporal Alexander Scott grabbed both flags and bore them to safety, thus earning the Medal of Honor which was issued September 28, 1897, for the act. Henry's command would eventually get back to Monrovia, discover a locomotive and empty passenger cars still standing idly on the track, and await the rest of Wallace's beaten army at the spot where the railroad crossed the National Road near New Market.[37]

Similarly, the Vermonters were still battling away on the skirmish line beyond the burning covered bridge on the Washington Pike, and they had to fight their way out of encirclement by Ramseur's men. First Lieutenant Davis led them single file back across the iron railroad bridge under a hail of bullets. He too would secure a Medal of Honor for such heroics, issued on

May 27, 1892. Hot on the heels of those skirmishers came Ramseur's yelling North Carolinians with Colonel Thomas F. Toon seizing the flag of his 20th regiment and leading it across the railroad bridge in pursuit of the fleeing enemy. The Federal field hospital at Gambrill's Mill was overrun, and hundreds of other bluecoats were also captured as they lost their way in the woods and hollows seeking the Baltimore Road. By 5:00 p.m., July 9, and perhaps even earlier, the main battlefield along the Monocacy had been cleared of organized fighting.[38]

Tyler's force held the stone bridge just long enough for Wallace and Ricketts to escape capture. Rodes' division now pressed forward too as Confederate victory was assured downstream. By 6:00 p.m., Colonel A. L. Brown and the 149th Ohio came under heavy pressure and were in danger of being overrun. A scratch contingent of the 159th Ohio Mounted Infantry under Captain Edward Leib, 5th U.S. Cavalry, failed to prevent the rebels from outflanking Tyler's final defensive position. Ramseur's breakthrough at the railroad bridge threatened Tyler's rear, and local citizens told the remaining Federals that "the main body of the army had moved out two hours before." Heavy Confederate shelling of the bridge area and rumors of retreat finally unhinged Brown's defense. His men suddenly broke, throwing guns and possessions away in panic. A brief rally in an orchard above the stone bridge enabled Brown to save 300 men, and he eventually rejoined the army at New Market about 8:00 p.m. Tyler and his staff, for their part, became separated from their command and took to the woods to avoid Confederate outriders in the neighborhood. They hid overnight with a Unionist family, and the next day went back into Frederick before following Wallace's defeated army to Baltimore. Tyler claimed that his party was "persistently" watched by rebel cavalrymen from Bradley Johnson's column, by this time wending its way to Baltimore on main roads to the north of the National Road. William H. James of Landstreet's 11th Maryland claimed disgustedly afterward that the charge that Wallace's force had run from the field, was "made by persons who were fifty miles off," and thus was absurd. But a decidedly jaded and beaten army welcomed citizens' buckets and pans of fresh water in towns like New Market as it retired in strung-out fashion all night and the next day.[39]

Tyler's brigade had accomplished its task. Similarly, at the other end of the battlefield, Clendenin's cavalrymen effectively screened that flank and rear for Wallace and Ricketts. After his morning bout with McCausland, the Illinoisan's fragmented command took no effective part in the fighting at the Araby farm, but hovered on high ground covering the Washington Turnpike to Urbana and the road from Buckeystown. Notwithstanding McCausland's heavy casualties at the hands of Rickett's infantrymen, the intrepid Confederate cavalryman had remounted his force while Gordon battled the Federals, and circled through Buckeystown, crossed the river, and rode to Urbana to gain Wallace's rear. Reaching that hamlet, the tired and thirsty rebels stopped to rest. Clendenin caught them off guard, made a rush into the center of town where a melee ensued. The bluecoats captured the "Night Hawk Rangers" flag of Company F, 17th Virginia Cavalry, and mortally wounded Major Frederick F. Smith, who lies buried with one of his troopers nearby. The unit's commander, Lieutenant Colonel William Cabell Tavenner, had been cut down earlier that day during McCausland's fighting on the Worthington-Thomas farms. The Federal cavalrymen then fought a delaying action until McCausland's command simply broke off pursuit. Clendenin retired with the bulk of his unit to New Market. One isolated segment, Companies C and I of the 8th Illinois Cavalry under Captain Levi A. Wells, however, fell back toward Washington via Sugar Loaf Mountain and would effectively harass Early's main force over the subsequent several days' march. The intensity of the cavalry's feuding at Monocacy was attested by one vignette involving Clendenin's adjutant. Having been "run down" in a corn field by a rebel, with only a fence between them, the Union horseman chose to ignore his opponent's repeated command to "surrender you son of a bitch." Instead, the Illinoisian fired several shots "for his mother," he claimed later, before finally being taken. Then, when his captor seemed to be out of ammunition, the adjutant wrenched his reins from the rebel's grasp and slipped off. Since the fence still separated the two men, there was little that the unarmed Confederate could do but shake his fist in anger.[40]

The Battle of Monocacy was over. However, just as Ricketts had predicted, the southern army was in no condition either to actively pursue Wallace or march for Washington that evening. The Confederates simply encamped on the battlefield or beside the Washington Road, where "we had plenty of Uncle Sam's coffee, sugar, pickled pork, and beans and crackers to do us several days," noted Virginian James Hutcheson. John Worsham recalled that he and his colleagues in the 21st Virginia set up camp in an orchard containing many Yankee wounded, some of whom they helped with food and water. Worsham and his friends then took a bath in the Gambrill Mill pond "which refreshed us very much." Every house and barn in the area became a temporary field hospital (many of which still stand), and the dead of both sides were eventually interred on the battlefield (to be reinterred after the war in Antietam National Cemetery and Mount Olivet Cemetery at Frederick). Some of the Confederate generals rode over the field counting heads and congratulating one another on the victory. After Breckinridge had emerged from a pleasant conversation with farm owner John Worthington, he rode over to tell John B. Gordon: "Gordon, if you ever made a fight before, this ought to immortalize you." Even Old Jube sought out Louisianan Zebulon York to tell him that he had handled his command well and that it had done its duty nobly. York told his Richmond friend that he would forever consider Early's words a compliment, coming from one of the Confederacy's "most cross-grained and faultfinding" generals.[41]

The Union prisoners (probably 600–700 of them) and the wounded from both sides were taken back into Frederick. The Confederate wounded would be sent immediately to hospitals at Winchester and elsewhere in the Shenandoah Valley. More seriously wounded rebels fell into Yankee hands when Frederick was retaken the next day by Federal cavalrymen and were sent to Baltimore hospitals and then on to northern prison camps. The Yankee prisoners, like fifteen-year-old William R. Browning of Company I, 149th Ohio National Guard, were stripped of valuables like combs, knives, and money, and turned over to the rebel infantry who claimed these prizes since they had done most of the fighting. Some Unionist ladies in Frederick ensured that the captives received food, but generally, the Confederate guards proved unfeeling when some of the prisoners tried to give their canteens to wounded comrades upon retracing their steps back to Monocacy Junction the next morning. Even more disheartening was the passage across the wreckage of the battlefield, where rebel soldiers busily scavenged among the Union dead for uniforms, equipment, and personal valuables.[42]

Early established his headquarters near the junction. He now knew that Grant had dispatched veterans to oppose his march on Washington. However, he could not be sure just how many or whether they had gone only to Baltimore, hence to the Monocacy, or also to the nation's capital. He knew that his own army had marched fourteen miles and fought a major battle that day and lost (by his own estimate) about 700 men killed and wounded. This figure was substantiated by Federal medical authorities when they returned to Frederick the next day and calculated rebel casualties on their own. Modern estimates, however, generally double that figure, as they have factored in McCausland's, Rodes's, and Ramseur's losses.* Equally important, the "short,

---

*The issue of Confederate casualties at Monocacy assumes importance only in the context of their impact on Early's ability to reach a decision in front of Washington. Albert E. Conradis' *Monocacy*, contended at the time of the battle's centennial that "accurate Confederate figures are not available," and that the ones usually cited failed to note losses other than in Gordon's division, since those coincided with the total suggested subsequently by Jubal Early in his 1867

Postwar View of Washington Turnpike Crossing (wartime covered bridge over Monocacy) from Wallace's Headquarters. Brook's Hill in background. (U.S. Army Military History Institute)

decisive, and bloody" action (as Gordon styled it), had cost significant numbers of officers, and in the Georgian's ranks at least, thirty per cent of his effective strength. This drained Confederate fighting power for the larger task ahead against Washington's fortifications. Early lost not only time, but a part of his first-line combat strength at Monocacy. Nonetheless, he directed that the army's wagon train, captives, and foraged livestock and supplies be conveyed across the Monocacy in preparation for resuming the march to Washington at first light. It is unclear just how the wagons and artillery got across the river in the absence of the covered bridge on the Washington

memoirs. Yet the Mount Olivet Cemetery at Frederick alone holds 408 Confederates killed in the battle, thus leading local authority Conradis to conclude that "it is not inconceivable that the Confederates lost between 1300 and 1500 killed and wounded," a figure quite believable since the Confederates played the role of aggressor at Monocacy. Dr. G. K. Johnson, Federal medical director at Frederick, at the time estimated rebel losses as variously as 150–275 killed in his official report, or 300 in a comment to contemporary newspapers, while suggesting that 430–435 Confederate wounded fell into Union hands upon the recapture of that city on July 10. (See Note 43.) Other students of this battle suggest that Confederate losses may have been 50 per cent more or less than those reported and that a safe estimate would be 1,000.

Turnpike, but farm fords, the Jug Bridge, country lanes, perhaps the railroad bridge, and most certainly the circular route through Buckeystown, enabled the Confederates to pass the army to the south side of the stream that night. In Gordon's view, the rebel victory at Monocacy had been won "at fearful cost," and practically by his division alone, "but it was complete, and the way lay open to Washington."[43]

Elsewhere that night, Wallace's defeated army could tally roughly 1,300 killed, wounded, but mostly missing. Nearly 700 of that number were in rebel hands, although one can never be absolutely sure of Civil War statistics. Stragglers trickled in over the next few days, the Federal wounded were recaptured when the Confederates evacuated Frederick on July 10, and unit commanders regrouped shattered commands and thus reduced loss figures with new roll-calls once Wallace's army returned to the Baltimore environs. Many of the Hoosier's soldiers grumbled about fighting superior numbers of the enemy and being simply overwhelmed in an unequal fight. When newspapers finally published news of the defeat, the North generally sighed that here was yet another example of military ineptitude, and asked when the war would ever end. Wallace told an aide after the battle, "this is the last of me," seeing his defeat as the excuse that Halleck had long sought to relieve him of command. According to Silas D. Wesson of Clendenin's cavalry: "We got whipped. What did they send us out there for? Why didn't Grant send more men? The rebs outnumbered us 10 to 1. The Maryland Home Guards run without firing a shot. The 6th Corps & us had it all alone." In truth, the Ohio guardsmen and the Maryland militiamen had performed as well as the veterans at Monocacy. Gordon had cracked Ricketts' veteran battle line, not that of Wallace's VIII corps contingents.[44]

Wallace tried to put the best face possible upon the defeat in his dispatches. His report to Washington at 2:05 p.m. the next day openly admitted that he had gone into battle with three objectives in mind: first, to keep open, if possible, the communication route by railroad to Harpers Ferry; second, to cover the roads to Washington and Baltimore; and third, to make the enemy develop his force. "I failed in all but the last," he said. In an expanded report written later in August, however, Lew Wallace praised the conduct of his soldiers, avowing "the fact speaks for itself. 'Monocacy' on their flags cannot be a word of dishonor." Orders had been given at the end of the battle to collect the dead in one burial ground on the battlefield suitable for a monument "upon which I propose to write: 'These men died to save the National Capital, and they did save it.'" In fact, this was by no means clear to anyone, least of all Wallace, on the night of July 9, 1864.[45]

Chapter Four

REBELS AT THE GATES

WASHINGTON CITY had been aflutter for days with reports of rebels upcountry. Every few hours the city's newspapers would "flash" another "extra" story that Confederates had invaded Maryland, and that Washington would be under attack within twelve hours. Then, still another "extra" would contradict the first, declaring it all to be an "idle scare." Writing home on July 8, 1864, Sergeant Reuben T. Prentice of the 8th Illinois Cavalry projected the complacency of a veteran on temporary duty in the capital. Most of his unit had gone up the Potomac with three days' rations and were said to be "in fine spirits all anxious to see a little excitement." He had been left behind with thirty men. There would not be much fighting for those of his regiment that had left town, he told his sister, because Early's people "are on more of a stealing expedition than a fighting one." He thought the task of driving them out of Maryland would be an easy one once "our Generals find what they have got to fight against and get their forces arranged to commence the attack." Nonetheless, the Battle of Monocacy dampened such optimism for many people.[1]

News from the Monocacy remained sketchy at first. *New York Times* reporter George F. Williams got aboard a train loaded with wounded from the battlefield and interviewed enough soldiers and a local farmer tending them so as to reconstruct the basic details of the fight. But most tabloids had to rely on a thinly-worded statement authorized by the War Department which informed the reader little more than that the Union had suffered another defeat, despite Wallace's apparent success in partially delaying the invading army. Lincoln and his advisers were slightly better informed, although the news came from a civilian source. The president had wired his friend, Baltimore and Ohio Railroad president John W. Garrett, at 5:15 p.m.: "What have you heard about battle at Monocacy to-day? We have nothing about it here except what you say." Garrett fired back the bad news two hours later. Admittedly it was heresay, he hastened to add, but Wallace had been beaten. One of the general's aides had carried the news to the Monrovia telegraph office whence it passed over the wires to Baltimore headquarters. By 11:40 p.m., Lincoln, Secretary of War Edwin Stanton, and Major General Henry W. Halleck, chief-of-staff, all read Wallace's own words in his final message from the "crossing of the Baltimore Pike and Railroad," near the battlefield. The message contained one chilling sentence in particular. "You will have to use every exertion to save Baltimore and Washington," noted the defeated commander.[2]

It took another seventeen minutes for Halleck to reply (by order of the President) for Wallace to rally his troops and "retard" Confederate progress on Baltimore. Nobody seemed concerned that the Hoosier general had left his headquarters without orders and gone to do battle on the Monocacy. No one argued that he should have retired toward Washington and further impeded Early's progress. With Wallace out of the picture, Halleck now turned to his chief, Ulysses S. Grant, for resolution of the crisis. One half-hour after contacting Wallace, Halleck alerted Grant to "a serious defeat at Monocacy Junction today." Even more significantly, "Old Brains" specifically cited Wallace's estimate of 20,000 Confederates on the loose in Maryland. This was no cavalry raid, in case anyone still harbored such illusions. Even Grant could no longer avoid that harsh fact. The Union's general-in-chief had fairly gloated just four days before in a letter to his financial adviser, J. Russell Jones: "We have the bulk of the Rebel Army in two grand Armies both besieged and both conscious that they cannot stand a single battle outside their fortifications with the Armies confronting them." He urged Jones to "be of good cheer and rest assured that all will come out right." Now, a small battle at some unknown railroad junction in Maryland threatened to undermine such confidence.[3]

Washington officials had already begun to sense something larger was brewing than a cavalry raid. Halleck's telegram on the afternoon of July 6 to Grant urged the strengthening of Washington's defenses. The commanding officer of those defenses wanted heavy artillerists returned from the Army of the Potomac, stated Halleck, for "one regiment of the latter is almost indispensable to mix with militia, who can scarcely fire a gun." Enough of the latter, or "100-day" men were on hand to garrison the works as infantry, he said, and, in fact, two battalions of the 9th New York Heavy Artillery had accompanied Ricketts' division to the Monocacy, without the knowledge of Halleck. A third battalion of that regiment was detoured to help at Washington, but Grant wanted all of these troops back (together with the rest of Ricketts' men) in time for a planned offensive at Petersburg later in the month. The general-in-chief seemed unaware that some 2,500 of the 3,500 dismounted cavalry, which he had also ordered back to be re-equipped and remounted at the local Giesboro cavalry depot at Washington, were sick or convalescent at best. It would take time to properly equip even those fit for service.

Veteran Reserve Corps regiments stood on alert from July 4 through 10, with Model 1842 "buck and ball" muskets with forty cartridges apiece, but continued their normal duties as exemplified by the 6th Veteran Reserve Corps which guarded a corral of government trains (manned by rebel deserters at Kendall Green), a little east of the government printing office. The 12th Veteran Reserve Corps was on duty with its Austrian-made muskets at Alexandria while the 10th Veteran Reserve Corps took the train from there back into the city and marched out to the northern defense line. Grant's own grim determination not to panic was reflected in his orders to his chief-of-

U.S. Depot of Army Clothing and Equipage, Washington, D.C. The influx of war workers into Washington, D.C., severely affected available housing, sanitation, and water for the population as well as the predominantly southern political sympathies of the old Washingtonians who might have aided the Confederates in capturing Washington. (U.S. Army Military History Institute)

staff to ensure that David Hunter return to Lee's supply lines west of Richmond as soon as possible. "If they succeed in nearly annihilating Ewell [Grant persisted in thinking that general commanded the Valley army] and Breckinridge, Hunter will be able to move through Charlottesville and utterly destroy the Railroads and Canals without the help of the troops sent from here," he contended. Grant was thinking of an offensive, not merely defending the capital.[4]

Grant was simply too far from the scene to understand the alarm rapidly spreading across the capital region. Halleck's telegrams and messages raised the issue, but had little impact on clarifying the situation. Grant, for his part, merely wanted to replace the presumedly incompetent Franz Sigel on the upper Potomac (even suggesting Major General Darius Couch, an old Army of the Potomac regular, now frantically trying to mobilize Pennsylvanians to defend their state). Halleck, meanwhile, sought to divert the XIX Corps (then arriving in Virginia from New Orleans) to Washington and Baltimore. He told Grant that Hunter "is too far off and moves too slowly," and any concern about naming some strike force commander like Couch to move independently against Early's 20,000–30,000 troops seemed premature. "Until more forces arrive we have nothing to meet that number in the field, and the militia are not reliable even to hold the fortifications of Washington and Baltimore," he declared. "If you propose to cut off this raid, and not merely to secure our depots," Halleck told Grant bluntly, "we must have more forces here."[5]

Grant and Halleck sized up the situation by telegraph as Wallace battled the Confederates along the Monocacy the next day. Grant reluctantly agreed to forward the XIX Corps even though he wanted everyone back before Petersburg by the eighteenth or twentieth of the month. He expressed a willingness to postpone "aggressive operations" if the rebel force north of the Potomac "can be captured or destroyed." But he was unclear as to how to accomplish that task, suggesting merely that Union forces should get south of Early and herd him northward while defending key depots and towns with small garrisons and militia. Grant's desire seemed clear enough. He wanted to deny Early any chance to escape and return to help Lee. When key staff members like Lieutenant Colonel Theodore S. Bowers told *Boston Journal* correspondent Charles Coffin that they were having "a little scare" at Washington, which would do them some good, and that Early's hodgepodge force of 25,000–30,000 would "not affect operations" at Petersburg, and that "the siege will go on," it disclosed much about Grant and his priorities. When yet still another aide, Lieutenant Colonel Eli Parker, wrote

"War Bulletin No. 5000" to Colonel William S. Rowley (whom he would succeed as Grant's military secretary in late August) that news from Washington and other northern points "have [sic] considerably agitated the even tenor of our ways," that "we cannot tell with any degree of certainty how large a force the rebs have up there," and that the Confederates in Maryland should never be permitted to escape, but "if they do an awful responsibility will rest somewhere," he merely reflected his commander's thinking. Grant had no feel for the situation, still had no appreciation of Lincoln's perturbation about the capital's safety, and had no real intention of interrupting his bulldog grip on Richmond-Petersburg.[6]

All this changed suddenly. At 5:30 p.m. on July 9, Grant ordered the rest of the VI Corps to Washington by water. One sentence in Halleck's final telegram of the previous evening had finally gotten his attention. "It is the impression that one-third of Lee's entire force is with Early and Breckinridge, and that Ransom has some 3,000 or 4,000 cavalry," stated the Washington official. Grant finally closed his own reply of 6:00 p.m., July 9 (sent in cipher) with the offer: "If the President thinks it advisable that I should go to Washington in person I can start in an hour after receiving notice leaving everything here on the defensive." At last, Ulysses S. Grant showed some evidence that he understood the significance of Early's advance against Washington, and that he had better respond to the president.[7]

President Abraham Lincoln entered the deliberations in earnest at this point. The Commander-in-Chief of the nation's armed forces had gone down to visit Grant not two weeks before. He had returned to Washington "sunburnt and fagged but still refreshed and cheered," noted John Hay, the president's personal secretary. The president retained full confidence in Grant, he said. Nevertheless, political issues loomed uppermost in the chief executive's mind as Early's little army prepared to strike north of the Potomac. Secretary of the Treasury Salmon P. Chase, a presidential aspirant in his own right that year, had resigned at the end of June. The first session of the Thirty-Eighth Congress had adjourned four days later amidst great hopes that Grant and Meade might give the nation a great victory at Petersburg in honor of Independence Day. The generals and their armies had not done so. Thereafter, Lincoln had pocket-vetoed a controversial reconstruction bill that would have imposed harsh requirements upon those seceded states desirous of returning to the Federal union. On July 6, he had suspended the writ of habeas corpus in Kentucky and proclaimed martial law there because so many Bluegrass residents had either joined or abetted Confederate guerrillas in the state. Two days later, the president proclaimed his support for a constitutional amend-

ment abolishing slavery but refused to sanction congressional authority to
end that institution. As events in western Maryland heated up, the tired
Lincoln and his family left the White House for their summer cottage on the
grounds of the Soldier's Home (or "Military Asylum" as it was called) beyond
the city limits near Fort Totten, D.C. The next day, he told *New York Tribune*
editor Horace Greeley that he would welcome anyone with a written peace
proposition that included both restoration of the Union and the end of slavery.
Presidential concern for political aspects of the Civil War at that moment
ended abruptly Saturday evening with the dire news from the Monocacy.[8]

Some Washington observers at the time stressed the confusion, even
panic, that seemed to pervade the highest circles of government. Other com-
mentators noted dread, but not panic, as officials like Secretary of War Edwin
Stanton made plans to protect families and personal assets as well as the
records of government from seizure by the rebels. Stanton told his clerk A.
E. H. Johnson, at one point, to take the secretary's personal $5,000, as well
as Mrs. Stanton's $400 in gold, and hide the money in Johnson's own home.
Other cabinet members like Secretary of the Navy Gideon Welles worried
more about the silence from the War Department, concerned either there was
too little real knowledge of the situation or a very great reluctance to communicate the danger. He was convinced that "there is both neglect and
ignorance here," and decided that Stanton and Halleck had implored Lincoln
to silence so as to prevent the spread of panic elsewhere in the north. Welles
dismissed Early's raid as not formidable if properly handled but admitted that
it might become so "from inattention and neglect." He thought the city and
government ill-prepared, and "a fierce onset could not well be resisted."
Welles's diary is filled with caustic references to ill-informed "dunderheads"
at the War Department and a somewhat scathing denunciation of the
wholesale lack of information available to him. President Lincoln, on the
other hand, continued to project calmness. To Thomas Swann and a group
of almost hysterical Baltimoreans, the president implored: "Let us be vigilant
but keep cool. I hope neither Baltimore nor Washington will be taken."[9]

Lincoln received a thorough briefing on the Monocacy defeat so that at
2:30 p.m. on Sunday, July 10, he could communicate directly with Grant.
The president outlined the situation. Hundred-day men and invalids defended the capital. There was no assurance of help from states like New York
or Pennsylvania, and Wallace's battered and beaten army could barely defend
Baltimore. Lincoln suggested that Grant retain his position at Petersburg,
but that he should personally lead the rest of the army north "and make a
vigorous effort to destroy the enemies [sic] force in this vicinity." The move

had a good chance for success if made promptly, and Lincoln closed: "This is what I think, upon your suggestion, and is not an order."[10]

Halleck's telegram to Grant an hour later reinforced the president's words. The chief-of-staff agreed with Grant's prescription of getting in Early's rear, "but unfortunately we have no force here for the field. All such forces were sent to you long ago." Typical of Halleck, however, he deferred the question of whether or not Grant should personally come to Washington. The general's response at 10:30 p.m. allayed the fears of everyone. He told the president that he had sent a full army corps under an excellent officer, "3,000 other troops," and was re-routing a 6,000 man-division of the XIX Corps, all of whom would be in the city by Monday night, July 11. He was ordering Major General E. O. C. Ord to take charge at Baltimore, and felt that the VI Corps under Major General Horatio Wright "will be able to compete with the whole force with Ewell and Early." When Hunter arrived from the west to close off the Confederates' escape route: "I have great faith that the enemy will never be able to get back with much of his force." Grant told his commander-in-chief: "I think on reflection it would have a bad effect for me to leave here." Lincoln replied resignedly the next morning that Grant's message was "very satisfactory." Perhaps a few people detected an underlying note of irritation as the president further suggested that the enemy would surely learn of Wright's arrival at Washington, and "then the difficulty will be to unite Wright and Hunter, South of the enemy before he will recross the Potomac." It was plain then that Washington, with its head-quarters' bureaucrats and civilian statesmen would have to fight their own battle to save the city without the guiding hand of the nation's top soldier.[11]

Grant had played out his immediate role in Washington's defense against Jubal Early. He would remain at City Point, directing Meade and Butler against the Richmond-Petersburg line and advising Halleck at long distance how to cope with the rebels in Maryland. Grant would suggest how to bring into service all citizens capable of bearing arms, how to collect other forces "about Edwards Ferry, and follow up and cut off retreat if possible." He even bowed toward the public outcry echoing throughout western Maryland by suggesting: "All losses sustained by loyal Citizens can be paid back to them by contributions collected from rebel sympathizers after the enemy is got rid of," thereby opening a subsequent Pandora's Box in the region. But, for the next two critical days, Grant and Meade spent much of their time trying to discover the precise whereabouts of Robert E. Lee and debunking Confederate deserter reports that the enemy's top commander had slipped away from his fortifications and also gone north to besiege Washington. Once more,

Bobby Lee had confounded his adversary. Moreover, it appeared on the weekend of July 9–10, 1864, that he was on the verge of accomplishing his scheme of relieving pressure upon himself and his army by threatening, maybe even capturing, the national capital.[12]

The July weekend was miserable in the nation's capital. Cold sweat of fear added to severe summer heat and humidity. It was one of the hottest and driest on record—no rain for forty-seven days! A Sunday school frolic for Washington blacks on the White House lawn the week before contrasted with dirty and disheveled ex-slave refugees who had stood in sullen silence just outside the gates—moot testimony to a war turned revolution. Old residents were reminded daily of how the conflict had altered their lives. The influx not only of the Freedmen but veritable armies of civilian clerks, including women to run the paperwork side of war, plus the dust in summer and mud in winter on city streets churned by marching feet and wagon wheels—all stood in contrast to the sleepy antebellum atmosphere of a southern town. Congress had adjourned on July 4th with House members rushing off to seek re-election in home districts later that year. Other residents, like political appointee Lucius E. Chittenden, or the Blair families who lived just beyond the District line near Sligo post office on the Seventh Street Road, reflected the customary approach of Washingtonians to summer. Old Francis Preston Blair and his son, Postmaster General Montgomery Blair, left town for a fishing trip in central Pennsylvania at the very moment Wallace and Early battled at Monocacy, scarcely forty miles distant. Their wives and children departed for the New Jersey shore. Meanwhile, Chittenden, Registrar of the Treasury, barely got his family off on the 6:30 p.m. train for New England that Sunday. It would be the last train out before the rebels cut the railroad north of Baltimore. Still, as lawyer Albert C. Riddle phrased it: "We were accustomed to the war, and in our neighborhood had heard the smothered thunder of more than one conflict." Presidential Secretary John Hay regarded that Sabbath day as rather quiet despite Monocacy, with "the usual flight of rumors but no special excitement."[13]

It naturally depended upon one's particular perspective. Attorney General Edward Bates noted in his diary that people had first made light of Early's advance as a mere raid "by a light party." He wondered how such a large army could have moved through the countryside undetected. "There must have been the most supine negligence or worse," he observed. Like Welles, Bates regarded "our Generals, Wallace, Segel et. cetera are helpless imbeciles," and concurred in the naval secretary's comment that "Stanton seems stupid, Halleck always does." Meanwhile, Secretary of State William

Seward's family waited anxiously to learn of their son's fate at Monocacy and rejoiced when news eventually came of his escape. Still, when Washington's population realized that Wallace's army had been all that stood between the capital and the Confederates, "there was general alarm," said the secretary's other son, Frederick. The influx of refugees from Frederick and upper Montgomery counties only added to the confusion. Piling wagons high with personal belongings, and driving livestock before them, many of these farmers were denied entry past the northern line of fortifications. News of their arrival preceded them, heightening the tension.[14]

Sunday morning, at least, reflected Washington's "lazy lassitude," but newsboys soon disturbed the quiet calling out headlines; "rebels a marchin' on to Washin'ton." *Chicago Journal* reporter Benjamin F. Taylor sent a dispatch home suggesting that the city "buys 'extras' and reads them; it hears rumors and believes them; it whistles and tries to look unconcerned." He had heard that a rebel sea raider lay off the mouth of Chesapeake Bay and was up to no good, that a dragging anchor had severed the telegraphic link with Grant leaving "no sign" from the general, that the enemy was advancing toward Laurel on the Baltimore railroad line but sixteen miles from the city, and had been seen out at Rockville on the Frederick Turnpike. Secretary Stanton cut short Lincoln's customary weekend retreat at Soldier's Home, sending word that it was too dangerous to remain so close to the front lines at Fort Totten. Chittenden walked in on Treasury officials filling mail sacks with notes and securities for safe passage away from the city aboard a government steamer. Nobody was quite sure just where danger lurked for rebel partisan John Mosby had frightened a group of picknickers across the Potomac at Falls Church, thus refuting local cavalry commander, Colonel Charles R. Lowell's cheery claim of "all quiet in this vicinity." Closet secessionists began to emerge within the city, reminding the transient northerners of the city's essentially southern character, and how the government had had to dramatically reorganize the city militia and flaunt regular troops in 1861 merely to install Lincoln in office. Alert provost guards quashed a nest of secessionists in Georgetown over the weekend and uncovered a half-finished Confederate flag ready for display when Early's men entered the city. Secessionists and their banner spent the next few days in a guard-house while blue-clad soldiers patrolled the roads and bridges to prevent collaborators from slipping out to tell Early about the weakness of the city's defenses.[15]

Questions about the true state of Washington's defenses loomed paramount in everyone's mind that weekend. The emergence of the city as more than merely the political nerve-center of the nation became apparent

On the Firing Line at Fort Totten. Manned by "100-day men," convalescents and limited duty troops, and a smattering of proficient heavy artillerists, forts such as Fort Totten (attacked by Early's army July 11–12) stymied the Confederates until reinforcements arrived from the Army of the Potomac. (U.S. Army Military History Institute)

as supply depots, armories, and convalescent centers vied with the government buildings for public view during the war years. Earlier scares had led to various military commissions and study of the capital's defense. Thousands of dollars and countless hours of work went into producing a "Fortress Washington," arguably the most heavily protected city in America at the time. Thirty-seven miles of forts, batteries, trenches, military roads, barracks, and other structures encircled the city, and extended downriver beyond Alexandria. Well over sixty forts and ninety-three additional field gun battery positions highlighted this complex. Army camps and storage facilities, hospitals and ordnance dumps clustered around each post. Strength figures on July 10 showed 31,231 officers and men with 944 heavy and 35 light pieces of artillery deployed to defend the place on paper. Unfortunately, many of the men were marginal soldiers—convalescents, militia, provost-marshal contingents. Their cannon were difficult to maneuver. The city lacked both the hardened maneuver force necessary to chase away an attacker and the trained artillery technicians required to service the heavy fortress guns.[16]

The paper strength compared favorably with what experts had claimed for several years was the minimal number of men necessary to defend Washington. A blue-ribbon panel in 1862 had provided expert opinion on this issue. Comprising the chiefs of engineers and artillery, the quartermaster general, the chief-of-staff to the general-in-chief, as well as Major General John G. Barnard, the engineer architect of this elaborate fort system, the group advocated a balanced defense by combined arms garrisons with a field maneuver element available in the Army of the Potomac itself. They had determined the city needed 25,000 infantry, 9,000 artillerists, and 3,000 cavalry—a total of 37,000 men emplaced in the city's defense works at all times. If the paper strength approached that sum in July 1864, Barnard nonetheless warned his superiors that the true numbers of men available to man the battlements against Early stood at barely 9,600. Moreover, he did not bother to raise the issue of the quality of these men.[17]

The absence of skilled technicians to work the heavy artillery posed the most serious problem. The scratch force of untutored, albeit zealous, men on hand hardly sufficed in July 1864. Ohio National Guard units (raised in the spring for garrison duties during the campaign season) were hardly veteran

Artillery Park, Washington Arsenal Grounds. Washington had become a vast supply base for the eastern theater of operations by 1864 as shown in this illustration of a Wiard gun artillery park. (U.S. Army Military History Institute)

Major (later Major General) John Gross Barnard, U.S.A. This highly intelligent, professional engineer officer designed and supervised construction of the elaborate system of field fortifications to shield Washington during the Civil War. (U.S. Army Military History Institute)

enough to stem the Confederate tide. Nor were the Invalid Corps or Veteran Reserve Corps of much promise. Barnard's able assistant, Lieutenant Colonel Barton S. Alexander, sent a long memorandum forward to Halleck on July 6 highlighting deficiencies among troops guarding the city's bridges. Alexander noted insufficient and neglectful sentries, lack of nightly removal of decking to ensure against cavalry raids, and the lack of protection against incendiary devices which saboteurs could place on or under the structures. Although Alexander did not note it, the whole fort line east of the Anacostia River (the area which Point Lookout escapees might be expected to threaten) was made up of isolated forts which were totally unsupported by intervening rifle trenches. Company-size units (the normal complement for each work) were stretched over two or three times their normal area of responsibility. Even worse, the whole fort line around the city showed signs of neglect with scrub growth and tall grass covering not only the earthworks themselves, but obscuring the fields of fire to the front and sides of each fort. The defenses of Washington literally presented a scruffy, unkempt, ill-prepared bulwark that July weekend. This fact greatly disturbed the city's Unionists.[18]

All that authorities could hope for was a sufficient show of force to bluff the enemy until Grant's veterans could arrive from Petersburg to save the city. However, such a display of bravado demanded cool and calculated risk-taking. It suggested adroit use of the interior lines of communication enjoyed by the Washington garrison. Men and equipment could be shifted rapidly to a threatened point on the perimeter, provided only a single point was under attack at any given time. Proper massing of artillery and infantry, even fighting behind ill-kept breastworks, could neutralize an enemy's superiority, provided there were skillful Union coordination and superb leadership on the field. Whether or not that was possible in the confusing circumstances of those July days was patently unclear. Adding to the confusion was a welter of requests for help from all over the region which flooded the War Department at this time.[19]

Many people naturally thought the rebels directly threatened their specific corner of the mid-Atlantic region. Stanton and Halleck managed to handle the situation at Washington, but it fell to state and local officials to muster their militia to protect their railroad lines, river crossings, and munitions plants, as well as the population centers of the area. Critical points like the Gunpowder and Bush river bridges north of Baltimore claimed attention, and the United States Navy was pressed into service to help there. Several small armed steamers were dispatched to the scene. Major Henry B. Judd gathered Delaware militiamen at Wilmington and sent them southward to help at the bridges, as well as out to the Du Pont powder works nearer the city. Five-hundred sailors as well as convalescents arrived from New York City to help at Baltimore, and Halleck wired Major General George Cadwalader to sweep Philadelphia hospitals for men to send to Washington. Colonel Samuel D. Oliphant, in fact, went by train from the capital to personally escort back some 1,200 of those invalids, and, in the end, had to detour by steamboats to convey these troops to the battlefront in the suburbs. General Barnard, recently returned from assignment at Grant's headquarters, implored Halleck on July 9 to request the return of trained heavy artillerists from the Petersburg lines. "The remnant of these regiments would furnish a full complement of experienced gunners to all the forts," he suggested, and would impart confidence among the militiamen, "and give to the defense a reliability which it cannot have, do what we may without them." Halleck most assuredly did not lack for general officers. Many volunteered from distant stations, and in one classic exchange, Brigadier General J. R. West telegraphed his availability from the comfortable parlor of New York's Fifth Avenue Hotel, only to receive back the full sting of Halleck's acerbic tongue. "We have five times as many generals here as we want, but are greatly in need of privates," said the chief-of-staff, "any one volunteering in that capacity will be thankfully received."[20]

Halleck became increasingly exasperated as the tension mounted in Washington. When Brigadier General Albion G. Howe (who succeeded Sigel in command at Harpers Ferry) asked for instructions, Halleck shot back: "I have no instructions to give, further than to open communication with General Hunter, and effect a junction with his army; after which all available forces of General Hunter's command should endeavor to reach Washington, or at least to open communication by the most available route." Hunter's pace eastward from Cumberland, Maryland was snail-like. Nobody, except Grant, expected him to play a significant role at this point. Still, Halleck's enjoinder to Howe hardly underscored Grant's order to mass forces and actively operate against Early's line of communications or retreat route, or more especially, to annihilate him. The Union high command relied on a static defense of the city, and it fell to Major General Christopher C. Augur, commanding the Department of Washington or XXII Corps, to organize the effort. The forty-three-year-old West Pointer was hardly brilliant, but he was capable enough. He had been associated earlier with various operations in Virginia and Louisiana under the Massachusetts politician-general, Nathaniel P. Banks. Now he would attempt to consolidate the defense against Early, operating from his departmental headquarters at Fourteenth and One-Half Street and Pennsylvania Avenue in downtown Washington. His primary assis-

Major General Christopher Columbus Augur, U.S.A. Commander of the Department of Washington-XXII Corps, he was in overall charge of the city's defense during Early's demonstration, July 11–12, 1864. (U.S. Army Military History Institute)

tant in the early going was Colonel Moses N. Wisewell, military governor of the city. Other figures would soon join the cavalcade of tactical leaders in the capital's defense.[21]

The snarled command became more apparent as the hours wore on. Halleck had ordered Major General Quincy A. Gillmore to save the city. Stanton introduced Major General Alexander McCook to such duty. Grant originally wanted to give Ord this mission, but the Monocacy defeat sent him to Baltimore. None of these men lacked experience. The thirty-nine-year-old Gillmore had spent most of the war on coastal campaigning, and had recently feuded with Ben Butler during the Bermuda Hundred operation between Richmond and Petersburg. McCook, younger than the others at thirty-five, was one of the "Fighting McCook" clan of Ohio. He too served under the cloud of the disastrous Chickamauga defeat the previous September. Things improved a bit when Gillmore eventually went out to take charge of the northeastern part of the defenses, while McCook set up a command post at the reserve camp to collect newly mustered units at the intersection of Fourteenth Street and Piney Branch Road near the T. Blagden

Major General Alexander McDowell McCook, U.S.A. Under War Department censure for faulty tactical conduct at the battle of Chickamauga in 1863, he was in charge of the northern defenses of Washington during Early's demonstration. (U.S. Army Military History Institute)

property and the Crystal Spring. Commanding the northern defenses in general on the eve of the crisis was a one-armed, convalescing twenty-seven-year-old veteran brigadier, Martin D. Hardin. Hardin's career was studded with gallantry and wounds—he was recuperating from his fourth (sustained on the North Anna) at the time Early's army appeared. Yet he was active enough to be out inspecting forts east of the Anacostia that Sunday afternoon, when news reached him about cavalry skirmishing north of Rockville on the way to Frederick. Galloping westward, Hardin reported at McCook's command post, listened to the Ohioan's complaints about inadequate troops, and learned that McCook planned to take over as commander of the northern defense line. Hardin would be assigned that portion of the works most likely to come under attack—the lines at Tennallytown where the turnpike from Frederick passed. That night, McCook and Lieutenant Colonel Alexander, now his engineer adviser, returned to the city, while Hardin stumbled on to his new assignment and reached Fort Reno about midnight.[22]

The Federal situation had not been helped by dispatch of Albion Howe's contingents to reinforce the Harpers Ferry garrison several days before. At 1:00 a.m. on July 10, Augur had responded to the pressure of Baltimore authorities and ordered the 10th Veteran Reserve Regiment (then encamped at Soldier's Home) to take the train to that city. It left at 8:45 a.m. Sunday morning. At that point, Hardin discovered that his "division" numbered only 1,800 infantry, a like number of artillerists, and but 60 cavalrymen. With these troops, he was to defend the whole sector from Fort Sumner on the Potomac to Fort Foote south of the Anacostia down the Potomac. Brigadier General Gustavus De Russy counted 4,000 infantry, 1,800 artillerists, and 50 cavalrymen for his defensive lines south of the Potomac (traditionally the most sensitive sector, but not so on July 10, 1864). Ironically, Colonel Benjamin F. Rosson's 147th Ohio National Guard had just finished a month in

Major General Quincy Adams Gillmore, U.S.A. In Washington under censure for faulty tactical leadership during the Richmond-Petersburg campaign, he was given control over a portion of the northeastern defense line and later over reinforcements from the XIX Corps. (U.S. Army Military History Institute)

the northern lines (manning posts from Forts Reno to Stevens), only to be sent back across the river to Fort Ethan Allen at this time. Augur could also muster several regiments of District of Columbia militia (aggregating 600 men), bits and pieces of four other cavalry regiments (800 men) from perimeter defense at Annandale, Virginia, some 1,000 miscellaneous and convalescing troopers from the Giesboro depot, and nine regiments of Veteran Reserves as well as a battalion of heavy artillerists doing provost duty in the city—at most an additional 4,000 extra muskets in total.[23]

Hardin's new sector on July 11 would be the crucial one. It initially contained one 1,000-man brigade comprising four companies of the 151st Ohio National Guard, five or six companies of light artillery, including one company of U.S. regular artillerists. These were all commanded by yet another convalescing veteran, Colonel J. M. Warner of the 1st Vermont Heavy Artillery. The works west of Rock Creek, eleven in number, mounted perhaps 100 guns ranging in size from 24- and 32-pound seacoast cannon, to 100-pound Parrott rifled guns. Lieutenant Colonel Joseph A. Haskin, USA, had perhaps 1,250 men of the 150th, 151st, and 170th Ohio National Guard, and two companies of volunteer heavy artillerists, plus invalids, to cover the expanse

Brigadier General Martin Davis Hardin, U.S.A. Veteran brigade commander in the Army of the Potomac, Hardin was convalescing from a fourth battle wound and the loss of an arm when asked to command the sector of forts initially tested by Early's Confederates. (U.S. Army Military History Institute)

100–pounder Parrott gun, Fort Totten, Military Defenses of Washington. During the defense of Washington, such heavy ordnance as this gun wrecked havoc on Confederate supply trains and camps in the rear, but were ineffective in the basically skirmish-battle in front of the fortification line itself. (U.S. Army Military History Institute)

of line eastward from Rock Creek to the Anacostia River—these forts mounting perhaps 126 guns in total. Warner soon shifted men forward from river batteries in his rear and placed them in weak spots between Forts Sumner and Reno. Other artillery companies (like Company A, 1st Wisconsin Heavy Artillery) came from as far away as Fort Lyon, below Alexandria, although authorities wanted to ensure proper strength in De Russy's lines to guard against Confederates crossing the river from Maryland and assaulting the southern works. When Major John W. Snyder's remaining battalion of the 9th New York Heavy Artillery arrived from Petersburg, per Grant's orders, it marched immediately to the works at Tennallytown. Perhaps the first of the Army of the Potomac "relief column" to reach Washington came with seven companies of the 25th New York Cavalry. Mustered into government service at Saratoga Springs and Hart's Island in New York Harbor from February on, it had been shipped to the Army of the Potomac for provost marshall duty and returned to D.C. for mounts just as Early's army threatened the city. This would prove to be their first test in combat, although their faded blue uniforms covered with Virginia dust seemed to project a veteran quality to friend and foe. They were among the first contingents seen by President

Abraham Lincoln, and the chief executive supposedly told one of its captains, "Our Capital is in a critical condition, and upon you and your good men depend the safety of the Capital; but should any of your command be captured, say nothing about the situation of Washington, and if they ask whose command you belong to, say the advance of the Sixth Corps."[24]

Proper intelligence about the Confederate approach was imperative for Washington officials. Despite the insufficient mounted troops, Major De Witt C. Thompson, 17th Pennsylvania Cavalry, commanded a camp on Muddy Branch northwest of Rockville, and he was ordered to shadow Early's flanks and report on the enemy's direction and intention. Lowell's 2d Massachusetts Cavalry shifted across the river from Falls Church and worked out of the lines at Tennallytown in similar fashion. Major William H. Fry of the 16th Pennsylvania Cavalry gathered together 500 men from the Giesboro depot and took this provisional regiment (reputedly representing every mounted unit in the Army of the Potomac) out to reconnoiter the country eastward from Rockville through Brookville and Leesborough and beyond to Laurel on the rail line to Baltimore. Fry soon fell in with Captain A. Levi Well's companies of the 8th Illinois Cavalry which had been cut off in the Monocacy fight and had retired via Sugarloaf Mountain. Fry and Wells turned northward from Rockville toward Gerrardsville, spoiling for a fight with the rebel vanguard. They would fire the opening shots of the battle for Washington. Yet, their main mission was gathering intelligence and passing such information back to the line of forts so that signal corpsmen and telegraphers might transmit that data downtown to the War Department, and thence around the perimeter of the defenses. Nearly every fort had its own signal station, and special telegraph offices were opened for the emergency at key posts like Forts Lincoln, Totten, Stevens, and Corcoran, as well as at Chain Bridge and Arlington.[25]

Jubal Early's army spent Saturday night on the Monocacy battlefield. Nobody bothered about the dead, but care was given to the wounded, and useful weapons and equipment were gathered from the fight. Then the march resumed before daybreak on Sunday with McCausland's battered troopers in the lead. The nine-mile long wagon train included prisoners and other booty. Ramseur's division stayed behind to protect a work party attempting to batter down the iron railroad bridge. Neither gunpowder nor solid shot from the artillery's 12-pounders had any effect, so Garrett's prized bridge survived despite all the fighting around it and subsequent attempts to destroy it. Other railroad facilities fared less well, as the Confederates burned everything else at the junction.[26]

Ramseur soon had his hands full holding off pursuing Federal cavalry as he hurried his men to close with the main part of Early's army. The march that day proved hot and tiring to Confederates and prisoners alike. Once more, heat, dust, and periodic skirmishing with a shadowy enemy dogged Early's veterans as they trudged through colorful little hamlets like Urbana, Hyattstown, and Clarksburg, where local "Secesh" occasionally turned out to cheer the marchers. One North Carolina reporter with the column found local residents to be very friendly to the Confederate cause and ready to join it. A Charlottesville, Virginia editor also in the ranks decided that such a welcome in the Old Line state could only mean that Washington itself would surely fall if Early attacked it. Sergeant Major John G. Young of the 4th North Carolina remembered how ladies rode horseback for miles just to see their cavalier heroes in gray, and volunteered their services as guides and couriers. He spoke too of "some few 'Marylanders'" joining the ranks for the campaign. Much of this may have resulted from a recent drawing of names for a conscription draft of Marylanders into the Union army which took place for the Fifth Congressional District at Ellicott's Mills on July 8. A heavy quota for Montgomery County, where Early's force was now passing, may have caused the ostensible display of support. Certainly the prisoners with the column told a different tale. They claimed that the tubs of water and barrels of crackers set out by locals such as Columbus Winsor of Urbana were for them, not the rebels. When one elderly woman in Clarksburg realized many of the dusty figures were actually Federals, she had exclaimed: "Why, those are our men! Why Union men, of course," bringing forth cheers from the dejected captives.[27]

Prisoner banter with their guards increased as the shared miseries of the march banded together friend and foe. One Confederate major proved an "exceedingly agreeable gentleman" in a discourse with a 9th New York "Heavy" concerning the origin of the sobriquet "Johnny" for the rebel fighting man. But there was precious little "dog-trotting" or "running" from the Monocacy to capture Washington quickly as claimed by Virginia cavalryman Alexander Hunter. The officers' constant urging to "close-up" was disagreeable to both Confederates and their prisoners, and everyone gratefully dropped beside the road to sleep once the sun set on the day's march of some twenty or more miles. Early's army could be found strung out from well above Gaithersburg almost to Rockville by Sunday night. Men and commands both straggled into the principal concentration point at Gaithersburg all night. The farm of Ignatius Fulks and his family attracted 1,800 cavalrymen, and their horses, haystacks, and the carcasses of butchered livestock soon attested to their rapacious appetites. John T. De Sellum and his sister

"Summit Hill" farm just south of town struggled to host Early and his generals as their "guests." A lively political discussion threatened to disrupt dinner as John Brown's 1859 raid on Harpers Ferry as well as the justness of the southern cause engaged the diners. De Sellum, a slaveowner, ardently defended the notion that the south should be "whipped back under the Constitution, Union, and Government of the United States with the rights and privileges she had before the war." One hot-headed colonel named Lee (perhaps it was Robert's own son?) responded to De Sellum, "You are an abolitionist—it is no use to blame the devil, and do the devil's work." Early and Brigadier General Arnold J. Elzey defused the situation, restored civility to the table, and "prevented a serious termination of the conversation."[28]

De Sellum was a prominent local citizen, who had donated land for construction of the Episcopal church and was well known as an adviser to the agricultural and scientific community in Washington. However, his southern sympathies and slave ownership failed to save him from Early's scavengers. The plunder began before the general arrived and continued all night and into July 11, as horses, beef, cows, bacon, tons of hay, and barrels of corn went off with the Confederates. With fences torn to pieces, confusion, and a night and day of horror as "our lives were in imminent danger," an aroused De Sellum finally accosted Early early the next morning and asked, "if he intended to give me up to be indiscriminately plundered." The crusty general replied that since De Sellum wasn't in sympathy with the Confederacy, "you can't expect favour or protection," but did write out an order leaving De Sellum and his sister two barrels of corn. Still, soon thereafter, rebel privates searched the De Sellum house for money and concealed arms as the sister managed to hide $3,000 and government bonds under her dress. Despite the general destruction and ruin at their hands, De Sellum subsequently hid three rebel soldiers from pursuing Federals although he caustically observed later: "How many of Early's men I directed to the North Pole or how many left by crossing the Potomac southward I only know by the large number of abandoned muskets left around my house." Early and his army were sacrificing valuable time, and not winning sympathy for their thievery in borderland Maryland.[29]

The initial sparring in defense of the nation's capital had already begun by the time De Sellum confronted the rebel host in his dooryard on Monday morning. Fry's cavalry had stopped at his place earlier on Sunday as it withdrew under pressure from McCausland after a fight at Gerrardsville. McCausland continued to push Fry back through Rockville to a hilltop about a mile south of the town. Rockville streets echoed with the sound of shots and then with the tramp of rebel feet. Random squads of outriders clashed with Union horsemen all over Montgomery County that day. One brash young Virginian from Greenbrier County, twenty-one-year-old William D. Scott of the 14th Cavalry, died in such a brush. Scott and his companions had been surprised while foraging at the Joseph A. Taney farm near Clopper's Mill. Mortally wounded, Scott fled to nearby "Woodlands," the Clopper family home, where a servant found him suffering on the front porch. He was taken in by the family and a doctor removed the bullet, but could not save his life. The family buried him secretly in front of the St. Rose of Lima Catholic Church. The fourth of seven children, Scott had three other brothers in Confederate service. When bitter feelings subsided in Montgomery County after the war, the United Daughters of the Confederacy erected a suitable headstone for his grave.[30]

This was roughly the situation as a new week opened. Early's main body of Confederates, hampered by prisoners and the baggage train, was strung out on the highway to Washington north of Rockville. Ramseur had finally closed with the main army by 11:00 p.m. Sunday night. At his point, the whole force lay about one day's hot march from the capital's fortifications. Reports from as far away as southern Pennsylvania noted: "Squads of rebel cavalry are infesting the mountain from Monterey to Frederick, stealing horses, and creating much alarm." The same could be said throughout the Frederick-Baltimore-Washington triangle. In fact, had Early retained control over his horsemen, they might have better served him in his main objective of threatening Washington. As it was, reports of those rampaging outriders as well as Bradley Johnson's main body of horsemen caused alarm bells to ring constantly in Baltimore. Wallace and Ricketts proved to be of little help for they were preoccupied in regrouping their commands at Ellicott's Mills. Far to the south at City Point, Ulysses S. Grant wired that two divisions of the VI Corps were on their way to help at Washington with the first contingents of the XIX Corps not far behind. Out on the Rockville Pike, Major Fry sent back the disturbing message at 5:00 p.m. that he and Wells were withdrawing, and he respectfully suggested that the forts in the Tennallytown vicinity should be strongly guarded "as the enemy's column is a mile long." Local residents along that highway suddenly realized they were in a war zone. Young Virginia Campbell Moore recounted years later how she and her family had attended a local church service when in rushed dusty, blue-clad troopers yelling: "Get these horses away from here and get to your homes—the Rebs are coming." The family then "slept in Confederate lines, breakfasted in Federal lines, dined in those of the Confederates and so on" for the next few

Hospital Ward in Armory Square Hospital, Washington, D.C. Wards like this were emptied of any wounded who could carry a firearm in order to man the Washington defenses against Early, providing a show of force that deterred the Confederates from attacking on July 11, 1864. (U.S. Army Military History Institute)

days. Indeed, the issue of the capital's safety hung in the balance that Sabbath. Early's rag-tag army was only a hair's breath from achieving the greatest Confederate triumph of the whole war. It all depended upon events of Monday morning.[31]

Few people slept well in Washington that night. Roads from the north were crowded with refugees spreading wild rumors. The city's streets filled with scurrying orderlies, convalescents, and clerks mustering with their commands. Two hundred and fifty less seriously wounded departed Campbell General Hospital alone, and Quartermaster General Montgomery C. Meigs personally supervised the gathering of his employees. Most civilians remained behind closed doors although a few "old negroes, young children, boys" reputedly slipped through Federal lines to enjoin Early's men to hurry because only a few government clerks manned the ramparts, claimed Virginia Private Alexander Hunter. Officers along the Union defense line kept pickets on alert and rifle pits fully manned, and additional units like the 7th Veteran Reserve Regiment, George W. Gile's brigade of convalescents, Snyder's New York heavy artillerymen, a company of the 151st Ohio National Guard, and Battery I, 2d U.S. Artillery, strengthened Colonel Warner's positions west of Tennallytown. It appeared that these troops would bear the brunt of the rebel assault in the morning.[32]

Monday, July 11, 1864, dawned clear and hot. The thermometer hovered in the mid-nineties over the next few days and debilitated defender and attacker alike. Picket posts of Ohio guardsmen on the south side of the Potomac out toward Great Falls brushed with scattered Confederate outriders

Major General Montgomery Cunningham Meigs, U.S.A. Quartermaster General of the Union Army, Meigs was not content to remain behind a desk during Early's attack on Washington. He organized his departmental employees (military and civilian) into battalions and personally led them to the northern defenses. (U.S. Army Military History Institute)

at first light, then scampered back to the safety of Fort Marcy near Chain Bridge. Lowell, with three squadrons of his Bay Staters and one from the 8th Illinois Cavalry, went out to the Old Stone Tavern area on the Rockville Pike and relieved Fry's tired troopers who were running out of ammunition. Accounts are unclear, but the day's action probably erupted in the vicinity of Rabbit's Creek between the Darcy and the Montrose post offices, somewhere near the Bethesda Presbyterian Church. McCausland's command slowly pushed back the outnumbered Federals to the Tennallytown heights, and approached the defenses of Washington in that sector via the Rockville Pike and River Road. The rebel advance, supported by horse artillery and at least one heavier artillery piece, elicited some fire from the guns of Fort Reno's sister forts like Bayard, Simmons, Mansfield, and Sumner to the west. Lowell, meanwhile, sent back "accurate and reliable information" about the enemy's advance, and the Federals atop the highest ground in the District at Tennallytown (430 feet above sea level) had a panoramic view. The signal station at Fort Reno alone overcame Early's numerical superiority for it could transmit reports about every move the dusty Confederate columns would make. The two sides skirmished briskly all Monday morning, as McCausland searched for weak points, and the defenders sparred back in turn. Hardin finally sent back an anxious message to Augur about noon, asking for more ammunition for Lowell's and Fry's Sharps and Burnside carbines, as well as forage for the hungry cavalry horses. Company M of Lowell's regiment ostensibly fought on foot, for some of their number claimed later that they had left their mounts at a "Camp Relief" in the city.[33]

McCausland could also report back to Early on what he found opposing him on the Georgetown Pike. He noted the strong line of hilltop fortifications stretching unbroken along the horizon. Tennallytown had been a popular Union training ground from the beginning of the war, and the tiny hamlet eventually became engulfed by a vast tent city of encamped volunteers. In the autumn of 1861, after the Bull Run disaster of that summer, authorities had become worried about low water in the Potomac and the possibility that the Confederates might attempt the very maneuver now being undertaken by Jubal Early. Army engineers laid out and volunteers constructed the first isolated forts such as Fort Pennsylvania (later renamed Reno in honor of fallen Major General Jesse L. Reno, killed at South Mountain in September 1862) at Tennallytown. Gangs of Freedmen or "Contrabands" had improved and expanded the defenses over the subsequent months so that an interconnected system of forts, batteries, rifle-trenches, abatis entanglements, and cleared fields of fire prevailed over the farmland and country lanes as well as the highways to the front.[34]

When McCausland and his scouts peered through their binoculars in the early morning haze, they saw a formidable line of works before them. Far to their right closer to the Potomac bristled Fort Sumner (843 perimeter yards and 30 guns), which commanded the river valley and the road constructed atop the city's aqueduct. Sabotage of that facility might have proven an inviting target, but there is no evidence that Early's people had the slightest inkling of its existence. Then came batteries Bailey and Benson, commanding the valley of Powder Mill Branch; Battery and Fort Mansfield (220 perimeter yards, 11 guns) as well as Fort Simmons (177 perimeter yards, 8 guns), all of which covered the property of the Unionist Shoemaker and Dean families (upon whose land these works had been constructed). Where the ancient River Road, the Rockville Pike (which had heard the tramp of English Major General Edward Braddock's troops a century before on their way to attack Fort Duquesne), and the Brookville Road all converged before entering Tenallytown, lay Fort Bayard (123 perimeter yards, 6 guns), and the strongest work of all, Fort and Battery Reno. Reno alone contained twenty-seven heavy guns, including a long-range 100-pound Parrott rifled cannon. All of this convinced McCausland that the topography and the defensive line would be far too strong for a direct assault, and he conveyed that impression back to Early at Rockville.[35]

Monday morning also witnessed an almost superhuman effort by Early and his officers to move the army forward from its overnight bivouacs. The Confederate column marched through Rockville (a town with a strong "Secesh" element according to Sergeant Major John Young of the 4th North Carolina). William Browning, an Ohio prisoner, captured at Monocacy, recalled the dead horses in the streets from a recent cavalry encounter, and one Unionist lady who fed him and offered to write and send letters home for the unfortunate Yanks. Another prisoner, from New York, noted that soon after passing through the town they were drawn up in line, thoroughly searched since money was "the chief object of rebel cupidity," and then paraded before General Breckinridge. He was "one of the finest looking men I ever saw," recalled the New Yorker years later. Yet he wondered if such a former Vice President of the United States "might and ought to be in a better business than seeking to destroy the place where, for four years, he had been the recipient of so many honors." Browning remembered too that sounds of distant gunfire closer to the city now reached them, and how rebel stragglers suddenly rushed past the captives intent upon being among the first to enter "and loot the city." One of the guards told the captives that the sound of those heavy fortress cannon was the sweetest music on earth. Browning snapped back that before the rebels took Washington they would be accommodated with plenty of sweet music, and when those same stragglers came rushing back several hours later, he taunted: "Why didn't you go into Washington?" The Confederates now replied dejectedly: "We would, only the cursed Yankees are throwing flour barrels at us," alluding to the heavy projectiles from the 24- and 32-pound guns in the forts.[36]

The struggle for the nation's capital shifted eastward as the day progressed. News of the Tennallytown works caused Early to side-slip away from the Georgetown Pike, searching for a place elsewhere to crack the Union lines. McCausland continued to demonstrate on the turnpike and River Road, but Early sent the bulk of his badly straggling force eastward toward another main thoroughfare into the city. The road he found was an old and well-maintained highway known as the Washington and Brookville Turnpike or simply the Union Road in Maryland, while in the District it bore the name Seventh Street Road (now Georgia Avenue). The whole army (wagons, artillery, prisoners, plunder, and the soldiery) turned eastward at Rockville onto what is now Viers Mill Road and passed Samuel Viers's grist mill on upper Rock Creek and then took New Cut Road to Mitchell's crossroads and Leesborough (now Wheaton). The column turned onto the turnpike leading southward past Sligo Post Office (now Silver Spring) toward the District line. Rodes' division took the lead followed by Ramseur, Gordon, the army train, with Echols in the rear, and Brigadier General Armistead Long's artillery batteries interspersed between the infantry divisions. The thermometer hit 94 degrees out at W. H. Farquehar's "Lonesome Hollow" farm near Sandy Spring in Montgomery County, and more dust and extreme fatigue swept across the marching Confederates. Georgian G. W. Nichols remembered being enveloped in clouds of dust and that many of his comrades fell by the roadside from exhaustion and sun stroke, "but we pulled on the best we could." Their officers rode up and down urging the men to "close-up" and promising them a chance to capture "Old Abe" in the White House. But, as Virginian John Worsham remembered, it had little effect for "our division [Gordon's] was stretched out almost like skirmishers." The turnpike might be mudless in winter due to its crushed flintstone base, but it was hard on sore feet and lungs in the dry summer, as the rebels discovered that day.[37]

The Federals spotted this huge dust cloud of marching Confederates. Signalers at Fort Reno (elevation 429 feet) and farther east at Fort Totten (elevation 330 feet) relayed the information about Early's flanking move. Captain James F. Berry of the 8th Illinois Cavalry also spotted the turning Confederates by midday from his outpost midway between the District line and Leesborough. He sent the word in to General McCook, who by now

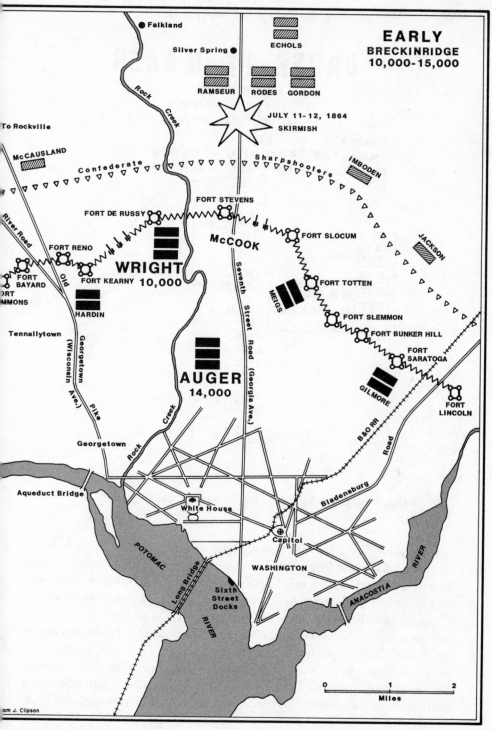

Early's Demonstration Before Washington, July 11–12, 1864, showing approximation of commands and commanders. (Cartography by William J. Clipson)

ORDER OF MARCH

ARMY OF THE VALLEY
MONDAY 11 JULY 1864
WEATHER: INCREDIBLY HOT

STARTING TIME: 3:30 A.M.
STARTING POINT: 4 MILES ABOVE ROCKVILLE. MD
DESTINATION: THE CAPITOL BLDG. 20 MILES DISTANT

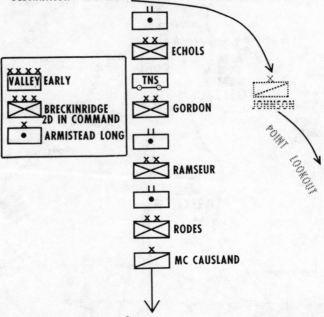

Order of March, Army of the Valley, July 11, 1864, as Early approaches the capital.

had come forward from the reserve camp and set up headquarters in the Mooreland Tavern at Brightwood, just south of Fort Stevens on the Seventh Street Road. McCook's meager forces took their places along the line from Fort Reno to Fort Totten, although the lines were admittedly stretched thin in places. McCook himself felt that "there never was before a command so hereogeneous [sic], yet so orderly," and he enumerated in his official report the ranks filled by hale and hearty soldiers, invalids and convalescents, and the government clerks, "each working with a singleness of purpose and willing to discharge any duty imposed upon him." McCook and others still worried about the exposed and tempting valley of Rock Creek and took great pains to fill that approach with fallen timber and brush. They thus channeled the axis of Early's approach onto the Seventh Street Road and directly at Fort Stevens. Here would occur the decisive combat for the City of Washington.[38]

Pickets from Captain A. A. Safford's Company F, 150th Ohio National Guard, learned just after breakfast that the enemy was coming. Many of "these boys from Oberlin" College had enlisted with the promise that they would never experience combat. Sergeant George R. Fackler established a picket command post just beyond the District line on the Seventh Street Road and stationed Corporal J. R. Hudson and three men at the so-called "Chestnut Post" near the toll gate where Piney Branch Road diverged from the Seventh Street Road in front of Fort Stevens, and headed out toward the Northwest Branch of the Anacostia River in Maryland. An additional three-man vedette took position atop a hill about a mile from the fort and in-between the other two stations. The Ohioans had watched all night as the flood of refugees and their possessions streamed toward the city. Private John Amos Bedient suggested that it seemed like a time of imminent danger and intense vigilance. "Several times during the night the muzzle of my cocked musket was within eighteen inches of men who only stopped at the third halt and click of the lock," he observed. In the words of yet another comrade, James Cannon: "The boys who had wanted to go to the front now found that the front had come to us." Before Fackler could gather up his pickets in an orderly fashion, the Confederates burst upon them, and the Buckeyes had to run quickly back to the lines at Fort Stevens, firing at the enemy in turn, but every man for himself.[39]

General Augur had also gone out to Fort Stevens at dawn, in preparation for touring all the northern front. He found the fort garrisoned by Safford's men, a portion of the 13th Michigan Battery under Captain Charles Dupont, and some convalescents under Lieutenant Henry L. Turner, 150th Ohio National Guard—about 209 men in all. He dispatched an aide to Colonel William Gamble, commanding a cavalry station at Camp Stoneman at Giesboro Depot, asking him to forward every available cavalryman, whether mounted or not. "Officers were assigned to commands rather promiscuously," recalled Lieutenant Samuel C. Smith of the 1st Maine Cavalry, and noted that he received command of seventy-five men from three different regiments. At daylight, in the later words of Sergeant A. G. Jacobs of Company B, 6th Ohio Cavalry, "we were . . . 'hoofing it' toward the Capital without our breakfast, but in the city, as we were on the move, we were well supplied with bread and butter and other eatables by citizens who thronged the way with baskets." Many of these troops were equipped with new Spencer

The Cavalry Depot at Camp Stoneman, Giesboro Point, Washington, D.C. Cavalrymen from this elaborate facility, who had been sent back from the Army of the Potomac for reequipment, went into the lines at Fort Stevens and successfully thwarted Early's advance until VI Corps reinforcements arrived on July 11–12, 1864. (U.S. Army Military History Institute)

repeating carbines. They passed throngs of excited refugees from upper Maryland, and "as we reached the Patent Office old men [clerks] could be seen pacing up and down the corridors with old muskets over their shoulders on guard duty," commented John H. Wolff of the 25th New York Cavalry after the war.

Augur also sent word to District of Columbia militia commander, Major General George C. Thomas, that it was time to put his men in the field. Despite Henry Halleck's aversion to the civilian clerks mustering to fight Early, Quartermaster General Montgomery C. Meigs enthusiastically called out his "troops," too. In the words of veteran Major and volunteer surgeon John V. Brinton (a former member of Grant's staff in the west): "The Secretary of War directed that all orderlies, messengers, military riffraff, the invalids, veteran reserve, and indeed every man in Government employ, who could put on a uniform, or carry a musket, should turn out in defence of the capital of his country." Yet this mobilization of resources took time and provoked many caustic remarks around the city. When Major William Doster, a provost marshal, asked for the location of militia headquarters at the shop of grocer-turned-militia-brigadier, Peter Bacon, the latter's brother answered, "damned if I know!" Such was the confusion of the moment.[40]

Meanwhile the Confederates straggled on past Leesborough toward the District of Columbia. The dusty men paid little attention to a roofless and uncompleted Grace Episcopal Church to their left just before they reached the crossroads known as Sligo (after the creek nearby). Ironically, some of them would find a final resting place in Grace Episcopal churchyard after the impending battle. Most of them caught sight of a country store (now the northwest corner of Georgia Avenue and Colesville Road), and immediately raided its well-stocked liquor cellar. They moved on past the Batchelder, Thomas, and Wilson properties—passing according to local lore, well into the early evening. Echols and Wharton's commands bivouacked on Batchelder's farm and on that of Postmaster General Montgomery Blair, called "Falkland." The first Confederate killed by Union pickets was buried close to the residence of a Mrs. Burns on the upper portion of the Blair estate. Mrs. Burns claimed to have conversed often with Early and Breckinridge and had overheard that they planned an all-out attack at dawn on Tuesday, July 12. Batchelder, Mrs. Burns, and Mr. Davis (the Sligo toll-keeper on the pike), all estimated rebel strength at about 20,000 men.[41]

The focal point for Confederate concentration became the two farms of the Blair family. In addition to Montgomery's place, his father's famous "Silver Spring" abutted the District boundary line at the Seventh Street Road. Here was the country show-place of the older Blair (whose Kentucky kinsmen were related to John C. Breckinridge), who had entertained the former Vice President as well as many other Washington notables in his time. Blair, in fact, had been the influential editor of *The Globe* newspaper during the presidency of Andrew Jackson and had served in that leader's so-called "kitchen cabinet." He had owned the famous Blair Mansion townhouse across the street from the White House in downtown Washington. While riding with his daughter Elizabeth one day just beyond the District line, one of the pair's horses bolted (accounts vary) and threw its rider to the ground beside a lovely, bubbling sunlit spring. Blair and Elizabeth were immediately taken by the site; he bought it in 1842, erected a country house in the French chateau style by 1845, and also constructed an artificial lake lined with flowers and a small island of honeysuckle in the center, with a lovely white marble statuette of a water nymph and an acorn-shaped summer pavilion adding to the atmosphere. A replica of that acorn-pavilion marks the spring site today

"Silver Spring," the mansion of Francis Preston Blair. During his Washington campaign, Early established his headquarters here and his soldiers enjoyed the cooling waters of the nearby "silver spring." (Montgomery County Historical Society)

on the East-West Highway just west of Georgia Avenue in the locale now named for Blair's "Silver Spring Farm."[42]

The elder Blair had moved permanently to Silver Spring in the early 1850s, leaving his city house to his lawyer son, Montgomery (counsel for Dred Scott in the controversial antebellum slave case and Lincoln's postmaster general from March 1861 until September 1864). The son also constructed his own country home, Falkland, and both estates became gathering places for Washington socialites as well as working farms (and encompassed much of the land which later became the town of Takoma Park). Union enlisted pickets and their officers from nearby camps and forts visited the places often and were always welcomed by the Unionist Blairs. Elizabeth Blair married a young naval officer from the Virginia family of Lee and spent the wartime period with her son and father at Silver Spring while Rear Admiral Samuel Phillips Lee was away on blockade duty. However, as noted previously, both properties were vacant at Early's approach. The southern general took posses-sion of Silver Spring for his headquarters, while his bedraggled soldiers basked in the refreshing waters of the spring and lake, and the officers discov-ered the Blair wine cellars. (The soldiery found the rum at nearby Barnes Tavern more amenable.) It is said that Early tried to protect the houses and properties during his occupation. However, since the Confederates soon bivouacked all over the grounds, such protection was predictably in vain.[43]

The Claggett family, whose property lay to the west of the Blairs and stretched from the Northern boundary stone of the District southward to the line of fortifications, was still another family affected by the rebel occupation of their land. There would be others in due course. One local resident, George Hobbs, recalled that he had just returned from field work for his noon meal when the opening shots of the fighting drove him and his family from their dinner table. He vividly remembered the beauty of the summer scene with meadows rich and green, orchards at their best, and waving rows of corn in the fields on each side of the Seventh Street Road. All of this changed quickly as shot and shell and scrambling men wrought havoc with the landscape. William E. Leach, Company K, 150th O.N.G., was the first Federal to be cut down by gunfire in the battle. Early reported later: "When we reached the sight of the enemy's fortifications the men were almost completely exhausted and not in condition to make an attack." Indeed, so many Confed-erates had dropped by the roadside or wandered off looking for water that the Confederate generals spent most of the day simply trying to corral their forces into line before the Yankee fortifications. Lieutenant Colonel David Lang led Colonel George H. Smith's 62d Virginia Mounted Infantry of Confederates past the Carberry (or Lay) house on the west side of the Seventh Street Road and the Rives (or Reeves) place across that road, in chasing Federal pickets and skirmishers. (Walter Reed Army Medical Center occupies much of that land today.)[44]

The brisk skirmishing, which distinguished the "battle" of Fort Stevens, kept up all afternoon between McCook's men and the lead Confederate divi-sion under Robert Rodes. Union participants remembered the blazing hot sun, the inadequate shelter afforded by wheat shocks on the picket line, and the cannon fire from the forts which endangered friend and foe alike. James M. Singer, a discharged veteran of the 19th United States Infantry, working in Meigs' Quartermaster department, noted how his comrades had been rushed out to seal a breach in the line and found the rebel sharpshooters already at work. "We about as politely informed them we were at home and prepared to receive callers," he noted. Many of these ersatz formations con-tained veterans like Singer, but lacked unit cohesion and elan.

The Union Skirmish Line at Fort Stevens, July 11–12, 1864, after a sketch by E. F. Mullen. This thinly manned but effective line of dismounted cavalry, convalescents, and militia effectively daunted the Confederate commander's plan to assault Fort Stevens. Note the house destroyed to prevent its use by sharpshooters. (The Soldier in Our Civil War, *II, 296*)

Confederates managed to push back the Federal picket line comprising the 150th O.N.G., 25th New York Cavalry, dismounted horsemen under Major G. G. Briggs of the 7th Michigan Cavalry, and the Veteran Reserves. Ammunition ran low at one point for the Federals, and an Ohio contingent commandeered a civilian buggy to brave enemy fire and rush a resupply to the skirmish line. The Buckeyes returned unscathed but their makeshift ammunition cart "was riddled, bed and spokes, by Confederate bullets." While no major Confederate assault took place, the heat of the skirmish action led to a frantic 1:00 p.m. message from the Fort Stevens signaler: "The enemy is within twenty rods (110 yards) of Fort Stevens." However, concentrated cannon fire from Fort De Russy to the west and Forts Slocum and Totten to the east, as well as Fort Stevens' own guns, lessened the danger. The heavier fortress cannon played upon the clouds of dust out in Maryland in an effort to disrupt the marching men and army trains. At one point, friendly fire endangered the lives of the Monocacy captives for their guards marched them directly down the Seventh Street Road into the face of the Union cannon fire. One New Yorker confessed his admiration for the welcome sound of this artillery was somewhat tempered with apprehension lest "some droppings fall on us." The 2d Pennsylvania Heavy Artillery cannoneers at Fort Slocum claimed the honor of firing the first cannon shots of the battle. Skilled and sarcastic veteran gunners at nearby Fort Totten noted: "A body of Confederate cavalry rode aimlessly to and fro along the edge of a wood, about five miles from our fort," completely undismayed by the show of Yankee firepower. Nevertheless, the fiery John B. Gordon became annoyed enough at the Union cannon fire to order up a battery of Parrott guns which, said one participant, "unlimbered in front of the brigade out in the open field in full view of the Yanks about four hundred yards away, and replied, knocking up the red dirt around the muzzles of the big fellows in the fort, while the enemy continued to aim at the moon and stars."[45]

The Federal skirmishers, led by the 25th New York cavalry and Briggs's 500–600 dismounted men (some of whom had reached the lines only that morning from Lighthouse Point on the James River via Baltimore), drove

Gun Drill at Fort Totten, Military Defenses of Washington. Quickly thrust into action against Early's Confederates, ersatz gun crews from militia, convalescents, and invalids had to replace the now-absent heavy artillerists, such as those shown here. (U.S. Army Military History Institute)

Early's Attack Stopped by Dismounted Cavalry and Militia, July 11, 1864, after a sketch by George H. Durfee. The skirmishing on that afternoon caused Early to hesitate and lose the opportunity of breaching the Union fortification line. (The Soldier in Our Civil War, II, 297)

the nettlesome Confederates back about 1:30 p.m., and established the Federal skirmish line some 1,100 yards from the earthworks. McCook claimed that affairs remained in that state for the rest of the day, since in his view, the enemy was not "developing any force other than their skirmish line." Confederate reports confirmed that the jaded rebels quickly dropped off into makeshift bivouacs in the afternoon heat or haphazardly supported their own sharpshooters up to dark. Captain Norris, of the 2d Provisional Pennsylvania Heavy Artillery at Fort De Russy, and Colonel John M. C. Marble of the 151st Ohio National Guard, who commanded both that fort as well as Fort Kearny to the west (including all intervening batteries like Smeade and Terrill), also reported heavy skirmishing west of Rock Creek by Colonel George W. Gile's Veteran Reserve brigade. Confederates trying to work their way through the abatis-filled creek valley proved particularly pesky, and sharpshooters in Claggett and other farmhouses to the front of the works took their toll of men in the works. Gunners sent 100-pound shells crashing at targets 4,000 or more yards away, beyond Silver Spring, as well as time, percussion, and case shells in the direction of the rebel skirmishers and sharpshooters at a 1,700–2,800-yard range. Local legend held that shellfire from Fort Reno reputedly dropped on a farm where the Naval Medical Center stands today in modern Bethesda. Marble declared solemnly: "We are assured by citizens . . . that the enemy was surprised at the accuracy of our fire at such distance, and from information since obtained we are led to conclude that the accuracy and activity of our artillery and skirmish line contributed largely to deter them from making the intended assault on Monday night." But skeptical rebels recalled that the shells ("which made a roaring noise like the passing of a railroad train") simply passed over their heads at "great altitude and burst to our rear, doing no damage to any one." I. G. Bradwell was more perceptive in that his fellow Georgians decided that Federal gunners were after the Confederate wagon train. Yet he too dismissed the shelling as producing nothing more than "a great contempt for the 'melish.'" Lieutenant Frank Wilkeson, Battery A, 4th United States Artillery, temporarily assigned to Fort Totten, declared the shooting to be the worst he ever saw and echoed Bradwell's contention that it was all the militia and departmental clerks' doing and that the enemy "did not pay the slightest attention to it." Nonetheless, North Carolina Sergeant Major John G. Young still pronounced the huge Union shells which he termed "nail kegs" to be "very unhealthy."[46]

Federal reinforcements from Meade's army began to arrive at Washington's Sixth Street wharves during this time. Lead elements of Major General Horatio Wright's VI Corps disembarked from steamers like *Essex*, while not far behind, contingents of the XIX Corps fresh from Louisiana left the *Crescent*. Only about 600 men from the 114th and 153d New York would actually land from the latter corps, but two battle-reduced divisions of Wright's men came off the gangways. All aboard had enjoyed the breezes off bay and river and the sights of Mount Vernon on the way up from City Point, but they were now completely taken aback by the wild enthusiasm of Washington's citizens anxious for their arrival. Even President Lincoln was on hand to greet them, munching on army biscuits as the men from Pennsylvania, New York, Rhode Island, and other northeastern states passed him. He joshed them from time to time about hurrying if they wanted to catch Jubal Early.[47]

Ever restless, the worried president had prowled the corridors of the War Department after returning Sunday evening from the Soldier's Home cottage. Annoyed at Stanton's ordering him back to the city and even more irritated when he learned that Assistant Secretary of the Navy Gustavus V. Fox had arranged a small escape steamer if the rebels broke into town, Lincoln did not intend to confine himself to the White House during the emergency. It is said he rode out to Tennallytown that morning to see what was happening.

He then went down to the docks to look for the reinforcements coming by river, and once Wright's men arrived, he insisted upon going out to Fort Stevens where a battle seemed to be taking place. He and his entourage made their way through townspeople, screaming that "it is the old Sixth Corps . . . the danger is over now," and on up the Seventh and Fourteenth Street roads to the defensive line. His cavalry escort unceremoniously hustled VI Corps marchers aside with brusque shouts of "give the road for the President" and clattered by in front of the carriage. Curiosity became so strong among the horde of civilians who, like Lincoln, wanted to see the battle, that many actually moved in among the soldiers in the rifle pits. The military finally banned anyone from approaching the lines without a pass. Of course, they could not keep the commander-in-chief from venturing into the battle zone.[48]

Confusion now arose over the use of the Federal reinforcements. Halleck attempted to orchestrate operations by directing Wright to move toward Chain Bridge and encamp behind the works at this point. He forbade the VI Corps commander from placing his veterans in the works "except in case of attack," and evidently intended the newcomers to form the maneuver element for operations against Early as orderd by Grant. All of this was quite premature, what with Fort Stevens and environs hard pressed at that moment. By 1:40 p.m., Halleck had countermanded the order and Wright's men backtracked to the Seventh Street Road with instructions to "rendezvous near the Military Asylum." Wright rode on ahead to meet with Augur and McCook, and to assure them that his men would arrive by midafternoon. It was now the VI Corp's turn to quick-march on dusty hot roads like the Confederates. George T. Stevens and his comrades in the 77th New York marveled at the bedraggled refugees they encountered on the march, suffered through the arduous trek, and made it to a make-shift bivouac behind Fort De Russy. Wright wanted to clean out the enemy sharpshooters, but was dissuaded by Augur and McCook in favor of allowing the veterans to rest while the militia and convalescents held their ground. Wright's men were peeved, one soldier declaring derisively: "There came out from Washington the most unique body of soldiers, if soldiers they could be called, ever seen during the war," and noted that "they gabbled and were evidently trying to keep up their courage by talking loudly and boastfully of their determination to hold the rifle pits at all hazards." Assuredly, more than one of those derided soldiers was probably like Major J. W. Crosby of the 61st Pennsylvania, who, despite an unhealed head wound from a previous battle, left his hospital bed, hired a horse, and rejoined his old unit behind the lines, saying, "I must go to my boys."[49]

Everyone expected a Confederate assault on the forts that afternoon. It never came. New York correspondent Sylvanus Cadwallader recounted how the rebels simply stacked arms up and down their line, built fires, and cooked their dinners before even commencing to skirmish with any resolve. A battery of artillery was unloaded in his brother-in-law E. A. Paul's dooryard (Paul was away with Hunter's forces, but his family remained in the house during the battle). Cadwallader always wondered at Early's inaction, for the Union lines could have been carried at any point, he observed, "with the loss of a few hundred men." A volley, a Rebel Yell, and a vigorous charge, would have given us Washington, claimed Virginia cavalryman John Opie. Major General John B. Gordon later boasted that he had actually ridden onto the Yankee breastworks at some point, and found them undefended with "space broad enough for the easy passage of Early's army without resistance." Certainly most of the dirty, heat-jaded Confederates lounging under shade trees on the farms, or sipping water from Frank Blair's Silver Spring, wondered about this. They claimed afterward to have seen the dome of the capital, viewed the city's church spires, and listened to the town clocks striking—all quite questionable given the topography and noise of battle in front of Fort Stevens—but they could never figure out why Early denied them a chance to capture the works and the city. Still, there were a few like Virginian John Worsham, who admitted that he saw "the most formidable looking [line of fortifications] I ever saw," and quietly gave thanks that the army had not been ordered to assault that position.[50]

Early had ridden forward upon his arrival and glimpsed "works which were feebly manned," he suggested in postwar reminiscences. Then, resting his horse while awaiting the arrival of Rodes' infantry, Old Jube queried a local farmer about the character and strength of Washington's defenses. "Nothing but earthworks," was the general's remembrance of the man's reply, and not a large force, the farmer had added, maybe 20,000 men in them. Suddenly, however, Early realized that earthworks "in the then state of the science of war" and defended by even 20,000 men presented a formidable obstacle. At the time, he merely shrugged and told his informant that if all that was by way of enemy opposition, "we would not mind that." However, Early was secretly worried.[51]

Alexander McCook's deployment of Briggs' dismounted troopers, the 25th New York Cavalry outside the works, and the rifle pits filled with all variety of men "defeated our hopes of getting possession of the works by surprise," said the Confederate chieftain after the war. In light of the general's encounter with the farmer at the time that he rode down the Seventh Street Road at the start, one may wonder if Early's heart was ever in a pitched battle to punch through the Federal works so soon after the Monocacy bloodletting. True, there was some idea of using Breckinridge's men to thrust southward in the Rock Creek valley between Forts Stevens and De Russy. But, scouting reports about that abatis-filled gulley dimmed that attraction. As the afternoon wore on, the appearance of even more faded blue uniforms in the opposing lines, the sharp skirmishing, heavy cannon fire, and determined Federal opposition reinforced Early's hesitancy. He and his generals all knew that their own ranks were thinned by the weather and the march. Early said it all in an 1881 account of his actions: "The whole command had then marched fully fifteen miles in very hot, dry weather and over exceedingly dusty roads, and was, of course, very much exhausted, many of the men having fallen by the way from heat and sheer exhaustion." Later claims that the Confederate generals had fallen victim to the bountiful wine cellar at the Blair mansion could hardly obscure this fundamental fact. To the army's ordnance chief, Colonel William Allan, "Our people were not up well enough to make an immediate dash on the city." It was as simple as that.[52]

The appearance of an unexpectedly large number of faded blue uniforms — whether worn by scratch contingents thrown together by Washington authorities or by veterans of the VI Corps then arriving—most certainly added to the rebel uncertainty. Yet, there was much more than the mere chimera of figures on the horizon which gave Early pause. A hint came later in memoirs of one George Haven Putnam, invalid at the time in a New Orleans hospital from XIX Corps service, but conversant with newspaper and comrade accounts of the Fort Stevens battle. He suggested that Washington authorities had adopted a course very exceptional from the point of view of military routine. He referred to placing practically the entire infantry defense force on the picket or skirmish line. Moreover, this force, according to Putnam, had been given instructions (again, "quite contrary to those usually given") to maintain a rapid fire "with the smallest possible pretext or even without pretext" and to shift places periodically to the right or left thus giving an impression of greater numbers. It seems too that a number of the Augur-McCook force had breech-loading carbines, given the predominant cavalry composition of the force, which provided increased rates of fire. Thus, to Putnam, the Union pickets at Fort Stevens on July 11, "succeeded in giving a very good impression (that is, an exaggerated impression) of their numbers," confounding Early's reconnaissance and decision to attack in force on the first day of the battle.[53]

Putnam's explanations notwithstanding, some Union commanders had worries of their own that afternoon. Brigadier General Frank Wheaton, commanding First Brigade, Second Division, VI Corps (and the whole division during the temporary absence of Brigadier General George W. Getty, still recuperating from a wound suffered in May at the Wilderness battle), reported the skirmish line had begun to waver and tire about 5:00 p.m. The accurate fire of some rebel sharpshooters located in an orchard succeeded in clearing Fort Stevens' guns of cannoneers for about twenty minutes, "so that it was impossible to man them." At least one Federal observer thought that a determined enemy drive at that moment could have taken the fort and then swept down the rifle pits on either side. "The line once broken, the work done, and the city would be in their possession," declared Lieutenant Edgar S. Dudley, 2d U.S. Artillery, then helping guard Fort Marcy on the Virginia side of Chain Bridge. Wheaton therefore secured orders to dispatch 500 men "to recover the line" held in the afternoon. This move was effected by sundown using Colonel J. F. Ballier's 98th Pennsylvania, Major Thomas McLaughlin's 102d Pennsylvania, and Captain James McGregor's 138th Pennsylvania which together drove Early's skirmish line back upon the main force of Confederates. Lieutenant Colonel J. S. Long's 93d Pennsylvania, and the 62d New York under Lieutenant T. B. Hamilton joined the fire-fight. Wheaton then established a more aggressive defensive line extending for two miles from the Battery Smeade–Fort De Russy area across the front of Fort Stevens, to a locale opposite Fort Slocum. This area, northward toward the District line, constituted the battle area at Fort Stevens.[54]

Abraham Lincoln appeared at some point during the afternoon or early evening proceedings. The historical record is unclear and observer memories are vague on this event. Some people claimed that the president had visited the post on Sunday, and, indeed, it may have been part of some humble sabbath gesture by the commander-in-chief seeking to inspire the troops. Members of the 150th Ohio National Guard, such as Lucian C. Warner and James C. Cannon, recalled that Lincoln had arrived in a barouche about noon that day, escorted by a troop of the Black Horse Cavalry. The tired-looking president had left the carriage hastily, entered Fort Stevens, and passed quickly from cannon to cannon as if making a formal inspection. Cannon remembered that the president had worn a yellowish linen coat and unbrushed high hat, and seemed more like some "care worn farmer in time of peril from drought and famine." Lincoln apparently returned to the fort on Monday, and still later in the day drove back to the War Department and regaled his friends in the telegraph office about the spirited fighting that he had witnessed, and drew a sketch map (since lost) of that action from his pocket. Other observers suggested that here was the first instance of Lincoln

President Lincoln at Fort Stevens after a contemporary sketch. According to legend, President Abraham Lincoln was under fire in this battle, which he, Mrs. Lincoln, and members of his administration were viewing. (The Soldier in Our Civil War, II, 297)

actually coming under enemy fire (the only such instance of any American president doing so while in office) and that some impetuous individual—soldier, officer, perhaps a civilian bystander—had shouted to the striking figure to get down off the Fort Stevens parapet before he got shot. Private John A. Bedient of the 150th O.N.G. claimed that honor, for one. Young Frederick Seward also claimed that he and his father, Lincoln's secretary of state, had accompanied Lincoln to the fort that day, and that other dignitaries like Secretary of the Navy Gideon Welles, as well as Mrs. Lincoln, and General Wright had also been present at the time. Indeed, this particular visit may have spawned the colorful tale of how Mary Todd Lincoln had swooned at the sight of wounded soldiers, prompting Lincoln to say that she would surely make a poor soldier if she always fainted at the sight of blood. A variant on this story attended the Lincolns' appearance at the fort the next day.[55]

Lincoln and his party presumably spent the night safely back in Washington. The soldiers in the trenches were less fortunate, and overall, the night of July 11–12 passed just as fretfully as the previous night. Stray reports of Mosby's partisans causing mischief upriver kept sentries alert on the south side of the Potomac, but nothing came of the reports. Union provost troops within the city dampened activity by the town's secessionists once more. Random picket fire kept both sides awake on the northern side of town, while even the Monocacy prisoners tried to scoop makeshift breastworks to guard against the fire coming from Union lines, and periodic bursts from the cannon made life unpleasant for the bivouacked rebels in the fields and woods out toward Silver Spring. VI and XIX Corps contingents continued to come into line, and about 9:00 p.m., Quartermaster General Meigs and his deputy, Brigadier General Daniel H. Rucker, arrived with 1,500 armed and equipped departmental employees. Lieutenant Colonel Joseph A. Haskin quickly escorted them by the light of a full moon to rifle pits between Forts Slocum and Totten—slightly away from the more sensitive and critical points in the defensive perimeter. An hour later, Colonel Francis J. Price also reported in with about 2,800 convalescents "organized into a provisional brigade composed of men from nearly every regiment in the Army of the Potomac," according to Alexander McCook. They too departed for the Fort Slocum sector as McCook anticipated "that the enemy would demonstrate farther to our right," and most of the Federal commanders frankly feared a night attack by Early's army. Some of the participants still wondered why the untrained men continued to man the front lines while the veteran soldiers remained in reserve. However, Halleck and Wright planned to keep the VI and XIX Corps troops as a containment reserve in case the rebels broke through the single defensive line, and then counterattack with them as part of a general offensive designed to annihilate the Confederates.[56]

The arrival of so many new commands and new faces added to the earlier organizational confusion. For those who did arrive and fell into line, a new command arrangement was published at 12:30 a.m. on July 12. Major General Quincy A. Gillmore would take command of that portion of the line from Fort Lincoln to Fort Totten. Meigs would command the portion from Fort Totten westward to Fort De Russy, including the main scene of action at Fort Stevens. Hardin would command from Fort De Russy further westward to Fort Sumner. Wright's VI Corps would remain in reserve (a provision which McCook apparently violated since he employed some of them for picket duty in front of Fort Stevens), and McCook would command the northern defense perimeter overall. In general, the defenders exuded confidence. Captain A. B. Beamish, 98th Pennsylvania, remembered that when one of Early's commissary sergeants wandered into Union lines by mistake about 10:00 p.m. and spotted VI Corps troops with their unmistakable Greek cross cap badges, the intruder had exclaimed: "If the Holy Cross of Christ Fellows are here, Gen. Early had better give up the idea of taking Washington." Little wonder, then, that General Meigs quietly fell asleep that night "in an orchard wrapped in a poncho, with my horse tethered to an apple tree."[57]

Chapter Five

THE PRESIDENT UNDER FIRE

S OME Federal soldiers had seen the northern defenses of Washington before. In fact, many of them had helped build the line of forts. Captain Aldace Walker of the 1st Vermont Heavy Artillery (originally 11th Infantry), could justifiably tell his father upon arriving back in the area with the VI Corps: "I have a familiar dating place" for his letters. Walker had spent his entire term of service between October 1862 and the unit's departure to join Grant in May 1864, within the northern defenses, particularly at Fort Stevens. He had helped with the dirty work of clearing land, laying out forts, roads, and outbuildings, and creating the complex protecting the city. He too had enjoyed periodic visits to the capital, and his men had chased livestock belonging to local farmers, and raided chicken coops as well as vegetable gardens to supplement their meager army diet. The Vermonters had watched freed slaves seek refuge among the New Englanders in camp. Walker himself spent time riding to the Military Asylum or Soldier's Home, attending services at Rock Creek Episcopal Parish, and often insinuating himself into the Blair family hospitality, especially at mealtime where he enjoyed the political banter. Postmaster General Montgomery Blair's daughter delighted him with her piano playing, and his letters projected a spirit of warmth with the civilian community as well as a sense of shared endeavor.[1]

Of course, not all the families in the area of the forts reveled in the names or missions of the occupiers of their farms and woodlands. Civilians like D. Colelazer (Coleglazer?), T. Carberry, C. A. Shoemaker, the heirs of W. Kurtz and Grammer families, Dr. Noble, W. King, M. H. White, J. Selden, J. Pilling, the Moreland and Lay families, Hoyl C. Bennett, L. Finchel, B. Jost, T. Mosher, Enos Ray, and William Brooke Bell may well have had different political leanings than the Yankee troops nearby. Their personal attachment to their land and homes and the safety of their families came first, and they may have regarded Abe Lincoln's Pets (as the Heavy Artillerists were derisively known) with some suspicion. But as months and even years passed, a spirit of friendly civility developed among the citizenry and soldiers. It survived relatively untroubled until Jubal Early's raid when both parties were thrust into the cauldron of actual war and destruction.[2]

Indeed, units like Walker's Vermonters or the 2d Rhode Island and 37th Massachusetts regiments probably grew to feel as much at home in this neighborhood as the civilian residents. Lieutenant Colonel George E. Chamberlin of the 1st Vermont "Heavies" returned to an area he knew well from previous experience while commanding Fort Totten earlier in the war. Rhode Islander Augustus Woodbury noted in July 1864: "Line of battle was formed in the camps occupied by the brigade during the winter of 1861–1862." Thus, many of the VI Corps returning on July 11 and 12 had been part of that earlier mass of Union soldiers who had helped with wholesale deforestation, confiscation of land, and destruction of homes and farm buildings—all judged detrimental to military efficiency during construction of the defense line early in the war. All of this had been accomplished in the name of protecting both the capital and the presumably loyal citizenry of the neighborhood.[3]

The key forts in what became the battle zone in July had all been laid out by Major, later Major General, John G. Barnard and his engineers. Fort De Russy stood on the western edge of Rock Creek Valley, and had been named for Colonel Gustavus A. De Russy, whose 4th New York Heavy Artillery had provided work details to construct the fort. Laid out on the farm of a "Mr. Swart" or Schwartz, it started as Camp Holt and became a popular attraction for weekend visitors because of its scenic surroundings. It commanded the well-traveled Milk House Road and crossing over the creek—the main east-west artery from the Georgetown or Rockville Turnpike eastward to Bladensburg. In fact, this road had provided the route used by the Montgomery County militia going to fight the British at that location a half-century before.[4]

When the 9th and 10th Rhode Island Infantry and 10th Rhode Island

Battery had occupied the premises at Fort De Russy, Major General Ambrose E. Burnside's wife and other garrison ladies visited their husbands and quickly discovered why the post had a reputation for flies, bugs, and lizards. Still, access to the creek provided opportunities for bathing parties, when that stream was not otherwise polluted by human and animal wastes from the fort and nearby camps. The fort itself was a trapezoidal work with a perimeter of 190 yards, and well-defined rifle pits to the front and flanks supported the work. Armament included three 32-pounder seacoast guns (mounted in a barbette), a 100-pound Parrott rifle (similarly mounted), five 30-pounder Parrott rifled-cannon (mounted in an embrasure), a 10-inch siege and a 24-pounder Coehorn mortar, and two vacant gun platforms for field pieces. Battery Smeade to the west provided additional supporting fire covering the Milk House Road. Unarmed batteries Kingsbury (nine platforms), "Battery to the Left of Rock Creek" (six platforms), and Sill (nine platforms), as well as additional unoccupied batteries and rifle-pits (all awaiting the intended influx of field army units to man them), could deliver a converging wall of fire on any enemy seeking to breach the abatis-filled Rock Creek entry through the lines. Off to the east, Fort Stevens provided additional intersecting fire for the guns of Fort De Russy.

Fort Slocum, sister fort immediately to the east of Fort Stevens on the Seventh Street Road, had also been laid out and constructed by Rhode Islanders. Men of the 2d Rhode Island had been named for their commander, Colonel John S. Slocum, killed at First Bull Run. The position was a strong one, with a fort of 653 perimeter yards covering the left fork of the Rock Creek Church Road and lanes leading out into Maryland. The fort mounted twenty-five guns and mortars with fifteen additional vacant platforms for field and siege pieces. Among its heavy armament were one 8-inch siege howitzer, two 24-pounder seacoast guns, four 24-pounder howitzers, seven 4.5-inch rifled-guns, six 10-pounder Parrott rifles, one 10-inch siege, and two 24-pounder Coehorn mortars. The guns all fired through embrasures. It too had supporting rifle pits and unarmed batteries.[5]

Further east stood Fort Totten, named for Brigadier General Joseph Totten, Chief of Engineers, United States Army. The fort and its advance battery occupied a commanding ridge which controlled the broad valley and country roads stretching before it to the north and east. The fort's 100-pounder could be trained to assist Forts Slocum and Stevens to the west. The other twenty guns and mortars included two 8-inch siege howitzers (in a barbette), eight 32-pound seacoast guns (in a barbette), three 30-pound Parrott rifles (in an embrasure), four 6-pound James rifles (in an embrasure), one 10-inch siege and one 24-pound Coehorn mortar. There were two vacant platforms in the 272-perimeter yard fortification. Fort Totten was an ever-popular post, due perhaps to the presidential cottage at nearby Soldier's Home. The Christmas of 1863 had witnessed a Yuletide visit of Imperial Russian naval dignitaries. Lieutenant Colonel Chamberlin of the 1st Vermont Heavy Artillery had written his wife that the fort had been selected "from among all north of the river as the one for them to see." Bands had played, thirteen-gun salutes had been fired, and there had been "quite a crowd to see the strangers," he noted. Seven months later the strangers were rebels not Russians, and the garrison included militiamen, not heavy artillerists.[6]

Nonetheless, the showpiece for this battle drama in the summer of 1864 would be Fort Stevens commanding the Seventh Street Road. The fort had been styled originally "Fort Massachusetts," as men of Brigadier General Darius B. Couch's brigade hailing from that state had been among its construction team. The vicinity of the fort also abounded with campsites of the volunteers at the outset of the war. "Camp Brightwood" was the name first applied to the scene (the name remains for this Washington neighborhood over a century and one-quarter later). Camp Stetson (1st Maine Heavy Artillery) and Camp Doubleday (76th New York) were also in the neighborhood as well as other regimental camps along the Rock Creek Ford Road. The Brightwood Hotel served as a community focal point, and the home of Matthew G. Emery stood nearby. Emery lost much timber and lumber from his property during construction of Fort Stevens, and both structures would be pressed into service as command posts and signal stations during the battle."[7]

Years later, Mrs. Anna Osborn, whose forebears resided in the vicinity of Fort Stevens (and who continued to live there three-quarters of a century later), recalled that her grandfather's house had been burned to make way for the fort and that neighborhood women had wept at the destruction of their own properties. The original Emery Church had been torn down in 1861 to make way for a magazine inside Fort Massachusetts, and when the fort was expanded the following year, there was more destruction against private property. One mourner at this time was a free black woman, Elizabeth Thomas, whose shanty fell because of the need for a second magazine in the new "Fort Stevens" (named for Brigadier General Isaac I. Stevens, killed at Chantilly in September). While weeping with her six-month-old baby in her arms beneath a large sycamore tree, "Aunt Betty" as she was known, watched German-speaking soldiers heave furniture and belongings out of her house and then demolish it. That evening, a tall, slender man, dressed in black, approached

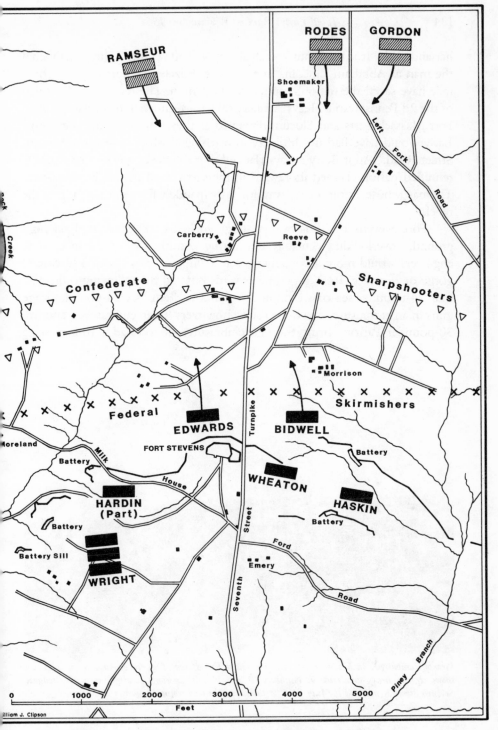

VI Corps attack, late afternon, July 12, 1964. (Cartography by William J. Clipson)

her and said: "It is hard, but you shall reap a great reward." She remembered the man as Abraham Lincoln. In any event, Elizabeth Thomas's misfortune may have saved the nation's capital for the Union. The regimental historian of the 2d Pennsylvania Heavy Artillery said as much when he declared: "Had Fort Massachusetts and Slocum remained as they were in 1862, then Jubal Early would have had no difficulty in reaching Washington on the Seventh Street Road." Aunt Betty always claimed that she never got her reward. The reunified nation claimed its reward in the sacrifice of people like Elizabeth Thomas whose home made way for an expanded fort which stopped the rebels.[8]

Fort Stevens by 1864 was a "large enclosed work, situated on high ground," overlooking generally undulating country for several miles. The engineers would more accurately term it a "lunette" possessing a stockaded gorge or rear face. Its 375-perimeter yards boasted the following ordnance: four 24-pounder seacoast cannon firing in a barbette, six 24-pounder siege guns in an embrasure, two 8-inch siege howitzers (in an embrasure), and five 30-pounder Parrotts firing through embrasures. It too had a 10-inch siege

View of Company F, 3d Massachusetts Heavy Artillery, Fort Stevens, Defenses of Washington. This view shows regular heavy artillerists at Numbers 10 and 11 gun positions, looking north with tollgate, Seventh Street Road, and the July 1864 battlefield in the background. (Library of Congress)

and a 24-pounder Coehorn mortar, plus three vacant platforms. Perhaps weaker than other forts in some ways, and commanding less rugged terrain, Fort Stevens may have been an inviting target to Early. The absence of veteran artillerists like Walker and his 1st Vermont comrades also made a difference. They had "the mortification of seeing the artillery entrusted to troops who could hardly load heavy ordnance with safety." "No use was made of the skill its members longed to exercise," said Walker in writing home about his unit once it returned with the VI Corps. The Vermonters, like the Rhode Island and Massachusetts veterans of these defenses, remained concealed in a forest behind the lines on July 11–12, while in Walker's irate words, "a grand Council of War decided how the so timely reinforcements should be employed."[9]

On Tuesday, July 12, Washington was cut off from the north by Bradley Johnson's raiders severing rail and telegraph lines north of Baltimore. Washington newspapers noted that reports about the rebels "are confusingly conflicting." Unionist citizenry—organized as Loyal Leagues—were mustered to help the military in both Baltimore and Washington. At the capital, Major General Abner Doubleday joined the bevy of commanders involved in the city's defense by organizing and commanding the Loyal Leagues there. Northern financial markets teetered as "greenback" currency (legal tender and lifeblood of business during the war) sank in value to thirty-five cents to the dollar. It required $285 in paper to pay for $100 in gold, and the monied class contended that "the government had only one chance in three of saving itself" from Early's threat.

Indecision continued to plague officials in Washington. Walker contended that President Lincoln, Secretary of War Stanton, General Halleck, as well as lesser leaders, all carefully discussed the situation but differed as to a solution. Whether or not to mount a vigorous attack on Early's besieging army, or merely to further develop the Confederates' intentions with a strong skirmish line preoccupied this "Council of War," said the Vermont officer. In fact, indecision seemed so rife on Tuesday that Assistant Secretary of War and Grant's own emissary at the capital, C. A. Dana, wired his superior at 11:30 a.m.: "There is no head to the whole and it seems indispensable that you should at once appoint one." Hunter would be the ranking officer if he ever arrived to coordinate operations in the rebel rear, but Stanton vowed to oppose that move on grounds of the aging warrior's recent proven incompetence against Early in the Shenandoah Valley. General Halleck "will not give orders as he receives them; the President will give none, and until you direct positively and explicitly what is to be done, everything will go on in the deplorable and fatal way in which it has gone for the past week," warned

Dana. Unfortunately, no immediate decision by the general-in-chief could have significant effect upon the battle taking place at Fort Stevens.[10]

The situation was just as indefinite on the Confederate side. Early had established his headquarters the previous evening in Francis Preston Blair's Silver Spring mansion, and, after dark, he summoned his senior commanders for a war council. Early, Breckinridge, Gordon, Rodes, and Ramseur met and sampled Blair's wine cellar. Time passed in this convivial setting as the generals toasted Breckinridge's presumed return to the Senate chamber in the morning. The Kentuckian reminisced about previous social gatherings in the Blair homes and spoke warmly of his distant kinsmen and what Washington meant to him personally. The atmosphere was probably quite heady by the time Early finally got down to business. He noted the army's position. Federals would be closing off the passes of South Mountain to the west as well as the upper Potomac crossings as Hunter's army moved into that area. The presumed presence of Army of the Potomac veterans in Washington's fortifications appeared to lessen chances for an easy victory there. Yet to have come this far and not attack also seemed to be folly. Failure at accomplishing General Robert E. Lee's orders haunted each one of the Confederate officers. Gordon, in one of his typically vague postwar utterances, claimed "there was not a dissenting opinion as to the impolicy of entering the city." After hearing them out, Early "determined to make an assault on the enemy's works at daylight next morning," unless information arrived showing the impracticality of such a plan. Just such information did come in from Bradley Johnson during the night. The cavalryman claimed interception of a telegram (later suggested as "fictitious" and purposely leaked to Baltimore secessionists so as to fall into Early's hands), which confirmed that two corps had arrived at Washington from Grant's forces before Petersburg. This effectively squelched Early's plan for an attack at dawn on Tuesday "until I could examine the works again," declared old Jube after the war. "As soon as it was light enough to see, I rode to the front and found the parapets lined with troops," he noted in his memoirs.[11]

Early later explained to Lee that the assault, even if successful, would have been attended "with such great sacrifice as would insure the destruction of my whole force before the victory could have been made available." Furthermore, had it proven unsuccessful, it would definitely have caused the destruction of his whole army, he said. He resolved, therefore, to maintain a demonstration during the daylight hours of July 12, and then retire toward the Potomac after dark. Early claimed that his infantry force numbered only 10,000 men, and, as was typical of Early, "a considerable part of the cavalry has proved wholly inefficient." True, Brigadier General Armistead Long's field guns could not have suppressed the heavier (albeit more unwieldy) fortress cannon of the Federals, but the absence of significant VI Corps field artillery on the field somewhat equalized that disparity. The fact was that, for whatever reason—the heat and jaded condition of Early's men, the shock of the Monocacy casualty figures, the Blair wine cellar, Federal reinforcements and stiffening resistance, the imprecise directives from Lee, or basic failure of nerve on the part of Early and his generals—the Confederates shrank from their planned assault on the morning of July 12. The "battle" would settle once more into skirmishing and sharpshooting, long distance and desultory artillery fire, and waiting for the covering darkness to escape. As G. W. Nichols of the 61st Georgia saw it: "We lay around all day (the 12th) and skirmished, and pretended like we would charge the enemy's works till night. . . ." Colonel E. N. Atkinson (replacing the wounded Clement Evans as brigade commander in Gordon's division) suggested in his campaign report: "Lay in line during the whole day—nothing of importance transpired. . . ."[12]

Tuesday came on "bright and glorious," remembered George T. Stevens of the 77th New York. The shallow valley (really little more than a swale) beyond Fort Stevens "presented a scene of surpassing loveliness, with its rich green meadows, its fields of waving corn, its orchards and its groves," he said. Lieutenant Colonel John N. Frazee, in command of Fort Stevens, opened up with three 30-pounder Parrott shells aimed at the Carberry house, 1,078 yards distant from Fort Stevens, and a like number aimed at the Rives' house, only 1,059 yards away. Similar fire was directed at an old camp about 1,950 yards out, a carriage shop at 2,075 yards away, and at a Confederate troop concentration in a grove of trees to the right of the Seventh Street Road, at 1,050 yards. Captain Joseph N. Abbey, 2d Provisional Pennsylvania Heavy Artillery, engaged in similar work with 4.5-inch Schenkl shells from Fort Slocum, firing at the Bramer house (3,000 yards distant), and the Blair house, 3,200 yards away. His fellow Pennsylvanian, Captain John Norris, performed like service at Fort De Russy. Together, the artillerists took great pride in their contribution to the battle that day since enemy sharpshooters occupied so many standing structures within rifle range of the Union lines. The Carberry, McChesney, Selden, Lay, and Rives places on the Seventh Street Road, the Noble farm on the left fork of the Rock Creek Church Road before Fort Slocum, and various structures to the front and right of Fort De Russy, provided havens for rebel marksmen all day to the discomfort of McCook's and Hardin's men. All told, cannoneers fired sixty-seven shots from Fort Stevens, fifty-three from Fort Slocum, and one hundred and nine from Fort De Russy during the course of the day's action on the twelfth.[13]

"The day wore away," recorded Quartermaster General Meigs. Colonel Charles R. Lowell took two squadrons of his 2d Massachusetts Cavalry out the River Road from the Tenallytown lines, and another column moved likewise on the Rockville Pike to drive Brigadier General John McCausland's gray-clad troopers back about one and one-half miles, with the rebels discarding arms, equipment, and retiring in some confusion. Alexander McCook's 7,886 front-line troops continued to have their hands full elsewhere on the lines with mounting casualties by mid-afternoon. Meigs' quartermaster units continued to bolster the northeastern lines, as a like number of sailors and Navy Yard workers under Rear Admiral Louis Goldsborough suspended labor on "the preservation of vessels and materials of war" and went into the trenches at Fort Lincoln where the turnpike and railroad to Baltimore entered the lines. As news trickled in about Bradley Johnson's raiders near that city, both Halleck and Barnard, the chief engineer, urged srengthening the garrisons in the forts east of the Anacostia River so as to close access to the city from that direction. An inordinate amount of reorganization and worry about proper allocation of commands continued to occupy the attention of the top brass. The latest organizational arrangements had Doubleday taking charge of the forts beyond the Anacostia, Quincy Gillmore commanding those from the Anacostia westward through Fort Slemmer (just east of Soldier's Home), Meigs supervising those all the way from Fort Totten to Fort Kearny beyond Rock Creek (thus the whole embattled front line facing Early), while Martin D. Hardin still retained charge of the sector from Fort Reno to the Potomac.[14]

Additional VI Corps troops arrived that day from Petersburg with soldiers such as Wilbur Fisk of the 2d Vermont stating that while they would have preferred rest camp instead of battle, knowing the enemy was making an invasion, despoiling the country, and robbing loyal citizens caused not a "word of murmuring" about the abrupt transfer. The passage upriver by Brigadier General David Russell's First Division elements repeated the previous day's saga of the Second Division of that corps. An anonymous crewman aboard the *George Leary* groused how "our beautiful clean beds, cots, et cetera, tumbled down in the hold to make room for horses, mules, cannon and soldiers," probably of Battery M, Fifth U.S. Artillery. Brigadier General Emory Upton's Second Brigade fire-eaters immediately got to squabbling over space aboard the craft and several members were knocked overboard in the fighting but managed to swim to safety. Nobody at the time knew that

Upton would emerge after the war as the army's top theorist on military policy before suicide cut short a brilliant and promising career. Chaplain F. C. Morse of the 37th Massachusetts admitted: "The officers are having a beautiful ride but for the men it is crowded and suffocating," and did not wonder at the rioting. Others like Colonel Joseph E. Hamblin, commanding the 65th New York, found the trip exhilarating. "To enjoy a cool breeze without blinding dust is a luxury we have not been accustomed to for months," he said. Hamblin thought the veterans "shall like fighting near the capital quite as well as in the trenches around Petersburg." Everyone took note of Fort Monroe and the watery graves of the USS *Cumberland* and *Congress* in Hampton Roads, as well as Fort Washington and Mount Vernon while passing up the Potomac. The 37th Massachusetts regimental band serenaded everyone while passing George Washington's ancestral seat. The night of July 11–12 passed on the water "as it was too dark to go on although we were in such a hurry," for fear of running aground.[15]

The Second and Third Brigades debarked at the Sixth Street wharves by mid-morning Tuesday and marched up Pennsylvania Avenue past the Treasury and White House (although few mentioned seeing President Abraham Lincoln this time). Sparser crowds greeted the Tuesday arrivals, leading W. F. Parish of the 15th New Jersey to note years later: "There was not a breath of air stirring, and the sun blazed down between the buildings soon had us dripping with perspiration and fairly panting with the confined heat." Coming off the transports with empty canteens, "thirst hardly described our condition. Did the citizens come out and welcome us with ice water, cakes, cookies, and glad words?" Not at all, he noted, for the streets were empty, the houses all shut tight, and he contrasted the scene with a captured Richmond at the end of the war where "on the main street at least, were quite a goodly number of men, no doubt our late enemies, who wished to see what the Yanks could do on parade." The Jerseymen, claimed Parrish, were heartily glad to reach the battle zone at Fort Stevens. In an unsubstantiated account, Augustus Buell of the 5th United States Artillery claimed a better reception for his unit. According to Buell, halts came at Sixth Street between "D" and "F" streets, and later at the large contraband camp on the Seventh Street Road (where Howard University now stands), as civilian admirers flocked to greet the new arriving veterans.[16]

The reinforcements now joined their VI Corps comrades of the Second Division in reserve among the pine trees behind Forts De Russy and Stevens. The 2d and 3d Vermont Regiments of the famed Vermont Brigade sent men directly into rifle pits between these two works—the very trenches they had helped dig two years before. The 1st Maine Battery also moved forward to provide greater fire support for the skirmishers, and a section was set up on either side of Fort Stevens, with a second section remaining in reserve. Recently remounted at Camp Barry and equipped with six 12-pounder Napoleon guns, it "was the only mounted battery on the field" and had fired seven shots in support of the action, according to the Maine Adjutant General's office. Captain A. M. Beattie led a relief team to the embattled skirmish line.

A sprinkling of civilians, like writer-naturalist John Burroughs, continued to enjoy the good fortune of securing passes from Colonel Moses Wisewell or simply eluded the sentries and reached the rear areas and front lines. Treasury Registrar Lucius Chittenden recalled leaving Willard's hotel about 3:30 p.m. with two companions, slipping past pickets at Meridian Hill (who held back the mass of civilians seeking to reach the "battle") and enduring the catcalls of half-drunken stragglers, skulkers, and even VI Corps veterans along their route out to Fort Stevens. "You are non-combatants who are coming out here to get up another Bull Run ain't ye?" shouted the soldiery, and yelled for Chittenden and his friends to "Skedaddle white livers!" The official reached the rifle pits to the right of Fort Stevens before a junior officer suggested their horse and buggy presented a target to sharpshooters. Leaving the rig behind the lines at a stable, they went by foot into the trenches and spotted Secretary of the Navy Gideon Welles conferring with radical Republican Senator Benjamin Wade of Ohio, about the evident lack of rebel strength and the superiority of the Union force. As Provost Major William Doster commented elsewhere that day: "The city shows no signs of alarms, except being subdued as children in a thunderstorm, listening and waiting for the issue." Doster, at least, found it profoundly interesting to "hear the rumbling of streetcars mixed with the rumbling of hostile cannon," citing one of pleasure and business, the other of death and agony. Already, the panic of the weekend had given way to resigned anxiety.[17]

Many observers once again saw the tall figure of President Lincoln return to his old stand atop the bullet-swept parapet of Fort Stevens. The historical record for Tuesday remains as imprecise as that of the previous day with regard to the president's itinerary. Secretary Welles noted in his diary that Lincoln conducted his regular Tuesday cabinet meeting at noon and expressed chagrin that so little was known about Early's intentions. The chief executive had sent an encoded message to Grant about 11:30 that morning, merely noting "vague rumors" about Lieutenant General James Longstreet's corps joining Early and that the general should "look out for its absence from your front." Then, sometime in the afternoon, the Lincolns and Secretary

Interior of Fort Stevens as President Lincoln Would Have Seen It. Shown here with Company F, 3d Massachusetts Heavy Artillery drawn up for the photographer in August 1865, the view had changed little since the previous summer when Lincoln viewed the battle from this fort. Supposedly he stood on the parapet behind the tree in this photograph when ordered off by Wright and others. (Library of Congress)

Stanton (with cavalry escort) had gone out to the lines at Fort Stevens. They visited the hospital behind the lines and accompanied by General and Mrs. Wright, the president's party made its way into the fort. Challenged by Sergeant Hiram Thompson of the 49th New York, they needed a pass signed by the Secretary of War authorizing entry. What a bag of prisoners it would have made had Early's men attacked and captured the fort at this time! In any case, as sniper bullets whistled overhead, and cannon boomed intermittently around him, the Lincolns, Wright, and possibly other bystanders in uniform mounted the forward parapet and took position as marked today by a simple bas relief and stone. Thus, the ever inquisitive President of the United States once again became the sole chief executive to experience hostile fire while holding office.[18]

High drama was in the air at Fort Stevens that afternoon. The hot sun, the acrid smell of black powder, the smokey landscape of the battlefield out front, all formed the backdrop for a man in dark suit and tattered stove-pipe hat standing atop a battle-swept parapet. Scarcely a mile away across the intervening battlefield stood an erstwhile Vice President and one of Lincoln's opponents in the 1860 presidential election (indeed, the favorite son of those southern states which subsequently seceded to form the Confederacy—John C. Breckinridge. Here was an ironic twist, a tableau truly capturing the symbolism of the Civil War—two American leaders now separated not merely by their political beliefs, but by the actual gulf of battle strife. Neither man probably knew the other was there, though they may have surmised it. Elsewhere that day, future leaders of a reunified country stood ready—men like Senators John B. Gordon of Georgia, Mark Hanna of Ohio, Edward V. Woolcott of Colorado, and philanthropist Lucian C. Warner to cite but a few. America past and America future came together at Fort Stevens, D.C., in a little known battle which held the fate of the nation.

The singing Minie balls and the thud and anguished cry of a member

President Abraham Lincoln under Confederate Fire at Fort Stevens, July 12, 1864. Here, for the only time in the nation's history, an American president actually came under hostile military fire. (From bas-relief by Schwizer, Lincoln Stone, Fort Stevens, courtesy National Park Service)

of the Presidential party hit by a rebel missile, complete what is known of Lincoln under fire that afternoon. Far more zesty (but unclear) is the sequence of events which caused Lincoln to descend from his precarious perch to safety and escape possible death or wounding that day. Camp stories, postwar reminiscences, and the forgetful memories of old men years later cloud the contemporary record. Major General Horatio Wright apparently entreated the president to remove himself from the parapet for he could not be responsible for Lincoln's safety, he said. Wright and Lincoln may even have haggled a bit about the constitutional prerogative of a president to view a battle in person. One account claimed that Lincoln felt "as Constitutional Commander-in-Chief . . . he had a right at least to watch a battle fought by his own troops," with the army officer retorting politely but firmly that "there was nothing in the Constitution authorizing the Constitutional Commander-in-Chief to expose himself to the enemy's fire where he could do no good!" Other accounts suggest an improbable longer dialogue between the two amidst flying shot and shell until Wright simply ordered his commander off the earthwork. Still other accounts suggest not Wright but possibly Frazee, the fort commander, various lowly privates in the Ohio National Guard, even free black "Aunt Betty" Thomas, may have uttered words causing Lincoln to leave his position. The most colorful account has then Captain (Brevet Lieutenant Colonel) Oliver Wendell Holmes noting the folly of the president's actions. Wright and the senior military figures present may have been more polite than the blunt comment attributed to both Holmes and Thomas, something to the effect of "Get down you fool!" Whoever truly moved the President of the United States to avoid death or maiming that Tuesday afternoon will be shrouded in the mists of history.[19]

Rebel sharpshooters at the Carberry house, for example, could see Abraham Lincoln. When Surgeon C. V. A. Crawford of the 102d Pennsylvania was shot beside the president, it was clear that the chief executive stood squarely in their rifle sights. Still, the ever enthusiastic president would periodically bob up from cover to peer once more over the top among a hail of bullets. From a distance of one hundred and twenty-five years, we can go no farther than historian John Cramer did in 1948. He noted that President Lincoln was indeed under hostile fire on two successive days, July 11 and 12, 1864. Men were shot near him. Mary Todd Lincoln and General Wright stood with him at some point on the Fort Stevens parapet (although it remains unclear that Mrs. Lincoln truly did so). Cramer proved that Lincoln responded to an authoritative request that he get out of harm's way—but made by whom or at what precise time could not be substantiated.

Ultimately, Lincoln and apocryphal tales are part of America's national heritage. We can go no farther with conjecture, perhaps, than Captain Aldace F. Walker of the 1st Vermont Heavy Artillery, who was present at the battle and who wrote home the next day: "The Generals and President and Secretaries, and cetera, were in the Fort looking on, Lincoln with a hole in his coat sleeve." Or, as Thomas Hyde of another VI Corps unit noted while sitting on the parapet himself that afternoon: "I saw the President standing on the wall a little way off." An officer between Hyde and the president, recalled the soldier, "suddenly keeled over and was helped off." Recalled Hyde in 1895: "Then a lot of people persuaded Mr. Lincoln to get down out of range which he very reluctantly did."[20]

Most of the stories about Lincoln at Fort Stevens came from eyewitness impressions emerging many years later as reminiscences about a Great Man and a Great Event. George E. Farrington of the 3d Vermont noted that he knew the president was there but did not see him, for "we were all busy watching the effects of the large shells from the fort and expecting to be ordered forward at any moment." B. T. Plugh of the 1st Wisconsin Heavy Artillery further observed a half-century later that Lincoln's party, including Colonel Lafayette C. Baker (the secret service chief), had visited Fort De Russy where he was posted and that the scene at Fort Stevens "was very similar" to what occurred at that fort during the fighting. Fifty years after the battle, W. Langford of Plugh's regiment claimed that when Lincoln (this time accompanied by Postmaster General Montgomery Blair) arrived at Fort Stevens where Langford was instructing 100-day men, the chief executive came over and singled him out with a cheery, "Well, well, is it possible you are the son of my old friend John W. Langford? I want to shake hands with you for you know your father and I were great chums." Nobody could be sure just when and where the affable Lincoln might turn up, and such events permitted great license with postwar memories of dedicated and patriotic Union veterans. C. H. Enos of the 122d New York, who served as a hospital steward at Fort Stevens during the battle, remembered consoling Mrs. Lincoln and Secretary of the Treasury Salmon P. Chase in their open carriage outside the fort that a surgeon, not the president, had been wounded. Enos was nowhere close to either Lincoln or Wright during the fighting, but somehow learned quickly of Surgeon Crawford's wounding, thus adding another dimension to legend.[21]

Of one thing we can be sure. Not only was Abraham Lincoln shot at, but, as commander-in-chief he was enjoined to actually issue an order during this battle. The moment came apparently just prior to his mounting the parapet, but even that remains uncertain. Either Wright or Frazee or someone else in authority secured the president's attention and noted how the rebel sharpshooters were employing cover afforded by civilian structures in the neighborhood. Another bystander saw this as a shrewd ploy for gaining approval to bombard those structures. Months later, Lincoln substantiated that: "I was present at Fort Stevens (I think) on the afternoon of July 12th 1864, when some houses in front were shelled by our guns, and understanding that the military officers in command thought it necessary [sic] the shelling of the houses proper and necessary, I certainly gave my approbation to its being done." Shortly thereafter, the presidential party was treated to a "real" battle as yet another official decided the time had arrived to push the Confederates back out of range, to clear the sharpshooter nests once and for all.[22]

The "Battle of Fort Stevens," in the sense of a well-defined attack with artillery preparation and text-book maneuver, came with the dusk assault by Colonel Daniel Bidwell's Third Brigade of the Second Division, VI Corps, against the Confederate skirmish line. Lincoln witnessed it and it provided the bulk of the casualties in the two-day action. The president's close call with death from sharpshooter fire undoubtedly caused McCook, Wright, and other senior military leaders to take more positive action. The orchard and shade trees on the Rives property, plus the Rives and Carberry or Lay houses on either side of the Seventh Street Road toward Silver Spring, seemed to protect Early's people. McCook found that Beattie's skirmishers from Getty's division of the VI Corps were inadequate, so he asked Wright to furnish a full brigade for the task. Nobody quite had the stomach for a pitched battle with Early's whole army (as preferred by Grant), but cleaning out skirmishers seemed simple enough.[23]

Lucius Chittenden colorfully described the scene. Standing on the rifle pits just east of Fort Stevens, he claimed to see almost two miles to Blair's Silver Spring mansion. He declared that the fields sloped gently down for about one-half mile to a brook, then rose with similar gradient to a low ridge about one and one-half miles further out. The slope immediately before the fort was devoid of vegetation, and beyond the stream lay the fine, wooden Carberry house replete with cupola and owned by a member of the Post Office Department. Slightly beyond lay the burnt-out shell of a house destroyed the previous day by the Federals. A small space around these two structures was cleared, and then beyond that came a wide tract covered with oak scrub, six to fifteen feet in height. Beyond lay a large wheat field in which the main body of Early's men could be seen, silhouetted against a large forest and the Roach house beside the road. The Blair properties stood across the District line in Maryland.[24]

To the east of the Seventh Street Road, noted Chittenden, was "a large open space from which the timber had been first removed, and the stumps left standing." A recently constructed earthwork, probably for field guns, stood a few rods from the rifle pits on a slight elevation. "To the left of this was a peach orchard in front of that a field of corn then an open space to the brook," noted the Treasury registrar. He also suggested that a few trees had been left standing in this space. A field with ten to twelve foot high brush could be seen across the brook, similar to that west of the Seventh Street Road. The Piney Branch Road, which departed Seventh Street Road at the toll booth heading northeast, cut across this swath, but a bridle path led to another well-appointed house surrounded by a large meadow and cultivated grounds. A large virgin forest intervened between that structure (opposite the Carberry place) and the Blair property. Confederate units occupied this area, while their skirmishers filled the brushy sections on both sides of the Seventh Street Road. Federal skirmishers could be found closer in, most probably occupying the cornfield and peach orchard. Today, city streets and residential neighborhoods occupy the area, but it was all rural in 1864 when Chittenden captured the sights and sounds of the battlefield. "Not a man was visible [in the brush]," he recorded, "but from every square rod of it as it seemed to me we could see the smoke and hear the report of musketry." The appearance of rapid discharges seemed peculiar to this civilian. A brief spurt of smoke, gentle diffusion through the atmosphere, and muted explosion due to distance "were like a constant popping instead of the regular roll of musketry," he noted.

Wright conferred with his division and brigade commanders, and decided that Brigadier General Frank Wheaton, temporarily commanding Brigadier General George Getty's Second Division, should undertake the assignment of clearing the front of the enemy. Colonel Daniel D. Bidwell's Third Brigade, Second Division would be the principal instrument, with Wheaton's own First Brigade as the immediate backup, while Colonel Oliver Edwards' Third Brigade of Russell's First Division would take a reserve position immediately in front of Fort Stevens and help if necessary. As it developed, elements from all these commands eventually got into the offensive. Bidwell deployed his units with the 77th New York (sporting a new flag) at the right flank position on the first line with the 7th Maine, and Bidwell's own 49th New York under Lieutenant Colonel G. M. Johnson. The 43d New York, 61st Pennsylvania, and 122d New York (a unit which had joined the brigade only two days before) formed the second line. According to plan, Bidwell would signify his readiness to begin the attack by waving the new flag of the 77th New York, and then the batteries of Fort Stevens and Fort

Brigadier General Frank Wheaton, U.S.A. Temporarily in division command, Wheaton supervised the late afternoon attack of VI Corps contingents designed to drive back Early's sharpshooters and skirmish line. (U.S. Army Military History Institute)

Colonel Daniel Bidwell, U.S.A., 49th New York, and commander, Third Brigade, Second Division, VI Corps. Bidwell's brigade led the July 12, 1864 assault in the "battle of Fort Stevens." Despite heavy losses to every regimental commander and to his own brigade, Bidwell drove back Early's skirmish line. (U.S. Army Military History Institute)

Slocum would rake the houses sheltering the troublesome rebel marksmen. Three salvos would be fired, and after the 36th shot (equaling the number of stars in the national flag at this time), the brigade would rush forward in the charge. Meanwhile, Bidwell's men lay upon their arms to avoid the still murderous enemy fire, which began to claim victims as soon as the Federals departed the shelter of the fortifications. They were all experienced at this sort of thing; most were veterans since the days of George B. McClellan's peninsula campaign of 1862. The 49th New York had even camped on this very ground in 1861 with 1,000 muskets in the ranks. Now they could muster only eighty-five men in the July heat, but as one survivor noted proudly in 1894: "This was the fourth battle that we had fought in defense of Washington—South Mountain, Antietam, and Gettysburg preceding." Anxious now to show their mettle before the younger men of the militia and the walking wounded of the convalescent corps, they later felt that none of the previous battles provided "any harder fighting or heavier losses in proportion to numbers engaged" than here at Fort Stevens, and "none was of more importance though [Fort Stevens was] scarcely known in history."[25]

Frank Wheaton received his orders from Wright and conveyed them to Bidwell about 5:00 p.m. It took the brigade commander about five hours to accomplish his mission, and there were anxious moments for the Union cause. Guns from Fort De Russy had to join the fray, and used the occasion to bombard troublesome sharpshooter positions in its front as well. The Napoleon cannon of the 1st Maine Light Artillery joined the heavier guns from the fort, and the battle became full-blown before it was over. Captain Charles Dupont of the 13th Michigan Light Artillery claimed the honor of "aiming the gun" that set one of the two target houses afire. Some twenty-five shots did the job on the Carberry house, claimed Daniel H. Bee of the 61st Pennsylvania, who watched the barrage. Milton Evans, one of the Ohio national guardsmen, contended later that five men jumped from the upstairs windows but were all that escaped from an estimated thirty marksmen in that structure. "The balance burned up," he observed calmly.

The artillery then concentrated upon the milling survivors in the road and fields surrounding the burning buildings. Bidwell's people sprang forward at the appointed time, carried the first ridge held by the skirmishers which bisected the Seventh Street Road, and pressed on. It was "as fine a bayonet charge as could be," wrote one gleeful survivor. But Confederate resistance stiffened beyond the Carberry and Rives properties. Major General Robert E. Rodes opened on the advancing Federals with his own artillery and even sent one or two of his own brigades to bolster the flagging skirmish line. Something of a full-scale fire-fight developed in the general vicinity of what is now the Walter Reed Army Medical Center. The high ground just north of that reservation also witnessed its share of the action as Edward's Third Brigade, First Division, and Wheaton's own brigade had to be sent to help out. Young William Eugene Ruggles from upstate New York recorded that his 122d New York ran out of ammunition, held their position beyond the Rives place for twenty minutes, and then "fell back, rallied again, charged them without ammunition, and drove them back again" before finally securing more bullets.[26]

The Confederates, on their part, claimed that they stopped Bidwell's advance three times and that they had not retired from the battlefield until after dark. Some Federals claimed a like number of repulses meted out to the rebels. The picket reserve of 150 men of the 102d Pennsylvania and an eighty-man detachment of Vermonters also got into the fight. Possibly the most colorful and complete discussion of the battle of July 12 from the southern perspective came with Colonel E. N. Atkinson's after-action report for Evans' brigade of Gordon's division. Noting that the Federals had started the later afternoon affair by firing the houses protecting the sharpshooters and then "made an attempt on our line," Atkinson noted that "they were driven back in our immediate front, but succeeded in driving the troops on our right back, which compelled the troops of this brigade, or rather the Fifty-third North Carolina Regiment and the sharpshooters, to fall back (the Thirty-second North Carolina Regiment was watching the right flank), and immediately the Forty-third North Carolina Regiment and the Forty-fifth North Carolina Regiment were deployed as skirmishers and ordered to the front." According to Atkinson, "they went up beautifully," joining the 53d North Carolina and the sharpshooters, and soon had a position established west of the Seventh Street Road. But those on the eastern side of the road "could not succeed in going quite as far as their original line." He claimed the men fought well, under heavy artillery fire from the Federals, while lacking any support from their own guns. Besides, said Atkinson, "the enemy had decidedly the advantage in position, but our men went up cheerfully and confidently."[27]

When the fighting was finished, the Federals retained the battlefield. The cost had been high—all Bidwell's regimental commanders had been cut down as well as 250–375 killed or wounded in a command which numbered barely 1,000 men. As S. A. McDonald of the 122d New York declared solemnly after the war: "That the percentage of killed was unusually large" was shown in comparison to Antietam, Chancellorsville, and Gettysburg, where, taken as a whole, Union losses in killed alone were "16.3 per cent of the aggregate killed and wounded." The figure at Fort Stevens in Bidwell's brigade stood at 35.8 per cent, he noted, with the 49th New York alone losing twenty-six of eighty-five men in its ranks. Victory had been gained, however, and the rebels driven back about a mile and pressure relieved on the Union defenses. The president and various civilian dignitaries delighted in seeing the pitched battle. But, as Private Ruggles observed: "I suppose they think it was a splendid sight, but we poor fellows could not see much fun in it."[28]

The 1st and 6th Veteran Reserve Corps regiments had their own little engagement when they dislodged Confederate sharpshooters from Claggett family buildings west of Rock Creek. Rebel cavalry activity some three and one-half miles beyond Fort Lincoln far to the east on the Baltimore Pike also caused Brigadier General Quincy Gillmore, commanding the sector, to anticipate an assault in his vicinity, but nothing took place there. Early's army was already beginning to fade from the scene, although few of the cocky rebels ever admitted that they had been bested in the day's action. Most of them saw the events of July 12th as "little more than a heavy skirmish" and one easily repulsed. But Monocacy captive William G. Browning of New York suggested that at the close of Bidwell's attack that afternoon, he and his comrades had been marched to the rear under heavy guard when, just then, "the whole rebel army came pell mell, almost a stampede" with infantry and the drovers and their captured livestock pouring across the fields, with artillery and cavalry seeking to escape by road. Lucius Chittenden claimed that he had seen a spirited mounted charge by the Confederates near the end of Bidwell's assault, which had been bloodily repulsed by Union forces. Certainly Early never admitted any impact made by the late afternoon and evening action, suggesting total casualties for the two-day affair to be eighty men, most of whom might have fallen on July 12. The Federal leadership realized that Bidwell's force was too small to accomplish much and held the enthusiastic soldiery in check rather than bring on even heavier action. Perhaps Major Henry Kyd Douglas of Early's staff captured the real importance of the "battle" by Bidwell and Rodes when he recounted an after-dark meeting between Early, Breckinridge, and Gordon at Silver Spring. Whether in "a droll humor, perhaps one of relief," recalled the staff officer, Early quipped in his falsetto drawl: "Major, we haven't taken Washington, but we've scared Abe Lincoln like hell!" Douglas answered incautiously: "Yes, General, but this afternoon when that Yankee line moved out against us, I think some other people were scared blue as hell's brimstone!" Was that true, asked Breckinridge with a laugh. "That's true," muttered Old Jube, "but it won't appear in history!"[29]

A silvery new moon shed its light upon the withdrawing Confederates and the details sent from the Union defensive line to collect the wounded that night. Casualty estimates varied predictably with Federal estimates approaching 400, the Confederates perhaps 200 more. Like all Civil War battlefields, Fort Stevens was a display of carnage and destruction to most onlookers. The militiamen and civilians had never seen such sights before as stretcher bearers and surgeons operated in rear area hospitals behind Fort Stevens making bloody heaps of amputated limbs. Some civilian doctors like W. J. C. Duhamel volunteered to help the army medics. Nathan Strain of Sunbury, Pennsylvania, underwent the butcher's knife that night, yet survived the war to claim membership in that select group of triplets who had all gone to save the Union. Out in front of Fort Stevens, the light of burning houses illuminated the scene with an eerie glow. "On all the floors, on the roofs, in the yards, within reach of the heat, were many bodies of the dead or dying, who could not move, and had been left behind by their [rebel] comrades," commented Lucius Chittenden, and "the odor of burning flesh filled the air; it was a sickening spectacle!" Within a day or so, Union dead had been collected and interred in a new battlefield cemetery, dedicated almost immediately by President Lincoln as "Battleground National Cemetery." Forty-one veterans of the Fort Stevens fight lie buried today in that hallowed ground on Georgia Avenue in northwest Washington. Seventeen Confederates were subsequently collected from the battle area and buried in a row in the dooryard of that roofless little Episcopal Church between Sligo Post Office and Leesborough which Early's men marched past during the affair before Washington. This was ironically the parish church of the Blair family, and even Jubal Early was so moved by its unfinished condition that he supposedly sent $100 to its rector, Dr. Josiaph Harding, to complete the structure. Another local story had the money intended for defraying the burial costs of the rebel dead. Federal troops would find Confederate wounded all over the countryside during the next few days, including some ninety seriously injured officers and men and their army doctor left at the Sligo Post Office. Some additional 200 prisoners also fell to the Federals in the wake of Early's retirement.[30]

Both Confederates and Federals alike destroyed property in the battle area. "Nearly all the houses were sacked by our men," admitted Sergeant Major John G. Young of the 4th North Carolina. Captain Robert E. Park of the 12th Alabama recorded that: "Many articles of male and female attire were strewn over the ground," suggesting that such conduct was contrary to orders but nonetheless practiced by many rebels who "exerted themselves to imitate the vandalism of Hunter and Milroy and their thieving followers while they occupied the fair Valley of Virginia." Park's regiment had encamped less than one hundred yards from Montgomery Blair's "Falkland" mansion near "Silver Spring." Somehow, during Early's withdrawal, "Falkland" went up in flames, as did a rented structure occupied by the family of famed *New York Times* correspondent Edward A. Paul. Guards had been placed at both houses to no avail. Some of the rebels told Mrs. Paul that they had tried to catch her husband twenty times to punish him for his vituperative comments and "we will catch and hang him yet." Greater respect for Francis Preston Blair by Breckinridge and Early probably saved "Silver Spring." However, even that mansion fell prey to ransacking and destruction of furniture and personal papers, as well as forays into the liquor supply by officers and men previously accustomed to applejack whiskey. Federal authorities became so enraged by this wanton conduct that generals such as Major General Benjamin F. Butler retaliated by sending a gunboat to burn the house and terrorize

Postmaster General Montgomery C. Blair. His "Falkland" mansion burned mysteriously at the end of Early's demonstration before Washington, leading to years of controversy as to its perpetrators and origin. His father's home, nearby "Silver Spring," was spared largely due to the intercession of cousin John C. Breckinridge and Jubal Early. (U.S. Army Military History Institute)

the wife of Confederate Secretary of War James A. Seddon near Fredericks-
burg, Virginia. Early and his officers genuinely deplored the destruction near
Washington, and he at least, expended much pen and ink in future years
trying to explain such actions as dastardly deeds by random sharpshooters or
stragglers, Union cannon fire, or rough and ready rabble in such units as the
Louisiana "Tigers" or 45th North Carolina, bent upon retaliation for Yankee
depredations in the Shenandoah. An officer of the 43d North Carolina,
Leonidus Lafayette Polk recounted that he understood that Maryland soldiers
in Early's force "struck a match to it," referring to the Postmaster General's
home. Early and Henry Kyd Douglas both dismissed any official sanction to
the burning by saying that it would have alerted the Federals that the Confederate army was retreating. The controversy raged for years, with even Union
veterans swearing that the Blair mansion was destroyed by Union artillery
fire.[31]

Years after the war, newspaper clippings noted that five or six families
in the vicinity of Fort Stevens lost their homes to the battle. Richard Butts,
W. Bell, J. McChesney, Abner Shoemaker, W. M. Morrison, and Mr. Lay all
suffered such loss. They further lost livestock and other property at the hands
of the two armies. In truth, Federal authorities were as callous as the Confederates in destruction of private property, especially after the battle. Driven to
ensure clear fields of fire should Early's army return, blue-clad soldiers and
laborers from the city spent nearly as much time tearing down obstacles as
policing the battlefield for the wounded. Chaplain F. C. Morse of the 37th
Massachusetts portrayed this sad scene in a letter home on July 13. Noting
the "piles of smoldering ruins now mark the place where happy union families
dwelt in peace," he also cited scores of axes wielded by "the strong arms of
colored prisoners [sic]" ruthlessly cut down the "most beautiful shade trees
of maple, locust, and other varieties." "Several large and beautiful peach-
orchards, the trees heavily laden with fruit have also been cut down," said
the cleric. Bitter local feelings lasted for generations toward the national
government in families whose property suffered after Early's raiders had left
the scene.[32]

A flood of stories about the battle began to surface by dawn of Wednesday, July 13. A Maine lieutenant doing signal duty atop the Fort Stevens
parapet had had a chair shot from under him the day before, and now regaled
listeners with the story that when rebel prisoners were brought in, one asked
if he was the officer who had been signaling during the battle. "Yes," had
replied the New Englander so that the Confederate said, "well I've been firing
at you all day." The Down Easterner shot back, "you had better improve your

aim." Then there was "Dog Jack," the prized bulldog mascot of the 102d Pennsylvania who had escaped unscathed from the battle. Less fortunate were three brothers—Aseph, John, and Horace Ellis. Aseph and John served together in Company A, 61st Pennsylvania while Horace was recuperating in a Washington hospital from wounds received while a member of the 7th Wisconsin. Horace left the hospital, secured a musket, took his place with his brothers, and witnessed the death of John in the fight. The surviving brothers buried John on the field, and Horace returned to the hospital, later rejoining his own regiment "with enhanced reputation as a courageous man, ready to do more than his duty." Some of those killed or wounded such as a Major Jones of the 6th Maine, or Private Matthew De Groff of the 43d New York, had fought while in transit to recruiting duties or even awaiting discharge from the army. Sergeant Richard Castle of De Groff's regiment wrote a poignant letter home just hours before meeting death on July 12. He told his family: "And if it comes my lot to fall in Battle, I will try to live so I can meet you both in heaven." Still others survived to secure promotions for their services at Fort Stevens, including Pennsylvanian Jacob Schmid, Captain George A. Armes of the 2d New York Heavy Artillery, and Quartermaster General Meigs, who received his brevet to a major general while out on the lines. For many, however, the name "Fort Stevens" would forever symbolize simply a lost limb, or "a vacant chair" at home.[33]

Fort Stevens opened the eyes of some like Lucius Chittenden. The Treasury registrar had never seen a battlefield, much less dead soldiers when he strode out on the field after Bidwell's attack. He was impressed with the extreme poverty of the dead Confederates he found there. One sharpshooter had body armor and a fine English rifle and cartridge box, but these had not prevented his death and were "the only things about him which did not indicate extreme destitution." Still another rebel's haversack contained merely "a jack-knife, a plug of twisted tobacco, a tin cup, and about two quarts of coarsely cracked corn, with, perhaps, an ounce of salt, tied in a rag." These were the belongings for the enemy soldier, marveled Chittenden, a foeman who had fought long and hard with Lee, and who had spent the previous six weeks marching more than three hundred miles with Early, ready to fight everyday, only to die a sharpshooter within sight of the nation's capital in some minor skirmish.[34]

Chittenden and his party returned to the city that night. Soldiers on their way to the front had warned of the victory and had merely drawn off into adjacent fields and bivouacked, leaving the roadway clear. Off to the east a single fortress gun sent a shell at intervals "with a screaming rush" after the retreating rebels, "like some wild animal growling his anger at the escape of his prey." The Vermont bureaucrat recorded that it was the last gun of Early's attack upon Washington. "We carried the news of the retreat of the Confederates to the city," he noted, adding its inhabitants slept soundly that night, "free from alarm or anxiety." Behind them at Fort Stevens, Ohio guardsmen and former Oberlin College student, Lucius Warner, noted that the soldiery spent the night by their guns expecting that fighting would resume at any time, but daylight showed no enemy in sight. In their wake, said the Buckeye, a few burned houses and scarred trees, dead bodies, and battered crops attested to the fact that Washington had barely escaped pillage and destruction. "And yet," noted Warner with a tinge of bitterness, "this is not recorded in the annals of the war as a battle, but only as a skirmish."[35]

Chapter Six

SIDESHOW IN
THE BALTIMORE SUBURBS

M OST of Jubal Early's cavalry missed the battles of Monocacy and Fort
Stevens due to another assignment. Brigadier General Bradley T.
Johnson of the mounted arm went to headquarters just south of Middletown
in Pleasant Valley sometime on July 8. He received the task of freeing Confederate prisoners at distant Point Lookout where the Potomac River merged
with the Chesapeake Bay. Johnson was probably in no mood for any wild
goose chase. He had been denied the opportunity to dash in and capture his
native town of Frederick due to the timidity of the cavalry chief, Major
General Robert Ransom. So a somewhat peeved Johnson looked upon the
new task with marginal enthusiasm. Attached to Old Jube "by my respect for
his intellect and by my warm love for his genuine, manly true character,"
claimed the Marylander later, he still told the general that the Point Lookout
mission "was utterly impossible for man or horse to accomplish." Early
brushed off his objections, and ordered him to depart the next morning,
avoiding Frederick, but lingering on the enemy's northern flank at the Monocacy until satisfied that the Confederates were "getting on all right" in their
attempt to cross the stream. Johnson and his command would then strike off
across country, cut railroad and telegraph lines north of Baltimore, sweep

Brigadier General Bradley Johnson, C.S.A. This trusted Maryland cavalry leader received the impossible assignment of raiding around Baltimore, striking to free Confederate prisoners at Point Lookout, and returning with them to rejoin Early's army in front of Washington. (U.S. Army Military History Institute)

south around that city, and push on to reach Point Lookout prison camp on the night of July 12. There, he would cooperate with Colonel-Commander John Taylor Wood's waterborne force and free an estimated 10,000 to 12,000 prisoners (perhaps more), and march them back to rejoin Early's army besieging Washington. Johnson flatly told his superior that the scheme gave ". . . me four days, not ninety-six hours [*Johnson's*] to compass near three hundred miles, not counting time lost in destroying bridges and railroads, but that I would do what was possible for men to do." The two soldiers saluted, and the brigadier departed to prepare his command for their mission.[1]

Johnson and 1,500 men left their mountainside bivouac promptly the next morning. The command numbered mostly southwest Virginians although a fair number of Marylanders were also present. Almost all of them were inappropriately armed with long muskets—a poor choice for mounted use. The lack of training and discipline concerned Captain George Wilson Booth, Johnson's adjutant. Potential, not proven quality, impressed Booth about them, although there seemed to be good material in the ranks and a few officers of merit and ability. Nonetheless, Johnson moved his men to Worman's Mill on the old Liberty Road, two miles north of Frederick, and awaited the sounds of Early's success farther south. Some of the gray-clad cavalry eventually participated in the pursuit of Wallace's beaten army, but the majority generally struck off toward Liberty, New Windsor, and Westminster, according to orders. Johnson himself confided their mission only to Booth, Captain Wilson C. Nicholas of his staff, and the brigade's ranking colonel, W. E. Peters of the 21st Virginia Cavalry.[2]

News of the rebel approach spread like wildfire through the region, said the *Carroll County Record*, thirty years later. Stores closed, fathers gathered wives and children behind shuttered windows and locked doors, and the vacant streets of tiny northern Maryland hamlets "seemed to moan a solemn dirge." When Johnson's force appeared at New Windsor, they demanded the reopening of shops. A number of robberies took place and telegraph wires were cut down, but Johnson was in a hurry so the raiders did not linger. Some rebels found ready access to pretty faces and warm victuals in the name of secession. By nightfall, Maryland Major (later Colonel) Harry Gilmor with twenty picked men went on and captured Westminster. His band charged into town with drawn sabres, thinking a force of 150 Federals garrisoned the place. They discovered instead numerous friends and some surprised citizenry who readily opened their shutters at their noisy approach. A message arrived from Johnson asking Gilmor to acquire 1,500 sets of clothing, shoes, and boots from the town's mayor. Dusk fell, the mayor could not rouse the council, and Gilmor personally persuaded Johnson to spare Westminster from the torch. Friends brought out bread and crackers for the troopers when Johnson's main force arrived, noted Virginian J. Kelly Bennette, and the southern horsemen swapped tales of the affluent fields and farms in this part of Maryland. Bennette, however, still missed the mountains of the Old Dominion, he said.[3]

Gilmor left just after breakfast on July 10, astride a new black mare, a gift from a Liberty, Maryland farmer. He had a new mission for his 2d Maryland Cavalry. Pushing through Reisterstown to Cockeysville, north of Baltimore, the Marylanders were to destroy the Northern Central Railroad tracks and bridges and pull down telegraph wires which linked tidewater with Harrisburg, Pennsylvania. Gilmor's weary men burned their first bridge across the Gunpowder River about three miles northeast of Cockeysville, tore up some track, and posted pickets on the Baltimore approach, until Johnson arrived. The brigadier reached Reisterstown about 9:00 a.m., his

Confederate Cavalry Ransacking New Windsor, Maryland. Small towns and individual farms north and west of Baltimore fell prey to rebel demands for supplies as shown by sketch artist Frederick Diehlman. (The Soldier in Our Civil War, *II, 301*)

outriders performing their almost daily ritual of gathering horses, and then followed Gilmor to Cockeysville, completing destruction of bridges and other targets. The new but strategically marginal Western Maryland Railroad escaped unscathed. Johnson then detached Gilmor on a special mission according to Early's direction. Gilmor was to move from Cockeysville eastward to destroy the Gunpowder River Bridge of the Philadelphia, Wilmington, and Baltimore Railroad, said to be heavily guarded by Yankee troops. For that reason, Gilmor was upset that Johnson allotted only a part of the 1st and 2d Maryland Cavalry battalions instead of a promised 500 men. According to Gilmor, the striking force comprised all the men "of my own command present with serviceable horses and fifty of the 1st Maryland, under command of Lieutenant W. H. Dorsey—in all about one hundred and thirty-five men." Gilmor, of course, knew nothing of the Point Lookout assignment, for which Johnson would need all the men possible and in top physical condition.[4]

Lurid tales of the rebels' approach now spread to the suburbs of Baltimore. One farmer and school teacher in rural northwestern Baltimore county noted in his journal for July 11, that the raiders lurked about in small squads with no one knowing when or where they would appear. He went about his chores but tried to hide livestock and grain like everyone else in the path of the invaders, and noted "terrible times," in his humble journal. Panic also began to appear in Baltimore City as newspapers and citizens on street corners caught the fever of the rebels' approach. The city was not as well fortified as its sister to the south. Threats to Baltimore's security had been more internal during the war years, as local secessionists constantly disturbed the city's tranquility. When Major General John A. Dix had assumed command of the Department of Maryland on July 24, 1861, he had immediately expanded Federal control over the venerable but bustling commercial city from the brick walls of Fort McHenry (that had so admirably defied the British in 1814). Dix had ordered erection of earthern forts on eminences like Federal

The Church Spires of Baltimore as Seen from Fort McHenry. The capture of Baltimore, which would have destroyed Union communications between Washington and the north, was never a major objective; however, the Baltimore suburbs were frequent targets of Confederate raids. (U.S. Army Military History Institute)

and Murray hills, and had armed all of them with seacoast guns, "all bearing upon and supporting each other, and so arranged that the whole city was at their mercy." This had effectively suppressed dissidence so that by June 1864, delegates to the National Union Convention (representing Republicans and some War Democrats) could gather in the city to renominate Abraham Lincoln for re-election. However, that was now a month past, as Johnson's Confederates bore down upon the town. Lew Wallace's force had gone out and met defeat at Monocacy, and the only defenders left seemed to be Yankees streaming back into the area with trainloads of wounded, and little sign of organized fight left in them. Federal and city officials ordered saloons closed until further notice at 8:00 p.m. on Saturday night, July 9, as they scrambled to put together some sort of token defense force. Just as in neighboring Washington, Baltimoreans met on the streets in animated conversation about their prospects for capture.[5]

Both soldiers and civilians now collaborated to ensure Baltimore's safety. Governor Augustus Bradford in May had called for enlistment of two 100-day service regiments, and he now asked for volunteers to complete the muster of the second one, the 12th Maryland. Response was feeble at first, and authorities had more luck securing horses than the men themselves. A special mayoral committee petitioned President Lincoln and the War Department for help but was rebuffed since all available troops were already in the field against Early's invaders. Brevet Brigadier General W. W. Morris assumed command of Baltimore's defense and received War Department permission to halt all reinforcements transiting the city in response to the emergency at Washington. Brigadier General H. H. Lockwood took charge "of all the forces called out by the mayor and officered by the Union Leagues of Baltimore." Brigadier General John Kenly took charge of the forts west of Jones' Falls, with headquarters at Fort Number 1 at the head of Baltimore Street, and Lockwood took command of those to the east of that point. Captain George A. Pope with a company of Union League loyalists marched out to Fort Number 7, overlooking the Northern Central Railroad near the Mount Royal Reservoir, and would remain there during the emergency. Companies of the 159th Ohio National Guard, local recruits from Camps Bradford and Carroll, and hospital convalescents all moved to help the work of defense. Major H. B. Judd, commanding to the north at Wilmington, Delaware, was advised to place guards at railroad bridges between Baltimore and his city and to organize and arm citizens and convalescents for the defense of his state, and particularly key military targets like the Du Pont powder works near Wilmington. Major General Darius B. Couch had likewise been rebuffed at Washington in his search for aid in defending Pennsylvania, and he was too involved with that mission to send any help to Baltimore.[6]

Alarm bells began to peal at dawn on Sunday in the Monument City. The governor and Mayor John Coleman now issued a joint proclamation declaring the danger "imminent" and news from the Monocacy spurred citizens with firearms to help construct and man additional fortifications. Black and white residents alike were pressed into service, and a total of 2,500 horses were gathered for emergency use. City resident Richard P. Thomas wrote to his brother serving in a reserve detachment at Sandy Spring, Maryland, that he was awaiting a home guard call-up, but really thought Washington and not Baltimore was the principal rebel target. He mentioned the press of thousands of cattle stirring in the city streets as country refugees sought to get their livestock away from the raiders. Drays and wagons carefully conveyed goods and government records to the harbor for shipment down the bay to safety should the enemy break into the city. Crowds gathered at the wharves and the railroad stations seeking to escape, and Morris suggested to Lockwood that street barricades be thrown up. Wallace arrived back in the city and took charge, moving remnants of his battered force into the city lines. Wagon trains and their escorts from as far away as Major General Franz Sigel's Martinsburg depot crossed the city and went into camp in the east end. William H. James of the 11th Maryland remembered returning home from Monocacy, having been separated from his comrades in their retreat, but proud that he had escaped with all his equipment and musket despite extremely blistered feet. "Upon my arrival at home I shaved, took a bath and put on clean clothes and after a few hours rest was all most myself again," he declared. He soon rejoined his reconstituted unit, encamped at Greenwood on Gay street beyond the main part of town. Extra police, wearing special identification ribbons denoting their status, now appeared on the streets. While business was not suspended, city officials did tighten travel restrictions and overall security, and intimidated any secessionists they found in the city.[7]

The Confederates' plan was working admirably. Gilmor left Cockeysville at noon on Sunday, feinting at Baltimore via Towsontown, turned east at Timonium toll gate to the old York Road, and thence to Meredith's bridge over the Gunpowder River. Finding no Federals, the Marylander decided upon one of his typical deviations. Leaving most of his command at the crossing, Gilmor went over to his home, "Glen Ellen," and visited his family. "I captured the whole party on the front steps" of the house, which was a replica of Sir Walter Scott's Abbotsford house in Scotland. After mutual displays of affection, Gilmor "treated them with kindness, and, upon detainment for a few hours, paroled and released them, and moved on with my command," he claimed. Johnson passed a similarly pleasant sabbath afternoon at his friend John Merryman's "Hayfield farm" near Cockeysville, and dispatched another trusted friend, Colonel James C. Clarke, to Baltimore City to learn about the defense of both Baltimore and Washington. Johnson admitted that "the charming society, the lovely girls, the balmy July air and luxuriant verdure of 'Mayfields'" was most inviting. But both Gilmor and Johnson wasted valuable time (if the Point Lookout mission still held precedence) in such relaxation. Gilmor spent the night in the saddle, dozing while riding across country toward Bel Air. Johnson finally departed "Hayfield," leaving two couriers behind to secure news from Clarke, and moved through lovely Green Spring Valley, encamping at John N. Carroll's "The Caves." It was during this ride that Johnson passed near Governor Bradford's country house and ordered its burning in the morning.[8]

Johnson's burning of Bradford's home in retaliation for Yankee depredations in the Shenandoah Valley remains controversial. One recent writer speaks of the arson as "an outstanding example of gentility," citing Confederate accounts of the affair. Supposedly, the officer sent to do the deed set fire to the house at dawn on Monday, but graciously allowed Mrs. Bradford to remove furniture and personal belongings, and actually ordered his men as well as several local citizens then in Confederate custody to help in the task. Governor Bradford had gone to Baltimore the previous day and had not returned to his country place, according to newspaper accounts at the time. Bradford's deposition seeking postwar claims for damages said otherwise. Mrs. Bradford had been awakened by the sounds of soldiers destroying furniture downstairs, had been handed the eviction order, and had little choice with flames already consuming the structure, he claimed. In any event, news of this action enraged northern sensibilities, especially those of Washington officials, in the same manner that Letcher's misfortune incensed Virginians. None of the activity had much military significance, but certainly indicated the blending of military and political acts during wartime. It also reflected much waste of time and energy that Johnson needed for completion of his primary assignment.[9]

More important was the intelligence gathered by Colonel Clarke in Baltimore. Johnson received it about midnight from the couriers posted at "Hayfields." Clarke related that all available rolling stock of the Baltimore and Ohio Railroad had been concentrated at Locust Point, and that transports offshore held XIX and VI Corps veterans ready to disembark and go by rail to relieve Washington. Johnson immediately sent a messenger to find Early with this news. The Marylander then moved on with his command. Monday's pace was leisurely, almost as if Johnson had no intention of rushing to reach Point Lookout. The day was just as warm for his men as for Early's main army battling Yankees forty miles away at Fort Stevens. Breakfast consisted of plundering two wagons en route to the Baltimore market with Painter's ice cream, just beyond Owing's Mills. While awaiting the return of the detachment torching Bradford's house, Johnson permitted his command to feast on this delicacy. Lacking proper utensils, the men used hats, rubber blankets, buckets, and old tins to carry the white stuff along with them. Most of the Virginians had never seen ice cream, were not too sure they really liked the "frozen vittles" or "frozen mush," as they called it. One angular rebel from Tazewell County stuffed his mouth full and "then clapped his hands to both sides of his head and jumped up and down. . . . It hurt so bad he forgot to spit it out," noted a comrade. More sensible "mountaineers" (as the Marylanders called the southwestern Virginians) thought the "beer" was nice but too cold. They simply filled canteens and enjoyed the ice cream later when it melted. Few of Johnson's command would ever forget the "buttermilk Rangers and their ice cream" caper near Baltimore in 1864.[10]

Moving slowly in the heat (hardly with the "hot haste" remembered by Johnson after the war), the Confederate column crossed Howard County outside Baltimore. They moved across the Baltimore and Ohio Railroad west of Woodstock, cut telegraph wires, tore up track, and skirted the remnants of Wallace's army, picking up stragglers on the way. Johnson enjoyed another detour for lunch with John Lee Carroll (later postwar governor of the state) at his "Doughoregan Manor" house. Johnson seemed oblivious to any Federal pursuit. In fact, Baltimore seemed even more frozen with fear than Washington. "The panic here is heavy and increasing," Wallace had wired the War Department that morning. He asked Henry Halleck for horses, since he had too few of his own to effectively pursue the raiders outside the city. Halleck naturally wired back another refusal, and aside from D. R. Clendenin's frayed 8th Illinois Cavalry, the absence of horses kept Wallace's command effectively sidelined while Johnson moved by. The Hoosier warrior continued to place new men in the defenses and strengthen all positions. One regiment took position in Baltimore Street between Eutaw and Canal, a second on Franklin Street between Eutaw and Holliday, and a third set up on Monument Street between Eutaw and Holliday. Another regiment went into position on Greene Street between Columbia and Franklin, and still another commanded the Bel Air Market and adjacent open space. Forts

Worthington, Marshall, Carroll, and various numbered batteries received men and artillery as Baltimore started to resemble Washington as a fortified city bristling with men and guns. Gilbert H. Bryson, the city surveyor, and Lieutenant John R. Meigs of the Army Engineers (coincidentally Quartermaster General Meigs's son), laid out and built new works like Fort Number 3 at Kirby's mansion on Kirby Lane; Fort Number 4 at the junction of Gilmor Street and Windsor Mill or Liberty Road; Fort Number 4½ at the head of Gilmor Street; and Fort Number 5 at the entrance to Druid Hill Park. By evening, Wallace got word that Grant was sending Major General E. O. C. Ord to take command at Baltimore. Wallace and Ricketts had done very little to hunt down and destroy the rebel cavalry raiders outside the city. The best they had done, perhaps, was what John Garrett reported to Edwin C. Stanton—the two generals had placed the Monocacy survivors "under proper discipline and control."[11]

The crisis had begun to abate by the time Ord arrived and consulted with Mayor Coleman and other officials. A thin blue line held Baltimore: Brigadier General John R. Kenly's Third Separate Brigade numbered only 25 officers and 721 men, and Colonel Charles Gilpin's Potomac Brigade was perhaps 1,461 men at most. The armed citizenry and weak units formed from convalescents, sailors, black recruits, and the remnants of Wallace's force swelled the total to about 10,000. However, the Hoosier would report a solid 13,413 soldiers present for duty in the department on his July strength returns, so there were more than enough men to cope with Bradley Johnson's command. If nothing more, the Confederate raid near Baltimore effectively enabled Union authorities to take measures to solidify their control of the city. The emergency enabled the governor to call up and organize the militia and may have served a better purpose as "muster day" than as a truly significant protection device. In fact, the confusion of "defending Baltimore" equalled that of Washington. Wallace and Ord had moments of conflicting responsibility until Halleck sorted it out for them by declaring that Wallace retained administrative control of the department while Ord "in respect to all military operations and movements, whether defensive or aggressive, . . . is by special assignment of the President the superior in command." The problem was that Ord did little more than either Wallace or Ricketts in trying to mount a pursuit and annihilation of Johnson's column.[12]

By the time that Johnson's men went into bivouac about 9:00 p.m. Monday night near Triadelphia on a Patuxent River tributary near the Howard-Montgomery County line, they had left behind them a trail of upheaval and Union ineptitude. "It was not the intention to do more than to threaten

Baltimore," declared Johnson's adjutant Captain Booth after the war. Baltimoreans failed to appreciate this fact at the time, and the mystery of Confederate intentions had been further compounded by Harry Gilmor's escapades that day. The Marylander had rested briefly on a farm near the Long Green or north branch of the Harford Turnpike on Sunday night. He set out again at dawn with his little band, crossed the Bel Air and Harford roads, cut telegraph wires about 5:00 a.m. and hence severed the communication link between Washington and Baltimore and the north. Superintendent A. J. Baldwin of the Independent Telegraph Company in Philadelphia so informed Couch at Harrisburg, although it was unclear what the general could do about it. "This would indicate that the rebels are making for the Gunpowder or Conowingo bridge, or both," Baldwin noted more helpfully. Gilmor's party ran into trouble just before reaching Kingsville on the Bel Air Turnpike. A Unionist farmer took offense when one of the Marylanders tried to remove a national flag from his house. The farmer blasted the soldier with buckshot and then took to the woods to escape. Gilmor's people retaliated by burning the house and barn, and then proceeded to Magnolia Station on the Philadelphia, Wilmington, and Baltimore Railroad just north of the Gunpowder River crossing, arriving about 8:30 a.m.[13]

The Confederates quickly captured the station and telegraph office, and within minutes also took two northbound trains. Among the prisoners were Major General William B. Franklin, sometime corps commander in the Army of the Potomac but more lately serving in Louisiana. The train also contained many women who flirted with the handsome young officer. The Confederates had strict orders not to rob or harm any passenger, although conflicting reports later surfaced concerning southern courtesy in this regard. Gilmor did parole several convalescents, but not the Yankee general, and he ensured that the civilians' baggage was carefully removed from the trains and placed unharmed in the station. The Marylander had other plans for the engines and cars. He would use them to set fire to the drawspan on the railroad bridge, thus supposedly incapacitating the structure for some time in the future. The engineer of the first train had rendered his locomotive inoperative, but the second train would serve nicely for Gilmor's scheme.[14]

Federal authorities had difficulty in deploying guards for the rail line as Johnson's raiders approached. Major Judd sent 100 convalescents to protect the ferry and railroad property at Havre-de-Grace on the Susquehanna River north of Magnolia Station. However, he had to reduce the time of the 100-day men in order to finish recruiting the 7th Delaware Infantry, and he eventually went in person to the crossings and put together a scratch detach-

ment of sailors and marines with a naval battery under Captain Thomas C.
Harris, USN, with a section of Pennsylvania artillery under Captain Stanis-
laus Mlotkowski. This force served as effective guards for the Conowingo
Bridge upstream. All vessels plying the Chesapeake and Delaware Canal were
pressed into service and sent to Perryville on the north bank of the Susquehanna to carry reinforcements from the north to Baltimore. Most important
for Gilmor's operation were the fifty men which Judd sent under Captain
Thomas Hugh Stirling to protect the Gunpowder River crossing. They met
Lieutenant Robert Price and thirty-two men from Company F, 159th Ohio
National Guard, who had been sent up from Baltimore and had been guarding the span day and night when Stirling's men arrived at 3:00 a.m. on July
10. Stirling and Price quickly agreed on responsibilities; the latter would
guard the western or Baltimore side, while the newcomers would cover the
eastern end or that closer to Magnolia Station.[15]

These bridge guards were totally incapable of withstanding even Gilmor's
small force of veterans. The Confederate leader sent a flag of truce to neutralize the opposition, which included a gunboat standing only three hundred
yards downstream. But the captain of the U.S.S. *Juanita* was unaccountably
unprepared to do battle. Gilmor's people ran the train onto the bridge slowly,
dispersed the Federal pickets, many of whom took to the water to escape,
and the train and bridge dropped hissing into the river, effectively severing
north-south travel by railroad. The *Juanita* shifted position to avoid being
set afire by sparks, and Gilmor simply signaled to her captain to come ashore
and carry the unharmed passengers north to safety.[16]

Both land and naval forces were quite unprepared for Gilmor's style of
operation. The demands of manpower elsewhere explained the army's reaction. Naval inadequacy, however, proved more disturbing since authorities
had been working for over a year to ensure bridge safety on the railroad. A
newsman had alerted the Navy Department on July 9 that the sector was
threatened, and Secretary Gideon Welles had ordered three gunboats to protect the Bush, Gunpowder, and Susquehanna crossings. The U.S.S. *Carituck*
went to Havre-de-Grace, the U.S.S. *Fuschia* made for the Bush River, and the
U.S.S. *Teaser* had been originally slated for the Gunpowder River. The latter
vessel's captain claimed that a leaky exhaust pipe had prevented him from
reaching his destination, while the *Fuschia* claimed later to have prevented the
burning of the Bush River railroad bridge, although Gilmor and band had
long gone by the time that vessel arrived on station. A few random stragglers
and deserters may have been all the enemy left in the area. Part of the navy's
problem was the vessels' drafts which hindered them from moving close

Major Harry Gilmor, C.S.A. This legendary Confederate cavalry raider temporarily disrupted Union communications north of Baltimore during Johnson's raid and participated in the burning of Chambersburg in late July 1864. (U.S. Army Military History Institute)

enough to effectively support the bridge guards ashore. More important was the specific culpability of Ensign William J. Herring, commanding the *Juanita*, for not having steam in his boilers. In sum, Gilmor conducted his operation virtually unmolested. Neither land nor sea forces served the Union cause at all well in the Gunpowder Bridge scuffle.[17]

Gilmor and his men left Magnolia Station by 4:00 p.m. on Monday. They planned to ride directly through Baltimore to gain the Franklin Turnpike, taking captives with them in buggies. However, a friend advised

Gilmor at the last minute that Federals had barricaded the streets of the city. So the Marylanders headed south on the Philadelphia Turnpike, turned westward to Towsontown via the Joppa and York roads, and evaded any pursuers by dark. Gilmor then sent Captain Nicholas Owings and twelve men to escort General Franklin and the other captives to Reisterstown, while the rest of the command tested Union picket lines closer to Baltimore. "A good many shots were fired but 'nobody hurt'!" was the report passed to local southern-sympathizing Madge Preston. Gilmor's own memoir embellished the fray. Eventually, the Confederates crossed the Northern Central Railroad at Rider's Switch and escaped. Gilmor and his thoroughly fatigued command stumbled onto Owings' party fast asleep near Hunt's Meeting House with no prisoners in sight. Franklin and his colleagues had made good their escape as the rebels slept beside the road.[18]

Gilmor was vexed by such negligence, but did not discipline his men. It was now daylight, and following food and more sleep, Gilmor's men combed the neighborhood for the prisoners eluding horsemen sent from the city's defenses, while their exhausted commander sought rest at the Seven Mile House in Reisterstown. Once more all together, Gilmor's men departed Pikesville about mid-afternoon and spent the night of Tuesday, July 12, at Randallstown. Local lore later held that Benjamin O. Howard, Gilmor's uncle and a former Maryland congressman (later recorder for the U.S. Supreme Court), kept his nephew from burning the government arsenal at Pikesville (enabling it to later serve as the Maryland Confederate Soldiers Home). Howard told Gilmor that the residents of the town were Confederate in sympathy and would suffer Federal retaliation for such an act. Gilmor left and took the next day to cross Montgomery County and rejoin Jubal Early's army on its retreat at Poolesville. Gilmor probably spared no hyperbole in later recounting his escapades at headquarters near Big Spring outside Leesburg, Virginia. He reported the loss of but seven men, only one of whom was killed. He had certainly baffled Baltimore officials even if Ord could wire Halleck at 10:00 p.m. Tuesday evening: "Have party out in pursuit of raiders, who are reported all over the country in force of from 5,000 to 7,000."[19]

If anything, Gilmor's party inflamed the country as far north as Wilmington, Delaware. A prisoner-of-war insurrection was suppressed by an alert garrison at Fort Delaware, south of that city. Emergency troops and wide-eyed refugees passed greetings at Conowingo and Peach Bottom crossings of the Susquehanna, but only a few outriders, guerrillas, or mere stragglers terrorized the countryside. Federal authorities certainly worried about mills and factories miles from any enemy force. Railroad repair crews soon fixed the burned-out drawspan on the Gunpowder Bridge, and a somewhat blasé E. O. C. Ord telegraphed from Baltimore on July 14 that little damage had been done by the raiders to property or persons, except passengers on cars had been robbed and horses taken wherever found. He lifted restrictions on travel in the city that same day. Yet for weeks thereafter any report about riders in the country toward the Susquehanna occasioned alarm. The Civil War as it affected northeastern Maryland provided good conversation for a long time.[20]

Meanwhile Johnson and the main force had passed a restless and hot Monday evening near Triadelphia. Warned that a Union cavalry force was bivouacked similarly at nearby Brookville, the Marylander ordered horses saddled and preparations made to attack the enemy. Scouts confirmed that the Federals had also been spooked by news of the rebels' presence and had departed in the night. When dawn broke on Tuesday, Johnson continued his way toward Laurel, where he intended to cross the Baltimore and Ohio's Washington branch. Scouts again brought news of a Federal force posted at Laurel, so the Confederates swung six miles closer to the capital, striking the tracks at Beltsville. They found only a harmless work crew and construction train at this point and immediately torched approximately twenty gondolas, ballast cars, and other railroad property. They also cut down eight telegraph poles serving thirteen different wires, thereby cutting service to the north and to Grant at City Point, Virginia. Union defenders inside the capital's fortifications at Fort Lincoln near Bladensburg saw smoke rising to the north. Three-hundred to five-hundred cavalrymen in blue (most of them dismounted veterans from the Army of the Potomac) went out to investigate. Their horses were green and proved unruly. Johnson deployed his men and guns from the Baltimore Light Artillery and quickly broke up the enemy's concentration, somewhere near the Paint Branch crossing about midway between Beltsville and Bladensburg. The rebels watched the Yankees "skedaddle in fine style" back to the safety of the city forts, spreading wild tales of large mounted forces in the Baltimore-Washington corridor.[21]

Rebel presence between Baltimore and Washington aroused panic at the state capital in Annapolis. Lew Wallace had already instructed Colonel A. R. Root and his militiamen to defend and protect the city at all hazards and to place the town under martial law, adding citizenry to the defense force. Business stopped in the city, and Unionists and secessionists alike dug trenches west of town. The U.S. Navy stationed a gunboat offshore and a steamboat at the Naval Academy wharf to spirit away important state papers and persons. The academy itself had long since transferred operations to

Newport, Rhode Island for the duration, and most of the military activity centered upon hospitals, convalescent centers, parole camps, and supply facilities. The state constitutional convention happened to be meeting at the time, and state officials offered their services even to the point of helping in the trenches. Nearby railroad guards at Annapolis Junction went on the alert, but Johnson's column brushed by everyone at this point. The Washington branch of the railroad suffered only minor damage.[22]

Union authorities expected Johnson's band to attack the capital's defensive lines between Forts Lincoln and Saratoga where the railroad and turnpike to Baltimore entered the fortifications. Johnson was content to search the area for horses and mules, several hundred of which were confiscated to provide changes of mounts for the dash to Point Lookout and to mount the more infirm prisoners found there. The Confederates now turned from Beltsville into southern Maryland on the road to Upper Marlboro. Just then, a courier rode up with news from Early. His arrival was fortuitous for the Maryland cavalryman. Johnson rationalized in his memoirs: "It was now the morning of Tuesday, the 12th. I was due that night at Point Lookout, at the southeast point of Maryland, in St. Mary's county." Once more he argued for the physical impossibility of men making that ride in the time available, explaining how he had canvassed the countryside to borrow fresh horses from his numerous friends and had replaced them as soon as the trotting men and mounts at the head of the column tired. He might then drop out and exchange his wornout horse for a fresh one and rejoin the tail of the column. "By this means I was enabled to march at a trot, which, with a cavalry column, is impossible for any length of time without breaking down horses," he explained. Broken-down horses quickly reduced the men's stamina too, he noted, but with fresh mounts: "I hoped to make a rapid march and get to Point Lookout early on the morning of the 13th."[23]

Johnson failed to explain how his diversions with friends had affected his timetable. Actually, the courier sent by Early now spared the Marylander that embarrassment. The man's message said that the Point Lookout raid was off, and that Johnson's force should rejoin the army near Washington. Of course, the messenger could provide no reason for the change of plans. In point of fact, poor security in Richmond had leaked the news of the naval side of the joint operation. Still, the scheme had been a good one. President Jefferson Davis and General Robert E. Lee had agreed to Colonel-Commander John Taylor Wood's idea of a waterborne assault on the Yankee prison camp. Wood discussed the plan directly with the general on July 2d, helped undoubtedly by his position as close adviser to the president. Lee thus wrote

Davis the next day: "I think under the blessing of a merciful Providence they will be successful and result in great good." He also sent a dispatch to Early to have Johnson effect the rendezvous with Wood's armed steamers "about the 12 Inst." Wood's job, meanwhile, would be to go to Wilmington, North Carolina and requisition men, firearms, and cannon from local commander Major General W. H. C. Whiting. He would then take the party through the Union blockaders, slip into Chesapeake Bay, disrupt the telegraph cable between Fort Monroe and Cherrystone Point, and appear off Point Lookout. Despite public talk about the planned expedition within both civilian Richmond and army circles, both Davis and Lee remained sanguine about its possibility of success.[24]

Wood experienced some predictable trouble in securing as large a caché of firearms as 20,000 muskets in a munitions-starved Confederacy. Yet, by July 9, he could wire Davis of his readiness. He had some 800 soldiers and sailors aboard the fast steamers *Let-her-B* and *Florie* and they were eager to accomplish their mission. As Virginia scion John Tyler, son of the former U.S. president, wrote Major General Sterling Price in distant Arkansas that day: "This I regard as decidedly the most brilliant idea of the war." The trouble was that men like Tyler were writing about it at all, thus openly broadcasting word of the mission. Davis therefore abandoned the mission the following day, telling Wood that the word had leaked out. He further explained, two days later, that the *New York Herald's* Washington correspondent had learned of the plan, causing that paper to suggest in its July 8th edition that "most of the prisoners at Point Lookout have been sent to Elmira, N.Y., and the remainder are being transferred as rapidly as possible." Both Davis and Lee therefore agreed the Wood-Johnson operation would be doomed to failure.[25]

Indeed, Major General Benjamin F. Butler had alerted the War Department about the scheme on July 7 stating: "A rebel deserter reports that it is part of Early's plan to attack Point Lookout and release the prisoners, amusing us meanwhile at Martinsburg." He added skeptically, "this is sent for what it is worth." General Ord wired similar skepticism about reports coincidental with Johnson's crossing the railroad near Beltsville. The alerted Navy Department increased its patrols off Point Lookout by July 8 and 9, although its blockading squadrons at sea learned nothing about the alert until after mid-month. At least some information about the Wood-Johnson raid was passed to Washington and acted upon. Furthermore, Union Commissary General of Prisoners authorities well understood the potentially inflammatory crowding together of thousands of prisoners of war in a twenty-five acre compound at

Point Lookout. Their response was to open a new POW depot in upstate New York, but just how many prisoners had been actually transferred to this new facility by the time of the planned Confederate strike remains unclear. Prison returns listed 14,747 for July with 4,528 prisoner transfers.

There can be little doubt that a successful strike would have freed some prisoners, perhaps even in the thousands. Since protective fortifications for the camp were not completed until July 27, this number of liberated POWS would have swelled Lee's ranks by a corps-size equivalent (provided, of course, that they made it back to Virginia). Thus, Wood was justifiably chagrined at the aborted plan; Johnson surely less so. Even as the Marylander refused to acknowledge the role his own delays played in the affair, he knew fully well at Beltsville on July 12 that he still faced a daunting eighty miles to his target. Johnson reluctantly turned his column back and headed westward to rendezvous with Early, not Wood, by evening. Some prisoners were apparently aware of Early's attack on Washington, but there is no evidence that anyone in the camp knew of the Wood-Johnson plan to liberate them.[26]

Johnson still had to move his force across the whole northeastern front of the capital's defenses before rejoining Early. Just when the horsemen encountered the Federal force near Paint Branch is unclear; Johnson claimed before arrival of Early's messenger, but his adjutant said the encounter took place afterward. Whenever the skirmish occurred, the Confederates subsequently passed unmolested, recruited a Maryland Agricultural College (now University of Maryland) official to guide them, and went "thence along the line of the Federal pickets, marching all night, occasionally driving in a picket, and expecting every moment to be fired upon from the works, within the range of which I was moving," explained Johnson after the war. Adjutant Booth expressed similar surprise at the enemy's inactivity, since a column of 1,200 or 1,300 men in the narrow roads with artillery, ordnance wagons, ambulances, and captured mules ("which we were driving along, loose, in the road") presented an inviting target. The Federals were content to let them pass; their tactics were solidly wedded to static defense from behind fixed fortifications. Booth led Johnson's worn-out column to the Rockville road by 9:00 p.m. on Tuesday. Rejoining the main army, Johnson reported in person to Early at midnight, and everyone hoped "to have a season of relief," recalled Booth. Such would not be possible, however, since Old Jube immediately posted Johnson's men with McCausland as the army's rear guard.[27]

The Marylanders and Virginians on this cavalry expedition felt some measure of success had been achieved by their efforts. A "besieged" Baltimore lacked food and fuel for over a week and the raiders had isolated Washington and the Monument City from the rest of the north for several days. The rebels approached two major population centers, defied their fortifications and garrisons, yet avoided pitched battle, and emerged unscathed. They had secured more horses and mules to add to Early's booty, while spreading havoc among the farmers and townspeople in the area. Still the immediate impact of the raid was disappointingly brief. The *Baltimore Sun* announced on July 15: "The excitement in this city attending the invasion of this State by the Rebels has almost completely abated." The principal rail and telegraph links with the north remained out of service only a week at best. Johnson's foray provided state authorities with the momentum to mobilize and register loyal militiamen, while Unionist sentiment rallied as never before in Baltimore. Mayor John Coleman authorized $10,000 from his council to be spent on bolstering the city's defenses. As compared to western Maryland, where Early's overall activity had a longer term impact on society and economy, the Johnson-Gilmor excursion to Baltimore and vicinity merely served to remind everyone that the rebellion was not over, and the rebels yet dangerous. After Major General Lew Wallace had been restored to full charge of the department on July 14, when Ord left to help pursue Early, the Hoosier addressed a circular "to the loyal citizens of Baltimore." The enemy having withdrawn, he noted, "and the impending evils of an invading force . . . having been removed," Wallace wanted to tender his personal thanks to those citizens who so ably had assisted government forces with courage and loyalty. The crisis had demonstrated latent Unionism in what had been formerly regarded as a hot-bed of secession.[28]

Sometime during the evening of July 15, Captain Pope formed his Union League company and marched them back to the clubhouse from Fort Number 7. They stacked arms in the yard and were dismissed, "leaving the Muskets and Tents and Blankets in the Captain's charge to be turned over to the United States." The Confederate threat to Baltimore was over. Civilian experiences with the invaders had varied, but few would forget the presence of Johnson and Gilmor so close to their homes. Many Marylanders resented that authorities had failed to adequately protect them from such invasion. One Baltimore girl wrote her aunt saying that the Confederates could have easily entered her city, and while not remaining long, they could have "done immense damage to our inhabitants in different ways." Young Rebecca Davis, daughter of Allen Bowie and Hestor Davis of "Greenwood" near Triadelphia and Rosbury Mills Post Office on the Howard-Montgomery County line, seemed to enjoy the successive visits by the Confederates under Johnson and Gilmor. The family still hid their livestock, and were neutral if not Unionist in sentiment. Yet the family shared meals with the raiders. Rebecca and her sister sang tunes like "Annie in the Vale" for a delighted Gilmor and his comrades, and received tunic buttons from the rebels in appreciation. She took away from her experience fond memories of "a most independent set, in highest spirits, easy and affable in their manners."[29]

The Davis family reserve was quickly broken down by the swashbuckling tone of Johnson's and Gilmor's men. Identification with the youth through kin and friendship allowed the Davis girls to dismiss any fears for these Confederates, and it helped Gilmor, in turn, to parole two of his lesser Gunpowder captives who were taken to the Baltimore lines by Allen Davis. Still, the family stayed alert so long as any hint remained of Early's continued presence on Maryland soil. Fears of horse-theft and personal molestation by rebel outriders gave the family anxious moments long after the last graycoats passed beyond the Potomac once again. But, they, at least, escaped the immediate public outcry in Baltimore for retribution and revenge against that city's secessionists. Arthur Christie and his wife (both British subjects) were arrested in late July for removing a national flag from the room of a Federal officer who boarded in the same house with them. Referred to Secretary of War Stanton, they were ordered out of the department and the state within twenty-four hours and could not return until the cessation of hostilities. Yet, one modern commentator has noted: "Political rhetoric and bitterness did not give way to severe and widespread reprisals." This was true, at least in the wake of the Johnson-Gilmor phase of Jubal Early's great raid in the summer of 1864.[30]

Chapter Seven

THE GRAY TIDE RECEDES

T HE gray dawn spread over the landscape widely extended in sight,"
Quartermaster General of the Union Army Montgomery C. Meigs
wrote expansively of the morning of July 13. "An occasional shot from a
suspicious picket and the low of a cow or the bray of a mule alone broke the
stillness of the morning, and at last the sun arose and all remained quiet," he
continued. Cavalry went out and reported back that the rebel positions stood
abandoned—a note quickly picked up by the day's newspapers. Further reports stated that Postmaster General Montgomery Blair's "Falkland" had been
burned, "old Francis P. Blair's house on the farm, turned topsy-turvey, all his
liquors consumed, and his papers ransacked," declared Meigs, with the enemy
in full retreat toward Rockville and the Potomac fords. The next twenty-four
to thirty-six hours would be critical in the race for those crossings. Yet, the
quartermaster chief said of the Union response: "We remained in position
till full daylight, and then, sent the men to their breakfast and continued our
work of clearing off obstructions to our fire and completing our entrenchments." The lack of immediate Federal pursuit would occasion controversy
over the succeeding weeks. Signal Corps Lieutenant J. Willard Brown stated:
"They have accomplished all they wished to or rather expected to,—carried
off all they needed from Maryland, while we were squat around Washington;
trembling in our boots." The rebels "can subsist now for six months, then

do it all over again in Maryland, Ohio, or elsewhere," he wrote bitterly to homefolks. In the words of one later historian, Colin R. Ballard, "the result was a lot of telegraphing in a game of cross purposes." Early was left not only to escape but "to pursue further adventures."[1]

Residents in the Sligo area around Blair's "Silver Spring" farm later testified that Early's army had begun departing about 7:00 p.m. on Tuesday, July 12, but that the rear guard of cavalry never left the area of the day's action much before 5:00 a.m. on Wednesday. These citizens watched the Confederates pass all night long, "and there were but three halts of fifteen minutes each," declared local farmer William Batchelder, near Leesborough. Local lore held that some of McCausland's cavalry took the old Georgetown Road rather than the Rockville Pike to effect their withdrawal and lost a cannon in a sink hole near the future site of the Bethesda Fire Department in the vicinity of the modern National Institutes of Health. Mr. and Mrs. Louis Rohrer reflected an experience in the area later incorporated into the Naval Medical Center on the pike, when they emerged in the morning to find the invaders gone but litter strewn everywhere from camps north of the house (which stood approximately where the tower of the complex now stands) and freshly dug graves beneath some locust trees out near the road. Out at Sandy Spring, Maryland, W. H. Farquhar cited in his daily journal, "things begin to loom much brighter," and would add later that evening, "a beautiful moonlight night for the young and happy." Sightseers who would soon visit "Silver Spring" noted how a shell fragment had clipped the foot off the statue standing in the springside pool, and killed a young rebel who had been drinking there at the time. His grave could be seen nearby. There was much to talk about in the wake of Early's raid on Washington.[2]

Indeed, curious urbanites from Washington swarmed out to view the rebel camps, line of battle, and damages at Silver Spring. One veteran claimed that President Lincoln had been out beyond the lines that night. Imaginative newspaper artists sketched scenes of Confederates cavorting among Blair's gardens, and tossing personal belongings from the family around the property. They reported finding inscriptions on one urn at Silver Spring from a "M. J. Alex.," Newberne, Pulaski County, Virginia to a "Miss B. B." claiming that "the rebels—Confederates—have, as far as possible, protected your house from destruction," which was more than the northern generals would have done "if you had been a rebel, as you call us." The writer claimed to have taken "the likeness of some one of your pretty lady friends," but that it was being safely preserved from ill-treatment "by a gentlemanly Southern." Captain Aldace F. Walker of the 1st Vermont Heavy Artillery found a ladies

The Fort Stevens Battlefield after the Fighting Ended. Only known photograph of the battlefield by E. H. T. Anthony. Note the destroyed house and rifle pits in the foreground, Seventh Street Road and toll booth at corner of Piney Branch Road, and area of Battleground National Cemetery beyond. (With Permission of Minnesota Historical Society)

carte-de-visite in the Blair house inscribed: "Taken from a pilferer for old acquaintance sake with Miss Emma Mason, and left at 11 p.m. here by a Rebel officer, who once knew her and remained behind to prevent this house from being burned by stragglers as was the neighboring one, 11 p.m., and no light. July 12, 1864."[3]

Actually, people back in Washington seemed perfectly happy to let the southerners go in peace. Quartermaster General Meigs would record his own view that while the rebels "had looked ugly and felt hard," during their two-day probing of the city's works, "they will not soon again insult the majesty of a free people in their National capital." The town's newspapers reported gleefully at the enemy's departure, while newsmen occupied themselves trying to calculate precisely just how many men Early had with him. Ben Taylor of the *Chicago Journal* contended the number was 30,000; Samuel Wilkeson of the *New York Tribune* speculated on 50,000 to 55,000; while a colleague from the crosstown *New York World* was positive that Confederate General A. P. Hill had some 45,000 to 60,000 graycoats poised just across the Potomac collaborating with Old Jube's 34,000 to 38,000 men. Whitelaw Reid of the *Cincinnati Gazette* was just as certain that Early never had more than 25,000 men, with only about one-third that figure "even within striking distance" of the city. He claimed that the fighting had been done solely by skirmishers while the majority of the Confederate raiders had been engaged in plundering the countryside and conveying vast quantities of livestock and foodstuffs back to Virginia. Hardly anyone among the newsmens' corps credited Major General Lew Wallace with much help in delaying the pace of Early's Confederates.[4]

President Abraham Lincoln's son Robert Todd Lincoln and his friend John Hay, the president's personal secretary, rode out to visit the scenes of the fighting and various headquarters early Wednesday morning. They encountered a flood of people held back for two days by provost guard details. Now everyone wanted to see real dead bodies, destroyed landscape, and the make-shift rebel breastworks which marked the high tide of Early's threat to Washington. Young Lincoln and Hay joined their friend, Captain Oliver Wendell Holmes of Major General Horatio Wright's staff behind the lines at Crystal Spring, and the trio then toured the army's encampment, "which was stretched in a loafer-like gypsy style among the trees." The VI Corps troops apparently were on alert to commence pursuit of the retreating Confederates, and Hay especially seemed impressed with the hitched and bridled artillery, but not the lounging infantry whom he described as "dirty, careless, soldierly in all else" but dress and deportment. The trio then moved on to Fort Stevens and "had a good view from the parapet of the battlefield of yesterday," but Hay and young Lincoln elicited no claim from Holmes that this was the spot where he had "ordered" the president to descend from on the previous afternoon.[5]

Hay, Lincoln, and Holmes then went to Major General Alexander McCook's headquarters and enjoyed a lager with their friends among the general's staff. They proceeded at a leisurely pace over to Meigs' headquarters for lunch with his deputy, Brigadier General Daniel Rucker. A fellow officer had been ordered to collect a burial detail, and so after becoming well for-

House Near Fort Stevens Hit by Shellfire. The neighborhood in front of the Federal lines where fighting occurred was shattered—structures were destroyed or battered, wheat and corn fields trampled, and orchards cut down by the soldiers. (Library of Congress)

tified with beer and a good meal, the trio ventured out onto the battlefield. They watched an "old sapper and miner" and fifty black freedmen laborers, as they passed the Seventh Street Road on their errand. They heard the sapper mutter to his workers: "Chief mourners, to the rear as pall bearers. Get our your pocket handkerchiefs" to counter the stench of dead bodies and animals. Hay and Lincoln, together with Holmes encountered several "apparently hearty and well-fed of late" prisoners who "expressed themselves anxious to get out of the Army," before they tired of this fun and went back into the city. There was still no indication that Holmes had seen young Lincoln's father during the battle.[6]

The *Washington Evening Star* proclaimed on July 13: "The Rebels Have Disappeared from Our Front," leaving their dead and wounded behind them. The paper boasted that measures had been taken for their immediate pursuit,

The Famous Sharpshooters Tree in Front of Fort Stevens. From a tree such as this, Confederate marksmen seriously threatened President Lincoln's safety on July 11 and 12, 1864. The site of this tulip tree, which was also used as a Confederate signal station, is marked by a plaque and two cannon balls retrieved from the battlefield farm of the Lay family nearby, now the modern Walter Reed Army Medical Center. (District of Columbia Civil War Centennial Commission)

although admitting a dearth of cavalry hampered Union actions unless soon joined by forces under David Hunter, Albion Howe, and Darius Couch from the upper Potomac. McCook pushed out two companies of skirmishers, flanked by horsemen "to gain all the information possible" at first light. However, they accomplished little more than "capturing" some 200 wounded and straggling rebels between Fort Stevens and Leesborough including eleven officers and ninety invalids at the Sligo Post Office. Rodes' Division Hospital yielded fifty-eight wounded and seven sick prisoners to the Federals. Colonel Charles R. Lowell's Massachusetts cavalrymen similarly rode out from Fort Reno and Tennallytown and discovered the retiring enemy about four and one-half miles from Rockville about 9:15 a.m., a rear guard which had departed the vicinity of Bethesda Church about four hours before. Lowell moved to within a half-mile of Rockville, uncovered the fast-moving retreat column from Silver Spring passing "by the old city road from Leesborough" heading for Poolesville and the river crossings nearby. Scouts off to Lowell's left on the river road to Offutt's Crossroads (modern Potomac) also discovered the rebel movement and, in scooping up stragglers, said of the Confederates "that they have been run to death" by forced marches "and that they were still expressing dismay" that "the Sixth Corps must be everywhere." Lowell advised his superiors back in the lines that "any serious attempt against Early's army with infantry must, I think, be made soon."[7]

Lowell now ran into resistance from Colonel William B. Jackson's rear guard. The Bay Staters suffered a serious rebuff both in the town of Rockville and just to the west along the banks of Watt's Branch, although Lowell's horsemen shot a number of rebels from their saddles with Spencer repeating carbines and captured Captain Wilson G. Nicholas of the 1st Maryland Cavalry, C.S.A. For the most part, they were soundly whipped, themselves losing an estimated sixty men captured. Twenty years later, one of the Federal wounded in this skirmish, James Hill, returned to thank his benefactor, local resident Margaret Bell. She had taken him inside her house under a hail of Confederate bullets, and nursed him until he could be transferred to a Washington hospital several days later. Lowell and his men withdrew about two miles south of town to re-form and take stock of the still dangerous Confederates.[8]

The key to catching Early's army lay with concentrating all manner of Federal forces in the region and cutting off his line of retreat. President Lincoln thought it possible and urged pursuit via the River Road, reported his private secretary. This required unity of purpose and coordination—something heretofore found completely wanting in the Federal effort. Again Lieutenant General Ulysses S. Grant, the general-in-chief, was too far away from the actual scene and tried to channel his ideas through his chief-of-staff and messenger, Major General Henry Halleck, whose role as half-strategist and half-operations director tended to only muddle the situation. Lincoln refused to intervene. Secretary of War Edwin Stanton proved as meddlesome as Halleck, and the plethora of generals and other officers involved with the early stages of the pursuit promised to continue the opera bouffe command arrangements prevailing during the "siege of Washington." Once Grant finally decided that General Robert E. Lee had not sent additional reinforcements to Early, he tried to clearly communicate his wishes to Halleck for implementation. Wright's maneuver force was to continue pursuing the Confederates as long as there was "any prospect of punishing" them, then return the VI and XIX Corps contingents to Petersburg for other operations. Kept informed, at least by Halleck and gadfly Assistant Secretary of War Charles A. Dana as to the details of Early's moves, Grant concluded that "by promptly pushing the enemy" Early could be driven from Maryland with great loss. Grant downplayed Early's vaunted numbers, while harboring doubts about any unity of pursuit because of communication difficulties. Yet, "if they will push boldly from all quarters," he claimed, then Early could be destroyed. The general-in-chief told Halleck bluntly on July 14, that if the enemy had indeed departed Maryland as everyone now contended, then "he should have upon his heels" all manner of veteran units, militiamen, cavalry, and "everything that can be got to follow." In a subsequently well-quoted phrase, Ulysses S. Grant flatly asserted that such pursuit should "eat out Virginia clear and clean as far as they go so that Crows flying over it for the balance of this season will have to carry their provender with them." Grant was clearly still thinking about starving Lee's army at Richmond-Petersburg, and not about defending Washington. Capital officials more predictably still focused on that concern and the possibility of Early turning around to once more threaten the city.[9]

Local families like that of Frederick L. Moore, who lived on the west side of the Rockville Pike (near the present Cedar Lane in Bethesda), scoffed at newspaper accounts of the intensity of the VI Corps pursuit of Early. Citing one alleged rear guard battle at "Duff's Run" nearby, Virginia Campbell Moore told her grandson in 1913, that by the time the Federals even reached the place, "the Confederates were across the river." In fact, more time was spent in policing up the wounded rebels and tubercular or heatstruck Federal pursuers than in chasing down the enemy, she claimed. Part of the problem lay with insufficient cavalry to harass Early's column, and authorities took too long to direct what few horsemen they had to move on both the River and Aqueduct (now MacArthur Boulevard) roads (which lay closer to the Potomac crossings), and interdict Early's line of retreat west of Rockville. Even Wright's infantry column was dilatory and confused. Coordination of such diverse commands as VIII Corps and Ricketts' division of the VI Corps from Baltimore with Wright's men at Washington took time. Approximately 4,200 XIX Corps "effectives" were still arriving from Louisiana, "most of whom spent the night in following the windings of the road that marks the long outline of the northern fortifications," claimed the corps historian later. By July 14, 192 officers and 2,987 men representing ten different regiments of that corps could be found in bivouacs at Tennallytown alone, suggesting how difficult it would be to develop a cohesive, cooperative force for pursuit of the rapidly disappearing Confederates. Wright finally got

Major General Horatio Gouverneur Wright, U.S.A. Commander of the VI Corps which relieved front-line defenders of Washington, he conducted a very deliberate but dilatory pursuit of Early into Virginia, fearing the Confederate's superior numbers. (U.S. Army Military History Institute)

his men moving on the Rockville Pike and on the River and Aqueduct roads by the afternoon of the 13th, and thought that Early had only a two hour start at that point. He sent Secretary of War Edwin Stanton a message at 3:30 p.m. stating: "I can assure yourself and the President that there will be no delay on my part to head off the enemy, and that the men I have will do all that the number of men can do." However, herein lay the rub; Wright contended he had only 10,500 men facing three or four times that number in the enemy force. The heat, dust, poorly coordinated and untrained wagoneers, and their unruly mules slowed them down. Wright made it to Offutt's Crossroads (present-day Potomac) by nightfall, but his column was strung out all the way back to the defensive line, and the men were quite played out by their fifteen-mile march. Vermont Captain Walker wrote his father that they had left Fort Stevens at 3:00 p.m. on the 13th and had marched all night past "new mules and green drivers with nary a mouthful to eat." Soon, Major General Quincy Gillmore, nominally commanding the XIX Corps elements, reported an injury suffered from a fall off his horse, and had to be replaced by Brigadier General William Emory. The open phase of the Federal pursuit had been shaky at best.[10]

The men in blue did not lack enthusiasm, however. Morale was high for the soldiers still basked in the limelight as saviors of the city. Men like George N. Carpenter of the 8th Vermont remembered debarkation from the *St. Mary* after their trip from New Orleans, and repeating the VI Corps feat of marching past the President and through the city to cheers and bouquets. Alanson Haines, chaplain to the 15th New Jersey, noted the comforting return of his unit to campsites near "Fort Kearny, upon which we had expended so much labor in the early days of our military life." One company of the 9th New York Heavy Artillery with Ricketts' division received a head of cabbage per man from one grateful citizen before leaving Baltimore, and they refused to be intimidated by cat-calls of "cabbage-head, cabbage-head" preferring to consider the vegetables a badge of honor for valor at Monocacy. When the New Yorkers got to Washington, they were met by President Lincoln and Secretary of State William Henry Seward, whose son commanded the regiment. One young member from Company D stepped forward to proudly display an eagle breastplate with a rebel bullet imbedded in it. "See, Mr. Lincoln," the youth exclaimed, "this saved my life at Monocacy; the force of the bullet knocked me down." The kindly chief executive examined the relic, showed it to Seward, then returned it saying: "Young man, keep that for your children and grandchildren, for future generations will prize that as the greatest heirloom you could possibly leave them."[11]

Although the Federal pursuit bogged down relatively early in the chase, Early and his officers drove their men relentlessly on the road to Poolesville. Outriders still foraged the countryside for stray livestock and other booty, and periodic rest stops enabled the Confederates to rip down telegraph wires and pile fences in the roadway to impede pursuit. That some Confederate Commissary officers actually paid for livestock and produce seized during Early's raid was attested to by a $120.00 voucher for sixty bushels of corn provided to Captain C. S. Hart by Montgomery County farmer A. Dawson during the army's retreat on July 14, 1864. Still, Early's army straggled badly. William Beavans of the 43rd North Carolina noted: "Marched all night [July 13] marching is very disagreeable and unpleasant. Got nothing to eat along the march except Dew Berries, which are numerous." Virginia artillerist

Henry Robinson Berkeley said this march was the toughest he had ever known, a claim echoed by cavalryman J. Kelly Bennette who added that he received nothing to eat for twenty-four hours except discarded scraps from other people's mess pans. Nearly everyone sought to ease their tired feet by "requisitioning" horses, and even Old Jube came close to losing his own mount at one point. More than one officer had to walk temporarily when his stead got "misplaced." Louisiana chaplain Father James B. Sheeran claimed the whole army looked more like demoralized cavalry as it neared the Potomac, and Monocacy captive Alfred Seelye Roe of the 9th New York Heavy Artillery wrote: "During the 13th we found our guards not quite so disposed to discuss the capture of Washington as they had been on Sunday and Monday." In fact, said W. G. Duckett, another New Yorker, they were "exceedingly waspish," and on very slight provocation shouted "Dry up, Yank." In fact, the guards simply let some of their prisoners slip away. Others continued the hot, enforced march of their captors.[12]

Early, in fact, gained a whole day on his pursuers, a lead which he never relinquished. His triumphant veterans splashed back across the Potomac at White's Ford near Poolesville on the morning of July 14, and fanned out over the Virginia hillsides to rest and take stock. Major General Robert Ransom's cavalry and several field guns covered the crossing and slowed Wright's advanced parties beyond Poolesville for several hours. Dismounting only the 8th Virginia Cavalry, the rear guard deployed as skirmishers for a noisy but effective containment action. By evening, they too had recrossed the river, and the two foes settled down to exchange long range cannon and musket fire across the stream. "We were all glad to get back to Dixie land," suggested G. W. Nichols, "for we never loved to cross the Potomac going north," a thought seconded years after the war by fellow Georgian, I. G. Bradwell. "Heaven be praised we are once more in the 'Old Dominion,'" uttered Virginia Cavalryman J. Kelly Bennette, adding that everything seemed to look better and brighter once they had gotten home. Early allowed his men two days' rest after their crossing. He sensed that Wright's Federals had no intention of immediately following his army across the Potomac.[13]

The head of Wright's expeditionary force eventually reached Poolesville late Wednesday afternoon, July 14. But the dusty column continued to stretch back to the District line. Emory's XIX Corps element encamped ten miles short of Poolesville. The march had been hot and fatiguing for the Federals as well, and reports received at the Seneca Creek crossing about rebel cavalry still off to Wright's flank at Darnestown kept him on edge. Many of his officers and men grumbled openly about the lack of water on this difficult march. (The 37th Massachusetts had its elation at being issued new Spencer repeating rifles cut short when it discovered the new cartridge pouches weighed far more than the old forty-round box used with the Springfield muskets.) At least the countryside was pretty and unspoiled by war, they noted as they crossed Montgomery County. Unable to secure hard data as to Hunter's whereabouts, frustrated by the lagging wagoneers, plagued by rumors of enemy cavalry on his flanks and the heat of his woolen uniform, a sweating Horatio Wright was quite perplexed by the time he fired off a late afternoon telegram to Halleck from his Poolesville camp. His 10,500-man expeditionary force was inadequate to cope with Early, he complained, "unless I overrate the enemy's strength." When a thoroughly disgusted President Lincoln heard about Wright's predicament, he exploded that the general "thinks the enemy are all across the Potomac but that he has halted and sent out an infantry reconnaissance, for fear he might come across the rebels and catch some of them." His chief was decidedly not happy, noted Presidential Secretary John Hay in his diary. Furthermore, a mere handful of rebel cavalry and artillery continued to prevent Wright from crossing the river.[14]

Wright and Early both gave their forces a two day respite. Only the execution of a deserter-turned-spy from the 67th New York highlighted the Federal stay in the fertile fields around Poolesville, according to soldier accounts. The bone-tired Confederates (with spoils and prisoners in tow) seemed to gain more from their repose in makeshift camps at places like Big Spring, two miles north of Leesburg. Rebel quartermasters counted the booty and began shipping it off to storehouses supplying Lee's army. The prisoners began their long march southward through Ashby's and Snicker's Gap toward the valley and eventually to rebel prison pens. The 21st Virginia Infantry received the task of taking captured horses to safety, and every foot soldier quickly found a mount. "I wish you could have seen the magnificent figure we presented on our march," wrote Lieutenant Overton Stager to a friend. However, this joy proved short-lived as the thirty-three mile trek though Union, Upperville, Paris, and across the mountains and Shenandoah River to Millwood in the valley was anything but pleasant. By the time the Virginians cut their charges loose to graze at Millwood, reported Sergeant John Worsham, "we were the most completely used up men you ever saw." Foot cavalry could not be converted quickly to mounted men, he decided, and so when the order to mount was given once more: "We were so sore and disabled that nearly all the men needed assistance in mounting." Meanwhile, back at Leesburg, Major Jedediah Hotchkiss and his cartography team spent their time sketching routes and actions of Early's expedition, and

Early Escapes to Virginia. On July 14, 1864, the Confederates escaped with their booty back to Virginia and encamped near Leesburg. (Alfred H. Gurney and Henry M. Alden, Harpers Pictorial History of the Great Rebellion)

everyone bathed and rested. Some of the officers and men accepted local hospitality since Leesburg was a hotbed of southern sentiment. North Carolina Sergeant Major John Young found time to take the 4th North Carolina Band to serenade some young ladies, among them the daughter of the Confederate minister to Great Britain. But such partying offended the sensibilities of straight-laced clergyman Father Sheeran of the Louisiana "Tigers," who personally intercepted some of the merrymakers and shamed the young officers about engaging in frolics within sight of the enemy.[15]

In one month and a day's time, decided Georgian G. W. Nichols, "we had fought four battles and marched 850 miles." Worsham of the 21st Virginia claimed he carried the scars of that march on his feet for the rest of his life. Ten million bushes of grain, large numbers of horses and cattle, and over $200,000 in good (meaning U.S.) money was the way Georgian officer W. R. Redding reported it in a letter to his wife. Captain Robert E. Park of the 12th Alabama recorded in his diary that "we have secured, it is said, over 3,000 horses and more than 2,500 head of beef cattle by this expedition," and concluded that such a gain would greatly help the Confederate Government. Early himself was more modest in his own tally of horseflesh, but in his July 14 report to Robert E. Lee, he flatly declared that "an immense amount of damage has been done the enemy."[16]

The Confederate army's inability to capture Washington may have been discussed in camp, although recuperation seems to have been more important to the soldiers. Nonetheless, Sergeant Major Joseph McMurran of the 4th Virginia noted in his diary: "It was thought that if we could have reached Washington about six hours earlier it could have been taken with comparatively small loss, but the game was not worth the sacrifice of life." Major William J. Pfohl, of the 21st North Carolina agreed, writing to a kinsman in Winston-Salem that a march of forty miles in twenty-six hours in the heat had effectively deterred them. "I do not think that the capture of Washington was contemplated by the authorities at all," he decided, and that only when Early had reached Rockville, twelve miles from the capital, and learned the true state of the Union defenses from McCausland that "he concluded to make the effort." Recalling that only 250 out of 1,600 men in his brigade had been actually present for duty ("a fair proportion throughout the whole army"), Pfohl, at least, wondered if they could have cracked the works, "which are of the most formidable character and if properly manned, would defy the largest army." Even then it seemed questionable to the North Carolinian "whether the taking of the place would have been any advantage to us, as we could not have held it but for a few days." Still, this army was different from the dejected army which had returned to Virginia the previous year following Gettysburg. "We are now victorious over enemies," McMurran waxed, having beaten the VI Corps at Monocacy, moved on Washington drawing Grant's army from Richmond, and made "the boldest march of the war." "Now the prospect of peace encourages all," he concluded. "Even the people of Maryland say that Lincoln will now have to make a proposition of an 'armistics.'" Nevertheless, there were probably other Confederates like Caleb Linker who wrote home that while they had gotten in sight of Washington and spent two days before the city, they had not really "accomplished anything."[17]

Southern newspapers seemed to give similarly mixed reviews to the operation. Certain Richmond sheets hinted that liquor might have caused the marginal success of Early's campaign, and more might have been expected from the audacious move. Mobile and Augusta (Georgia) editors expressed confidence that the peace movement in the north and European recognition might have been enhanced by the invasion across the Potomac. They thanked Old Jube for the booty, thousands of head of livestock, and temporary relief of the Shenandoah Valley from Yankee invaders. However, predictable fault was found in his failure to capture Washington or Baltimore. Senior leaders in his army tended to agree. Brigadier General Stephen Ramseur cited the heat and dust, but "we have accomplished a good deal," he proudly wrote his wife, and he expected more success in the future. For his part, Early apologized to Lee in his campaign report, written during the rest at Leesburg. He felt that Washington simply could not have been captured or the Point Lookout prisoners freed, once the massive resources of the Lincoln government had been brought to bear against the expedition. "Washington can never be taken by our troops unless suprised when without a force to defend it," he declared bluntly. Early also told his chief that he would rest his tired army for a day and then march for the sanctuary of the Shenandoah Valley. After receiving a dispatch from Lee (dated July 11) while still at Leesburg, Early appended an afterthought: "I will retreat in forced marches by land toward Richmond."[18]

Most of Lee's guidance, as contained in his July 11 dispatch, had been overtaken by events by the time Early re-crossed the Potomac. Still, Lee cautioned that by reading northern newspapers, Early might learn what forces were being arrayed against him, and then strike them independently before they could unite their efforts. Louisiana brigadier Zebulon York postured in his after-action report on July 22d, that: "The sight of Washington's dome and fortifications fired anew my men, and they would have hailed with joy the command for an assault and moved with intrepidity to its execution. But confiding in the wisdom of their leader, they withdrew at his bidding and acquiesced in any direction for their zeal." Aware of such spirit, Lee indicated that Early's mission was not yet over. In the discretionary manner of far too many of Lee's directives, he told his lieutenant: "In your further operations you must of course be guided by the circumstances by which you are surrounded, and the information you may be able to collect, and must not consider yourself committed to any particular line of conduct, but be governed by your good judgement." He particularly wanted Early to "retire into the Valley and threaten and hang upon the enemy's flank should he push on toward Richmond." Nowhere did he order Early "to retreat in forced marches by land" back to the main army as Early indicated he would do in reply to Lee's dispatch. Surely Early could see the continued value of keeping reinforcements away from Grant and Meade. As Lee told Secretary of War James Seddon on July 19: ". . . so far as [Early's] movement was intended to relieve our territory in that section [Lynchburg and the Valley] of the enemy, it has up to the present time been successful." Lee hinted that further results could be anticipated from Old Jube's actions.[19]

In point of fact, Early faced danger from a new quarter. Major General David Hunter's Army of West Virginia was now slowly reappearing in the theater of operations. Just when strong talk of Hunter's replacement could be heard in Washington, he and his forward elements reached Martinsburg,

West Virginia as Early's army battled before Fort Stevens. Perhaps Grant retained too much confidence in his old friend from their days in the Department of the Missouri at the beginning of the war. He wired Washington that while Hunter possessed a tired and demoralized force, it could still move up the Shenandoah Valley either holding a large body of the enemy or slip across the Blue Ridge and devastate the Virginia Central Railroad between Charlottesville and Gordonsville as per Grant's favorite scheme. The general-in-chief still did not fully appreciate the disastrous impact of Hunter's ill-advised withdrawal from Lynchburg through the West Virginia mountains. The retreat had opened the path for Early's operation north of the Potomac and especially against Washington, and had ruined the administration's confidence in the aging general. Grant particularly chided Assistant Secretary Dana for Washington's carping criticism of the "brave old soldier" whose courage (in Grant's opinion at least) had impressed the rebels and who had acted (in Grant's words) with "great promptness and great success." The Union's senior military leader was quite incorrect about Hunter. Worst of all, he still failed to understand the administration's paranoia about the capital's safety. Grant was entering extremely soft ground, and only the strong words of Dana, relayed through Grant's aide, Brigadier General John A. Rawlins, brought Grant to his senses.[20]

Dana at last was able to alert Grant to a potentially dangerous situation. On the one hand, Dana noted a malicious presence in "the obstinate prudence of Gen. Halleck" in sending Wright's force outside the fortifications in pursuit of the escaping Early. He also cited the president's reluctance to interfere in the conduct of operations and the nearly frantic reaction of radical Republican congressmen and senators to all the inaction. On the other hand, Dana warned Rawlins pointedly on July 19 that talk had begun in Washington blaming Grant specifically for the disgraceful raid. Dana cited the reasons: Grant as commander-in-chief had responsibility for the whole field of operations; his previous stripping of trained garrisons from Washington's forts had left their defense in the hands of mere militia; Grant himself had sent Hunter on the ill-fated Lynchburg operation, thus paving the way for Early's march down the valley and on to the capital. Additionally, said the assistant secretary, critics cited Grant's inaction in allowing Hunter to retire to the Ohio and his tardiness in actually responding with sufficient relief troops from Meade's army, "till it is too late to do anything more than begin a useless pursuit of any enemy whose escape with all his plunder we are impotent to prevent." Many in Washington viewed Grant's campaign as a total failure and its leader as hesitant as Halleck in resolving the gnawing problems of command and control. In Dana's candid view, the revolting spectacle of the siege of Washington "with all its circumstances of paltroonery and stupidity" was as yet too prominent in people's minds and "its brand is too stinging" for cool judgment. It appeared, said Dana, that all this pointed to a resounding defeat at the polls for Lincoln and "a thousand other things almost as fatal to the country."[21]

Events played on in northern Virginia independent of communications between Washington and City Point, although camp gossip suggested that Wright's soldiers knew exactly what was transpiring. A staff officer brought back an order from Washington, noted Vermonter Aldace F. Walker in the VI Corps, whereby Grant had directed "for us to make up an expeditionary force of our own Corps, the 19th, Hunter's and Sigel's forces, men from Baltimore and all about, all under Wright to follow the rebs and live on the country." At least, this was how "we understand it," said Walker, even though at that very moment the XIX Corps with "only two small divisions of our Corps, with some cavalry and artillery" were advancing toward Winchester. "Our two poor little divisions, though called the two best in the Army of the Potomac, would not stand much show against their big army, but we shan't catch them anyway," he admitted.[22]

Meanwhile, Hunter spent two days re-outfitting his force at Martinsburg while awaiting the arrival of the rest of his men from Cumberland, Maryland. Re-establishing communication lines with Washington took time and, for the most part, kept him out of touch with the War Department. Once more, only the intrepid work of railroad president, John W. Garrett, appraised Washington of what Union forces were doing on the upper Potomac. By July 14, elements of Hunter's army had reached Harpers Ferry and passed on to Knoxville, Maryland, apparently on the trail of a long-departed Early. Here, Hunter received a dispatch from Wright at Poolesville, asking him to join forces at Leesburg, Virginia, across the Potomac. Hunter immediately sent forward Brigadier General Jeremiah Sullivan with 7,000 infantry and 2,000 cavalry under former French and now Union officer, Brigadier Alfred Duffié. Using the towpath of the Chesapeake and Ohio Canal, these forces crossed at Knoxville and Berlin, Maryland, and headed south. They were within striking distance of Early's force as they passed through Lovettsville. Then, instead of pressing on directly to Leesburg (as Wright had requested), Sullivan followed Hunter's wishes to turn right through Hillsborough and Purcellville to reach Aldie at the edge of the mountains. Here the Little River Turnpike (from Alexandria just below Washington) divided into the Ashby's Gap Turnpike to the west and the Snicker's Gap Turnpike to the northwest. Sullivan's marching column would have directly bisected Early's line of retreat from Leesburg through Snicker's Gap, had he not encamped at Hillsborough on the night of July 15. Here he lost his opportunity to cut off Early from the valley sanctuary. However, he may also have saved his tiny command from annihilation at the hands of the larger Confederate force. Wright, now compelled to follow Early onto Virginia soil, splashed across White's Ford on July 16, while friendly fire support from his artillery suppressed the remaining enemy rear guard. Some 23,000 or more Federals stood on the threshold of a pincer movement which could have destroyed Jubal Early's raiders by a coordinated effort.[23]

The Federals, like the rebels several days before, found the river bed stony, slippery, and full of holes, even though it was only two or three feet deep. Nonetheless, they frolicked in the refreshing waters, stripping naked, or at least to underdrawers, and made the crossing with firearms and clothing held aloft to keep them dry. All of this delighted various onlookers, including a bevy of black washerwomen standing on the bank trying to decide how they too might cope with a stream crossing in petticoats. After the passage, remembered Frederick W. Wild of Alexander's Baltimore Battery, the men piled their wet drawers in company stacks. "How they afterwards got them, and how they were distributed among the men, I do not know," he shrugged. John B. Southard of the 49th New York wrote his sister in Rexford Flats, Saratoga County, that after crossing the Potomac they were all soon dust-covered once more and "I would have liked to see [the soldiers], marching threw [sic] the flats the peopel [sic] would [have] thought they were mud statues marching." Wright's forces soon outdistanced the wagon train in spite of the dust and heat. By this time, however, Sullivan realized his predicament, and held back from closing with the Confederates. Sometime near noon on July 16, David Hunter's other division commander, Brigadier General George Crook, rode up to Hillsborough, took over command from Sullivan whom he considered imcompetent or even cowardly, and sent off Duffié's horsemen to find the enemy. Duffié tracked down Early's vedettes at nearby Waterford and then uncovered the whole Confederate army—men, animals, and vehicles—all slowly moving westward on the road to Snicker's Gap. The lead brigade of Yankees, led by Colonel William B. Tibbit and about 300 men with several artillery pieces, pitched into the rebel column on the outskirts of Purcellville shortly after noon.[24]

A slashing Union attack cut through the Confederate wagon train which Early had positioned midway between infantry elements in the column. The cavalrymen had little difficulty cutting out over one hundred horses and mules, some eighty wagons, ambulances or other conveyances, and grabbing fifty to sixty prisoners. If infantry support had been available, Tibbit might have accomplished even more. But Rodes' division learned of the commotion and came running to beat off the attackers. Lieutenant George Whittaker Wills of the 43rd North Carolina claimed that thirty of the vehicles were retaken, and the angry rebels even made off with two artillery pieces of the Federals. Still, he admitted "there was a good deal of excitement for a while." Captain Robert Park of the 12th Alabama recorded in his diary that Doles-Cook's Georgia and Battle's Alabama brigades double-timed two miles to catch the retiring Union horsemen. "The idea of Confederate infantry trying to catch Yankee cavalry, especially when the latter is scared beyond its wits, is not a new one at all," he observed, and would doubtless be repeated in the future, for "a frightened Yankee is *unapproachable*." Some of the southerners actually welcomed Tibbit's success for many of the burned wagons had contained Maryland plunder, hoarded by the rebel quartermasters. Everything from a pin or ladies kerchief to fine boots, broad cloth, hoops, and any quantity of dress goods which "these pilfering selfish fellows had appropriated and concealed," noted North Carolinian Leonidus Lafayette Polk disgustedly. "Hurrah! for these Yankee raiders say *we*," he added in a note to his wife, adding that what he and his comrades needed was good army clothing, not plundered civilian garb.[25]

Duffié's cavalry also skirmished later that evening with some of Brigadier General William Jackson's rear guard Confederates near Wood Grove northwest of Purcellville. Be that as it may, in the main, Early was allowed to escape to bivouacs that night both in and beyond Snicker's Gap in the Blue Ridge. The next day, July 17, he crossed the Shenandoah River and encamped his forces in strong positions near Berryville. To one postwar commentator, Crook and Wright had "now come together just in season to allow Early to slip between them." Indeed, with their men hot, haggard, and in as foul temper from marching conditions as the Confederates, and with Wright's veterans straggling badly (even some taking to ambulances for relief), Crook and Wright both decided to rest for the night. Crook's command encamped around Purcellville while their leader reported for orders to Wright, bivouacked six miles back toward Leesburg in Clark's Gap. Wright told Crook to push ahead in the morning and force Snicker's Gap and the ferry crossing of the Shenandoah River beyond. Wright would follow to lend a hand. It was clear that the VI Corps commander was holding back, knowing that Grant wanted his soldiers returned to Petersburg just as soon as it became evident that Early was no longer a serious threat. As modern historian Jeffrey

Brigadier General George Crook, U.S.A. One of Hunter's division commanders, whose lackluster coordination of pursuit operations with Wright after Early's return to Virginia enabled the Confederates to elude capture and return to the Shenandoah Valley. (U.S. Army Military History Institute)

Wert concludes: "The whole expedition had become simply one of pushing Early's rear, a tactical reconnaissance in-force."[26]

Grant's continuing detachment from events along the Blue Ridge sapped the Federal pursuit. News from Halleck only reinforced the general-in-chief's advisory role. On July 15, Grant told Halleck that in the event of any recurrence of a Confederate raid northward, "there should be an immediate call for all the troops we are likely to require," and that Washington, Baltimore, and Harpers Ferry should be designated as "schools of instruction" with all troops raised east of Ohio sent to those points. Union officials would then always have the benefit of increased force, in Grant's view, and such force could be rapidly improved by contacts with veteran troops. Furthermore, if Hunter found it impossible to reach and cut the Virginia Central Railroad, then he should make all the mountain valleys south of the Baltimore and Ohio Railroad "a desert as high up as possible." Grant explained that he did not intend to burn houses, but merely to remove "every particle of provisions and stock" and to warn the population to leave. He scoffed at the offensive capabilities of any Confederate force from Virginia to Georgia, and declared that "Early could never capture any important point with a force even of 30–50,000 men so long as the main union army is within thirty hours of the Capitol." Grant clearly relied on his superior capabilities for rushing reinforcements back to the capital region if needed. He bluntly informed Halleck that he saw no further use for Wright to follow the enemy when Early was a full day's march ahead of him.[27]

Grant hammered on this theme for the next week or more. By the 17th, he envisioned Early turning westward to reach the Ohio, possibly via Pittsburgh, but never venturing directly north of the Potomac again. Nevertheless, he took the precaution of sending back regiments whose term of service was scheduled to expire by August 20 as a guard for the capital, and advised Halleck that he might retain the services of the heavy artillery units sent back. Then, in the first real indication that he finally was beginning to comprehend that the core of the problem lay with lack of unified command, he sent a ciphered message designed "to prevent a recurrence of what has just taken place in Maryland." The Susquehanna, West Virginia, Middle, and Washington departments were to be consolidated under one single commander who would control "all troops that cooperate in any movement of the enemy toward Maryland or Pa." The only trouble was that the man whom Grant had in mind, Major General William B. Franklin, was unacceptable in Washington. Grant received no reply for three days. He repeated his idea. At this point, the general-in-chief discovered the full power of Halleck's ability to delay or obstruct the proceedings.[28]

Henry Halleck may have been styled "Old Brains" in army circles, but he was also vainglorious and vindictive. He had been Grant's superior officer in the west before moving to Washington as general-in-chief himself, in the summer of 1862. While Halleck became enmeshed in the political intrigues of the wartime capital, he also came to understand the hopes and fears of Stanton and Lincoln. Statutorily loyal to his successor by 1864, he privately felt slighted at now coming under Grant's command. Halleck still tried to dabble in strategic formulation, to alter organizational responsibilities, and to shape the war in his own view. He interfered in ways which bemuddled and delayed implementation of orders. On the other hand, he was a vital link in the three-way command arrangement between City Point, Washington, and the field armies. Furthermore, he occasionally offered sage advice that a more pragmatic general like Grant avoided only at his own peril.[29]

When Halleck finally reported back to Grant about the reorganization scheme, he noted Washington's opposition to Franklin. He was a member of the old McClellan clique, said Halleck in a July 21 dispatch, was besmirched by the intrigues of 1862, and was not politically viable with the Radicals on Capitol Hill. Moreover, Halleck (like Assistant Secretary of War Dana several days before) attempted to enlighten Grant on the Washington political climate of that moment. Writing on July 19, Halleck suggested a bit patronizingly: "The recent raid into Maryland seems to have established several things which it may be well for us to keep in mind." First, it showed that while Grant operated south of the James with Lee between him and Washington, the Confederate leader could make a pretty large detachment unknown to the Federals for a week or ten days and send it against Washington or into the valley. Second, Hunter's army, which, in government's view, comprised the only troops north of Richmond actually available for field service, was entirely inadequate to hold West Virginia, the Baltimore and Ohio Railroad, and at the same time resist any considerable raid north of the Potomac. Third, reliance could not be placed upon northern militia who might not come out at all, arrive late, or prove unsatisfactory in numbers and quality. Finally, said Halleck bluntly, the Washington and Baltimore garrisons were entirely unfit for the field and inadequate for defense. Had it not been for the timely arrival of the VI Corps veterans during the recent crisis, "both cities would have been in great danger." So long as Grant had operated "between Washington & the enemy," with the Army of the Potomac covering Maryland and Pennsylvania, Halleck had been agreeable to stripping garrisons and guard troops for Grant's needs which might otherwise have formed the reserve for the capital region. But circumstances had changed with Grant's passage across the James, and "I am decidedly of [the] opinion that a larger available force should be left in this vicinity."[30]

Halleck agreed that reinforcements could be sent from the James, as done at Fort Stevens, but only if the government knew of the size and mission of the raiders. This would be impossible without a superior cavalry force, which was not then present nor likely to appear, since Early's men had stripped the country of animals and provisions necessary for such a mounted force. Furthermore, if Early had utilized the fords between Harpers Ferry and the capital—fordable due to low water at that moment—and moved directly on either Baltimore or Washington, or if the VI Corps had been delayed twenty-four hours, then one or the other of those large depots of supplies would have been in gravest danger. Was it safe to repeat the risk? queried Halleck. "Is not Washington too important in a political as well as military point of view, to run any serious risk at all?" As for Grant's fabled schools of instruction, Halleck pooh-poohed the suggestion by noting: the army was not receiving one-half the number of recruits as it discharged; volunteering had virtually ceased; anticipation of anything from Lincoln's latest call for 500,000 new men issued on July 18 was suspect; and unless the country braced itself for adoption of an "efficient and thorough draft," then replacement for the wastage of the army could not be secured. As for the principal problem, "so long as Lee is able to make any large detachments, Washington cannot be deemed safe, without a larger & more available force in its vicinity." Ironically, these were the same arguments made by President Abraham Lincoln to his earlier field commander, Major General George B. McClellan, two years before.[31]

It is not altogether clear what precise impact either Halleck or Dana had upon Ulysses S. Grant. The general was not far off in his postwar statement: "It seemed to be the policy of General Halleck and Secretary Stanton to keep any force sent [to the Shenandoah] in pursuit of the invading army, moving right and left so as to keep between the enemy and our capital; and, generally speaking, they pursued this policy until all knowledge of the whereabouts of the enemy was lost." Grant wanted but one policy—seize the initiative, find, fix, and fight Early to the death. Halleck and Stanton counseled another in screening the capital region from invasion and capture. While both permitted Meade's Army of the Potomac to concentrate on defeating Lee, this confusion in the Washington region led to inertia and confusion for the remainder of July and into August. Grant, at least, followed Halleck's and Dana's advice and permitted Washington officials to retain Wright's veterans until, said Grant, "the departure of Early is assured or other forces are collected to make his presence no longer necessary." He also drily asked Halleck: "If Early has halted about Berryville what is there to prevent Wright and Hunter from attacking him?"[32]

Grant had a point. While Early had gone into camp around Berryville on July 17, he was prepared to dispute the river crossings of the Shenandoah. Ramseur and Gordon took positions controlling Castleman's Ferry on the main Leesburg-Winchester Road. Rodes moved two miles downstream to guard Rock's Ford. Jackson's cavalry departed northward to cover the Charlestown route into the area while Imboden's troopers went in the opposite direction to protect the Millwood approach. A relaxed Major General John C. Breckinridge, confident that he could hold the crossings for Early, departed later that sabbath morning to find an Episcopal Church service in Berryville. The enterprising fighting men in the army began canvassing the neighborhood, and as one lady at nearby "Bloomfield" farm recounted, she and other women spent the next two days feeding hungry soldiers and mending their socks. Such kindness still did not prevent Private Billy Beavans of the 43rd North Carolina from noting in his diary that while the girls were pretty enough "they are not strong secesh enough for me in these parts."[33]

Both Crook and Wright did nothing that Sunday, perhaps in the belief that the rest would do their tired soldiers some good. One Maine soldier, James M. Gasper, said he and his comrades simply "lay on the hill in the woods all day," while Vermonter Aldace F. Walker "lay in a beautiful grove" all day waiting for orders to get up. Two days later he wrote his father that "we are living pretty well nowadays; have just learned how," and reported foraging beyond the picket lines for butter, chickens, and blackberries. Meanwhile, Duffié's cavalry were more active, combining with Colonel James A. Mulligan's brigade of the 23rd Illinois and 10th West Virginia Infantry as well as nearly 1,000 dismounted cavalrymen to push the Confederate rear guard through Snicker's Gap, and attempt a crossing of the Shenandoah River at Castleman's Ferry. The Federals were rebuffed three times by an artillery-infantry force strongly posted at the crossing. Both sides now prepared to dispute this vital passage on the river and entry into the Shenandoah Valley. By noon, Monday, July 18, Confederates posted on the heights west of the ferry could see blue-coated columns descending toward the river from the gap. The Federals had just completed a leisurely march from Purcellville to tiny Hamilton where, noted Lieutenant Colonel Mason W. Tyler of the 37th Massachusetts, "flags and handkerchiefs waved as we passed." By mid-afternoon, the flood plain at Castleman's Ferry was covered with Early's pursuers, with some preparing for battle while others like the 14th New Jersey simply settled down to cook dinner from all the liberated hogs, chickens, honey and potatoes they had confiscated from "supposed rebel Virginians." Wright ordered Crook, breveted Major General that very day, to send a task force downstream (north) to cross the river, and establish a bridgehead to outflank the ferry. Crook designated Colonel Joseph Thoburn's augmented division for this task.[34]

Thoburn's three brigades made their way undetected over narrow, stony roads, and quickly crossed the river at a place known to both sides as "Island Ford." A handful of rebel pickets barred the way as Crook and Wright watched the proceedings from a vantage point two hundred feet above the valley floor. The pickets quickly fell into Federal hands and told their captors that two Confederate regiments, supported by Gordon's and Wharton's divisions under the overall command of John C. Breckinridge, were about three miles distant near Webbtown and Wickliffe with Rodes and Ramseur off to the north covering approaches from Harpers Ferry. Early was in the area in person, and the whole Confederate army was on alert. Thoburn, taken aback by news of such strong opposition, passed the information back to Crook, who in turn told Thoburn to hold his bridgehead, but not advance on the ferry. He would have Wright send reinforcements.[35]

Thoburn advanced his three brigades in two lines and posted them on the so-called "Westwood" farm, the first behind a bluff some seventy-five yards from the river, the second behind a low stone fence along a road on the riverbank. The terrain gradually sloped upward from these positions to an adjacent ridge on which "Cool Springs" farm soon bristled with Rodes' full division, having been alerted to the Yankee's crossing. A "warmly contested" two-hour conflict developed in the late afternoon as Rodes attacked the Federal positions. Confederate participants remembered a desperate slaughter as their side charged to within forty yards of the stone fence and eventually routed a portion of the defenders, many of whom drowned while re-crossing the river. The Federals, too, described an ambitious fight with artillery as well as infantry involved. One savage Confederate attack routed Lieutenant Colonel Samuel B. Young's Provisional Brigade of dismounted cavalry, comprising a patchwork of seventeen different units scrapped together from Washington, Maryland, and Virginia camps, hospitals, and rear echelon posts and completely lacking in cohesion. They broke for the rear, many panic-stricken troopers drowning as they tried to swim the treacherous Shenandoah to safety. Darkness allowed Thoburn to extricate his battered force, completely baffled at the lack of promised support from the VI Corps. The Federals suffered over 400 casualties, most in "their posterior parts," Louisiana Father Sheeran noted ungenerously. The Confederates lost nearly that many due to their succession of attacks to drive Thoburn into the river. Among the dead were Colonel James Hall Wood (14th North Carolina), Colonel William Allison Owens (52nd North Carolina), and Lieutenant Colonel Walter Scott Stallings (2nd North Carolina). Indeed, the action at Island Ford or Cool Spring farm was as costly to Rodes' division as Monocacy had been for his comrade John B. Gordon. One Tarheel brigade lost more than twenty-five per cent of its effective strength because of the division commander's determination to capture the Federally-held stone fence. On the Federal side, the costly withdrawal across the river left "the Shenandoah blue with their uniforms and crimson with their blood" in the words of one rebel onlooker. Feelings were so bitter in the neighborhood that when Colonel Daniel Frost (commanding the 11th West Virginia and Crooks' third brigade) suffered a mortal wound literally on the edge of kinsman Eben Frost's "Cool Spring" farm, the latter (an ardent secessionist) refused to visit him on his death bed, and said that it would not have happened if his cousin had stayed at home.[36]

Crook and Wright failed to agree on the proper course of action during the battle, creating harsh feelings between them and their commands. VI Corps veterans scoffed at the ineptitude of Crook's people, many of whom were thought to be mere 100-day men. The Army of West Virginia soldiers held a grudge from then on against Wright and his corps for failing to provide support for Thoburn. Wright explained this away, claiming that the fight was lost anyway and that he wanted to slide northward to Key's Gap for better coordination with the rest of Hunter's army coming south from Martinsburg. Whether timidity, changing priorities, or in Crook's disdainful postwar view that "incompetency or worse" governed Wright's conduct of the Cool Spring fight, it was clear that once more as an independent commander, the VI Corps leader had failed to aggressively pursue Lincoln's and Grant's wish that Early's army be destroyed.[37]

That night, and all the next day, Confederates and Federals picked and sniped away at one another across the three hundred yards of water in the Shenandoah River. Duffié with 2,000 cavalry passed to the south through Ashby's Gap and stormed across the Shenandoah on the old road through Millwood to Winchester. However, they could not hold this position. The 37th Massachusetts fired its Spencer rifles and claimed a number of rebel pickets shot down. Yet no major resumption of battle took place; both sides simply wanted a rest. The Confederates dug shallow graves for friend and foe alike on their side of the stream and mourned lost comrades. The Confederate dead would be reinterred eventually in the Stonewall Cemetery and their erstwhile enemies in the National Cemetery at Winchester. Some of the 37th Massachusetts callously drove in a flock of some farmers' sheep and made mutton of them. "The owner of the sheep came around (an old man) scolding about losing his sheep and wanted pay for them," noted the regimental historian. The soldiers chatted pleasantly and told him if he was a Unionist he would get paid. "The old man got into the wrong crowd to get much sympathy," thought the Bay Staters. "We wanted a change in our bill of fare." Yet other soldiers like Elias Pillet of the 114th New York found refreshment in the surrounding countryside. "In front, rolled the Shenandoah River, its murmuring faintly heard in the stillness of the evening; hundreds of camp fires dotting the undulating farms around," he noted while beyond, the North Mountain range lifted its dark head skyward and the moon rose in its fullness over Snicker's Gap. Yanks and Rebs alike had grown jaded about battle and hard marching, but at least a few remained sensitive to "a landscape which might challenge the admiration of the world."[38]

Early received reports that more Federals under Brigadier General William Averell, a cavalry leader not entirely trusted by either Hunter or Crook, were moving on Winchester from Martinsburg, thereby threatening his rear. Therefore, during the night of July 20, Early withdrew his army from the Shenandoah River line to the valley turnpike, bent on regrouping at Strasburg. But he also sent part of his command on another forced night march to counter Averell's threat and cover the army's changing position. Young, combative North Carolina brigadier Stephen Ramseur and his men made the wearisome trek with two batteries and the cavalry of Jackson and William Vaughn. By this time the ardors of a month of marching had taken their toll and led to the Confederates' undoing. Ramseur, possibly misled by reports from Vaughn that he faced a mere reconnaissance force, rushed headlong into premature combat with Averell's whole division at Stephenson's Depot (also styled Rutherford's Farm or Tavern), north of Winchester. The Confederates were outflanked and rather badly cut up. The *Richmond Enquirer*, always seeking scapegoats, described it as "the deplorable affair in which Ramseur's division was humiliated in the dust." Four hundred southerners fell, among them Colonel Francis H. Board, 58th Virginia; and Brigadier General Robert Doak Lilley was captured. "Seldom has a Confederate defeat been so squarely acknowledged," was the way one writer later saw it. Even the distraught Ramseur acknowledged to his young wife back in North Carolina that his men "behaved shamefully," and that for the first time he was deeply mortified at the conduct of his troops. The affair temporarily became a *cause celibre* through the Confederate army, even at Petersburg, and Ramseur expended many words in every letter home throughout August bemoaning how his critics misunderstood what actually happened. Carrie Clack with the 23rd North Carolina summed it all up when he noted ". . . owing to the Comdg Genls. neglect, or want of the exact locality of the enemy, it suffered an inglorious rout; a perfect panic, with scarcely any one hurt, the blame is taken off the troops, & rests on Ramseur, Brig. Genl. comgd. Div."[39]

Early rushed Rodes' command back to aid the routed Ramseur while Averell unaccountably refrained from pushing on into Winchester. Meanwhile, Wright and Cook finally crossed the Shenandoah on July 30, discovered Early gone from their front, and surveyed the little battlefield still replete with half-covered shallow graves and the flotsam of conflict. They marched on to Berryville, with the 2nd Connecticut Heavy Artillery leading the advance brigade. Suddenly Wright, conceiving "the object of the expedition to be accomplished," about-faced and ordered his men to return for what he informed Halleck would be a "two days easy march" to Washington. One unimpressed Vermonter later decided: "The conclusion that Early had abandoned the Valley seems to have been hastily reached and perhaps was founded on what he was expected to do, than on actual information concerning his movements." Crook would move on to an eventual rendezvous with Averell at Kernstown just south of Winchester in an exposed position, inviting Confederate response. The valley had been returned to David Hunter's sole responsibility.[40]

In what turned out to be an anabasis bordering upon irresponsibility, Wright's "easy two day march" turned out to be a grinding race to get back to the steamboats at Washington to help Grant at Petersburg before Early's men returned to Lee's army. Notwithstanding later reminiscences of Yankee fanfare to impress rebellious Leesburg with unfurled banners and bands playing joyously as the troops marched through town, Wright's veterans basically remembered the march with bitterness. Many were virtually shoeless and "walked along nearly asleep on their feet." Rainstorms offered scant relief and overnight encampments at Goose Creek and Difficult Run failed to quench thirst, hunger, or the desire for longer periods of sleep. Mosby's guerillas hung on their flanks and rear, gobbling up stragglers, and various plans to trap the partisans failed as always. Animals likewise suffered from lack of proper forage and shoes. Relief came only on July 23, when the expedition closed on Washington's fortifications and went into camps stretching from Tennallytown back across the Chain Bridge. While Wright rode on to headquarters seeking orders, his tired army bedded down to savor mail from home, collect back pay, and wonder about their next destination. One lieutenant and eight enlisted men from the 23rd Pennsylvania ("Birney's Zouaves") went out on the town and had a lively time on a single pass between them! "I am quite contented so long as we do not take transports for Petersburg," noted Colonel Joseph E. Hamblin of the 65th New York. He shuddered thinking about another season of heat and dust near Richmond. Frankly, said Hamblin, the cooler mountain breezes had restored the vigor that had drained his men's strength campaigning from the Rappahannock to the James. Heavy rain showers saturated the Washington encampments, but nobody noticed so long as the generals did not require more marches like the one just concluded. Estimates varied, but the soldiers figured that most of them had spent the previous two weeks traveling upwards of 500–600 miles, 170 to 175 of which had been by foot! As Vermont captain, soon to be major, Aldace F. Walker wrote his father at the time, the Wright expedition "aboutfaced" to return to Washington: "We are on our way back to base and reliable communications again. What has been done meanwhile we know nothing of, and of what we have done we know little."[41]

Chapter Eight

UNITY OF COMMAND ACHIEVED

MAJOR GENERAL HENRY HALLECK dutifully notified Grant at 10:00 a.m. on July 22, 1864 that Major General Horatio Wright had broken off pursuit of Jubal Early's retreating Confederates. Wright and his men had returned to Washington en route to Petersburg per Ulysses S. Grant's instructions. "In my opinion," said Halleck, "raids will be renewed as soon as he leaves; but you are the judge whether or not a large enough movable force shall be kept here to prevent them." Major General David Hunter had flatly announced the inability of his Army of West Virginia to cope alone with the Confederates in the Shenandoah Valley, and Assistant Secretary of War Charles A. Dana privately advised Grant that only half an army actually filled Hunter's ranks. Halleck suggested that even President Abraham Lincoln looked to Grant for a solution. Grant obliged at 6:00 p.m. the next evening, wiring that Wright would return to Petersburg with his VI Corps. The XIX Corps could remain to protect Washington while Hunter should take up "such of the advanced positions suggested by him as his judgement will best protect the line of the Potomac." An exasperated Grant wrote his old political sponsor, Illinois congressman E. B. Washburn saying, "Maryland raid upset my plans but I will make an attempt to do something before many days." When he queried Dana the following day: "How does the pursuit after the enemy shape up? Have they been compelled to drop any of their plunder and have we killed, captured or scattered any of their forces to speak of?" The assistant secretary replied negatively. The pursuit had been "an egregious failure"; Wright and Crook had accomplished nothing with Wright starting back to Washington "as soon as he got where he might have done something worth while." Early had gotten off with the plunder and Hunter was not expected to do much. "Had Wright remained in the valley," said Dana, "the combined forces might have made a fine campaign at least against the rail roads and the crops."[1]

Once more it was business as usual in Washington. Government officials seemed content to forget Early and return to running the affairs of state. If residents may not have slept quite so soundly, "free from alarm or anxiety," as implied by Treasury registrar Lucius Chittenden, shops had reopened promptly and trains ran northward on schedule again. Georgetown bargemen and businessmen were distraught over lost revenue following rebel destruction of the Chesapeake and Ohio Canal upriver. However, most citizens became complacent as the District militia disbanded and the government clerks went back to normal schedules. True, Quartermaster General Montgomery C. Meigs (who never forgot his two-day experience commanding troops in the field) kept his quartermaster employees proudly drilling regularly, but military officials generally breathed more easily once Early's men returned south of the Potomac. People even began to speak of the whole affair as a hoax perpetrated by the newspapers. Correspondent Noah Brooks overheard several carefree soldiers passing the equestrian statue of George Washington on Pennsylvania Avenue in the West End, remark: "What Brigadier is that? Old Uncle Jake Andrew Jackson?" "Nawh," drawled a reply, "that's Wash-tub-a-ridin on a contract hoss." Washington had indeed returned to its norm.[2]

There was an underlying unease, a lack of fulfillment mixed with relief that the raiders were gone. Political circles reflected this ambivalence. This was an election year, and one of re-election for Lincoln and his administration. The summer seemed the darkest hour of the war to many observers fretting about the vote. Washington and the whole north had been frightened by the audacity of Early's invasion. Union generals, including the great Grant, seemed unable to end the rebellion militarily. Hunter, Crook, and Wright could not even bring Early to bay. An American president had been besieged in his own capital. Faith in the Union cause wavered. Attorney General Edward Bates recorded in his diary: "Alas! for the impotence or treachery of our military rulers! The raiders have retired across the Potomac, with all their booty safe! Nobody seems disposed to hinder them." Postmaster General

Montgomery Blair (whose own property losses totaled $20,000 or more) reputedly caused an uproar in one cabinet session by pronouncing that all the officers in command were "poltroons" and too cowardly to fight a handful of scraggly rebels. At least Lew Wallace had been willing to do so. Secretary of the Navy Gideon Welles said: "We have done nothing," adding that it seemed more gratifying to self-pride to believe there were so many of the Confederates that this alone allowed Early to get off with "considerable plunder scot free." One former Army of the Potomac corps commander from the McClellan era, and now on duty at Columbus Ohio, Major General Samuel P. Heintzelman, noted in his personal journal: "I suppose Genl. Halleck wants an alarm signal fired upon and Mr. Stanton to have cannon placed in the streets. I am very glad I am not thus involved." No wonder the caustic editor of the New York-based *Army-Navy Journal* declared: "The annual expedition of the Confederate forces into Maryland and Pennsylvania has been inaugurated this year at about the usual time, and with rather more than the usual success." He further suggested that it might well "furnish July almanac makers with another 'about this time may be expected' passage for their wares." The prestigious *Times* of London of July 25 pronounced that the Confederacy was more formidable than ever before. Clearly something had to be done to overcome the image of Early's success in besieging Washington and causing the initiative to pass to the Confederacy.[3]

Citizens elsewhere also thought something should be done. Maryland farmers and tradesmen did not think Early's raid was a hoax. Many returned to devastated properties and lost revenue from stolen livestock and grain. Frederick County businessman Thomas Gorsuch wrote to his brother Robert in neighboring Carroll County that while his city had escaped serious damage by paying the ransom, "the community surrounding it [was] pretty well stripped of everything; stock, money, clothing and everything [the rebels] could use or get away." Frederick City tailor and shopkeeper Jacob Englebrecht echoed that observation recording that the county had suffered "to the amount of two or three millions of dollars." Elihu Rockwell wrote to Mrs. E. R. Coleman in Canadaigua, New York, deploring the acts of people "raised among us, [who] once enjoyed all the rights and immunities of citizens" and noted that his family urged him to leave the locale. He recounted rebel atrocities against Union wounded after Monocacy and hinted that the atmosphere was ripe for retribution. The appearance of David Hunter in the area provided the opportunity for hard-bitten Unionists like Major John I. Yellott of the 1st Maryland Potomac Home Brigade with the pretext for exacting such retribution. A wave of terror descended upon western Maryland. Suppression of secessionist newspapers, such as John W. Baughman's *Frederick Citizen,* and deportation of southern-sympathizing families beyond the Potomac were initiated. The arrest or harassment of local Frederick residents Harriet Pettit Floyd, the Baughmans, Isaac Reich, and the Ebert families reflected the ill-will raised in the wake of Early's invasion of Maryland.[4]

Once Major General Lew Wallace returned to active command of the Middle Department, VIII Corps, he took an active hand in Frederick County restitution efforts on behalf of the Unionists there. He ordered twenty-five Liberty District residents of the county to indemnify Thomas Harris $11,010.08 for the destruction of his barn during Early's raid. He sent a survey officer out to Ishmael Day's burned-out farm near Kingsville, north of Baltimore, and decreed that all "disloyal and disaffected persons residing within five miles" of the place were to reimburse Day based on their tax roll liabilities. Even Baltimore City smarted under his stern rule with local "secesh" going underground, as engineers and U.S. Colored Troops labored to finish the fortifications around town. Not a few people rejoiced when Lieutenant Colonel David Clendenin's rowdy 8th Illinois troopers left town and things quieted down. The cavalrymen had gotten quite liquored up after Monocacy, and one ruffian Daniel "Coon Creek" O'Connor of Company B had been shot dead in a duel with a comrade. Better that these Yankees left to chase the rebels, for most southerners in the city would have agreed with exiled merchant-owner of the Baltimore *Daily Exchange,* William W. Glenn, who declared disgustedly that Early's expedition "has done nothing, but capture a rail road train and burn Governor Bradford's and Mr. Blair's houses." So both loyalists and secessionists looked to the future from different perspectives in the wake of Early's intrusion. Most of all, neither group hoped to see war pass their way again.[5]

Within the army, at least Horatio Wright's men received a portion of their wishes concerning the future. They would not be returning to the heat, dust, and vermin (much less death) of the Petersburg trenches very soon. Within the week, however, they would be grousing about having to tramp the hardpan of Maryland and Shenandoah highways.

Again, the cause would be Jubal Early, as he had successfully feigned retreat, eluded pursuit, and still emerged dangerous with his Valley Army at Strasburg, south of Winchester, by July 23. The wounded from various fights for Shenandoah River crossings had gone on to temporary hospitals at Mt. Jackson and Harrisonburg and eventually to more permanent rehabilitation facilities at Charlottesville and Richmond. Some even went home on furlough. Others, who were sick and lame from as far back as the Lynchburg affair such as John O. Cassler (33d Virginia) and 2d Lt. J. E. Green (commanding sharpshooters of Company 1, 53d NC), now rejoined the army. Those contingents which Early had left behind guarding captured stores at Martinsburg before Monocacy (if they escaped the return of Hunter's and Sigel's forces) also rejoined, and the "Tom Cobb Infantry" of the 38th Georgia once more took their rightful place in the ranks. All of Early's ranks were much thinner (if still as feisty and combative, and given to profanity and hard drink as ever). Cassler noted that his division had been reduced considerably ever since two-thirds of it had been captured in May at Spotsylvania, "and kept losing men all the time, with no recruits possible except possibly a few from the hospitals." His brigade and regiment (the 33d Virginia) were down to 500 and 100 men, respectively. Five Virginia regiments could muster an average of only 45 men each and the three Virginia brigades in the division were consolidated into one. Richard Colbert of Company C, 9th Louisiana Infantry wrote home, "tired of being pulled and hauled about as we are," noting that only 79 men were left in his regiment and only 30 or 40 in a sister regiment. He feared that the Louisiana Brigade would lose all the glory it had previously won in Virginia through consolidation. One civilian commented that the old Stonewall Brigade no longer had the spirit left to animate them. Nonetheless, the Valley Army remained formidable.[6]

Jubal Early had new plans for his veterans. Like the Union VI Corps, they would not be returning to the Petersburg lines. Learning of Wright's return to Washington, Old Jube decided to further implement Lee's original instructions in June. His army always welcomed any chance to further thrash Hunter's people for the earlier depredations in the Valley. Corps remained to be gathered for the Confederacy, the rebuilt Baltimore and Ohio Railroad awaited renewed interruption, and upper Maryland and southern Pennsylvania beckoned for further incursions. Division commander Stephen D. Ramseur commented that the Richmond newspapers were "pitching in" to Early for not capturing Washington, although in the North Carolinian's view, the Confederates would have been repulsed with great loss and then "these same Wiseacres would have condemned him for recklessness." Early needed something to reinspire his men and improve his image at the same time. Commencing about July 23, he embarked on a second phase of his summer campaign—a phase often overlooked as part of the story of his raid against Washington. Nonetheless, Early's actions in late July were just as important because of their impact on the confused Union command structure.[7]

Early realized that Hunter's maneuver force under Brigadier General

George Crook had taken an exposed position just south of Winchester at Kernstown. President Lincoln had queried Hunter (now headquartered at Harpers Ferry) on the 23d: "Are you able to take care of the enemy when he turns back on you, as he probably will, on finding that Wright left?" The answer was a resounding negative.

Crook's 12,000 men were organized into three divisions of infantry plus Brigadier General William Averell's cavalry division. Once again they proved no match for Early's veterans. Cavalry skirmishing occupied the 23d. The next morning, Federal troopers discovered not merely a rebel reconnaissance coming north on the valley road, but Early's whole army. Crook got most of his force into position behind Hogg's Run, while the flamboyant Irish-American Colonel James Mulligan pushed his division forward and ran into the advancing Confederates of John B. Gordon. By noon the battle settled into something of a slugfest. Crook ordered Colonel Joseph Thoburn's Third Division (still battered from the Island Ford fight on July 18) to make a flank attack via a long wooded ridge west of Kernstown. Things seemed favorable to the Federal side until Averell unaccountably tarried in making a similar maneuver east of the highway. Major General John C. Breckinridge led a much wider sweep in this direction and thus got around Crook's left flank. As Ramseur and Gordon swept north in two lines astride the valley road, the Kentuckian's command attacked to the Federals' left. Mulligan and Colonel Isaac Duval's Second Division fought bitterly, but the Irish-American was cut down with a mortal wound as the blue-clad ranks broke and ran. Crook's beaten army fled back past the old Opequon Meeting House and graveyard through Winchester. Admitted Yankee losses totaled 1,185 with nearly 500 captured. Cavalry Colonel Alfred Duffié later blamed Colonel J. C. Higgins (his Second Brigade leader) for "shameful mismanagement" of the army's wagon train, which soon clogged the retreat route and "the road was strewn with cannon boxes, wagons, ambulances, and old broken-down horses that were killed and left in the road," as one rebel noted. Seventy-two wagons and twelve caissons soon filled the air with smoke and fire as Federals abandoned them to the enemy. Major Eugene Blackford of the 5th Alabama infantry noted: "A perfect panic prevailed amongst them from the beginning and they drove like sheep. . . ."[8]

Blackford recounted the "extraordinary battle in which the hand of the almighty was more plainly raised in our behalf than in any other of the war." He claimed that Confederate pursuit broke down from sheer exhaustion, for the rebels "were anxious to come up with the men who had been guilty of the fearful outrages we had all interrupted, during Hunter's advance." There would have been an awful reckoning, he declared zestfully, but at least there had been a glorious battle in which an enemy army of 15,000–20,000 had been routed by a considerably smaller Confederate force with but 150 killed, wounded, and missing. Blackford's fellow Alabamian, Captain Robert E. Park of the 12th Infantry commented in his diary: "As I have said before, it seems to be impossible to catch a running Yankee. They are as fleet almost as race-horses." The Confederates would have liked to have accomplished more and Early blamed his cavalry for not effecting complete annihilation. Still, some of his units, like Rodes' infantry, had marched twenty-seven miles, fought a sharp battle, and needed rest. Confederates like Brigadier General R. D. Lilley, captured earlier at Stephenson's Depot, were recaptured. Crook himself escaped on the macadamized turnpike, but dense clouds of dust mixed with the smoke of burning vehicles to foul the clear valley air. Heavy rains pelted friend and foe alike on July 25, as the dejected Federals wound their way back through Bunker Hill and Martinsburg. "This makes the third time our Brigade have run the Yankees through Winchester," observed Louisianan T. E. Morrow. Sergeant Major John G. Young of the 4th North Carolina, noted that the streets of that town were filled with ladies and "nearly all had a plate of provisions." Harpers Ferry seemed to be the sole place of refuge for the Federals, recorded Young's fellow Tarheel, John E. Walker of the 6th Regiment, "when old Early's foot cavalry gets after them." He added that Crook's defeat left Early "monarch of all he surveys."[9]

Crook's defeated army recrossed the Potomac on July 26 and attempted to regroup in the vicinity of Sharpsburg, Maryland Heights, and Pleasant Valley. Hunter had replied directly to Lincoln's pointed question about handling Early's resurgent army at 9:00 a.m. on July 23 by declaring: "My force is not strong enough to hold the enemy should he return upon us with his whole force," but had added that reconnaissance had not "led me to apprehend such a movement." Lowly Union signalman David Seibert had also written home to his father the day before from Harpers Ferry saying: "It is now perfectly safe to come if you desire to come down. How soon the railroad was finished here! The cars now run through again."

The Second Battle of Kernstown squashed both sentiments. Early and the rebels were loose again in the lower valley and travel such as Seibert had in mind was unsafe. To underscore that fact, the Confederates once more ripped up fifteen miles of the newly relaid railroad from Martinsburg to Harpers Ferry on July 26 and 27. As North Carolina Lieutenant Leonidus Lafayette Polk of the 43d Regiment told his wife by letter: "It seems to be Gen. Early's determination to *damage* it some this time." Skirmishing oc-

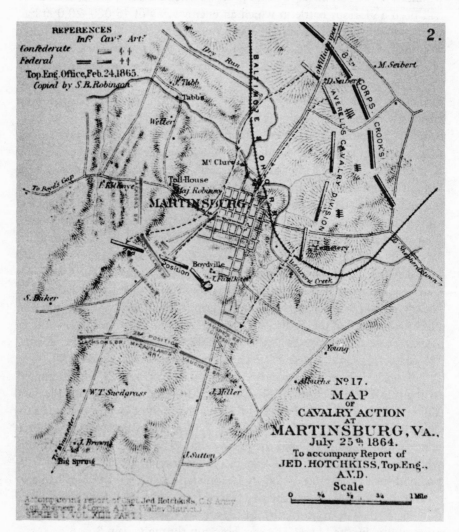

Map of the Cavalry Action at Martinsburg, West Virginia, July 25, 1864, by Confederate cartographer Jedeidiah Hotchkiss. Actions such as this proved that various Army of West Virginia leaders (like Crook and Averell) were no match for the wily Early whose Confederate troops continued to dominate the lower Shenandoah Valley. (Official Records Atlas, Plate LXXXII)

curred at Martinsburg, Charlestown, and Duffields Station with the Federals always at a disadvantage. Two days later Early's cavalry crossed the Potomac headed for southern Pennsylvania and western Maryland. Gray-clad infantry splashed across the river once more and moved on to Hagerstown. This despite Crook's wire to Hunter on July 27: "I am well satisfied that it is not their intention to move north, but to collect all supplies in the vicinity of Winchester; besides General Early's troops are in no condition to make any hard marches." Whatever the Union estimates of Early, he had resoundingly answered Grant's question to Assistant Secretary Dana on July 24 about the state of Federal pursuit![10]

Washington authorities immediately ordered both VI and XIX Corps to stop their embarkation for the return to Petersburg. Secretary of War Edwin Stanton telegraphed Grant's headquarters at 9:00 a.m. on July 24: "The pursuit of Early on the whole has proved an egregious blunder," adding that Wright and Crook "accomplished nothing" and that the VI Corps commander had returned "as soon as he got where he might have done something worthwhile." Once again the Lincoln administration was displeased with events and once more Army of the Potomac veterans took up the march against Early. Recently promoted Major Aldace F. Walker of the 1st Vermont Heavy Artillery wrote his father: "We were happy as clams in our good luck in re-entering the Defenses of Washington, and now we are equally vexed at our removal. But we can stand it all I reckon," adding that he pitied the poor, exhausted men. Indeed, the Union troops marched in rapid succession from the environs of Washington to Frederick, and on to Charlestown and Halltown in the valley, and then back again to the Frederick area. Seventy-two miles in seventy-two hours was the way the wearied Yanks saw it; "the fastest marching we ever done," wrote Anson B. Shuey of the 93d Pennsylvania to his wife on August 1.[11]

The unit historian of the 11th Vermont computed a total trek of seventy-five miles in fifty hours, and reported the men were marching nearly barefoot because his unit had missed re-outfitting at Washington following their return from chasing Early to the Shenandoah. Two hundred men of the VI Corps reputedly fell sick from sunstroke with a few deaths reported. Drought conditions, temperatures in the upper nineties, and only a five-minute break per hour attended the march. Finally, Wright (now teamed once more with Crook under Hunter's command) reported his men too exhausted and scattered to move that morning. Indeed, regimental histories, as well as soldiers' letters and reminiscences, all recount Union stragglers strung out all over that section of Maryland and West Virginia. Cavalrymen and their horses were simply played out with most commands counting a handful of men mustering on any given day. Exhausted Federals hid out in barns and haylofts helped by local blacks and Unionists until their commands countermarched and they could rejoin the ranks. Halleck's harsh marching orders permitted no surcease, and by the end of the month these very troops were close to mutiny. Captain Andrew Cowan, commanding the 1st New York Light Artillery, recalled years later that they marched back and forth to Harpers Ferry so much that Early's men dubbed them derisively, "Harpers Ferry Weeklies," alluding to the name of the popular monthly tabloid of the war period. "It was a zig-zag, tiresome game they played with the wily enemy," declared the 8th Vermont's historian. "Whoever may have been the first to propose the theory of perpetual motion," wrote another Vermonter, the VI Corps proved to have been "the first to demonstrate its possibility by actual practice." Walker's 1st Vermont "Heavies," while taking much joshing from the other regiments for having once again lost their soft assignment in Washington's forts, did gain relief by encamping beside the Monocacy on the old battlefield. Toward nightfall on Sunday, July 31, a mere corporal's guard of the respective regiments of the famed Vermont Brigade struggled back into Frederick, and even their chronicler admitted the men had reached their limit. Strung out for fifteen or twenty miles to the rear with thousands lying exhausted in the woods for want of food and water, the march cost the VI Corps as much as a major engagement due to disabled personnel, declared G. G. Benedict. It was absolutely needless, he declared; "it was a piece of General Halleck's 'spectacular strategy.'" A demoralized Major Aldace Walker wrote his father on July 29, that in the army's broken condition if the Confederates cut across through White's Ford and Poolesville to get at Washington, "they would take the city without any trouble, for there is nothing left of a garrison, and how we would have to hump it towards Washington again."[12]

Part of the cause for this excessive maneuvering lay with escalation of Confederate cavalry activity, and the rather insufficient intelligence effort of the Federal horsemen. Everyone and their horses were played out from aimless chasing of shadows, claimed First New York Cavalry historian, William H. Beach. John Mosby's partisan rebel bands roamed with abandon, gobbling up an ambulance train near Harpers Ferry, then crossing the Potomac on July 30 and capturing a picket post of the 8th Illinois Cavalry near the mouth of the Monocacy River. The more serious (and subsequently controversial) cavalry endeavor resulted from Early's direct order to brigadiers John McCausland and Bradley Johnson to carry the taste of Hunter's brand of warfare against civilians to the Cumberland Valley of southern Pennsylvania and thence westward to Cumberland, Maryland. This was the infamous Chambersburg Raid, and it reflected the increasing war-weariness and willingness to involve noncombatants by both sides. The latest raid's implications for Early, Washington, and the Lincoln government manifested themselves since it truly revealed Union command ineptitude, as well as Grant's intense desire to rid the Shenandoah of Old Jube's menace once and for all.[13]

The Chambersburg affair stemmed to a large degree not only from Hunter's depredations at Lexington, but also from ill-will resulting from Early's Confederates foraging through Maryland. Hunter determined to pursue the hard-line policies of forcing an oath of allegiance upon possible rebels and compensating Unionist suffering and losses. In consequence of sympathy displayed by some Frederick countians for the Confederates, Hunter issued an order on July 18, directing Major John I. Yellott, First Maryland Potomac Home Brigade Infantry, to enforce the oath-taking or arrest "all persons who are known by Union citizens to have given such information" to the rebels or enabled Early's men to take Unionist property. The males were to be put in prison at Wheeling, West Virginia and their families sent to Confederate lines. Yellott was to seize the secessionists' houses to be used "for hospitals, government offices, and store houses," and to sell the furniture at public auction "for the benefit of Union citizens" of Frederick "who are known to have suffered loss of property from information given by these persons." The edict was enforced with a vengeance.[14]

Hunter carried this policy a step further when dealing with disloyal citizens in the lower valley, or what by this time was West Virginia. His implementation of Grant's instructions about devastating the rebel breadbasket of the Shenandoah (but not private residences), as conveyed by Halleck on July 17, led Hunter into questionable activities. Both sides were by now truly concerned about this business. Hunter's depredations had included burning Maryland governor Augustus W. Bradford's home outside Baltimore, as well as Postmaster General Montgomery C. Meig's "Falkland" place near Washington. Early denied responsibility for both these acts, but rumors flew. Hunter issued orders on July 17 for Captain F. G. Martindale of the First New York (Lincoln) Cavalry to go to Charlestown and to "burn the dwelling house and out-buildings of Andrew Hunter, not permitting anything to be taken from there except the family." This particular Hunter was the general's distant cousin who had been instrumental in the prosecution of the anti-slavery raider John Brown at the local courthouse and was a member of the Virginia Senate. General Hunter's action therefore caused quite a stir in the neighborhood. Furthermore, additional secessionist houses were targeted by

Martindale's orders, including "Boydville" belonging to Charles J. Faulkner at Martinsburg, "Fountain Rock" belonging to Andrew R. Boteler, a member of the Confederate Congress, and nearby "Bedford" owned by Edmund J. Lee, a first cousin to the Confederacy's premier general.

President Lincoln intervened personally to spare Faulkner's "Boydville" mansion, but Hunter planned to burn all of Charlestown should the place harbor any guerrillas. At least one staunch Unionist, John W. Garrett of the Baltimore and Ohio Railroad, expressed opposition to such acts, if only because it threatened further retaliation against his line. In sum, Hunter's latest round of retribution against secessionist civilians for acts committed by Confederate soldiers ignited a tinder-box in the lower Shenandoah Valley.[15]

Early was determined now to ransom several northern towns to reimburse the local Jefferson County, West Virginia families who had lost their homes and property to Hunter's men. For this distinction, he chose Chambersburg in the agriculturally-rich Cumberland Valley, as well as Cumberland in the upper Potomac coal fields. Early's aide, Major Moses Gibson, prepared an order which the general signed "as he did not wish it thought he could hide behind his adjutant general, A. S. Pendleton." The order directed McCausland and Johnson to take their 4,000 troopers and receive a ransom, or else burn the towns. Departing northward on July 29, Major Harry Gilmor's two battalions seized McCoy's Ford across the Potomac west of Hagerstown and brushed aside Averell's outposts. Opposed by elements of the 12th and 14th Pennsylvania Cavalry, and regulars under Lieutenant H. T. McLean from the Carlisle Barracks north of Chambersburg, the rebel column pressed on. Skirmishes at Clear Spring and elsewhere kept the Federals off guard. Averell's troopers pursuing on the parallel valley pike to the east were burdened with wagons and refugees and neutralized. The lighter Confederate raiding party continued to push McLean's scratch force—now joined by several cannon of the 1st New York Artillery—back through Mercersburg and St. Thomas. By 5:00 a.m. on July 30, the Confederates appeared on the western edge of Chambersburg. McLean escaped with his men and covered Averell's train as far north as Shippensburg. By this time, McCausland and Johnson were no longer concerned about McLean. At 5:30 a.m., McCausland sent a delegation of Virginia troopers from the 8th Cavalry and 21st Battalion into Chambersburg along with various staff officers, including the intrepid Marylander Colonel Harry Gilmor, to demand the ransom specified in Early's orders. While the main cavalry force waited on the outskirts of town, the delegation ate breakfast at the Franklin Hotel, engaged private citizen J. W. Douglas to find the town burghers, and watched in irritation as

Brigadier General William Woods Averell, U.S.A. Hunter's cavalry commander who was involved in numerous actions against Early's men in the valley. He was unable to prevent McCausland's burning of Chambersburg, Pennsylvania, on July 30, but finally defeated his opponent on the upper Potomac, August 7, 1864. (U.S. Army Military History Institute)

Brigadier General John McCausland, C.S.A. Best known for his late July raid north of the Potomac and the burning of Chambersburg, Pennsylvania, in retribution for Yankee depredations in the Shenandoah Valley. (West Virginia Department of Culture and History)

none of the residents seemed to take the raid very seriously. Chambersburg was given six hours to raise $500,000 in greenbacks or $100,000 in gold. It was Hagerstown, Middletown, and Frederick all over again.[16]

Chambersburg civic leaders could not raise the required sum and may have delayed purposely to await Averell's arrival. McCausland insisted they had to carry out their orders if payment was not forthcoming, and around noon, rebel troopers carried kerosene from one of the stores and started the fires which quickly spread across town. Hundreds of buildings were destroyed with property damage exceeding $1,600,000. Personal property losses reached $900,000 with perhaps one-third of the 6,000 residents rendered homeless and one dead in the flames. The Pennsylvania legislature eventually granted survivors $900,000 in benefits, but claims with the national government remained unresolved over a century and a quarter later. Colonel William Peters commanding the 21st Virginia refused to carry out orders for the burning and was subsequently placed under arrest for insubordination. The town's masonic hall was spared thanks to intervention by a rebel Mason. But Lieutenant Calder Bailey and two other Confederates, who somehow got left behind, were murdered by the irate citizenry. Three babies were also reputedly born during the excitement.[17]

Meanwhile, fearful that Averell would catch them, McCausland and Johnson swept away to the west and headed for Hancock and Cumberland. When they tried to ransom Hancock the next day, the Confederates fell to quarreling among themselves when Marylanders in Johnson's outfit refused

Ruins of Chambersburg, Pennsylvania, Burned July 30, 1864, by Confederates under McCausland. This incident reflected the downturn in the civilized conduct of war in the eastern theater and in Early's campaign against Washington. (Library of Congress)

to torch their fellow Old Line State town. Only the arrival of Averell prevented a breakdown in discipline and permitted McCausland's command to escape and try their luck at Cumberland. That town's defenses thwarted the raiders, and McCausland and Johnson had to flee across the Potomac in eluding Averell and other equally stalwart homeguards and Federal railroad guards. Finally Averell caught up with the Confederates in a surprise attack on August 7. McCausland and Johnson were routed with the loss of over 500 men and 678 horses, plus all the command's artillery. This disaster avenged Chambersburg and effectively destroyed Early's mounted arm for future service, even though survivors eventually rejoined the valley army at Winchester.[18]

Early reputedly told a Williamsport, Maryland reporter on August 6, that he had sent McCausland to ravage Pennsylvania because he did not wish to create depredations in Maryland, which he still hoped would become a member of the Confederacy. He suggested that he condoned the burning of the Bradford residence outside Baltimore as well as the mansion of Montgomery Blair outside Washington, even though he had not ordered either act. He pointedly remarked how he had set a special guard over Blair's father's place at Silver Spring. Remorse was not in Old Jube's makeup, and the war was taking its toll on human sensitivities.

Writing from Charlestown, West Virginia ("one of the prettiest towns in the valley"), on August 23, Major Eugene Blackford of the 5th Alabama talked about the burning of the local Andrew Hunter place by David Hunter. "The burning of Chambersburg however will put a stop to all this," he told his mother. While he could never execute such an order himself, "I look upon it as one of the very best that could have been issued." Jubal Early had the same impression, although for years after the war he bore the stigma of that act. Although he took full responsibility as he explained to one correspondent in 1882, Early claimed; "I would have been fully justified, by the laws of retaliation in war, in burning the town without giving the inhabitants the opportunity of redeeming it." Blackford claimed at the time—and he was hardly alone—that the Chambersburg action "will do more to put a stop to the villainess of the enemy than any thing we have ever done." Far from exciting a spirit of revenge, he thought, "fear alone was the passion roused" among the citizens of Pennsylvania and Maryland.

Ironically, the Chambersburg Raid may have hardened the hearts and minds in some unexpected circles. Baltimoreans met at the Light Street Methodist Church in that city on August 4 for the purpose of raising funds for the relief of the suffering people of Chambersburg. Young Rebecca Davis of "Greenwood" in upper Montgomery County, Maryland—who had thrilled at the visits by Bradley Johnson's and Harry Gilmor's youthful troops earlier—recorded her impression of the Chambersburg burning: "Much do I deplore the act by them and wish they should have refrained from following similar examples set them." She had remonstrated with the young gray-clads of Johnson's command imploring them to "return good for evil," only to be told "we have tried that three years, Miss, been twice to Penna. respecting private property and what have we in return?" "God grant we may be humbled and purified as a people in this sore, this chastisement," she now wailed in her journal. Yet, in Early's army, Sandie Pendleton wrote his brother on August 8 from Bunker Hill, Virginia: "I think we have struck a blow in the right direction" in burning Chambersburg, adding that he was glad the Richmond newspapers "stand up to it so well."[19]

The July 1864 Confederate invasion north of the Potomac and most direct threat to the cities of Washington and Baltimore finally captured Grant's attention. All along, he had thought that subordinates could handle the problem. Jubal Early's hovering presence endangering Washington, and the raid upon Chambersburg and Cumberland finally galvanized the government's top soldier into action. He realized that lack of unified command in the region was the issue as he wrote to Lincoln on July 25 (with John Rawlins carrying the letter personally to the chief executive). Grant gave the chief his plan for a single department or "military division" to be commanded, if not by the inept Franklin, then even by George Gordon Meade, leader of the Army of the Potomac. Citing the breakdown in telegraphic communication between Washington and City Point during the Fort Stevens crisis, Grant spoke specifically about twelve- and twenty-four-hour delays which had hampered him in giving positive orders and directions concerning local situations. What he needed, Grant told the president, was one man "having no care beyond his own command," who could station his troops to best advantage, and, who from personal examination of the terrain and local conditions could "adopt means of getting the earliest information of any advance of the enemy, and would prepare to meet it." Grant told Lincoln that all he asked was that one general officer, "in whom I and yourself have confidence," should command the whole.[20]

Grant also wanted to send Major General Philip Sheridan and his cavalry against the Virginia Central Railroad to entice Early away from the lower valley and capital region. He also planned to get on with Meade's offensive at Petersburg, either against the southside railroads or via a mine explosion under Lee's main line. All of this served as a backdrop to the pivotal events of the last week in July, when Early again disrupted Grant's timetable and

Major General Philip Henry Sheridan, U.S.A. The Union's inability to defeat or even properly coordinate operations against Jubal Early led to the appointment of Sheridan to battle the Confederates in the Shenandoah Valley and finally free Washington from southern threats. (U.S. Army Military History Institute)

caused the general to mutter "everybody is scared and want[s] reinforcements." He narrowly avoided being recalled to Washington for consultations with the president, and ordered Major General Benjamin F. Butler, the dyspeptic commander of the Army of the James north of Petersburg, to dispatch all remaining XIX Corps personnel back to the capital. Meade was also instructed to order back a fully-mounted and equipped cavalry division to bolster affairs on the upper Potomac. However, Lincoln was not to be denied a talk with his senior military man and took a steamer to meet with the general at Fort Monroe on Sunday morning, July 31. It was a bleak moment; explosion of the great mine beneath Lee's line had been badly bungled the day before in the "Battle of the Crater," and hard decisions were in order. News of the Chambersburg raid proved that nobody really had a handle on affairs. It was possibly the darkest moment in Grant's conduct of the war to date.[21]

Lincoln's five-hour consultation with Grant remains a mystery. Little was said about it, then or later, although Lincoln had arrived with a cryptic note on the back of Grant's acceptance telegram for the get-together: "Meade & Franklin/McClellan/Md & Pa." Obviously the central issue was unity and aggressiveness of command. The president would not hear of either Franklin or Meade for the upper Potomac, and mere mention of McClellan was divisive enough in that election year. Aside from that, the two midwesterners of humble origin now leading the government probably talked out the situation with common sense. Whether or not Phil Sheridan's name came up is not known, but this was the name that Grant sent forward for approval the day after the Fort Monroe meeting. Here was yet another midwesterner who had fought tenaciously at Perryville and Stones River, and who had wrested control of Missionary Ridge from the enemy at the Battle of Chattanooga. Grant's confidence and a good public press had vaulted the young (thirty-three year old) major general to the forefront of Grant's lieutenants. Opposition arose predictably from old War Department hands at Sheridan's youth, but Grant was now visibly irritated at their machinations as well as the inability of Wright, Crook, or even Hunter to resolve the Jubal Early question. Hunter might remain in place as regional commander (and out of the way of the action), but Grant wanted Sheridan put in charge of operations "south of the enemy and follow him to the death." Lincoln deferred to Grant's wishes, with an obsequious Halleck falling into line on August 3: "Had you asked my opinion in regard to Genls Hunter and Sheridan it would have been freely and frankly given; but I must beg to be excused from deciding operations which lawfully and properly belong to your office." Grant simply blew past that bit of pique with Special Order No. 68 on August 2, directing Sheridan and his staff to Washington.[22]

It was Lincoln who really settled matters in his 6:00 a.m. telegram on August 3, 1864. Agreeing to Sheridan's assignment and Grant's strategy for Early's destruction, the commander-in-chief chided his senior military leader to examine all the dispatches "and discover if you can, that there is any idea in the head of any one here of getting south of the enemy and pursuing him to the death." Within two hours of receipt of this message at noon on August 4, Grant boarded his dispatch boat for Washington to take the train to meet with David Hunter to "see what is required to drive the enemy out of Maryland and Northern Virginia." The move was fully one month overdue.[23]

Grant frankly thought all this was a brief, if necessary, interruption of his principal work at Petersburg. Perhaps everyone but the general fully expected that the aging and somewhat befuddled Hunter would now ask to be relieved of command. The War Department had little confidence in his ability to accomplish anything with regard to Early. However, Grant maintained that Hunter and Sheridan could effect a pincer movement and trap the Confederates if his old friend wished to remain in the game. After visiting Lincoln, Stanton, Halleck, and Sheridan at the capital, Grant took the 3:00 p.m. train for Monocacy Junction. Here he found the VI Corps, part of the XIX Corps, the Army of West Virginia, and various cavalry units lounging around Frederick and along the sylvan banks of the Monocacy, trying to recuperate from weeks of chasing the rebels. They had been positioned "to cover Baltimore and Washington against the column that went to Chambersburg," noted Vermont Major Aldace F. Walker. But that force had proven a very small one, and now he added, "we seem to be waiting for further developments of the enemy." Staff Captain Robert Cornwall wrote his wife asking if she had ever seen 16,000 men bathing in a river at one time, and told her how Brigadier General James B. Ricketts' popular wife had captured the hearts at headquarters with her beauty and charm. The whole assemblage projected more an air of frolic than serious business. Grant's arrival changed all that, sending a ripple of excitement and expectation through the camps.[24]

Grant had no time for nonsense. He immediately called a senior conference at Colonel C. Keefer Thomas's battle-scarred "Araby" house on the Monocacy battlefield. Options and strategy occupied the agenda of the assembled leaders in one of the mansion's upper rooms. Grant wanted to know what Hunter knew of Early's whereabouts and the older man's response was vague. Halleck's myriad conflicting orders had caused more confusion and senseless countermarching. Halleck's dispatch of thousands of troops to help Hunter had left the latter with the task of organizing the army and not coping with Early. He had simply lost track of his adversary. An obviously displeased Grant noted that if Hunter could not find Early, then he (Grant) surely could. A general advance of the army was immediately ordered from Frederick to Halltown, West Virginia some four miles southwest of Harpers Ferry. If that didn't get Early's attention and draw him out, then nothing would. Sheridan would take command of the maneuver force, and Hunter could remain at division or department command headquarters at Cumberland, Baltimore, or anywhere which suited him. At 8:00 p.m. Grant drew up Hunter's specific orders, and they were typical of Grant. "Bear in mind," said Grant, "the object is to drive the enemy South, and to do this you will want to keep him always in sight." "Be guided in your course, by the course taken by Early," he told Hunter. Furthermore, the Union forces pushing up the valley should leave nothing that would invite the Confederate to return.

Anything not useful to the Federal army should be destroyed, although that did not include houses and buildings. Inform the people, said Grant "that so long as an Army can subsist among them, recurrences of these raids must be expected, and we are determined to stop them at all hazards."[25]

Hunter now realized he was being shelved. He requested relief from assignment, which Grant accepted and wired Washington to have Sheridan take the morning train for the junction. Grant noted later in his memoirs that Hunter said that he did not want to embarrass the cause, "thus showing a patriotism that was none too common in the army." Grant remained over-night at Monocacy to meet Sheridan as the warm summer evening echoed with locomotive whistles and the clatter of the trains moving the "Army of the Shenandoah" to forward positions beyond the Potomac. The next morn-ing, after a cordial breakfast with the Thomas family (where six-year-old Virginia Thomas told an amused Grant that her father was "a Rebel when the Rebels are here and a Yankee when the Yankees are here"), the general-in-chief made his way back to the junction to await Sheridan's arrival. Their meeting was brief—a handshake, a salute, and a simple gesture of confidence. Sheridan boarded a westbound train for his appointment in the valley; Grant returned eastward back to City Point. Young signalman David Seibert wrote his father from Harpers Ferry on August 7: "We expect some work is on hand and I expect something will be done now."[26]

Jubal Early's threat to Washington and the Lincoln administration was over. Philip Sheridan's campaign to destroy Early and his army was about to begin. The whole issue had been settled by conference in a few hours, on the very ground where Early had fought and won a battle on July 9, but suffered the crucial delay in securing the grand prize—the capture of Washington. The previous month had seen a president under fire and the political fate of the Union hanging by a mere thread. It had witnessed the eleventh hour arrival of the relief force from Grant's armies, despite that general's disbelief that it could have happened in the first place. The heat, the dust of daily marching, and delays because of carousing and foraging on the approach to the capital region, had all cost Early a chance for glory. His summer campaign against the north was over; the military power of the Confederates in the east, for yet one more invasion north of the Potomac, quite spent. When Sheridan and Grant parted ways at Monocacy Junction on August 7, the unswerving path had begun toward a fateful meeting at Appomattox Court House the following April.

Chapter Nine

※

BATTLE REMEMBRANCE

I F Jubal Early's campaign against Washington was over by the end of July 1864, the Union's struggle against Early's army was not. This quest required at least three more months of maneuvers and bloody encounters at Opequon, Fisher's Hill, and Cedar Creek. It did not really end until Phil Sheridan's ultimate destruction of the remnants of Early's once proud Valley Army at Waynesborough, Virginia, in March 1865. Thousands more would fall, including Confederate generals Robert Rodes and Stephen Ramseur, as well as Early's trusted staffer Alexander (Sandie) Pendleton. Misery and retribution would attend these months of combat for both soldiers and civilians alike. The delay at Monocacy, the near-miss at Fort Stevens, Sherman's capture of Atlanta in September, and "Little Phil's" success in the valley that autumn, all combined to surmount the earlier Union crisis of July. Together they re-established allegiance to the republic and victory at the polls for the Lincoln administration.[1]

This is not to say that Confederate general Robert E. Lee ever quite gave up his idea of threatening Washington as a device to relieve pressure at Richmond-Petersburg. He wrote Confederate president Jefferson Davis on July 23: "A mounted force with long range guns might, by secret and rapid march, penetrate the lines south of the Potomac, and excite the alarm of the authorities at Washington, but if its approach was known, I fear the defenses

227

south of the river could be manned in time to prevent it." Lee now realized the limitations of his scheme. He was warned by Early that the only way to get into Washington was when the city was unprotected. And that was not likely to occur again. Nonetheless, by early August, Lee sent Lieutenant General Richard H. Anderson with a division of infantry and some cavalry to Culpeper, and hoped to detach Major General Wade Hampton's horsemen for another assault, "should the enemy's forces move west of the Blue Ridge range, leaving Washington uncovered." Grant's relentless pressure at Richmond-Petersburg prevented Hampton from riding north, and Anderson's force was dissipated reinforcing a harassed Early against Sheridan.

Early's campaign proved costly in still another way. Breckinridge's "corps," for example, carried 19,611 officers and men on the rolls as of July 15, 1864 and its return from Maryland, but could count only 63 officers and 4,237 men present (excluding Wharton's brigade of perhaps 1,000 effectives). The casualty figures for Gordon's and Echols' divisions in the Maryland campaign numbered 1,027 or 25 per cent (although some of the nearly 8,000 officers and men absent on that date might eventually straggle back to the army). Gordon alone lost 767 of his approximate 3,500-man division in fighting between Maryland Heights, Monocacy, and on the Shenandoah River during the retreat, he admitted. In short, Early dissipated his army's fighting strength on the Washington campaign. Now, in late summer, he faced an even bigger test by an overwhelmingly superior force of the enemy. In fact, with Sheridan, Early now entered a life-or-death struggle for his very survival.[2]

By early September, Lee realized the strategic game of threats to Washington was a thing of the past. He wrote Davis on September 1: "As matters now stand, we have no troops disposable to meet movements of the enemy or strike where opportunity presents, without taking them from the trenches and exposing some important point." It was merely a question of time—Grant had won the strategic war in Virginia, and Lee knew it.[3]

Grant believed that relentless pressure at Petersburg-Richmond and reliance upon Sheridan's army to thwart Early was sufficient to protect the nation's capital. He urged Sheridan several times in August and September to draw upon the unusually large Washington garrisons for reinforcements. All requests failed when faced by the administration's continued paranoia for the city's safety, as communicated through telegrams from Major General Henry Halleck, the chief-of-staff. Early occasionally feinted as if to move north of the Potomac, but the burden of "threatening" Washington now passed to the partisan band of Lieutenant Colonel John Mosby and other roving bands of irregulars. The "gray ghost," as he was styled, harassed pickets and rear areas close to the city down to the end of the war. Yet, in the end, he too failed to do major damage, and appeared more the irritant than the threat.[4]

Washington's garrisons remained a backwash of multi-hued units and marginally efficient troops. Colonel J. Howard Kitching, of the 6th New York Heavy Artillery, had brigade command of thirteen forts and wrote his father on August 17: "General Auger told me that I would find things in very bad shape, and indeed I do. There has been no system in the management of the command till everything has gotten wrong and foremost." The New York "Heavies" had been sent back by Grant to help guard the capital, and then supported Sheridan's forces where Kitching lost his life at the battle of Cedar Creek in October. On paper at least, Washington remained protected by 20,000 to 30,000 effectives and 1,000 cannon during autumn and winter. Quartermaster General Montgomery C. Meigs continued to muster, train, and inspect his clerks, who openly boasted of drilling from 3:00 to 4:00 p.m. in "Uncle Sam's blue." The army's engineers continued to work on the earthworks to strengthen them against an enemy threat which would never materialize again.[5]

More worrisome to local citizens around Washington than any repetition of Early's raid were "the things left behind after a great inundation," as Montgomery countian W. H. Farquhar recorded in his private journal on July 13, 1864. He alluded to the "slime and ugly crawling creatures"— stragglers from Early's ranks who mounted a reign of terror in the Sandy Spring area for some months thereafter. The Ashton country store was robbed in September, and eleven guerrillas under a "Captain Bowie" ransacked A. G. Thomas's establishment in Sandy Spring as late as October. This band was later apprehended in a pitched battle about five and one-half miles southeast of Rockville. As Farquhar noted, these events showed that "person and property were no longer safe from outrage" in the region.[6]

The end of the war in April 1865 brought no end to the memories of Early's passage the year before. In time, farms and residences were restored and the beauty of the Shenandoah Valley and upper Maryland areas was renewed. Confederate and Union soldiers, for the most part, returned home to bind up old wounds. However, there were a few such as Old Jube himself, John A. McCausland, and John C. Breckinridge, who were doomed by choice or indictment to wander in exile during the early years of Reconstruction. An embittered Early first sought refuge in Mexico before returning, unreconstructed, to Lynchburg to resume his law practice. He also managed the

Louisiana lottery for a time, and engaged in many of the postwar wrangles between southern veterans about events long past. Early would expend much pen and ink trying to explain his actions during the Washington campaign before his death in 1894. His fellow Virginian, John McCausland, likewise went off to Mexico and on to Europe before settling back in southwest Virginia. On the other hand, Breckinridge's experience was different.[7]

A grand jury in the District of Columbia handed down a high treason indictment against both Breckinridge and Confederate president Jefferson Davis (both former United States officials) on May 26, 1865. Breckinridge's charge included leading troops against the capital of the United States, killing government soldiers and citizens, and destroying property during the July 1864 incursion. Signatories to this indictment included Francis P. Blair, Sr., John P. Clagett, Martin D. Hardin, Thomas L. Maury, M.D., George E. Kirk, and John H. McChesney. Blair, Clagett, and McChesney all owned property directly affected by the fighting at Fort Stevens which involved Breckinridge. Martin D. Hardin had participated in the battle on the Union side and it is probable that all of them had vested interests in the outcome. Some writers in the northern press even hinted that Davis and Breckinridge should hang for their crimes. Although the case never went to trial, the Kentuckian and former Vice President of the United States wandered from Canada to Europe, tasting fame and high society before returning home to the Blue Grass and the practice of law.[8]

Among Early's subordinates, John Brown Gordon returned to Georgia to become an ardent advocate for restoration of home rule and became so popular that he was elected senator three times and governor once. He helped organize the United Confederate Veterans, and became its first commander-in-chief before his death in 1904. He, like Early, wrote controversial memoirs. Robert Ransom, Jr., became a government civil engineer in New Bern, North Carolina and died in 1902. Other brigade and regimental leaders went home and engaged in law, business, and even the ministry. Former Brigadier General Clement A. Evans edited a twelve-volume *Confederate Military History* which contributed to the Civil War period of southern history. Others followed Gordon's lead to become active in Confederate veteran affairs. They recalled devotion to their cause and on occasion offered insights about Early's abortive campaign against Washington.[9]

Federal "alumni" from Early's campaign followed different paths in their postwar careers. Naturally, some remained in the army and advanced to powerful positions. They included: Christopher Augur, John C. Barnard, Quincy A. Gillmore, Henry Halleck, Alexander McCook, Montgomery C. Meigs, and Horatio Wright. Others, such as Lew Wallace, Max Weber, Franz Sigel, and William Averell, profited from service to the winning side through lucrative diplomatic or political appointments from postwar American presidents like their old general-in-chief, Ulysses S. Grant. Lower-ranking officers and enlisted men returned home and used their military service to begin careers in politics, business, law, or education. Some, like Joseph A. Goulden, late of the 25th New York Cavalry, gained the House of Representatives; others, such as George K. Nash, one of the "Oberlin College boys" in the 150th Ohio National Guard, served as his state's governor from 1900 to 1904. Many contributed to northern veteran organizations such as the Military Order of the Loyal Legion and the Grand Army of the Republic. A few, like Wallace, left superb reminiscences which help illuminate campaigns like the operation against Washington in 1864. Martin D. Hardin, like John McCausland of Early's force, lived to be counted among the oldest surviving general officers of that conflict—Hardin dying in 1923 and McCausland four years later.[10]

Veterans read accounts of Early's campaign and wrote their own versions seeking vindication or recrimination. Early entered the fray. Writing from exile in Havana, Cuba, on December 18, 1865, he declared: "My force, when I arrived in front of the fortifications of Washington, on the 11th of July 1864, was 8,000 muskets, three small battalions of artillery, with about forty field-pieces, of which the largest were 12-pounder Napoleons, and about 2,000 badly-mounted and equipped cavalry, of which a large portion had been detached to cut the railroads leading from Baltimore north." Within two years he wrote his memoirs in which he noted the reasons for his actions (never necessarily admitting failure) before Washington. The heat, the strength of the fortifications, the superior Union signal communications, the absence of friendly intelligence or help from Washington secessionists, and arrival of Grant's veterans, all contributed to Early's decision not to attack the city. He wrote that his "small force" had been "thrown up to the very walls of the Federal Capital, north of a river which could not be forded at any point within 40 miles, and with a heavy force and the South Mountain in my rear—the passes through which could be held by a small number of troops." Early dismissed critics who blamed his delays in the lower valley, and claimed that "an examination of his narrative would show that not one moment was spent in idleness." He declared everyone was employed in a productive manner to remove obstacles to the army's advance. Success to Early was found in the fruits of actions by Gilmor and Johnson before Baltimore and the large cache of supplies and livestock carried back to Virginia by the army. In a footnote, Early again denied blame for the burning of Montgomery Blair's house, "though I believed that retaliation was justified by previous acts of the enemy."[11]

Old Jube was back in print by the early 1870s and he refuted newspaper accounts as to the mission, strength figures, and nature of his actions in front of Washington. He solidified his position around a core of issues which denied any notion of a definite "attack" on the city. Early claimed that, "no attack was made by my troops, either upon Fort Stevens or upon any other portion of the fortifications of Washington." Furthermore, "General Lee did not expect that I would be able to capture Washington with my small force." The great Confederate general's orders were "simply to threaten that city," since "my only chance of capturing it depended upon its being found without any garrison." Early reiterated that the object of the campaign was to cause Grant to withdraw from Richmond. Lee "would have been gratified if I could have taken Washington," but when Early suggested that idea during talks in late June, Lee "remarked that it would hardly be possible to do so."[12]

In 1881, Early presented his view of the facts before public scrutiny in an article for the *Southern Historical Society Papers*. He particularly defended his somewhat changed strength figures, again explained the Blair house affair, and reiterated the nature of Lee's original orders. However, the focus was on numbers. Early had studied Major General John G. Barnard's famous report on the defenses of Washington and its assertion that, based on reliable government estimates at the time, Early's army numbered up to 22,420 officers and men with sixty pieces of artillery. This was incorrect, claimed Early, as he assigned his own set of force figures by individual commander: Breckinridge 2,104; Rodes 3,013; Gordon 2,544; Ramseur 1,909; and 3,000 cavalrymen, or a total of 12,570. Arrayed against him, noted Old Jube, were "over fifteen thousand men available for duty in the trenches and in connection there with on the front against which my advance was made before I got within reach of the works." He further added at least 14,000 reinforcements from Grant's forces, with over 20,000 men "in my rear at Harpers Ferry." It was obvious, even at this early date, that everyone had some axe to grind on the issue. Early was establishing a rationale for his failure to take the city. On the Union side, Barnard sought a substantiation for the $1,500,000 engineering project that he had conducted during the war—the vaunted defenses of Washington.[13]

Early attracted both followers and enemies through the years, all of whom in some way commented upon his conduct of the Washington operation. Staffer Major Henry Kyd Douglas undoubtedly captured the positive side to Early's successful operation (in southern eyes). He considered the smallness of the army, continuous marches from Richmond to Washington through the Valley and upper Maryland, and the contests with Hunter, Sigel, and Wallace. Douglas declared: "His daring raid to Washington's doorstep displayed rapidity, audacity, and skill, [and] Early was justified in claiming 'it is without parallel in this or any other modern war.'" Early's old friend from Lynchburg, John W. Daniel, recorded a stirring apologia in 1894 when he stated that within a thirty-day period, with less than 14,000 men Early had:

1. Driven Hunter's army of 18,500 out of the field.

2. Bottled up Sigel's force of 6,000 at Harpers Ferry.

3. Defeated Wallace's army of 6,000–7,000 at the Monocacy, and sent it fleeing into Baltimore.

4. Diverted from Grant's army the Sixth Corps and a part of the Nineteenth Corps.

5. Transferred the seat of war from central and Piedmont Virginia to the borderline of northern Virginia on the Potomac, where it began three years before and occupied fully 60,000 men to oppose him.

Daniel, however, suggested that the hope that Washington might be captured "was never either a design or expectation." Unlike McClellan before him, Grant would not be forced to abandon operations on the James, and hence neither Early's nor Lee's armies could be transferred to the northern border. Memories were mellowing and the truth changed with the passage of time to the old veterans.[14]

Nonetheless, there were critics even among former Confederates. Their negativism lay rooted in a comment by Douglas. Suggesting that Early "never has and never will receive the credit he deserves," the Maryland Confederate suggested that all the glories of that early and mid-summer "were overclouded and forgotten in the disasters of the autumn." Certainly, Early's fiery old subordinate, John Brown Gordon, was not one to lavish praise on his old commander's record. The man whose men had borne the brunt of the heavy fighting at Monocacy and had given Early that victory claimed to have personally ridden onto Washington's breastworks at some point and found them empty. "Undoubtedly we could have marched into Washington," he claimed in 1904. Yet, Gordon really excoriated Early for his lack of "official courage, or what is known as the courage of one's convictions." According to Gordon, Early was an able strategist and "one of the coolest and most imperturbable of men under fire and in extremity." But he would not act upon subordinates' suggestions (especially one supposes when the subordinate was Gordon), and did not trust the accuracy of scouting reports (perhaps an allusion to Early's mistrust and ignorance of the role of cavalrymen). Or it may have been that Early, the epitome of bachelorhood, simply resented the presence of Mrs. Gordon always by her husband's side in camp. The Georgian included these comments in those passages of his memoirs concerning the Washington campaign. He implied that Old Jube displayed these traits on that raid, although readily admitting: "In the council of war called by General Early there was not a dissenting opinion as to the impolicy of entering the city."[15]

It was the rebel cavalrymen who seemed to dislike and rebuke Early most in later years. John Opie, one of the scouts from the 5th Virginia Cavalry, admitted that if the army had entered Washington it would have plundered and left the city in ruin, so it was best it had not been captured. Yet Early had lost a golden opportunity to immortalize himself by capturing the capital, and in Opie's opinion, Early "was about the only man in that army who believed it impossible to accomplish." The strongest comments about the army's leader in that campaign came from fellow Virginian Alexander Hunter. To Hunter, the fatal mistake of the war had been made in placing Early in command of the Valley Army because "it shortened the war fully a year." Constantly alluding to the way it would have been if Jackson had lived, he rebuked Early for tippling in Blair's wine cellar from a keg of old peach brandy. "He drank long and deeply from that keg, and sank into a deep slumber which lasted for hours, and from which nothing could rouse him; and that is why the order to advance was not given." Of all the participants in the campaign, only Hunter, in his reminiscences, directly contradicts Early's account of actions taken before Fort Stevens. Hunter claimed that "a steady stream of all kinds of emissaries of the Southern sympathizers came" to meet the skirmishers. He said that blacks and young children all told one tale: "Come in at once, there are only Department clerks in the trenches. Don't delay, but come at once." In Hunter's opinion, the rank and file of the army never forgave Early for not letting them enter the city. From that day, he noted, the veterans fought well, but "never with dash, and firm determination to do or die." They no longer displayed the spirit which had made them victorious on previous battlefields.[16]

Maryland cavalryman, George Wilson Booth, veteran of Bradley Johnson's column, flatly declared in 1907 that Early had failed in all three of his missions—"first and principally" to compel Grant to detach sizable numbers of troops and thus relieve the pressure on Lee; second, "if circumstances so turned out as to make possible, the capture of Washington itself," which would have necessitated abandonment of operations before Richmond, "with the possibility of creating an impression abroad which could be turned to our advantage"; and third, to free the Point Lookout prisoners. Booth especially cited the Confederacy's lingering hope of European recognition as turning on the success or failure of Early's raid. Booth attributed Early's failure mainly to delays and lost time in crossing the Potomac into Maryland. But he also noted the impact of the Monocacy delay and the opportune arrival of the VI Corps, which Booth claimed "was altogether unforeseen; it was one of the accidental features which became prominent in war by reason of the great results which hinge on such occurrences." Citing what by now was the litany of inferior forces, Booth held that once Early got to the capital "to assault so superior a force behind strong entrenchments, on which the skill and labor of the federal engineer had been devoted for nearly three years, would have been rashness approaching to folly or madness," and so it became mandatory to withdraw promptly.[17]

Union participants in this campaign were far less combative in postwar accounts. Their side had won both the battle for the capital and the war. Blame for the near disaster was freely accorded Washington authorities, but no individual generals were cited except for the unfortunate David Hunter and Franz Sigel. Grant set the tone in his deathbed memoirs, delivering credit to Lew Wallace for his actions at Monocacy which weakened the attack on Washington. "General Wallace contributed on this occasion, by the defeat of the troops under him," proclaimed Grant, a greater benefit to the Union cause than "often falls to the lot of a commander of an equal force to render by means of a victory." That their earlier differences in the west had been reconciled by Wallace's singular act during Early's campaign may even have been deduced as early as September 1864. Writing to his wife from Baltimore on the twelfth, Wallace had noted that a recent visit to the front had occasioned a reception by Grant "with utmost cordiality and kindness." In short, said Wallace, Grant seemed to be taking pains to forget that there had ever been "anything of an unpleasant nature between us." Grant proffered no combat command to Wallace at anytime during the remainder of the war, and the Hoosier general spent the period in administrative duties. After the war, he served on a military commission which tried the conspirators in the Lincoln assassination, and presided over the court-martial which tried and condemned the infamous Confederate commander of the Andersonville prison compound. He went on to the governorship of the New Mexico territory and later served as minister to Turkey. Of course, he is best known as the author of *Ben Hur: A Tale of the Christ*. His sacrifice at Monocacy certainly helped save the capital and defused animosities with Grant and the War Department.[18]

Final victory and Grant's acclaim as chief architect shielded both him and Horatio Wright from the glare of censure for performance in July 1864. Grant's overdue recognition of the verity of Jubal Early's threat, and Wright's sluggish pursuit after the battle at Fort Stevens, were lost in the larger events of the final year of the war. Wright's weakness bore out again in October in the near-disaster of Cedar Creek. At any rate, the brotherhood of West Pointers and victors of the Union kept the matter to themselves. Wright served ably through the final days of conflict, became military governor of Texas during the Reconstruction period, and ended his army career as chief engineer. He presided over river and harbor improvements as well as the completion of the Washington Monument in the nation's capital.[19]

Years later there was a rekindling of interest in the details of Early's raid among Union veterans. Quartermaster General Montgomery C. Meigs, whose own postwar career provided varied and honorable service to his country, fondly recalled his own battlefield command in July 1864 during the crisis. So did Martin Hardin, as well as countless other enlisted men who

Washington, D.C. — The Grand Review of Union Armies, May 1865, from a sketch by James E. Taylor. The completed capitol dome in the background, the victorious Union armies on the march on Pennsylvania Avenue, and the cheering spectators aptly reflect the emergent Washington. (Library of Congress)

embellished the tales of their regiments with each retelling. From those accounts sprang the image of poorly defended trenches, the worthless militia and convalescents, the heroic relief by the VI Corps, and Lincoln under enemy fire. Lost to history were the proud memories of Ohio national guardsmen and the quartermaster and other government clerks who held the line before Wright's command arrived from Petersburg. At least a few of those Ohio "100-day men," like William J. Gleason of Company E, 150th Ohio National Guard, returned home with parchment certificates of honorable service and "national thanks," signed by President Lincoln in late 1864. Through the years, the old veterans of Fort Stevens exchanged greetings and war stories through the pages of their magazines, such as *The National Tribune.* They scolded one another on errors of fact and memory and gradually rebuilt the impression of a momentous event out of proportion to its actual size. As S. A. McDonald, late of the 122d New York, stated in 1894: "The whole affair was of no great magnitude as compared with Antietam, Chancellorsville, or Gettysburg, but the forces engaged outnumbered the combatants in the first battle of the Revolutionary war and the Union loss was far greater than that sustained by the Continental army at the historic battle of Bennington. The fighting was sharp and lively, the percentage of killed and wounded was unusually heavy, and the peculiarity of the surroundings was calculated to invest it with more of the dramatic than attached to any other minor engagement of the war."[20]

The thinning ranks of veterans were proud when some of their members erected monuments to valorous deeds on the Monocacy and Fort Stevens battle sites. The 14th New Jersey monument was the first one erected at Monocacy on July 11, 1907, followed the next year by that of Pennsylvania. The sum of $1,500 was raised in Frederick in the late 1870s for the beautiful Confederate memorial, which still presides above more than 400 southern graves in Mount Olivet Cemetery in that city. Union dead from Monocacy found integrated resting places at Antietam National Cemetery, and lost the distinction of their service at Monocacy. In Washington itself, tiny Battleground National Cemetery holds not only the remains of 41 Federals from that battle, but monuments to the 98th Pennsylvania (erected 1891), 122d New York (1903), Company K, 150th Ohio National Guard (1907), and 25th New York Cavalry (1914). The cemetery became the focal point for Memorial Day ceremonies honoring the fallen from all America's wars. A granite shaft marked simply "Confederate" took its place over the 17 dead southerners from Fort Stevens, when they were reinterred near a rebuilt Grace Church in Silver Spring. The church structure known to the generation

Battleground National Cemetery, Washington, D.C., August 1865. Established within two weeks after the battle on the very battlefield itself, forty Union fallen (a veteran of the battle was subsequently added, to total forty-one graves) lie buried here. The cemetery may be visited today on Georgia Avenue (Seventh Street Road) in northwest Washington. (U.S. Army Military History Institute)

of the war had burned in 1896, and two years later the erection of a trolley line on Georgia Avenue (Seventh Street Road) moved the gravesite to the present location. Other Confederates probably lie in churchyards and private cemeteries all over the capital region as mute testament to the passage of Early's invaders during the Civil War.[21]

There were other ways in which the memory of the Fort Stevens action was preserved. The small village of Leesborough was so grateful for Brigadier General Frank Wheaton's success in saving them from rebel occupation that they renamed the town for him. Brigadier General George Getty chose to settle on a farm about two miles from Silver Spring after the war. Montgomery Blair rebuilt "Falkland" where he and his descendants lived until 1958, when the house and grounds gave way to the Blair Shopping Center (although neighboring, aging apartments later bore the Falkland name). The "Silver Spring" farm of Blair's father lasted until 1955 when it too was razed.

The Sligo community had long since taken the name of that famous property for its town name. While the spring dried up because of construction in the area over the years, a replica acorn and statue were rededicated on the site. A gas station at the corner of Colesville Road and Georgia Avenue in the center of modern Silver Spring marks the site of the country store and its liberated liquor supply from July 1864.[22]

Post-Civil War expansion of the nation's capital directly affected the historic environment at Fort Stevens, although Monocacy was spared from construction blight for over a century. However, preservation efforts on behalf of both battlefields have been a twentieth-century phenomenon, spurred by commercial development and consummated by a history-minded citizenry.

The resolution of the war for the Union meant that Washington could expect growth and population expansion. A city with a pre-Civil War population of about 75,000 added another 100,000 within twenty years of Appo-

Confederate Monument, Grace Episcopal Church, Silver Spring, Maryland. This simple granite shaft on Georgia Avenue marks the final resting place of seventeen of Early's men, killed before Fort Stevens, gathered up and interred in this then-country churchyard, where ironically the Blair families worshipped.

mattox. New government employees, businessmen, and professionals flocked to the community although the true urban center remained south of Boundary Street (now Florida Avenue) for years. The populace also began to move to the suburbs such as Tennallytown, Brightwood, Silver Spring, and Rockville. While still basically rural, the commercial development of farmland (that had been the battlefield of 1864) accompanied this trend. Work crews of the land developers now changed the city's rural landscape to urban neighborhoods, streets, and modern conveniences, where the fateful events of Early's raid had once taken place.

Ex-slaves and other squatters gravitated to Union camps and forts all over the south during the war, and the military defenses of Washington served as beacons to these people. In 1865, forts like Reno, Kearny, De Russy, Stevens, Slocum, and Totten (all of which had seen action during July 1864) reverted to their original landowners' possession. By 1873, one commentator stated that all the city's old forts had been dismantled, stripped of ordnance and appurtenances, and anything usable had been taken by the civilian owners. Black migrants sold scrap metal from the old forts for a living, but grass was creeping "nearer and nearer the magazine." The landowners fought the squatters for their land, and Giles Dyer re-established his original ownership at Fort Reno only through lengthy court battles about military occupation of the place. His heirs sold the land to Newall Onion and Alexander Butts, two postwar real estate operators, and new patterns for land use took shape.[23]

The realtors subdivided the property and a racially mixed area of shanty-type houses went up around what was once Fort Reno. Streets came in the 1880s, and the community of Tennallytown or Fort Reno thrived despite some local friction. Original residents whose ancestors (both black and white) dated to colonial Maryland and Virginia, found European immigrants moving in as the old Rockville or Georgetown Turnpike gave way to modern Wisconsin Avenue. The remains of the Civil War defenses remained visible until the construction of a major city reservoir at Fort Reno in 1900, but the land to the north of the defensive line at this point (scene of McCausland's demonstration) rapidly passed to housing and commercial uses. To the east of Fort Reno, another veteran of that fight, Major George Armes, became involved in the vast development schemes of Nevada Congressman and later Senator Francis G. Newlands and his Chevy Chase Land Company. In fact, there is reason to believe that the pair hatched the whole land acquisition idea while surveying the countryside from Armes' "Fairfield" house, located on Grant Road near the Battery Rossell and Forty Kearny sites. At that time

(1889), everything between Tennallytown and the Fourteenth Street Road (east of Rock Creek, and south of the Fort Stevens area), remained rural and was bisected only by a few country lanes. The vast development of this region via the Chevy Chase Land Company and other groups would take place over the next generation with the extension of modern Connecticut Avenue from downtown. Construction of the Metropolitan Branch of the Baltimore and Ohio Railroad westward through Montgomery County before the turn of the century and consequent opening of "bedroom communities" from Takoma Park, Forest Glen, and Kensington to Rockville and beyond, for example, encroached upon areas through which Early's army had foraged, marched, and encamped during its stay before Washington in 1864. Development of homes in the so-called Capitol View Park (one of the county's first sub-divisions in 1888) virtually obliterated the one section of high ground where some Confederates might well have caught a glimpse of the capitol dome from the wartime farm of Thomas Brown, just west of the Washington-Brookville Turnpike north of Sligo and "Silver Spring."[24]

The valley of Rock Creek was preserved as a public park in 1890, effectively saving several batteries and trenches from Broad Branch to Fort Stevens. Fort De Russy still provides one of the most agreeably visual remnants of the defenses of Washington. A military guide to the nation's capital produced two years later suggested there was still evidence of earthworks to the west at Fort Sumner, Fort Bayard, as well as Fort Reno ("including the emplacement for the 100-pounder Parrott rifle"). The extension of Connecticut Avenue had cut away Battery Rossell. Fort Kearny was gone, but the works to the east (all the way to Fort Stevens beyond the park) remained in good viewable shape. The guide noted that the line to the east of the Seventh Street Road remained similarly constituted with the exception of Fort Slocum, where only the old well and an auxiliary battery to the west, with its trench-linkage to the fort, were still intact. Fort Totten near Soldiers Home was in "very good condition." The guide took special note of Fort Stevens, stating that "some of the buildings and fences here bear evidence of quite a lively time," with bullet holes still visible.[25]

There were unhappy landowners near Fort Stevens who never got over the fact that the area had been a battlefield. James Mulloy of the Metropolitan Police in the city sought recompense from the Quartermaster Department two weeks after the battle for damages done to his planned homestead where the government had set up Battleground National Cemetery. He claimed on July 23, 1864 that the dead bodies contaminated his spring water which made the property unfit for habitation. It took him three years to collect

$2,650.35 in damages, which were paid on August 1, 1868. Residents gradually restored their land. The Seventh Street Road or Georgia Avenue followed the pattern of that major artery to and from the city and served as a convenient drawing card for urban construction. A stone replacement structure heralded the rebirth of the Emery Methodist Church on the site of the original Fort Massachusetts. Elizabeth "Aunt Betty" Thomas reconstructed her modest home from materials left over from Fort Stevens and still awaited President Abraham Lincoln's promised "reaping of a great reward." One Union veteran of the battle, Corporal Lewis Cass White, Company H, 102d Pennsylvania, returned to the area and saw the neglected state of the old fort, and was determined to settle there and preserve the ground over which he and his comrades had fought so hard. He purchased the northwest corner of the Georgia Avenue-Piney Branch Road intersection, built a large house, and in time constructed two more for his children and grandchildren. The point was the original location of the Civil War era tollgate, viewed by White and others as the highwater mark of Early's raid. Major General Horatio Wright had identified the precise location of Lincoln's vantage point at the battle during an 1893 reunion. In 1900, White, together with Generals Thomas M. Vincent, Frank Wheaton, George Getty, Fred C. Ainsworth, John C. Breckinridge, and others, formed a "Fort Stevens–Lincoln National Military Park Association," designed to preserve the place where President Lincoln had stood under Confederate fire.[26]

Washington wanted to improve its appearance by the turn of the century, but within the bounds of orderly development. The so-called McMillan Commission in 1901 sought ways of improving the park system and advanced the idea of memorializing the old forts within this system. They also proposed a "fort drive" to connect the sites in a continuous, picturesque boulevard encircling the city. The next year, the Fort Stevens–Lincoln National Military Park Association proposed Congressional creation of a national park at Fort Stevens. But the resultant Senate bill proposed preservation of the line of northern defenses from Fort Reno to Fort Totten in three separate parcels of about 2.65 acres, linking up with other government land at Fort Reno ("now a reservoir"), a school lot near Connecticut Avenue containing old earthworks, Rock Creek Park already preserving Fort De Russy and various batteries, another school lot east of the creek through which ran rifle trenches and the Battleground National Cemetery. The "fort drive" boulevard also played a role, although Fort Stevens would be the principal attraction, noted Association chairman, General Vincent. War Department commissioners would supervise development of the park, much as they were doing at battlefields elsewhere in the country. They would also "ascertain and definitely mark the lines of battle of all troops engaged in the battle of Fort Stevens and points of interest connected with the fortifications of defenses of the national capital during the Civil War."[27]

The rural complexion of Brightwood would have permitted accomplishment of this goal at the time. Newsmen seemed sympathetic in their coverage of the plan. Vermont Senator Redfield Proctor, a Civil War veteran himself as well as former Secretary of War, introduced the Association-sponsored legislation. It died quickly. Senator William Warner of Missouri introduced a similar bill again in 1906. Again, it went nowhere. William Van Zandt Cox, nephew of Ohio congressman "Sunset" Cox, purchased some of the Fort Stevens site in order to preserve it and took charge of the historial committee of the Brightwood Citizens Association. None of the plans developed, although President Theodore Roosevelt, at least, attended the unveiling of a so-called "Lincoln Stone," at Battleground National Cemetery on the fortieth anniversary of the battle.[28]

The lack of recognition, and the run-down, debris-laden condition of old Fort Stevens irked veterans' groups as well as the Fort Stevens Association. Only a rude board nailed to a small tree marked the site. Cox and White secured $250 by public appeal and on November 7, 1911, supervised the placement of a three-ton boulder (five and one-half feet high by three feet in diameter and drawn from the battlefield near the site of the new Walter Reed Army hospital on the old Carberry property). This was placed atop the parapet marking the spot where Lincoln stood under fire. Four 32-pounder cannon balls surrounded the base of the marker. These projectiles had also been recovered from the field after having been fired from the fort by Captain Jewett's artillerists in 1864. Between 400 and 500 people witnessed the ceremony, led by Major General Leonard Wood, the VI Corps Veterans Association, and various patriotic societies. Even "Aunt Betty" Thomas and the sculptor Richard Seek of Tennessee (himself a Union veteran) were present for the reading of the roll of Union and Confederate dead, and the unveiling of this rather ungainly boulder.[29]

One of Jubal Early's old artillery commanders during the campaign and later congressman from Louisiana, Floyd King, delivered some nonpartisan remarks at the 1911 ceremony. Eulogizing Lincoln by noting the assassinated leader's friendship for the south (ironic since King probably harbored few such thoughts in 1864), the ex-Confederate solemnly declared forty-seven years later that he was heartily glad that Early's army had failed to capture Fort Stevens. Veterans' groups would continue to hold reunions at the site,

1911 Commemoration at Fort Stevens. In the foreground, note Elizabeth "Aunt Betty" Thomas who awaited her "great reward," supposedly promised by President Lincoln in 1862. (District of Columbia Civil War Centennial Commission)

and the VI Corps Association dedicated a bronze bas-relief on July 12, 1920 which depicted the president, Wright, and Surgeon Crawford under fire on the spot. J. Otto Schwizer's sculpture definitely improved the bland boulder, but interest groups still could not secure federal legislation to preserve the site.[30]

The situation at Fort Stevens took a downward turn by 1925. Despite all preservation efforts, the place had become a public eyesore and dumping ground for trash. Many people simply assumed the government owned the site, as it did Battleground National Cemetery. Legislation once again went before Congress in February of that year, and it was forwarded to the War Department (which administered the military parks at that time) for comment. However, Secretary of War John W. Weeks vetoed the idea of acquiring Fort Stevens, claiming that while President Lincoln may have been there under enemy fire—an "historically important and interesting" fact—he did not consider it sufficient to warrant government preservation. In a somewhat classic definition of what at the time was considered a rationale for military parks, Weeks stated: "I feel that a national military park should be a piece of ground of considerable extent, the site of an important military engagement in which a comparatively large number of troops was involved, the outcome of which had a definite military and political effect."[31]

Developers now began to nibble around the very edges of the Fort Stevens perimeter as subdivisions were started in the area by May 1925. Legislation was again introduced in February 1928 seeking to devote $25,000 to the acquisition of the property, but highly accelerated economic and social forces worked against preservation in this expanding area of Washington. The title of an article in the Washington *Star* of January 15, 1934 heralded: "Marker which etches Lincoln now symbolizes glory in the dust heaps." Finally the government acquired what remained of Fort Stevens and its immediate vicinity in a series of separate transactions between October 15, 1925, and May 13, 1933. Supervised by National Park Service landscape architect Robert P. McKean, the Civilian Conservation Corps carefully restored the western magazine of the fort and the parapet upon which the Lincoln stone rests even today. Substituting concrete for the original wood in revetments, gun platforms, and magazine interior, the 1930s restoration captured the style and detail of the Civil War work. Installation of a bas-relief diagram of the 1864 fort occurred in September 1936 through the offices of the Grand Army of the Republic and Daughters of Union Veterans of the Civil War.[32]

Periodic clean-up of the grounds, remounting of replica cannon, and commemorative exercises on Memorial Day as well as on the anniversary have continued the memory of Battleground National Cemetery and Fort Stevens despite the ever-changing urban neighborhood and public neglect of the sites. A reenactment of the tableau depicting Lincoln under fire took place in the one-hundredth anniversary of the event during the Civil War centennial. Modern streets, businesses, and residential blocks have obliterated the original farmland, although visitors can stand both where Lincoln stood in the fort and also on the site of the famous "sharpshooters" tulip tree on the grounds of the Walter Reed Army Medical Center to the north of both Fort Stevens and Battleground. Two 100-pounder spherical shots, fired either from Forts De Russy or Totten and found on the Thomas Lay or Carberry farm, decorate a marker to this tree. The tree itself grew just north of a rise in the ground that shielded the lower part in defilade from Fort Stevens, a fact sensed even yet by the alert onlooker. One may ponder how history might have been different had sharpshooter bullets found as their target not a lowly army surgeon, but the president of the United States.[33]

The effort to preserve Monocacy parallels that of Fort Stevens. Long in

Union Unit Memorials at Battleground National Cemetery. The battle to save Fort Stevens and Monocacy was fought by local citizens' and veterans' groups who by the 1920s and 1930s had succeeded in securing national protection for the sites.

coming, preservation of this battlefield was also largely a product of the Great Depression era. The year 1928 found Frederick countians like Judge Glenn Worthington (student and author concerning the battle as well as landowner and descendant of John Worthington who resided on part of the field) advocating a memorial park on the site. Local efforts simply did not penetrate U.S. government barriers despite the battle's historical significance. Responding to such sentiment, E. D. Pope, editor of the influential *Confederate Veteran*, wrote in his February issue that year: "The national government has never even so much as placed markers on the battlefield to indicate where this tremendously important and moot sanguinary battle occurred." The cause took on a new tenor that spring when Congress studied a bill to make the battle site a Federal park.[34]

The intention of the Monocacy Battle Field Association, of which Judge Worthington, Charles Mc. Mathias, James H. Gambrill, Jr., and Robert E.

Restored and Preserved Battlements of Fort Stevens at the Time of the Battle Centennial in 1964. Note the Lincoln Stone atop the parapet where the president came under Confederate fire. (District of Columbia Civil War Centennial Commission)

Delaplaine were prime movers, turned out to be limited to roadways through private property, rather than government acquisition of working farmland. Their guide was the so-called "Antietam model," where interpretive markers placed along several miles of roadway through the battlefield enabled visitors to appreciate the historical events. Monocacy had changed little since the battle; land prices stood at about $100 per acre, and the battlefield itself covered about 200 acres. Re-routing of the main Frederick-Washington highway south of the river had left the Union monuments at the foot of Araby's entrance lane, isolated from ready access. The New Jersey monument adjacent to the railroad was already inaccessible from the new highway where 2,100 to 2,800 motor vehicles passed daily. Bushes, briars, and public neglect threatened the monuments and the battlefield just as they had at Fort Stevens. Worthington and his comrades felt obligated to do their patriotic duty to preserve the place, so long as their invaluable farmland was not lost to private use.[35]

An Act of Congress, dated June 21, 1934, authorized establishment of the Monocacy Military Park. The original bill provided for land donation to the government at no cost (this was, after all, a period of great financial stringency and national privation). Congress did authorize $50,000 for development, but none of it was spent since no matching funds could be obtained at the local level. The project languished from the Second World War period through the Civil War Centennial, as state markers fell into neglect and obscurity. Finally, local supporters succeeded in achieving national historic landmark status for the site in December 1973, and Congress passed legislation three years later for a 1,200 acre Monocacy National Battlefield. Significant boundary expansion, interpretive program planning, and public awareness activities promised to give Monocacy its due by the late 1970s. President Jimmy Carter (following in the footsteps of Franklin Delano Roosevelt in 1934) signed a bill in November 1978 authorizing expenditure of $3,500,000 at Monocacy. All of this came not a moment too soon, as the commercial expansion of Frederick and Interstate Highway 270 (which cut directly through the area of John B. Gordon's assault of James B. Ricketts' line late on July 9, 1864) threatened to engulf the area. Today, National Park Service development, spurred by the 125th anniversary commemoration of the battle, lends support to the belated fame and credit due this long-overlooked battle which many observers felt truly saved Washington from capture.[36]

Monocacy and Fort Stevens stand as monuments to the passing of great armies during Jubal Early's raid on Washington in 1864. Could Early have captured Washington? Could he have held the capital if he had smashed through the Federal defense lines? The war might have gone differently if he and his ragged army had succeeded in that quest. Grant may have been recalled to rectify the situation; he, too, may have been unable to conquer the ubiquitous band of Confederates. Surely the Lincoln administration would have gone elsewhere to fight the war and battle for its own political survival. Speculation is not part of history; Early did not conquer Washington or capture the Lincoln government. We do not know conclusively that this was even the strategy of his superiors. What is known is that he was deterred by dust and heat, the heroic stand of Wallace and Ricketts on the Monocacy, and the stalwart defenders of Fort Stevens (whether militia, government clerks, or Meade's veterans). Perhaps contributing to the failure to capture Washington was Early's own hesitancy in the face of long odds, the relief from the heat by spirits from old Frank Blair's wine cellar, and the imprecise directives from his own chief, the magnificent Lee. What Early accomplished was to buy time for the Confederacy—a nine-month reprieve on life for the Lost Cause—no more, no less.

Early's raid ended the south's real hope of achieving peace through capture of the enemy capital. It ended Robert E. Lee's hope of relieving pressure upon his army and defending the south's seat of power at Richmond. The campaign tested men's wills; the brilliant strategic gamble of Bobby Lee contrasted with the tenacity of Grant and the patience of Abraham Lincoln, and the homefront will power of north vs. south. Tactical leadership was weak in this campaign. The Thermopolyean stand of Lew Wallace contrasted with the celtic rush of John B. Gordon and Robert Rodes to effect a bloody battlefield decision at the cost of campaign goals. The imprecision of mission stands out clearly, with Federal force commanders remaining unaware that annihilation and not merely repulse of the Confederates remained uppermost in Grant's thinking. On the southern side, Early's army could not equally accomplish the divisive tasks of ceaseless foraging, capturing a distant prison compound, and threatening or even capturing Washington. Early's own genius sparkled in outwitting Hunter at Lynchburg, opening the Valley once more, and leading his force virtually undetected to the gates of the capital. However, his reputation sagged badly when he lost control of his force by allowing widespread foraging, and unnecessarily high casualties in the Monocacy delay. This delay cost him the ultimate prize of the war which lay within his grasp—the capture of Washington.

Old Jube was no Jackson. His men knew it and the army performed accordingly. Yet, these were not the same men who followed the gallant

Stonewall two years before. These were weary, ill-clothed, malnourished, undisciplined troops who were possibly more interested in plunder and liquor than maintaining discipline necessary for total victory. They accomplished part of the army's mission in replenishing Confederate supplies and threatening the enemy capital, but attainment of the ultimate victory lay beyond them. Given their condition by the hot July of 1864, perhaps even the presence of their beloved Jackson might not have made much difference, despite the lackluster performance of their opponents.

Certainly the Federal performance was little more than a narrow escape from disaster. Grant's fixation with Lee at Richmond-Petersburg nearly cost him the nation's capital. The War Department huddle of Stanton, Halleck, and their bureaucratic subordinates attempted to fill the void. In Grant's absence, they muddled through with poorly-serving field commanders such as Hunter and Sigel. Undependable telegraphic technology hampered everyone in staying informed. Even after three years of warfare, Union responses were slow and indecisive. Veterans like Horatio Wright and his maneuver force subordinates proved incapable of proper cooperation and collaboration with George Crook in catching Early and destroying his army. This was the ultimate Federal mission, whether in the name of fulfilling Grant's aims before Richmond-Petersburg or the Lincoln administration's goal of safeguarding Washington. Achievement of timely unity of command and effective prosecution of the war in the east was effectively delayed by inadequate leadership at all levels on the Union side in this campaign.

The men in blue—whether militia or veterans—accomplished what they could, given the leadership void. From Monocacy to Fort Stevens they performed well enough to get by in defensive positions and served adequately in the task of thwarting Confederate capture of Washington. However, diluted by integration of veteran units with rear echelon battalions, militia, and fortress garrisons, in July 1864 they were not yet prepared to battle to the death with the wily and wiry veterans from the Army of Northern Virginia. David Hunter may not have been too far off when he told Grant at their "Araby" house meeting just prior to his relief, that he needed all his time for organizing an army out of the disparate pursuit force collected against Early. That was precisely what Phil Sheridan found out during the month of August before he could accomplish his mission in the Shenandoah. By this stage of the war, perhaps Billy Yank was less anxious than Johnny Reb to make those headlong charges in battle which only resulted in mass death and injury. Force development and organizational effectiveness had become prerequisites for the final campaign.

Finally, Early's campaign introduced the ugly involvement of the civilian community in warfare, which had been largely avoided up to this time in the eastern theater. Marylanders no longer rejoiced at the sight of either army, as the soldiery ransacked their region indiscriminately. True, aid and comfort went to the fighting men on both sides in time of need, but it was increasingly repaid by looting and destruction of food, livestock, and personal property. As New York private John B. Southard noted during Wright's pursuit of Early: "We are after the rebs that robed [sic] the Marylanders and they made a grate [sic] many union men that were rebs [,] about two thirds that they robed [sic] were C.S.A. and it turned them Union." The war had taken a sour turn, and the war-weary populace came to realize it. David Hunter's depredations in the Shenandoah were not merely countered by the burning of prominent officials' residences north of the Potomac, but by other countless and unreported injustices perpetrated by both sides—all in the name of retribution. True civil war began to surface from beneath the veneer of civilized conflict in which persecution of citizenry (for example, at Charlestown, Martinsburg, and Chambersburg) sullied the image that modern America has retained about a war of brothers fought by errant knights and inspired yeomanry.[37]

We return to study Early's raid as we do the war as a whole and principally in the light of those supposed knights and yeomanry. During the expedition against Washington, we marvel at the bone-weary resilience of men in blue and gray tramping the hard-pan roadways of the Shenandoah and Maryland, braving ungodly heat and dust, as well as cannon fire and musketry. Whether to the high-spirited Louisiana "Tiger" or to the wide-eyed Ohio militiaman from the collegiate ranks at Oberlin, the 1864 invasion provided stern lessons in death and privation, victory and defeat, and the brotherhood of arms. Beautiful scenery and friendly ladies aside, the fighting men provided the backbone of the story of Early' raid. They never forgave Old Jube for denying them the chance to sack Washington and capture Uncle Abe, nor Henry Halleck's idiotic orders sending them marching and counter-marching in pursuit of enemy shadows. Survival, not glory, provided the daily fare for the men in blue and gray in the summer campaign of 1864.

Moot testament to the passing of great hosts during this raid comes less from studies of generalship or rumors of liquored command conferences at the Blair mansion. Even the apochryphal tales of who really told Abraham Lincoln to descend from the parapet at Fort Stevens pale before the monuments to the fallen. Battleground National Cemetery and the tiny country churchyard of the new suburbanite Grace Episcopal Church in Silver Spring hold the key to the saga. Farther away at Mount Olivet Cemetery in Frederick or Antietam National Cemetery stand the silent headstones marking the meaning of Monocacy. Probably yet undiscovered and unmarked burial spots for other fallen soldiers across the region provide the true testimonial to why either army fought within the shadow of the Great Capitol of the United States. Men's lust to cover the land with roads and residences or nature's periodic destruction of great trees that once sheltered the sweltering, suffering fighting men cannot completely erase the human dimensions of an event like Early's raid.[38]

What then can be said of that event? Without Early's campaign, the war would possibly have been over by Christmas. Not just Savannah, Georgia but also Richmond and Petersburg could have been Yuletide gifts to President Lincoln. Conversely, could Early have succeeded in this most risky Confederate undertaking? One elderly veteran of the 25th New York Cavalry thought as late as 1915: "If Gen. Early had the proper pluck, he could have gotten into Washington. . . . our skirmish line was thrown out in single file over a large front." Lieutenant Frank Wilkeson, assigned to Battery A, 4th United States Artillery (and witness to the battle at Fort Stevens), thought he knew the answer too. "I unhesitatingly answer, yes," he contended, adding that the southern general could have taken the city without losing more than one thousand men. "But," said the skeptical Wilkeson, "if he had taken it, his poorly-clad, poorly-fed, impoverished men would inevitably have gone to plundering, would inevitably have gotten drunk, and stayed drunk, and he would have lost his entire army." That is the bottom line for Early's raid—the Last Confederate Invasion—in July 1864.[39]

Appendix A

ARMY OF THE VALLEY DISTRICT
(Second Army Corps; Army of Northern Virginia)

Lieutenant General Jubal A. Early, commanding
Rodes' Division (Maj. Gen. Robert E. Rodes)

Battle's Brigade (Brig. Gen. Cullen A. Battle)
  3d Alabama Infantry
  5th Alabama Infantry
  6th Alabama Infantry
  12th Alabama Infantry
  61st Alabama Infantry

Grimes' Brigade (Brig. Gen. Bryan Grimes)
  32d North Carolina Infantry
  43d North Carolina Infantry
  45th North Carolina Infantry
  53d North Carolina Infantry
  2d North Carolina (Battalion) Infantry

Cook's Brigade (Brig. Gen. Philip Cook)
  4th Georgia Infantry
  12th Georgia Infantry   (all fragmentary regiments)
  21st Georgia Infantry
  44th Georgia Infantry

Cox's Brigade (Brig. Gen. William R. Cox)
1st North Carolina Infantry
2d North Carolina Infantry
3d North Carolina Infantry
4th North Carolina Infantry
14th North Carolina Infantry
30th North Carolina Infantry

Ramseur's Division (Major General Stephen D. Ramseur)

Lilley's Brigade (Brig. Gen. Robert Lilley)
13th Virginia Infantry
31st Virginia Infantry
49th Virginia Infantry
52d Virginia Infantry
58th Virginia Infantry

Johnston's Brigade (Brig. Gen. Robert D. Johnston)
5th North Carolina Infantry
12th North Carolina Infantry
20th North Carolina Infantry
23d North Carolina Infantry

Lewis' Brigade (Brig. Gen. William Lewis)
6th North Carolina Infantry
21st North Carolina Infantry
54th North Carolina Infantry   (all fragmentary regiments)
57th North Carolina Infantry
1st North Carolina Battalion Sharpshooters

Breckinridge's Corps (Major General John C. Breckinridge)

Gordon's Division (Major General John B. Gordon)

Evans' Brigade (Brig. Gen. Clement A. Evans / Col. E. N. Atkinson)
13th Georgia Infantry
26th Georgia Infantry
31st Georgia Infantry
38th Georgia Infantry
60th Georgia Infantry
61st Georgia Infantry
12th Georgia (Battalion) Infantry

York's Brigade (Brig. Gen. Zebulon York) (consolidated)

Hays' old brigade (Louisiana Tigers) (Col. W. R. Peck)
5th Louisiana Infantry
6th Louisiana Infantry
7th Louisiana Infantry   (all fragmentary regiments)
8th Louisiana Infantry
9th Louisiana Infantry

Stafford's old brigade (Col. E. Waggaman)
1st Louisiana Infantry
2d Louisiana Infantry
10th Louisiana Infantry   (all fragmentary regiments)
14th Louisiana Infantry
15th Louisiana Infantry

Terry's Brigade (Brig. Gen. William Terry) (consolidated)

Jackson's old 1st or "Stonewall" brigade (Col. J. H. S. Funk)
2d Virginia Infantry
4th Virginia Infantry
5th Virginia Infantry
27th Virginia Infantry
33d Virginia Infantry

Jones' old 2d brigade (Col. R. H. Dungan)
21st Virginia Infantry
25th Virginia Infantry
42d Virginia Infantry
44th Virginia Infantry
48th Virginia Infantry
50th Virginia Infantry

Stuart's old 3d brigade (Lt. Col. S. H. Saunders)
10th Virginia Infantry
23d Virginia Infantry
37th Virginia Infantry

Echols' Division (Brig. Gen. John Echols) (formerly Breckinridge's and Elzey's divisions)

Wharton's Brigade (Brig. Gen. Gabriel C. Wharton)
30th Virginia Infantry Battalion Sharpshooters
45th Virginia Infantry

50th Virginia Infantry
51st Virginia Infantry

Echols' Brigade (Col. George S. Patton)
22d Virginia Infantry
23d Virginia Infantry (battalion)
26th Virginia Infantry (battalion)

Vaughn's Brigade (Brig. Gen. Thomas Smith)
36th Virginia Infantry
45th Virginia Infantry (battalion)
60th Virginia Infantry
Thomas' Legion (dismounted)

Ransom's Cavalry Division (Major General Robert Ransom)

Imboden's Brigade (Brig. Gen. John Imboden / Col. George Smith)
18th Virginia Cavalry
23d Virginia Cavalry
62d Virginia Mounted Infantry
Unauthorized Virginia Cavalry Battalion

McCausland's Brigade (Brig. Gen. John McCausland)
14th Virginia Cavalry
16th Virginia Cavalry
17th Virginia Cavalry
25th Virginia Cavalry
37th Virginia Cavalry Battalion

Johnson's Brigade (Brig. Gen. Bradley T. Johnson)
1st Maryland Cavalry Battalion
8th Virginia Cavalry
21st Virginia Cavalry
22d Virginia Cavalry Battalion
34th Virginia Cavalry Battalion
36th Virginia Cavalry

Jackson's Brigade (Brig. Gen. W. L. Jackson)
2d Maryland Cavalry Battalion
19th Virginia Cavalry
20th Virginia Cavalry
46th Virginia Cavalry Battalion
47th Virginia Cavalry Battalion

Horse Artillery (10–14 guns)
Jackson's Co. Va. Horse Artillery (T. E. Jackson) with McCausland Brigade

McClanahan's Co. (Staunton) Va. Horse Artillery (McClanahan) with Imboden's Brigade

Baltimore Light Artillery (2d Maryland) (Griffin) with Johnson's Brigade

Lurty's Va. Battery (Lurty) with Jackson's Brigade

Artillery (Brig. Gen. Armistead L. Long)
   (approximately 36–40 guns)

Braxton's Battalion (Major Carter M. Braxton)
   Allegheny Artillery (Va.) (Carpenter)
   Lee Artillery (Va.) (Hardwicke)
   Stafford Artillery (Va.) (Cooper)

King's Battalion (Major J. Floyd King)
                  (Major William McLaughlin)
   Wise Legion Artillery (Va.) (Lowry)
   (Centreville Rifles, Lowry's Artillery)
   Lewisburg Artillery (Va.) (Bryan)
   Monroe Battery (Va.) (Chapman)

Nelson's Battalion (Major William Nelson)
   Amherst Artillery (Va.) (Kirkpatrick)
   Fluvanna Artillery (Va.) (Massie)
   Milledge Artillery (Ga.) (Milledge)

(Composition of horse artillery unclear. May have included all or some of the following: 2d Maryland Battery (Griffin), Charlottesville Battery (Va.) (T. E. Jackson), Roanoke Battery (Va.) (Lurty), Staunton Battery (Va.) (McClannahan), 1st Stuart H.A. Battery (Va.) (Johnston), Lynchburg Battery (Va.) (Shoemaker), Ashby Battery (Va.) Thomson).

Recapitulation: Early's forces included 67 infantry regiments, 6 battalions of infantry (or fragments), plus 11 regiments and 9 battalions of cavalry, as well as three battalions (nine batteries) of field, upwards of seven batteries of horse artillery. The force may have comprised as many as 20,000 men at some point, while losses in this campaign probably numbered from 1,500 to 2,000.

Sources:

Brad Coker, *The Battle of Monocacy* (Baltimore, 1982), 44.

Albert E. Conradis, "The Battle of Monocacy," in Frederick Civil War Centennial, Inc. *To Commemorate the One Hundredth Anniversary of the Battle of Monocacy* (Frederick, 1964), Appendix II, 35.

George E. Pond, *The Shenandoah Valley in 1864* (New York, 1883), Appendix D, 273.

U.S. War Department, *The War of the Rebellion; The Official Records of Union and Confederate Armies* (Washington, 1880–1901), I, 37, pt. 1, 1003–1004.

Frank Vandiver, *Jubal's Raid* (New York, 1960), 172.

Jeffrey D. Wert, *From Winchester to Cedar Creek; The Shenandoah Campaign of 1864* (Carlisle, 1987), 316–317.

Appendix B

TROOPS IN THE DEPARTMENT OF WASHINGTON (XXII) CORPS

Major General Christopher C. Augur, as reported June 30, 1864

Headquarters
Signal Corps
US Veteran Reserve Corps (two companies)

District of Washington (Col. Moses N. Wisewell)

First Brigade, Veteran Reserve Corps (Wisewell)
    1st Regiment
    6th Regiment
    9th Regiment
    19th Regiment
    22d Regiment
    24th Regiment

Not brigaded
    150th Pennsylvania Volunteer Infantry, Co. K
    18th Regiment US Veteran Reserve Corps (from Second Brigade VRC)
    Union Light Guard (Ohio cavalry)
    US Ordnance Detachment

Haskin's Division (Lieut. Col. Joseph A. Haskin) *

First Brigade (Col. William H. Hayward)
13th Michigan Battery
14th Michigan Battery
150th Ohio National Guard
1st Pennsylvania Artillery Battalion (four companies)
1st Rhode Island Light Artillery, Battery D
4th US Artillery, Battery A

Second Brigade (Col. John M. C. Marble)
New Hampshire Heavy Artillery, 1st Company
1st Ohio Light Artillery, Battery L
151st Ohio National Guard
170th Ohio National Guard
2d US Artillery, Battery I

Third Brigade (Lieut. Col. John H. Oberteuffer)
Massachusetts Heavy Artillery (3d Heavy Artillery)
6th Independent Company
7th Independent Company
8th Independent Company
9th Independent Company
10th Independent Company
11th Independent Company
12th Independent Company
14th Independent Company

Forte Foote, Md. (Capt. Ira McL. Barton)
Maine Coast Guard, Company B
New Hampshire Heavy Artillery, 2d Company

Cavalry Depot (Col. George A. H. Baker)
US Veteran Reserve Corps (two companies)

Cavalry Division (Col. William Gamble)
Detachments from Army of the Potomac (dismounted)
8th Illinois Volunteer Cavalry (seven companies)

Fort Washington, Md. (Col. Horace Brooks)
Maine Coast Guard, Company A
4th US Artillery (regimental headquarters)

*Headquarters, Washington City. Troops at Batteries Cameron and Reno, Forts Baker, Bunker Hill, Davis, Du Pont, Foote, Greble, Lincoln, Mahan, Meigs, Reno, Ricketts, Slocum, Snyder, Stanton, Stevens, Sumner, Totten, and Wagner—all.

District of Saint Mary's, Md. (Col. Alonzo G. Draper)
    139th Ohio National Guard (eight companies)
    4th Rhode Island Volunteer Infantry
    36th US Colored Troops
    10th US Veteran Reserve Corps (two companies)
    11th US Veteran Reserve Corps
    20th US Veteran Reserve Corps
    2d and 5th US Cavalry (detachment)
    2d Wisconsin Battery

Artillery Camp of Instruction (Brig. Gen. Albion P. Howe)
        Camp Barry, D.C. (Maj. James A. Hall)
    Maine Light Artillery, 3d Battery (C)
    New York Light Artillery, 6th Battery
    New York Light Artillery, 17th Battery
    5th US Artillery, Battery F
    5th US Artillery, Battery L

District of Alexandria (Brig. Gen. John P. Slough)

Second Brigade, Veteran Reserve Corps (Col. William H. Browne)
    3d Regiment
    11th Regiment (Point Lookout, Md.)
    12th Regiment
    14th Regiment (Camp Distribution)
    18th Regiment (Washington)
    20th Regiment (Point Lookout, Md.)

Not brigaded
    1st District of Columbia Volunteer Infantry (four companies)
    2d District of Columbia Volunteer Infantry
    8th Illinois Cavalry, Company D*
    1st Michigan Cavalry, Company D*
    Pennsylvania Light Artillery, Battery H

Rendezvous of Distribution (Lieut. Col. Samuel McKelvy)
    14th Regiment Veteran Reserve Corps

Provisional Brigades (Maj. Gen. Silas Casey)
    23d US Colored Troops (detachment)
    27th US Colored Troops (detachment)
    31st US Colored Troops (one company)

---

*Constituting, with detachment of 12th Veteran Reserve Corps, the command of Lieut. Col. Henry H. Wells, provost-marshal, Defenses South of the Potomac.

De Russy's Division (Brig. Gen. Gustavus A. De Russy)*

First Brigade (Col. John C. Lee)
1st Maine Battery (A)
Maryland Light Artillery, Battery A
Maryland Light Artillery, Battery D
1st New York Light Artillery
5th New York Battery
13th New York Cavalry, Company C
145th Ohio Volunteer Infantry
147th Ohio Volunteer Infantry
164th Ohio Volunteer Infantry
169th Ohio Volunteer Infantry
1st Pennsylvania Light Artillery, Battery H
1st Pennsylvania Light Artillery, Battery G
2d US Artillery, Battery G

Second Brigade (Col. W. Smith Irwin)
16th Indiana Battery
16th Massachusetts Battery
Massachusetts Heavy Artillery, 3d Company
Massachusetts Heavy Artillery, 15th Company
1st New York Artillery, Battery F
136th Ohio National Guard
142d Ohio National Guard
166th Ohio National Guard
Pennsylvania Light Artillery, Battery C
Pennsylvania Light Artillery, Battery F
Pennsylvania Light Artillery, Battery I
1st Rhode Island Light Artillery, Battery H
1st US Artillery, Battery E
1st West Virginia Light Artillery, Battery C
1st Wisconsin Heavy Artillery (one company)

Cavalry Brigade (Col. Charles R. Lowell, Jr.)
2d Massachusetts Volunteer Cavalry
13th New York Volunteer Cavalry
16th New York Volunteer Cavalry

---

*Headquarters, Arlington, Va. First Brigade at Forts Cass, C. F. Smith, Craig, Corcoran, Ethan Allen, Marcy, Tillinghast, Whipple, and Woodbury. The Second Brigade at Battery Rodgers and Forts Barnard, Berry Ellsworth, Fransworth, Garescheo, Lyon, O'Rorke, Reynolds, Richardson, Scott, Ward, Weed, Willard, Williams, and Worth—all Defenses South of the Potomac.

Recapitulation: Augur's command reported present for duty 518 officers and 13,986 men serving 484 heavy and 33 field guns in 87 forts and batteries north of the Potomac with 426 officers and 10,737 men serving 466 heavy and 6 field guns in 76 forts south of the Potomac. Thus, according to report, he could bring to bear in defense of Washington, ostensibly 944 officers and 24,723 men with 950 heavy and 39 field guns from a fortification system numbering 163 forts, batteries, and rifle trenches which circumvented the city (including Alexandria).

Sources: US War Department, *War of the Rebellion: The Official Records of the Union and Confederate Armies* (Washington: 1880–1901), I, 37, pt. 1, 697–700.

Appendix C

TROOPS IN THE DEPARTMENT OF WEST VIRGINIA

Major General David Hunter as reported June 30, 1864

Signal Corps
Capt. Franklin E. Town

First Infantry Division (Brig. Gen. Jeremiah C. Sullivan)

First Brigade (Col. Augustus Moor)
18th Connecticut Volunteer Infantry
2d Maryland Eastern Shore Infantry
28th Ohio Volunteer Infantry
116th Ohio Volunteer Infantry
123d Ohio Volunteer Infantry
N.B. According to a separate return of the 1st Brigade, Col. George D. Wells commanding, it consisted at this date of the 34th Massachusetts, battalion of the 5th New York Heavy Artillery, and the 116th and 123d Ohio.

Second Brigade (Col. Joseph Thoburn)
34th Massachusetts Volunteer Infantry
5th New York Heavy Artillery (four companies)
1st West Virginia Volunteer Infantry
12th West Virginia Volunteer Infantry

Second Infantry Division (Brig. Gen. George Crook)

First Brigade (Col. Rutherford B. Hayes)
23d Ohio Volunteer Infantry
36th Ohio Volunteer Infantry
5th West Virginia Volunteer Infantry
13th West Virginia Volunteer Infantry

Second Brigade (Col. Carr B. White)
13th Ohio Volunteer Infantry
91st Ohio Volunteer Infantry
9th West Virginia Volunteer Infantry
14th West Virginia Volunteer Infantry

Third Brigade (Col. Jacob M. Campbell)
54th Pennsylvania Volunteer Infantry
3d and 4th Regiments Pennsylvania Reserve Corps (six companies)
11th West Virginia Volunteer Infantry
15th West Virginia Volunteer Infantry

Artillery (Capt. James R. McMullin)
Kentucky Light Artillery, 1st Battery
Ohio Light Artillery, 1st Battery

First Cavalry Division (Brig. Gen. Alfred N. Duffié)

First Brigade (Col. William B. Tibbits)
1st Maryland Potomac Home Brigade
1st New York (Lincoln) Cavalry
1st New York (Veteran) Cavalry
21st New York Cavalry

Second Brigade (Col. John H. Oley)
1st West Virginia Cavalry
3d West Virginia Cavalry
5th West Virginia Cavalry
7th West Virginia Cavalry

Third Brigade (Col. William H. Powell) N.N. Ordered transferred to Crook's division on 24 June.
34th Ohio Mounted Infantry
2d West Virginia Cavalry

Artillery Brigade (Capt. Henry A. Du Pont)
Maryland Light Artillery, Battery B
New York Light Artillery, 30th Battery

1st West Virginia Light Artillery, Battery D
5th US Artillery, Battery B

Reserve Division (Maj. Gen. Franz Sigel)

Stations, Monocacy to Sleepy Creek (Brig. Gen. Max Weber)*
17th Indiana Battery (light artillery battalion)
Loudon (Va.) Rangers (two companies)
1st Maryland Potomac Home Brigade
5th New York Heavy Artillery (eight companies)
32d New York Independent Battery
135th Ohio Infantry
152d Ohio Infantry
160th Ohio Infantry
161st Ohio Infantry
Wrigley's Independent Company Engineers, Pennsylvania
1st Pennsylvania Light Artillery, Battery D (light artillery battalion)
1st West Virginia Light Artillery, Battery A (light artillery battalion)
Camp Distribution

Stations, West of Sleepy Creek (Brig. Gen. Benjamin F. Kelley)†
1st Illinois Light Artillery, Battery L
16th Illinois Cavalry, Company C
2d Maryland Potomac Home Brigade, Company F
2d Maryland Potomac Home Brigade, Company K
153d Ohio Infantry
154th Ohio Infantry
3d Company Ohio Cavalry
1st West Virginia Cavalry, Company A
1st West Virginia Light Artillery, Battery E
1st West Virginia Light Artillery, Battery F
1st West Virginia Light Artillery, Battery H
1st West Virginia Cavalry, Company A
6th West Virginia Cavalry
6th West Virginia Infantry
Engineer troops (Campbell)

---

*Headquarters, Harpers Ferry with troops at Black Creek, Bolivar Heights, Cherry Run, Duffield's Depot, Harpers Ferry, Martinsburg, Maryland Heights, Monocacy, Point of Rocks, and Sleepy Creek.

†Troops at Buckhannon, Clarksburg, Cumberland, Grafton, Greenland Gap, Green Spring Run, New Creek, and Paw Paw.

Miscellaneous

Frederick, Md.
132d Company, US Veteran Reserve Corps

Wheeling, West Virginia
West Virginia Exempts

Recapitulation: Hunter's force of two infantry and two cavalry plus a reserve division reported 1,079 officers and 27,408 men with 34 heavy and 44 light artillery pieces.

Source: US War Department, *War of the Rebellion: The Official Records of the Union and Confederate Armies* (Washington: 1880–1901), I, 37, pt. 1, 701–704.

Appendix D

TROOPS IN THE MIDDLE DEPARTMENT (VIII CORPS)

Major General Lew Wallace, as reported June 30, 1864

First Separate Brigade (Brig. Gen. Erastus B. Tyler)
    1st Maryland Eastern Shore Infantry (two companies)
    3d Maryland Potomac Home Brigade
    144th Ohio Infantry

Second Separate Brigade (Bvt. Brig. Gen. [Col.] William W. Morris)
    131st Ohio Infantry
    137th Ohio Infantry

Third Separate Brigade (Brig. Gen. John R. Kenly)
N.B. Including District of Delaware
    Baltimore (Alexander's) Battery, Maryland Light Artillery
    1st Maryland Eastern Shore Infantry (eight companies)
    Smith's Independent Company Cavalry (Maryland)
    11th Maryland Infantry
    149th Ohio Infantry
    159th Ohio Infantry
    3d Pennsylvania Artillery, Battery H
    71st Company US Veteran Reserve Corps
    72d Company US Veteran Reserve Corps
    89th Company US Veteran Reserve Corps

95th Company US Veteran Reserve Corps
96th Company US Veteran Reserve Corps
143d Company US Veteran Reserve Corps
Miscellaneous Detachment US Veteran Reserve Corps

Annapolis, Md. (Col. Adrian R. Root)
1st Maryland Eastern Shore Infantry, (Company I)
144th Ohio (detachment)
149th Ohio (detachment)
118th Company US Veteran Reserve Corps
119th Company US Veteran Reserve Corps

Recapitulation: Wallace's forces numbered 265 officers and 6,027 men.

Source: US War Department, *War of the Rebellion: The Official Records of the Union and Confederate Armies* (Washington: 1880–1901), I, 37, pt. 1, 704.

Appendix E

TROOPS IN THE DEPARTMENT OF THE SUSQUEHANNA
Major General Darius N. Couch, and
DEPARTMENT OF THE EAST
Major General John A. Dix as reported on June 30, 1864

Department of the Susquehanna (Couch)

Philadelphia, Pa. (Major General George Cadwalader)
    186th Pennsylvania Infantry
    46th Company US Veteran Reserve Corps
    51st Company US Veteran Reserve Corps
    52d Company US Veteran Reserve Corps
    53d Company US Veteran Reserve Corps
    55th Company US Veteran Reserve Corps
    57th Company US Veteran Reserve Corps
    59th Company US Veteran Reserve Corps
    105th Company US Veteran Reserve Corps
    131st Company US Veteran Reserve Corps
    162d Company US Veteran Reserve Corps

Harrisburg, Pa. (Lieut. Col. James V. Bomford)
Patapsco (Maryland) Guards
1st New York Light Artillery, Battery A
50th Company US Veteran Reserve Corps

Pottsville, Pa. (Lehigh District) (Capt. Josiah C. Hullinger)
21st Pennsylvania Cavalry, Company D
50th Company, US Veteran Reserve Corps

Pittsburgh, Pa. (District of Monongahela) (Brig. Gen. Thomas A. Rowley)
(Capt. Edward S. Wright)
21st US Veteran Reserve Corps, Company I
109th Company US Veteran Reserve Corps

Chelton Hill (Camp William Penn), Pa. (Lieut. Col. Louis Wagner)
43d US Colored Troops, Companies H, I, K
45th US Colored Troops (three companies)

Carlisle Barracks, Pa.
Cavalry Depot
Draft Rendezvous

York, Pa. (Surg. Henry Palmer)
108th Company US Veteran Reserve Corps, 2d Battalion

Chambersburg, Pa.
US Signal Corps detachment

Department of the East (Dix)

City and Harbor of New York (Brig. Gen. P. Regis De Trobriand)
7th New York (battalion) Infantry
15th New York State National Guard
20th New York Battery
28th New York Battery
3d US Infantry
6th US Infantry
7th US Infantry, Companies A, B, D, E, G, I, K
31st US Colored Troops (detachment)

Recapitulation: Couch numbered 59 officers and 811 men; Dix counted 221 officers and 3,354 men.

Source: US War Department, *War of the Rebellion: The Official Records of Union and Confederate Armies* (Washington: 1880–1901), I, 37, pt. 1, 705–706.

Appendix F

ORGANIZATION OF FEDERAL FORCES AT MONOCACY—JULY 9, 1864

Major General Lew Wallace, Commander

Middle Department (VIII Corps) (Wallace)

First Separate Brigade (Tyler)
  1st Maryland Potomac Home Brigade (5 companies)
  3d Maryland Potomac Home Brigade
  11th Maryland Volunteer Infantry
  144th Ohio National Guard (3 companies)
  149th Ohio National Guard (7 companies)
  Baltimore Battery (Alexander) (6 guns)
  Blockhouse howitzer (Wiegel) (1 gun)
  Small Mountain howitzer

Cavalry (Clendenin)
  8th Illinois Volunteer Cavalry (7 companies)
  Loudoun (Va.) Rangers (Cos. A, B)
  159th Ohio Mounted Infantry
  Wells's Mixed Cavalry Detachment

Third Division (VI Corps) (Brig. Gen. James Ricketts)

First Brigade (Truex)
  14th New Jersey Volunteer Infantry

106th New York Volunteer Infantry
151st New York Volunteer Infantry
87th Pennsylvania Volunteer Infantry
10th Vermont Volunteer Infantry

Second Brigade (McClennan)
9th New York Heavy Artillery (two battalions)
110th Ohio Volunteer Infantry
122d Ohio Volunteer Infantry
126th Ohio Volunteer Infantry
138th Pennsylvania Volunteer Infantry

VI Corps units at Monrovia, Md. (Staunton)
6th Maryland Volunteer Infantry
122d Ohio Volunteer Infantry (detachment)
67th Pennsylvania Volunteer Infantry

Recapitulation: Wallace had at his command all or portions of seventeen infantry regiments, four cavalry units, one field gun battery, plus unattached howitzers guarding the railroad bridge over the Monocacy. His strength approximated 2,500 VIII corps, plus cavalry and 4,500–5,000 VI corps veterans. His losses totaled approximately 1,294–1,968 killed, wounded, and missing.

Sources: Brad Coker, *The Battle of Monocacy* (Baltimore, 1982), 31, 49.

Glenn H. Worthington, *Fighting for Time* (Frederick, 1932), 259–260.

US War Department, *War of the Rebellion; A Compilation of the Official Records of the Union and Confederate Armies* (Washington: 1880–1901), I, 37, pt. 1, 200, 202.

Appendix G

FEDERAL TROOPS AT THE BATTLE OF FORT STEVENS, JULY 11–12, 1864

Department of Washington (XII Corps)
(Major General Christopher C. Augur)

8th Illinois Volunteer Cavalry (one squadron) (Wells)
Provisional Cavalry Regiment (Fry)

Northern Defenses of Washington (Maj. Gen. Alexander McD. McCook)

7th Michigan Volunteer Cavalry (detachment) (Darling)

First Division (Brig. Gen. Martin D. Mardin)

First Brigade (Col. James M. Warner)
Forts Reno, Bayard, Simmons
9th New York Heavy Artillery, Company B
151st Ohio National Guard (one co.)
2d US Artillery, Battery I

Fort Kearny
9th New York Heavy Artillery (one co.)
151st Ohio National Guard, Company K

Battery Smeade
    9th New York Heavy Artillery, Company E (½ co.)
    151st Ohio National Guard, Company I

Fort De Russy
    9th New York Heavy Artillery, Company L (½ co.)
    151st Ohio National Guard, Companies C, G
    1st Wisconsin Heavy Artillery, Company A

Operating in sector from Forts Sumner to Slocum
    2d Massachusetts Volunteer Cavalry
    25th New York Volunteer Cavalry
    1st Ohio Light Artillery, Battery L
    147th Ohio National Guard
    151st Ohio National Guard
    Provisional Cavalry (dismounted men, 2d Cavalry Division, Army of the Potomac)
    First Brigade, Veteran Reserve Corps (6 regiments) (Gile)
    7th Veteran Reserve Corps

Second Brigade (Lieut. Col. Joseph A. Haskin)
Fort Stevens
    13th Michigan Battery
    150th Ohio National Guard, Company K
    convalescents
    1st Maine Light Artillery

Fort Slocum
    14th Michigan Battery
    150th Ohio National Guard, Company G
    2d Pennsylvania Heavy Artillery

Fort Totten
    150th Ohio National Guard (balance)
    Quartermaster Department clerks (Rucker)
    2d Pennsylvania Heavy Artillery

Provisional Division (Maj. Gen. Montgomery C. Meigs)*

First Brigade (Brig. Gen. Daniel C. Rucker)
    Quartermaster clerks
    Provisional brigade (detachment)

*The Provisional Division manned the lines from the right of Fort Stevens to Fort Totten and beyond, with its Second Brigade dispatched to Fort Saratoga at 4 p.m., July 12, to help Major General Quincy Gillmore deter the anticipated move by Bradley Johnson's column in that

Second Brigade (Brig. Gen. Halbert E. Paine)
2d District of Columbia Volunteer Militia
Quartermaster clerks, Washington Depot (3 cos.)

Third Brigade (Col. Francis Price, Col. Addison Fransworth, Col. Charles M. Alexander)
Reserve Provisional Brigade
hospital convalescents and
distribution camp troops

Lines east of Fort Totten (Maj. Gen. Quincy A. Gillmore)

XIX Corps elements
2d District of Columbia

VI Corps (Maj. Gen. Horatio G. Wright)

First Division

First Brigade (Col. William H. Penrose) (arrived July 11)
4th New Jersey Volunteer Infantry
10th New Jersey Volunteer Infantry
15th New Jersey Volunteer Infantry

Second Brigade (Brig. Gen. Emory Upton) (arrived July 12)
2d Connecticut Heavy Artillery
65th New York Volunteer Infantry
67th New York Volunteer Infantry
121st New York Volunteer Infantry
95th Pennsylvania Volunteer Infantry
96th Pennsylvania Volunteer Infantry

Third Brigade (Col. Oliver Edwards) (arrived July 12)
6th Maine Volunteer Infantry
37th Massachusetts Volunteer Infantry
23d Pennsylvania Volunteer Infantry

---

direction. The Quartermaster Department Office Battalion under Captain J. J. Dana relieved Veteran Reserve Corps contingents throughout the Department of Washington for service in the threatened sector, stationing a company of clerks at each of the following locations:
Nineteenth Street Wagon Park
Clothing Store— H Street near Nineteenth Street
Eastern Branch Stables and Corral
Kendall Green Corral and Stables
Workshops, Corrals, Stables on F Street between Twenty-First and Twenty-Third Streets
Alexandria area

82d Pennsylvania Volunteer Infantry
119th Pennsylvania Volunteer Infantry
49th New York Volunteer Infantry
2d Rhode Island Volunteer Infantry (Bn)
5th Wisconsin Volunteer Infantry (Bn)

Second Division (Brig. Gen. George W. Getty) (absent)

First Brigade (Brig. Gen. Frank Wheaton) (arrived July 11)
62d New York Volunteer Infantry
93d Pennsylvania Volunteer Infantry
98th Pennsylvania Volunteer Infantry
102d Pennsylvania Volunteer Infantry

Second Brigade (Col. Lewis Grant) (arrived July 11?)
2d Vermont Volunteer Infantry
3d Vermont Volunteer Infantry
4th Vermont Volunteer Infantry
5th Vermont Volunteer Infantry
6th Vermont Volunteer Infantry

Third Brigade (Col. Daniel D. Bidwell) (arrived July 11)
7th Maine Volunteer Infantry
43d New York Volunteer Infantry
49th New York Volunteer Infantry
77th New York Volunteer Infantry
122d New York Volunteer Infantry
61st Pennsylvania Volunteer Infantry

(from Artillery Brigade) (Col. Charles H. Tompkins)
1st Maine Light Artillery, 1st Battery (Cowan) (arrived July 11)

XIX Corps (Maj. Gen. J. J. Reynolds) (absent)

First Division (Brig. Gen. William H. Emory)

First Brigade (Col. George L. Beal) (arrived July 11)
114th New York Volunteer Infantry (detachment)
153d New York Volunteer Infantry
(rest of brigade arrives July 13)

Recapitulation: Estimates suggest that on July 10, 1864, Federal forces available for the defenses north of the Potomac numbered 3,716 officers and men, with an additional 5,887 south of the Potomac. McCook's aide, Colonel Norton P. Chipman, claimed the status of US forces on July 12 numbered 6,271 officers and men in the lines from Fort Totten to Fort Stevens, with 7,765 manning the line from Fort Stevens to Fort De Russy for a total of 14,036 directly opposing the Confederate thrust via the Seventh Street Road axis. Major General John G. Barnard, Chief Engineer, computed a total of 20,400 officers and men participating in the city's defense, including 4,400 Veteran Reserve Corps and 2,000 Quartermaster employees and soldiers, and miscellaneous contingents. Wright's VI corps numbered about 10,000 officers and men (by his computation), while possibly 500–800 XIX corps troops could be added to the Federal force.

Sources: Frederick H. Dyer, *A Compendium of the War of the Rebellion* (New York, 1959 edition), I, 308–313, 379–382.

George E. Pond, *The Sheanandoah Valley in 1864* (New York, 1883), 65-66. 256-257.

US War Department, *War of the Rebellion: A Compilation of the Official Records of the Union and Confederate Armies* (Washington, 1880–1901), I, 37, pt. 1, 230–285.

Bibliography

Primary Sources — Archival

Alabama Department of Archives and History, Montgomery, Alabama
  Cullen Andrews Battle papers
Duke University, Durham, North Carolina
  Confederate States of America, Archives, Army, Miscellaneous Officers and Soldiers Letters
  Edwin Hardin papers
  Journal of Anonymous Crewman, Steamer *George Leary*
  Edmund Jennings Lee papers
  T. A. Meysenburg Notes on Battles around Martinsburg, Va.
  Robert Smith Rodgers papers, History of Second Eastern Shore Regiment, Maryland Infantry
  Mary Eliza (Fleming) Schooler papers
Fort Ward Museum and Historic Site, Alexandria, Virginia
  Defenses of Washington collection
Frederick County Historical Society, Frederick, Maryland
  Elbert Baughman family papers
  Robert Cornwell papers
  Edward S. Delaplaine collection
  Thomas Gorsuch papers
  Battle of Monocacy files
  Rich family papers
  Elihu Rockwell papers
  Joseph Urner reminiscence
Huntington Library, San Marino, California
  James W. Eldridge collection
  John Page Nicholson collection

Illinois State Historical Library, Springfield, Illinois
    Reuben T. Prentice papers
    William R. Rowley papers
Library of Congress, Washington, D.C.
    Thomas L. Feamster diary
    Samuel P. Heintzelman papers
    Montgomery C. Meigs papers
Maryland Historical Society, Baltimore, Maryland
    Augustus Bradford papers
    I. G. Bradwell papers
    Carey scrapbook
    Civil War Miscellaneous collection
    Rebecca Davis diary
    Harry Gilmor papers
    Rinehart diary
    Richard P. Thomas papers
Massachusetts Historical Society, Boston, Massachusetts
    F. C. Morse papers
Montgomery County Historical Society, Rockville, Maryland
    John T. De Sellum letters
National Archives and Records Administration, Washington, D.C.
    Record Group 77, Records of the Corps of Engineers, Defenses of Washington
    (see also cartographic records under this heading)
New York Historical Society, New York, New York
    John Fleming recollections
    J. Stoddard Johnston Notes
    Naval History Society collection
        James H. Rochelle
    Southard Family papers
North Carolina Department of History and Archives, Raleigh, North Carolina
    Augustus Clewell papers
    Thomas F. Toon papers
    John G. Young diary
North Louisiana Historical Association Archives, Centenary College of Louisiana, Shreveport, Louisiana
    Richard Colbert letters
Tulane University, New Orleans, Louisiana
    Association of the Army of Northern Virginia papers
U.S. Army Military History Institute, Carlisle Barracks, Pennsylvania
    Civil War Miscellaneous collection
        Richard Castle papers
        James M. Gasper papers

Henry Ivins papers
George E. Kimball papers
Paul Lounsberry papers
Jacob A. Schmid papers
Anson B. Shuey papers
Civil War Times *Illustrated* collection
David B. Lang papers
Silas D. Wesson papers
Harrisburg Civil War Round Table collection
Seibert Family papers
Lewis Leigh collection
Eugene Blackford papers
Sondus W. Haskell papers
Overton Steger papers
James Sheeran diary
U.S. *Department of the Interior, National Park Service, Rock Creek Nature Center, Washington, D.C.*
Battleground National Cemetery files
Defenses of Washington files
Fort Stevens files
University of Georgia, Athens, Georgia
John B. Gordon family papers
University of North Carolina, Chapel Hill (Southern Historical Collection), Chapel Hill, North Carolina
William Allan books
William Beavans books
J. Kelly Bennette diary
Carrie E. Clack papers
James E. Green diary
William R. Gwaltney papers
Thomas Butler King papers
John Paris papers
Leonidus Lafayette Polk papers
Stephen D. Ramseur papers
W. R. Redding paper
Richard Woolfolk Waldrop papers
William Henry Wills papers
Frank E. Vandiver Private Collection, College Station, Texas
Lucius C. Chittenden, "A Chapter for My Children to Read," unpublished
    manuscript
Vermont Historical Society, Montpelier, Vermont
Aldace F. Walker letters

Virginia Historical Society, Richmond, Virginia
    Millard Bushong/Jubal A. Early papers
    District of Columbia Supreme Court, Davis and Breckinridge indictments
    Robert E. Lee Headquarters papers
    Buckner McGill Randolph diary
    Rufus Woolwine diary
Virginia State Library and Archives, Richmond, Virginia
    Joseph McMurran diary
Western Reserve Historical Society, Cleveland, Ohio
    W. H. Hayward papers

Primary Sources — Printed

Newspapers and Periodicals

Army and Navy Journal
Baltimore Sun
Frank Leslies Illustrated Newspaper
Frederick *News*
Harpers Weekly
Middletown (Maryland) *Valley Register*
Montgomery County (Maryland) *Sentinel*
Richmond *Sentinel*
Washington *Post*
Washington *Star*
Washington *Times Herald*

The National Tribune

(Veterans' Reminiscences Chronologically)

D. E. McLean (25th New York Cavalry) July 16, 1885
S. A. McDonald (122d New York) April 12, 19, 1894
R. I. Cowden (49th New York) June 7, 1894
G. S. Orr (77th New York) June 28, 1894
J. H. Wolf (25th New York Cavalry) November 9, 1899
R. R. Lord (25th New York Cavalry) February 22, 1900
R. Guyton (139th Pennsylvania) March 29, 1900
L. Blosser (151st Ohio) April 12, 1900
C. O. Welch (2d Massachusetts Cavalry) April 12, 1900
S. J. Weiler (Cavalry) April 5, 1900
J. F. Loeble (98th Pennsylvania) April 26, 1900
R. R. Lord (25th New York Cavalry) May 31, 1900

J. G. Bridaham (Cavalry) July 19, 1900

Veteran (102d Pennsylvania) August 2, 1900

A. F. Jackson (1st Maine Cavalry) August 9, 1900

A. G. Jacobs (6th Ohio Cavalry) August 23, 1900

M. B. Aldrich (6th Veteran Reserve Corps) September 20, 1900

A. C. Fletcher (1st Veteran Reserve Corps) September 27, 1900

D. H. Mangan (102d Pennsylvania) September 27, 1900

C. Porter (11th Vermont) September 27, 1900

I. A. Hawk (102d Pennsylvania) September 27, 1900

J. Commons (1st Rhode Island Cavalry) November 1, 1900

D. W. Shaw (12th Veteran Reserve Corps) August 22, 1901

W. V. Cox, March 26, 1903

Oliver Edwards, August 20, 1903

"150th Ohio," October 15, 1903

E. French (19th Veteran Reserve Corps) August 11, 1904

E. A. Fuller (77th New York) December 29, 1910

F. Filler (14th Ohio) June 1, 1911

G. M. Eichelberger (6th Maryland) June 29, 1911

D. O. Bowen (1st Maine Heavy Artillery) December 28, 1911

J. M. Singer (19th United States Infantry) February 8, 1912

J. D. Shuman (13th Michigan Battery) March 7, 1912

A. A. Safford (105th Ohio) April 4, 1912

D. H. Bee (61st Pennsylvania) April 11, 1912

J. C. Clevenger (1st New Jersey Cavalry) June 27, 1912

G. E. Farrington (3d Vermont) July 11, 1912

F. S. Morgen (Cavalry) August 1, 1912

A. G. Jacobs (6th Ohio Cavalry) August 8, 1912

C. Crowell (New Jersey) August 16, 1912

O. Pelton (VI Corps) February 27, 1913

L. Carswhite [Cass White] (102d Pennsylvania) March 6, 1913

S. R. Averill (13th Pennsylvania Cavalry) October 9, 1913

W. F. Parish (15th New Jersey) January 15, 1914

J. H. Wolff (25th New York Cavalry) January 22, 1914

B. T. Plugh (1st Wisconsin Heavy Artillery) April 23, 1914

J. A. Goulden (25th New York Cavalry) October 1, 1914

E. French (19th Veteran Reserve Corps) November 19, 1914

J. H. Smith (43d New York) April 29, 1915

G. Fernald (14th Veteran Reserve Corps) July 8, 1915

E. H. Fuller (77th New York) July 22, 1915

D. M. Wilcox (10th Massachusetts) July 29, 1915

A. Cowan (1st New York Battery) September 23, 1915

W. Langford (1st Wisconsin Heavy Artillery) September 23, 1915

W. N. Siggins (1st Veteran Reserve Corps) October 7, 1915
Comrade Peterson (Dismounted Cavalry) December 2, 1915
R. I. Smith (22d Veteran Reserve Corps) January 20, 1916
C. H. Enos (122d New York) March 23, 1916
M. Evans (147th Ohio) March 30, 1916
J. T. Metcalf (5th United States Cavalry) August 3, 1916
C. W. Armstrong (2d Pennsylvania Cavalry) October 17, 1918
W. V. Cox, June 12 and August 14, 1919
A. H. Skinner, September 11, 1919
E. Turner (2d Vermont) October 9, 1919
A. G. Jacobs (6th Ohio Cavalry) July 15, 1920
J. McElroy, July 22, 1920
D. Dibble (25th New York Cavalry) September 16, 1920
S. J. Weiler (2d Pennsylvania Cavalry) September 30, 1920
P. Soule (5th New York Cavalry) October 14, 1920
W. H. Woodburn (25th New York Cavalry) July 14, 1921
S. J. Weiler (2d Pennsylvania Cavalry) August 24, 1922
J. C. Cannon (150th Ohio) October 12, 1922
E. M. Gardner (150th Ohio) October 4, 1923
M. King (7th Maine) October 18, 1923
S. A. Smith (49th New York) December 6, 1923
W. O. Hedrick (1st Massachusetts Cavalry) December 20, 1923
A. E. Cobb (9th New York Heavy Artillery) December 27, 1923
H. A. Shisey (15th Maine) January 3, 1924
O. J. Demmon (8th Illinois Cavalry) January 17, 1924
F. S. Morgen (1st Pennsylvania Cavalry) June 12, 1924
J. H. Wolff (25th New York Cavalry) September 18, 1924
A. McIntosh (150th Ohio) July 30, 1925
C. L. Shurger (9th New York Heavy Artillery) October 15, 1925
J. Brogan (65th New York) December 31, 1925

Documents—Government

Barnard, John Gross. *Report on the Defenses of Washington.* Washington: Government Printing Office, 1871.

Maine, State of, Adjutant General's Office. *Annual Report, 1864.* Augusta: State Printer, 1865.

U.S. Congress, Fifty-Seventh, First Session, Senate Document 433. *Fort Stevens-Lincoln National Military Park,* June 26, 1902. Washington: Government Printing Office, 1902.

—————, Sixty-Eighth, Second Session, House of Representatives. Hearings before Committee on Military Affairs, *To Commemorate Battle of Fort Stevens,* January 12, 1925. Washington: Government Printing Office, 1925.

_____, Sixty-Eighth, Second Session, House of Representatives. Hearings on House Report 1537, *To Establish a National Military Park at Fort Stevens,* February 20, 1925. Washington: Government Printing Office, 1925.

_____, Seventieth, First Session, House of Representatives. Hearings before Committee on Military Affairs, *To Establish a National Military Park at Battlefield of Monocacy, Maryland,* April 13, 1928. Washington: Government Printing Office, 1928.

U.S. Navy Department. *Official Records of the Union and Confederate Navies in the War of the Rebellion.* Washington: Government Printing Office, 1894–1927. 30 volumes.

U.S. War Department. *War of the Rebellion: A Compilation of the Official Records of the Union and Confederate Armies.* Washington: Government Printing Office, 1880–1901, 128 volumes and atlas.

Documents—Other

Basler, Roy P., editor. *The Collected Works of Abraham Lincoln.* New Brunswick: Rutgers University Press, 1953.

Dowdey, Clifford and Louis H. Manarin, editors. *The Wartime Papers of R. E. Lee.* New York: Bramhall House for Virginia Civil War Commission, 1966.

Dowdey, Clifford, editor. *The Wartime Papers of R. E. Lee.* Boston: Little, Brown, and Company, 1961.

Dyer, Frederick H. *A Compendium of the War of the Rebellion.* New York: Thomas Yoseloff, 1959 edition. 3 volumes.

Freeman, Douglas Southall. *Lee's Dispatches: Unpublished Letters of General Robert E. Lee to Jefferson Davis and the War Department of the Confederate States of America 1862–1865.* New York: G.P. Putnam's Sons, 1957.

Simon, John Y., editor. *The Papers of Ulysses S. Grant.* Carbondale, Illinois: Southern Illinois University Press, 1967– . 15 volumes.

Illustrated Works

Guerney, Alfred H. and Henry M. Alden. *Harper's Pictorial History of the Great Rebellion.* Chicago: McDonnell Brothers, 1866. 2 volumes.

Moat, Louis S., editor. *Frank Leslie's Illustrated History of the Civil War.* New York: Mrs. Frank Leslie, 1895.

Mottelay, Paul F. and T. Campbell-Copeland, editors. *The Soldier in Our Civil War.* New York: Stanley Bradley, 1885. 2 volumes.

Memoirs, Diaries, Reminiscences—Civilian

Bates, David Homer. *Lincoln in the Telegraph Office: Recollections of the United States Military Telegraph Corps During the Civil War.* New York: Century Company, 1907.

Beale, Howard K., editor. *The Diary of Edward Bates, 1859–1866.* New York: De Capo Press, 1971 edition.

Beauchamp, Virginia Walcott, editor. *A Private War: Letters and Diaries of Madge Preston, 1862–1867.* New Brunswick: Rutgers University Press, 1987.

Brooks, Noah (Herbert Mitgang, editor). *Washington D.C. in Lincoln's Time.* Chicago: Quandrangle, 1971 edition.

Carpenter, F. B. *Six Months at the White House with Abraham Lincoln; The Story of a Picture.* New York: Hurd and Houghton, 1867.

Chittenden, Lucius E. *Recollections of President Lincoln and His Administration.* New York: Harper and Brothers, 1891.

Dana, Charles A. *Recollections of the Civil War; With the Leaders at Washington and in the Field in the Sixties.* New York: D. Appleton and Company, 1898.

Dennett, Tyler. *Lincoln and the Civil War in the Diaries and Letters of John Hay.* New York: Dodd, Mead and Company, 1939.

Doster, William E. *Lincoln and Episodes of the Civil War.* New York: G.P. Putnam's Sons, 1915.

Emerson, Edward W. *Life and Letters of Charles Russell Lowell.* Boston: Houghton Mifflin and Company, 1907.

Marks, Bayly Ellen and Mark Norten Schatz, editors. *Between North and South: A Maryland Journalist Views the Civil War; The Narrative of William Wilkens Glenn, 1861–1869.* Rutherford, N.J.: Fairleigh Dickinson University Press, 1976.

Moore, Virginia Campbell. "Remembrances of Life Along the Rockville Pike During the Civil War," *The Montgomery County Story,* Volume 27, Number 4 (November 1984), 127–142.

Poore, Ben Perley. *Perley's Reminiscences.* Philadelphia: Hubbard Brothers, 1886. 2 volumes.

Quinn, William R., editor. *The Diary of Jacob Engelbrecht.* Frederick, Md.: Frederick County Historical Society, 1976.

Riddle, Albert Gallatin. *Recollections of War Time: Reminiscences of Men and Events in Washington, 1860–1865.* New York: G.P. Putnam's Sons, 1895.

Seward, Frederick W. *Reminiscences of a War-time Statesman and Diplomat, 1830–1915.* New York: G.P. Putnam's Sons, 1916.

Staudenraus, P. J., editor. *Mr. Lincoln's Washington: Selections From the Writings of Noah Brooks, Civil War Correspondent.* South Brunswick: Thomas Yoseloff, 1967.

Stearns, Amanda Akin. *The Lady Nurse of Ward E.* New York: Baker and Taylor, 1909.

Tuckerman, Charles K. *Personal Recollections of Notable People.* New York: Dodd Mead and Company, 1895. 2 volumes.

Welles, Gideon. *Diary.* Boston: Houghton Mifflin, 1911. 2 volumes.

Memoirs, Diaries, Reminiscences—Confederate Military

"An Old Comrade," *A Sketch of the Life and Services of Major John A. Harman, Chief Quartermaster.* Staunton, Va.: "Spectator" Job Print, March 1876.

Barnett, Hoyt. "Recalls Gen. Early's Raid," Washington *Post*, July 14, 1935, 47.

Booth, George Wilson. *Personal Reminiscences of a Maryland Soldier in the War Between the States*. Baltimore: By Private Circulation, 1898.

Bradwell, I. G. "Early's Demonstration Against Washington in 1864," *Confederate Veteran*, XXII, Number 10 (October 1914), 438–439.

_____ . "Early's March to Washington in 1864," *Confederate Veteran*, XXVIII, XXVIII Number 5, (May 1920), 176–177.

_____ . "In the Battle of Monocacy, Md.," *Confederate Veteran*, XXXVI, Number 2 (February 1928), 55–57.

_____ . "On to Washington," *Confederate Veteran*, XXXVI, Number 3 (March 1928), 95–96.

_____ ."The Battle of Monocacy, Md.," *Confederate Veteran*, XXXVII, Number 10 (October 1929), 382–383.

Casler, John O. *Four Years in the Stonewall Brigade*. Girard, Kansas: Appeal-Publishing Company, 1906, and Dayton, Ohio: Morningside Bookshop, 1971 edition.

Coffman, J. W. "Burning of the Blair House," *Confederate Veteran*, XIV, Number 7 (July 1911), 336.

Crenshaw, Edward. "Diary of Captain Edward Crenshaw," *Alabama Historical Quarterly* (1930), 449–450.

Daniel, John W. "General Jubal A. Early," *Southern Historical Society Papers*, XXII (1894), 281–340.

Douglas, Henry Kyd. *I Rode With Stonewall*. Chapel Hill: University of North Carolina Press, 1940.

Durkin, Joseph T., editor. *Confederate Chaplain; A War Journal of Rev. James B. Sheeran, c.ss.r., Fourteenth Louisiana, C.S.A.* Milwaukee: Bruce Publishing Company, 1960.

Early, Jubal A. "The Advance on Washington in 1864," *Southern Historical Society Papers*, 9, Numbers 7 and 8 (July/August 1881), 297–312.

_____ . *Autobiographical Sketch and Narrative of the War Between the States*. Philadelphia: J.B. Lippincott, 1912.

_____ . *A Memoir of the Last Year of the War For Independence, in the Confederate States of America, Containing an Account of the Operations of His Commands in the Years 1864 and 1865*. Lynchburg, Va.: C.W. Button, 1867.

_____ . "Early's March to Washington in 1864," in Robert Underwood Johnson and Clarence Clough Buel, editors. *Battles and Leaders of the Civil War*. New York: Century Company, 1884. 4 volumes.

_____ . (Frank Vandiver, editor). *War Memoirs*. Bloomington: Indiana University Press, 1960.

Gilmor, Harry. *Four Years in the Saddle*. New York: Harper and Brothers, 1866.

Gipson, Moses. "Valley Campaign of General Early," *Southern Historical Society Papers*, 34 (1906), 212–217.

Gordon, John B. *Reminiscences of the Civil War*. New York: Charles Scribners, 1904.

Hunter, Alexander. *Johnny Reb and Billy Yank.* New York and Washington: Neale, 1905.

Hutcheson, James A. "Saved the Day at Monocacy," *Confederate Veteran*, XXIII, Number 2 (February 1915), 77.

Johnson, Bradley T. "My Ride Around Baltimore in 1864," *Journal of the United States Cavalry Association*, II, Number 6 (September 1889), 250–260.

Long, Armistead Lindsay. *Memoirs of Robert E. Lee.* New York: J.M. Stoddart and Company, 1886.

McDonald, Archie P., editor. *Make Me a Map of the Valley; The Civil War Journal of Stonewall Jackson's Topographer.* Dallas: Southern Methodist University Press, 1973.

Mettam, Henry C. "Civil War Memoirs: First Maryland Cavalry, C.S.A.," *Maryland Historical Magazine*, 58, Number 2 (June 1963), 139–170.

Opie, John N. *A Rebel Cavalryman with Lee, Stuart, and Jackson.* Chicago: W.B. Conkey, 1899.

Park, Robert E. "Diary," *Southern Historical Society Papers*, I (1876), 370–386.

Rich, Edward R. *Comrades Four.* New York: Neale, 1907.

Runge, William H., editor. *Four Years in the Confederate Artillery; The Diary of Private Henry Robinson Berkeley.* Chapel Hill: University of North Carolina Press, 1961.

Scott, W. W., editor. "Diary of Captain H.W. Wingfield," *Bulletin of the Virginia State Library*, XVI, Numbers 2 and 3 (July 1927).

Taylor, Walter H. *Four Years With General Lee.* New York: D. Appleton, 1878.

Worsham, John H. *One of Jackson's Foot Cavalry; His Experience and What He Saw During the War 1861–1865.* New York: Neale, 1912, and Jackson Tennessee: McCowat-Mercer Press, 1964.

Memoirs, Diaries, Reminiscences—Union Military

Abbott, Samuel A. *Personal Recollections and Civil War Diary, 1864.* Burlington, Vt.: Free Press, 1908.

Alvord, Henry E. "Early's Attack Upon Washington, July 1864," in Military Order of the Loyal Legion of the United States, District of Columbia Commandery, *War Papers Number 26*, April 1897, 3–32.

Armes, George A. *Ups and Downs of an Army Officer.* Washington: McGill and Wallace, 1900.

Beamish, A. B. "Battle of Fort Stephens [sic] Near Washington, D.C. July 12, 1864, A Little Different Version," *Grand Army Scout and Soldiers Mail* (Philadelphia) Saturday, July 10, 1886.

——————. "The Attempted Capture of Washington," *Veteran's Advocate* (Concord, NH), June 15, 1886.

Blanding, Stephen F. *In the Defense of Washington or Sunshine in a Soldier's Life.* Providence: Freeman, 1889.

Brinton, John H. *Personal Memoirs of John H. Brinton, Major and Surgeon, U.S.V.* New York: Neale, 1914.

Buell, Augustus. *The Cannoneer: Recollections of Service in the Army of the Potomac by a Detached Volunteer.* Washington: National Tribune, 1890.

Cadwallader, Sylvanus. (Benjamin P. Thomas, editor). *Three Years with Grant.* New York: Alfred A. Knopf, 1955.

Clark, Roderick A. (Corporal Company F, Fourteenth New Jersey). "Reminiscences," *National Tribune*, April 15, 1886.

Croffut, W. A., editor. *Fifty Years in Camp and Field: Diary of Major General Ethan Allen Hitchcock.* New York: G.P. Putnam's Sons, 1909.

Dix, Morgan, compiler. *Memoirs of John Dix.* New York: Harper and Brothers, 1883. 2 volumes.

Dudley, Edgar S. "A Reminiscence of Washington and Early's Attack in 1864," in Military Order of the Loyal Legion of the United States, Ohio Commandery, *Sketches of War History 1861–1865.* Cincinnati: Robert Clarke and Company, 1888, I, 107–127.

Freeman, Daniel B. (Company G, Tenth Vermont), "A Day's Skirmish," *National Tribune*, March 18, 1897.

Gobin, John Peter Shindel. "Lincoln Under Fire," in Military Order of the Loyal Legion of the United States, Commandery of Pennsylvania, *Abraham Lincoln Memorial Meeting, February 13, 1907.* Philadelphia: n.p., 1907, 13–15.

Grant, Ulysses S. *Personal Memoirs.* New York: Charles L. Webster, 1885. 2 volumes.

Hamblin, Deborah, compiler. *Brevet Major General Joseph Eldridge Hamblin.* Boston: Privately printed, 1902.

Hardin, Martin D. "The Defence of Washington Against Early's Attack in July, 1864," in Military Order of the Loyal Legion of the United States, Illinois Commandery. *Military Essays and Recollections.* Chicago: A.C. McClurg and Company, 1894, 121-144.

Hyde, Thomas W. *Following the Greek Cross.* Boston: Houghton Mifflin, 1895.

James, William H. "Blue and Gray I; A Baltimore Volunteer of 1864," *Maryland Historical Magazine*, XXXVI, Number 1 (March 1941), 22-33.

Jenkins, Albert F. "Letter, June 12, 1893," *First Maine Bugle, Campaign III, Call 3* (July 1893), 97.

Kitching, John B. *"More Than Conqueror," or Memorials of Col. J. Howard Kitching.* New York: Hurd and Houghton, 1873.

McDougle, W. T. (Company K, One Hundred and Twenty-Sixth Ohio). "Account of Monocacy," *National Tribune*, February 21, 1884.

O'Ferrall, Charles T. *Forty Years of Active Service.* New York: Neale, 1904.

Perkins, George. *A Summer in Maryland and Virginia or Campaigning with the One Hundred and Forty-Ninth Ohio Volunteer Infantry.* Chillicothe: School Printing Company, 1911.

Porter, Horace. *Campaigning with Grant.* New York: Century Company, 1906.

Putnam, George Haven. *Memories of My Youth, 1844-1865*. New York: G.P. Putnam's Sons, 1914.

Robertson, Peter (One Hundred and Sixth New York). "Monocacy and the Gallant Stand of the One Hundred and Sixth New York," *National Tribune*, January 24, 1884.

Rosenblatt, Emil. *Anti-Rebel: The Civil War Letters of Wilbur Fisk*. Croton-on-Hudson: By Author, 1983.

Shaw, William H. *A Diary as Kept by William H. Shaw during the Great Civil War from April 1861 to July 1865*. N.P., n.d.

Smith, Samuel C. "Detailed from Dismounted Camp," First Maine Bugle, *Campaign III, Call 3* (July 1893), 24-27.

Stevens, George T. *Three Years in the Sixth Corps: A Concise Narrative of Events in the Army of the Potomac from 1861 to the Close of the Rebellion, April, 1865*. New York: D. Van Nostrand, 1870.

Stewart, Alexander Morrison. *Camp, March and Battle-field or Three Years and a Half with the Army of the Potomac*. Philadelphia: James B. Rodgers, 1865.

Taylor, Benjamin Franklin. *Pictures of Life in Camp and Field*. Chicago: S.C. Griggs, 1875

Tyler, Mason Whiting (Wiliam S. Tyler, editor). *Recollections of the Civil War with Many Original Diary Entries and Letters Written from the Seat of War and with Annotated References*. New York: G.P. Putnam's Sons, 1912.

Wallace, Lew. *Lew Wallace; An Autobiography*. New York: Harper and Brothers, 1906). 2 volumes.

Warner, Lucier Calvin. *The Story of My Life During Seventy Eventful Years, 1841-1911*. New York: Privately printed, 1914.

Wilkenson, Frank. *Recollections of a Private Soldier in the Army of the Potomac*. New York: G. P. Putnam's Sons, 1898.

Unit Histories—Confederate

Bartlett, Napier. *Military Record of Louisiana*. New Orleans: L. Graham and Company, 1875 and Baton Rouge: Louisiana State University Press, 1964 edition.

Clark, Walter E., editor. *Histories of the Several Regiments and Battalions from North Carolina in the Great War 1861–1865*. Raleigh: E.M. Uzell, 1901. 5 volumes.

Delauter, Jr., Roger V. *Sixty-Second Virginia Infantry* [Virginia Regimental Series]. Lynchburg: M.E. Howard, Inc., 1988.

Fonerden, C.A. *A Brief History of the Military Career of Carpenter's Battery*. New Market, Va.: Henkel and Company, 1911.

Goldsborough, W. W. *The Maryland Line in the Confederate Army, 1861–1865*. Baltimore, Md.: Kelly, Piet and Company, 1869 and Guggenheimer, Weil and Company, 1900.

Iobst, Richard W. and Louis H. Manarin. *The Bloody Sixth; The Sixth North Carolina Regiment Confederate States of America.* Raleigh: North Carolina Confederate Centennial Commission, 1965.

Jones, Terry L. *Lee's Tigers; The Louisiana Infantry in the Army of Northern Virginia.* Baton Rouge: Louisiana State University Press, 1987.

Kenan, Thomas S., compiler. *Sketch of the Forty-Third Regiment North Carolina Troops (Infantry).* Raleigh: n.p., 1895.

Murray, Allan J. *South Georgia Rebels; The True Wartime Experiences of the Twenty-Sixth Regiment Georgia Volunteer Infantry, Lawton-Gordon-Evans Brigade, Confederate States Army 1861–1865.* St. Mary's Ga.: By Author, 1976.

Nichols, G. W. *A Soldier's Story of His Regiment (Sixty-First Georgia) and Incidentally of the Lawton-Gordon-Evans Brigade Army of Northern Virginia.* n.p., 1898 and Kennesaw, Ga.: Continental Book Company, 1961 edition.

Park, Robert E. "The Twelfth Alabama Infantry, Confederate States Army," *Southern Historical Society Papers,* 33 (1905), 193–296.

Robertson, James I. *The Stonewall Brigade.* Baton Rouge: Louisiana State University Press, 1963.

Smith, W. A. *The Anson Guards; Company C, Fourteenth Regiment North Carolina Volunteers 1861–1865.* Charlotte: Stone Publishing Company, 1914.

Stegeman, John F. *These Men She Gave; Civil War Diary of Athens, Georgia.* Athens: University of Georgia Press, 1964.

United Daughters of the Confederacy, Georgia Divison, Oglethorpe County Chapter 1292, Lexington. *This They Remembered; The History of the Four Companies . . . Who Went from Oglethorpe County to Serve in the War Between the States.* Washington, Ga.: Washington Publishing Company, 1965.

Wallace, Lee A., Jr. *Fifth Virginia Infantry* [Virginia Regimental Series]. Lynchburg: H.E. Howard, Inc., 1988.

Wellman, Manly Wade. *Rebel Boast: First at Bethel—Last at Appomattox.* New York: Henry Holt, 1956.

Unit Histories — Union

Beach, William Harrison. *The First New York (Lincoln) Cavalry, from April 19, 1861 to July 7, 1865.* New York: Lincoln Cavalry Association, 1902.

Beecher, Harris H. *Record of the One Hundred and Fourteenth Regiment, N.Y.S.V.* Norwich: J. F. Hubbard, Jr., 1866.

Benedict, George Grenville. *Vermont in the Civil War.* Burlington: Free Press Association, 1888. 2 volumes.

Bidwell, Frederick David, compiler. *History of the Forty-Ninth New York Volunteers.* Albany: J.B. Lyon, 1916.

Bowen, James L. *History of the Thirty-Seventh Regiment, Massachusetts Volunteers in the Civil War of 1861–1865.* Holyoke: Clark W. Bryan and Company, 1884.

Brewer, Abraham T. *History of the Sixty-First Regiment Pennsylvania Volunteers, 1861–1865.* Pittsburgh: Art Engraving and Printing Company, 1911.

Brown, J. Willard. *The Signal Corps, U.S.A. in the War of the Rebellion.* Boston: U.S. Veteran Signal Corps Association, 1896.

Cannon, James Cannon. *Memorial, One Hundred and Fiftieth Ohio, Company K.* n.p., 1907.

——————. *Record of Service of Company J, One Hundred and Fiftieth O.V.I., 1864.* n.p., 1903.

Carpenter, George N. *History of the Eighth Regiment Vermont Volunteers, 1861–1865.* Boston: Press of Deland and Barta, 1886.

Clark, Lewis H. *Military History of Wayne County, N.Y.; The County in the Civil War.* Sodus, N.Y.: Lewis H. Clark, Hulett and Gaylord, 1881. [Ninth New York Heavy Artillery].

Farrar, Samuel Clarke. *The Twenty-Second Pennsylvania Cavalry and the Ringgold Battalion 1861–1865.* Pittsburgh: Twenty-Second Pennsylvania Ringgold Cavalry Association, 1911.

Gleason, William J. *Historical Sketch of the One Hundred and Fiftieth Regiment Ohio Volunteer Infantry: Roster of the Regiment.* n.p., 1899.

Haines, Alanson A. *History of the Fifteenth Regiment New Jersey Volunteers.* New York: Jenkins and Thomas Printers, 1883.

Hard, Abner. *History of the Eighth Cavalry Regiment Illinois Volunteers During the Great Rebellion.* Aurora, Ill. By Author, 1868.

Haynes, Edwin M. *History of the Tenth Vermont.* Rutland: Tuttle, 1894.

Irwin, Richard B. *History of the Nineteenth Army Corps.* New York: G. P. Putnam's Sons, 1893.

Lewis, Osceola. *History of the One Hundred and Thirty-Eighth Pennsylvania.* Norristown: Wills, Tredell and Jenkins, 1866.

Mark, Penrose G. *Red, White, and Blue Badge, Pennsylvania Veteran Volunteers, A History of the Ninety-Third Regiment.* Harrisburg: Aughinbaugh, 1911.

Nash, Eugene Arus. *A History of the Forty-Fourth New York Volunteer Infantry in the Civil War, 1861–1865.* Chicago: R.R. Donnelley and Sons, 1911.

Newcomer, C. Armour. *Cole's Cavalry; or Three Years in the Saddle in the Shenandoah Valley.* Baltimore: Cushing and Company, 1895.

Niebaum, John H. *History of the Pittsburgh Washington Infantry: One Hundred and Second (Old Thirteenth) Regiment Pennsylvania Veteran Volunteers, and Its Forebears.* Pittsburgh: Burgum Printing Company, 1931.

Pellet, Elias Porter. *History of the One Hundred and Fourteenth Regiment New York State Volunteers.* Norwich: Telegraph and Chronicle Power Press Printers, 1866.

Prowell, George R. *History of the Eighty-Seventh Regiment, Pennsylvania Volunteers.* York: Press of the York Daily, 1901.

Roe, Alfred Seelye. *History of the Ninth New York Heavy Artillery.* Worchester, Mass.: By Author, 1899.

Schilling, T. C. and M. C. Peirce. *Roster of the One Hundred and Forty-Seventh Ohio Volunteer Infantry with Age at Enlistment, Post Office Address and Deaths as Far as Could be Ascertained.* West Milton, Ohio: Radabaugh Brothers Printers, 1913.

Shaw, Horace and Charles J. House. *The First Maine Heavy Artillery.* Portland: Privately published, 1903.

Smith, A. P. *History of the Seventy-Sixth New York Volunteers.* Cortland: Privately published, 1867.

Swinfen, David B. *Ruggles' Regiment: The One Hundred and Twenty-Second New York Volunteers in the American Civil War.* Hanover and London: University Press of New England, 1982.

Terrill, J. Newton. *Campaigns of the Fourteenth Regiment New Jersey Volunteers.* New Brunswick: Daily Home News Press, 1884.

Twenty Third Pennsylvania Regiment Survivors Association. *History of the Twenty-Third Regiment Pennsylvania Volunteer Infantry.* Philadelphia, n.p., 1904.

Vaill, Theodore F. *History of the Second Connecticut Volunteer Heavy Artillery.* Winsted, Conn.: Winsted Printing Company, 1868.

Walker, Aldace F. *The Vermont Brigade in the Shenandoah Valley, 1864.* Burlington: The Free Press Association, 1869.

Walker, William C. *History of the Eighteenth Regiment Connecticut Volunteers in the War of the Rebellion.* Norwich: Regimental Committee, 1885.

Ward, George W. *History of the Second Pennsylvania Heavy Artillery.* Philadelphia: By Author, 1904.

Wild, Frederick W. *Memoirs and History of Captain F. W. Alexander's Baltimore Battery of Light Artillery.* Baltimore: Press of the Maryland School for Boys, 1912.

Woodbury, Augustus. *The Second Rhode Island: A Narrative of Military Operations.* Providence: Valpey, Angell and Company, 1875.

Secondary Sources—Books

Adams, F. Colburn. *Siege of Washington, D.C. Written Expressly For Little People.* New York: Dick and Fitzgerald, 1867.

Alexander, Theodore, et al., editors. *Southern Revenge: Civil War History of Cham-*

bersburg, Pennsylvania. Shippensburg, Pa.: White Mane Publishing Co. for Greater Chambersburg Chamber of Commerce, 1989.

Ambrose, Stephen E. *Halleck: Lincoln's Chief of Staff*. Baton Rouge: Louisiana State University Press, 1962.

Andrews, J. Cutler. *The North Reports the Civil War*. Pittsburgh: University of Pittsburgh Press, 1955.

_____ . *The South Reports the Civil War*. Princeton: Princeton University Press, 1970.

Ballard, Colin R. *The Military Genius of Abraham Lincoln*. Cleveland and New York: World, 1952.

Bean, W. G. *Stonewall's Man; Sandie Pendleton*. Wilmington: Broadfoot Publishing Company, 1987.

Beitzell, Edwin W. *Point Lookout Prison Camp for Confederates*. Abell, Md.: By Author, 1972.

Bok, Edward W. *The Americanization of Edward Bok*. New York: C. Scribner's Sons, 1920.

Brown, Lenard E. *Forts De Russy, Stevens, and Totten; General Background*. Washington: National Park Service, February 1968.

Bushong, Millard K. *Old Jube: A Biography of General Jubal A. Early*. Boyce, Va.: Carr Publishing Company, 1955.

Catton, Bruce. *Never Call Retreat* [Centennial History of the Civil War]. Garden City: Doubleday, 1965.

Coker, Brad. *The Battle of Monocacy* [Honors Monograph Series, College of Liberal Arts, University of Baltimore]. Baltimore: University of Baltimore, 1982.

Cooling, Benjamin Franklin and Walton H. Owen. *Mr. Lincoln's Forts; A Guide to the Civil War Defenses of Washington*. Shippensburg, Pa.: White Mane Publishing Company, 1988.

_____ . *Symbol, Sword and Shield; Defending Washington During the Civil War*. Hamden, Ct.: Archon, 1975.

Cramer, John Henry. *Lincoln Under Enemy Fire: The Complete Account of His Experience During Early's Attack on Washington*. Baton Rouge: Louisiana State University Press, 1948.

Davidson, Isobel. *Real Stories from Baltimore County History*. Hatbbro, Pa.: Tradition Press, 1967.

Davis, William C. *Breckinridge; Statesman, Soldier, Symbol*. Baton Rouge: Louisiana State University Press, 1974.

Denison, George T. *Modern Cavalry*. London: Bosworth, 1868.

District of Columbia, National Guard, Engineer Platoon of the Engineer Corps. *Guide to and Maps of the National Capital including the Fortifications*. Washington: F.L. Averill, 1892.

Farquhar, Roger Brooke. *Historical Montgomery County, Maryland—Old Homes and History*. Baltimore: Monumental Printing Company, 1952.

Farquhar, W. H. *Annals of Sandy Spring or Twenty Years History of a Rural County in Maryland.* Baltimore: Cashings and Bailey, 1884. 2 volumes.

Federal Writers' Project, Works Progress Administration. *Washington City and Capital* [American Guide Series]. Washington: Government Printing Office, 1937.

Freeman, Douglas Southall. *Lee's Lieutenants; A Study in Command.* New York: Charles Scribners, 1950. 3 volumes.

_____. *R. E. Lee: A Biography.* New York: Charles Scribners, 1935. 4 volumes.

Gallagher, Gary W. *Stephen Dodson Ramseur, Lee's Gallant General.* Chapel Hill: University of North Carolina Press, 1985.

Getty, Mildred Newbold. *Grace Episcopal Church, 1857–1957.* Silver Spring: Privately published, 1957.

Goldsborough, E. Y. *Early's Great Raid . . . Battle of Monocacy.* n.p., 1898 and Frederick, Md.: The Historical Society of Frederick County, 1989.

Goode, Paul R. *The United States Soldiers' Home; A History of Its First Hundred Years.* Richmond: William Byrd Press, 1957.

Hagerman, Edward. *The American Civil War and the Origins of Modern Warfare.* Bloomington: Indiana University Press, 1988.

Hale, Laura Virginia. *Four Valiant Years in the Lower Shenandoah Valley, 1861–1865.* Strasburg, Va.: Shenandoah Publishing House, 1968.

Haley, William D., editor. *Philip's Washington Described; A Complete View of the American Capital, and the District of Columbia.* New York: Rudd and Carleton, 1861.

Helm, Judith Reck. *Tenleytown, D.C.; Country Village into City Neighborhood.* Washington: Tennally Press, 1981.

Hibben, Henry B. *History of the Washington Navy Yard 1799–1889.* Washington: Government Printing Office, 1890.

Holman, Doree Germaine and Gertrude D. Bradley. *Old Bethesda—Bethesda Not So Old.* Gaithersburg: Franklin Press, ?????

Jones, Virgil Carrington. *Ranger Mosby.* Chapel Hill: University of North Carolina Press, 1944.

Klein, Frederick Shriver, editor. *Just South of Gettysburg: Carroll County, Maryland in the Civil War.* Westminster, Md.: Carroll County Historical Society, 1963.

Lee, Richard M. *Mr. Lincoln's City; An Illustrated Guide to the Civil War Sites of Washington.* McLean, Va.: BPM Publications, 1981.

Leech, Margaret. *Reveille in Washington 1860–1865.* New York: Harper and Brothers, 1941.

Lewis, Thomas A. *The Guns of Cedar Creek.* New York: Harper and Row, 1988.

_____, and the editors of Time-Life Books, *The Shenandoah in Flames; The Valley Campaign of 1864.* Alexandria, Va.: Time-Life Books, 1987.

Manakee, Harold R. *Maryland in the Civil War.* Baltimore: Maryland Historical Society, 1961.

Maurice, Frederick. *Robert E. Lee: The Soldier.* Boston: Houghton, Mifflin, 1925.

McClure, Stanley. *Guide Leaflet to the Defenses of Washington.* Washington: National Park Service, 1956.

McKee, Irving. *"Ben-Hur" Wallace; The Life of General Lew Wallace*. Berkeley: University of California Press, 1947.

Meaney, Peter J. *The Civil War Engagement at Cool Spring, July 18, 1864*. Berryville, Va.: Privately printed, c. 1980.

Michel, Robert E. *Colonel Harry Gilmor's Raid Around Baltimore*. Baltimore: Erbe Publishers, 1976.

Miller, David V. *The Defenses of Washington During the Civil War*. Buffalo, N.Y.: By Author, 1976.

Mitchell, Mary. *Divided Town; A Study of Georgetown, D.C. During the Civil War*. Barre, Mass.: Barre Publishers, 1968.

Morris, George S. and Susan L. Foutz. *Lynchburg in the Civil War, The City—The People—The Battle*. [Virginia Civil War Battles and Leaders Series] Lynchburg: H.E. Howard, Inc., 1984.

Nevins, Allan. *The War for the Union*. New York: Charles Scribner's Sons, 1971. 3 volumes.

Newman, Harry Wright. *Maryland and the Confederacy*. Annapolis: By Author, 1976.

Nicolay, John G. *A Short Life of Abraham Lincoln*. New York: Century, 1907.

_____, and John Hay. *Abraham Lincoln: A History*. New York: Century, 1904. 10 volumes.

Plank, Will. *Banners and Bugles: A Record of Ulster County, New York and the Mid-Hudson Region in the Civil War*. Marlborough, N.Y.: Centennial Press, 1963.

Plum, William R. *The Military Telegraph During the Civil War in the United States*. Chicago: Jansen, McClurg, and Company, 1882. 2 volumes.

Pond, George F. *The Shenandoah Valley in the Civil War*. [Scribner's Campaigns of the Civil War] New York: Charles Scribner's Sons, 1883.

Proctor, John Clagett. *Washington, Past and Present*. New York: Lewis Historical Publishing Company, 1930. 4 volumes.

Randall, Ruth Painter. *Mary Lincoln: A Biography of a Marriage*. Boston: Little, Brown, 1953.

Reid, Whitelaw. *Ohio in the War: Her Statesmen, Her Generals, and Soldiers*. Cincinnati: Moore, Wilstach, and Baldwin, 1868. 2 volumes.

Scharf, J. Thomas. *History of Baltimore City and County*. Philadelphia: Louis H. Everts, 1881.

_____. *History of Western Maryland: Being A History of Montgomery, Carroll, Washington, Allegheny, and Garrett Counties*. Philadelphia: Louis H. Everts, 1882 and Baltimore: Regional Publishing Company, 1968 edition. 2 volumes.

Shingleton, Royce Gordon. *John Tyler Wood, Sea Ghost of the Confederacy*. Athens, Ga.: University of Georgia Press, 1979.

Sluby, Paul E., Sr., compiler. (Stanton L. Wormley, editor). *Civil War Cemeteries of the District of Columbia Metropolitan Area*. Washington: Columbian Harmony Society, c. 1982.

Smith, Elbert B. *Francis Preston Blair*. New York: Free Press, 1980.

Smith, Fred. *Samuel Duncan Oliphant: The Indomitable Campaigner.* New York: Exposition Press, 1967.

Stackpole, Edward J. *Sheridan in the Shenandoah; Jubal Early's Nemesis.* Harrisburg: The Stackpole Company, 1961.

Stepp, John W., compiler and editor, with I. William Hill. *Mirror of the War; The Washington Star Reports the Civil War.* New York: Castle Books, Inc. for The Evening Star Newspaper Company, 1961.

Strode, Hudson. *Jefferson Davis: Tragic Hero; The Last Twenty-Five Years 1864–1889.* New York: Harcourt, Grace, and World, 1964.

Todd, Charles Burr. *The Story of Washington.* New York: G.P. Putnam's and Sons, 1887.

Toomey, Daniel Carroll. *The Civil War in Maryland.* Baltimore: Toomey Press, 1983.

Vandiver, Frank. *Jubal's Raid; General Early's Famous Attack on Washington in 1864.* New York: McGraw-Hill, 1960.

U.S. Department of the Army. *The Medal of Honor.* Washington: Government Printing Office, 1948.

Warner, Ezra J. *Generals in Blue; Lives of the Union Commanders.* Baton Rouge: Louisiana State University Press, 1964.

_____ . *Generals in Gray; Lives of the Confederate Commanders.* Baton Rouge: Louisiana State University Press, 1959.

Weigley, Russel F. *Quartermaster General of the Union Army: A Biography of M. C. Meigs.* New York: Columbia University Press, 1959.

Wert, Jeffrey D. *From Winchester to Cedar Creek: The Shenandoah Valley Campaign of 1864.* Carlisle, Pa.: Mountain Press, 1987.

Whitmore, Nancy F. and Timothy L. Cannon. *Frederick: A Pictorial History.* Norfolk: Donning and Company, 1981.

Williams, T. J. C. and Folger McKinsey et. al. *History of Frederick County, Maryland.* Baltimore: L.R. Titsworth, 1910 and Regional Publishing Company, 1967 edition. 2 volumes.

Worthington, Glenn H. *Fighting For Time or the Battle That Saved Washington and Mayhap the Union.* Frederick: Frederick County Historical Society, 1932 and Shippensburg, Pa.: Beidel Printing House, 1985.

Secondary Sources — Articles

Abbot, Henry L. "Biographical Memoir of John Gross Barnard," in *Professional Members; Corps of Engineers United States Army, and Engineer Department at Large,* V (January–December 1913), 83–90.

Carey, Richard. "When Gilmor Threatened Baltimore," Baltimore *Sun*, December 1, 1929.

Cohen, Roger S., Jr. "The Defenses of Washington Located in Montgomery County During the Civil War," *The Montgomery County Story,* IV (February 1961), Number 2, 1–4.

Conradis, Albert E. "The Battle of Monocacy; The Battle That Saved Washington From Capture," in Frederick County Civil War Centennial, Inc. *To Commemorate the One Hundredth Anniversary of the Battle of Monocacy, "The Battle That Saved Washington."* Frederick: Frederick Civil War Centennial Inc., 1964, 8–60.

Cooling, Benjamin Franklin. "Civil War Deterrent: The Defenses of Washington," *Military Affairs*, XXIX (Winter 1966), Number 4, 164–178.

Cowen, Benjamin R. "The One Hundred Days Men of Ohio," in W. H. Chamberlin et al., editors. Military of the Loyal Legion of the United States, Ohio Commandery, *Sketches of War History 1861–1865*. Cincinnati: Robert Clarke Company, 1903, V, 361–383.

Cox, William V. "The Defenses of Washington: General Early's Advance on the Capital and the Battle of Fort Stevens, July 11 and 12, 1864," *Records of the Columbia Historical Society*, IV (1901), 1–31.

_____ . "Fort Stevens, Where Lincoln Was Under Fire," in Marcus Benjamin, compiler and editor. *Washington During War Time; A Series of Papers Showing the Military, Political, and Social Phases During 1861 to 1865*. Washington: Byron S. Adams, 1902, 53–70.

Decker, Harry L. "Pendleton, Artillery Genius Under Lee, Was Pastor of All Saints Church Here," in Frederick County Civil War Centennial, Inc. *To Commemorate the One Hundredth Anniversary of the Battle of Monocacy, "The Battle That Saved Washington."* Frederick: Frederick Civil War Centennial Inc., 1964, 56–60.

Delaplaine, Edward S. "General Early's Levy on Frederick," in Frederick County Civil War Centennial, Inc. *To Commemorate the One Hundredth Anniversary of the Battle of Monocacy, "The Battle That Saved Washington."* Frederick: Frederick Civil War Centennial Inc., 1964, 42–55.

Duncan, Richard R. "Maryland's Reaction to Early's Raid in 1864: A Summer of Bitterness," *Maryland Historical Magazine*, 64, (Fall 1969), Number 3, 248–279.

Engelman, Robert. "Fellowship of the Rings," Washington *Post*, June 25, 1989.

Getty, Mildred Newbold. "The Silver Spring Area, Part I," *The Montgomery County Story*, XII, Number 1 (November 1968), 1–8.

Grabenstein, Joseph. "History Is Just a Hike Away," *St. John's* [High School] *Quarterly*, 4 (Autumn 1983) Number 1, 11 and (Winter 1984) Number 2, 2.

Hamilton, Clay and Charles T. Jacobs. "Greenbrier Civil War Soldier Buried in Maryland," Lewisburg (West Va.), *The West Virginia Daily News*, October 11, 1983.

Hicks, Frederick C. "Lincoln, Wright, and Holmes at Fort Stevens," *Journal of the Illinois State Historical Society*, 39 (September 1946), Number 3, 323–332.

Kohn, Benard. "Restored Civil War Fort is New Sightseeing Shrine," Washington *Sunday Star*, July 4, 1937.

Lee, Blair. "The Day Confederates Marched into Montgomery County History," *The Montgomery Journal*, June 28, 1989.

Levy, Claudia. "Capitol View Park: A Step Back in Time," Washington *Post*, May 13, 1989.

Lewis, Thomas A. "There in the Heat of July," [Early's Raid on Washington], *Smithsonian*, 19 (July 1988), Number 4, 66–75.

"Lincoln at Fort Stevens," *Civil War Times Illustrated*, 17 (July 1978), Number 4, 33.

"Lincoln Incident Recalled," Washington *Post*, July 5, 1964.

McElroy, John. "Fort Stevens as National Park Favored as Tribute to Lincoln," Washington *Star*, June 27, 1923.

"Memorial Park on Monocacy Battlefield," *Confederate Veteran*, XXXVI (February 1928), Number 2, 44.

Morseberger, Robert E. "The Battle That Saved Washington," *Civil War Times Illustrated*, XIII (May 1974), Number 2, 12–17, 20–27.

Nevin, D. R. B. "Fort Stevens," *United Service Journal*, 2 (July 1889), Number 2, 37–45.

"Oberlin and the Civil War," *Oberlin Today*, 22 (First Quarter 1964), Number 1, 3–11.

Proctor, John Clagett. "Preservation of Historic Fort Stevens," Washington *Sunday Star*, July 8, 1945.

_____ . "Washington and Environs," Washington *Sunday Star*, 1928–1949.

Sherwood, John. "Lincoln Under Fire, Fort Stevens Guns to Boom," Washington *Evening Star*, July 10, 1964.

Smith, Edward, "When the Confederates Came to the Capital," Washington *Post*, July 9, 1989.

Smith, Everard. "Rebels at Washington: Lincoln under Enemy Fire and Wheaton's Attack," *St. Albans* [School] *Review* (Spring 1967,) 3–15.

Stackpole, Edward J. "The Day the Rebels Could Have Marched into the White House," *Civil War Times*, II (February–March 1961), Number 10, 5–6, 19.

Stinson, Byron. "The Invalid Corps," *Civil War Times Illustrated*, X (May 1971), Number 2, 20–27.

"The Civil War as Reported by the Star One Hundred Years Ago, Confederate Menace Capital," Washington *Star*, July 12, 1964.

Vincent, Thomas McCurdy. "Early's March on Washington," in Marcus Benjamin, compiler and editor. *Washington During War Time; A Series of Papers Showing the Military, Political and Social Phases During 1861 to 1865*. Washington: Dyron S. Adams, 1902, 47–52.

Warrington, J. Lee. "In Defense of Washington," *AAA World*, Potomac Division, III (May-June 1983), Number 3, 21.

Wert, Jeffrey E. "The Snicker's Gap War," *Civil War Times Illustrated*, XVII (July 1978), Number 4, 30–40.

Wesley, Edward. "Rebels in Frederick; Battle Expected at Monocacy," *Fredericktonian*, January 16, 1978.

"When Early Came," Washington *Evening Star*, October 12, 1895.

Wilson, W. Emerson. "City Prepares to Fight Invaders," Wilmington (Del.) *Morning News*, July 15, 1964.

Worthington, Glenn H. "The Battle of Monocacy," *Confederate Veteran*, XXXVI (January 1928), Number 1, 20–23.

Secondary Sources—Unpublished

District of Columbia Civil War Centennial Commission. "Commemoration Ceremony on the One Hundredth Anniversary of the Battle of Fort Stevens at Fort Stevens, July 11, 1964."

Eckert, Ralph Lowell. "John Brown Gordon: Soldier, Southerner, American." Ph.D dissertation, Louisiana State University, 1983, 2 volumes, and Ann Arbor: University Microfilms International, 1984.

Fenton, Charles Wendell. "Early's Raid on Washington," Army War College, March 1916.

Gatchel, Theodore Dodge. "Early's Raid on Washington, June–July 1864," M.A. thesis, American University, 1933.

Hampton, Wade. "The Raid on Point Lookout; A Study in Desperation," Research paper, American University, August 1970, copy in Maryland Historical Society.

Kindmark, Robert G. "John Gross Barnard: His Civil War Career and Military Writings," Research paper, Allegheny College, April 1978.

Minney, Elton D. "The Battle of Monocacy; An Individual Study Project," Army War College, 1988.

Pickering, Abner. "Early's Raid in 1864, Including the Battle of the Monocacy," Army War College, 1913–1914.

Smith, Everard Hall. "The General and the Valley: Union Generalship During the Threat to Washington in 1864." Ph.D dissertation, University of North Carolina at Chapel Hill, 1977 and Ann Arbor: University Microfilms International, 1977.

U.S. Department of the Interior, National Park Service, National Capital Region, Rock Creek Park. "Battleground National Cemetery," unpublished flyer, n.d.

Notes

Chapter 1

1. Edgar S. Dudley, "Reminiscences of Washington and Early's Attack in 1864," Military Order of the Loyal Legion, Ohio Commandery, *Sketches of War History 1861–1865*, v. 1, p. 109.

2. Letter, Eugene Blackford-sister, May 14, 1864, Lewis Leigh Jr. Collection, US Army Military History Institute (MHI), Carlisle Barracks, Pa.

3. U.S. War Department, *The War of the Rebellion; A Compilation of the Official Records of the Union and Confederate Armies* (Washington, 1880–1901), series I, volume 33, pp. 827–829; hereinafter cited *ORA* with reference to series, volume, page, accordingly.

4. *Ibid.*, pp. 794–795.

5. For a discussion of the broader role of the capital in the war in the east, see the authors, *Symbol, Sword, and Shield; Defending Washington During the Civil War* (Hamden, Ct., 1975), chapters 1–7.

6. John G. Barnard, *A Report on the Defenses of Washington*, (Washington, 1871), p. 123.

7. *ORA*, I, p. 33, pp. 729–730, 733.

8. *Ibid.*, pp. 770, 807–808, 879–880, 887–888, 897, 992, 1009, also 36, pt. 1, 3; pt. 2, 652, 825. Grant's correspondence has been conveniently collected by John V. Simon, editor, *The Papers of Ulysses S. Grant* (Carbondale and Edwardsville, 1967–), with Volume 10 and 11 relevant to this time-frame. Hereinafter cited Simon, Grant papers, with relevant volume.

9. *ORA*, I, p. 33, pp. 879–888, 897.

10. Clifford Dowdey and Louis H. Manarin, editors, *The Wartime Papers of R. E. Lee* (Boston, 1961), pp. 774–775; *ORA*, I, 37, pt. 1, pp. 707–758 inter alia.

11. Dowdey, *Ibid.*, pp. 627, 767, 806; *ORA*, 1, 32, pt. 2, pp. 541–542, 566–567; Bradley T. Johnson, "My Ride Around Baltimore in Eighteen Hundred and Sixty Four," *Journal of the United States Cavalry Association*, I, #6 (September 1889), pp. 250–251.

12. Frank Vandiver, *Jubal's Raid* (New York, 1960), pp. 18–19; Millard Bushong, *Old Jube* (Boyce, Va., 1955), pp. 26–37.

13. John W. Daniel, "Jubal A. Early," in Edward Daniel, compiler, *Speeches and Orations of John W. Daniel* (Lynchburg, 1911), p. 520; Henry Kyd Douglas, *I Rode with Stonewall* (Chapel Hill, 1940), p. 33; G. Moxley Sorrel, *Recollections of a Confederate Staff Officer* (Jackson, Tenn., 1958 ed, p 50; Lee A. Wallace, *Fifth Virginia Infantry* (Lynchburg, 1988), p. 60.

14. Jubal A. Early, *War Memoirs* (Bloomington, 1960 ed.), p. 371; *ORA*, I, 37, pt. 1, p. 346.

15. Moses Gipson, "The Valley Campaign of General Early," Richmond *Times Dispatch*, August 26, 1906, quoted in *Southern Historical Society Papers*, v. 34 (1906), pp. 212–213; Letter, Leonidus L. Polk-wife, June 16, 1864, Polk papers, Southern Historical Collections, University

303

of North Carolina Library, Chapel Hill (hereinafter cited SHC/UNC); Dowdey and Manarin, *Lee's Wartime Papers*, pp. 701, 707; J. Cutler Andrews, *The South Reports the Civil War* (Princeton, 1970), pp. 407–408.

16. Daniel, *Speeches*, 541; Vandiver, *Jubal's Raid*, pp. 37–38; *ORA*, I, 37, pt. 1; W. G. Bean, *Stonewall's Man, Sandie Pendleton* (Chapel Hill, 1959), p. 204; William Allan, "Reminiscences," 20, Allan papers, SHC/UNC.

17. William C. Walker, *History of the Eighteenth Connecticut* (Norwich, NY, 1885), p. 261; on the Lynchburg campaign, see Vandiver, *Jubal's Raid*, pp. 32– 55; Edward J. Stackpole, *Sheridan in the Shenandoah* (Harrisburg, 1961), pp. 38–44; *ORA*, I, 37, pt. 1, pp. 93–160 incl.; and Everard Hall Smith, "The General and the Valley; Union Leadership During the Threat to Washington in 1864," unpublished doctoral dissertation, University of North Carolina, Chapel Hill, 1977, pp. 119–136; J. Kelly Bennette, diary, June 18, 1864, SHC/UNC; F. H. Gurtler, "Hunter at Lynchburg," *The National Tribune*, March 7, 1912.

18. Walker, *Ibid.*, pp. 274–275; *ORA, Ibid.*, pp. 101–102, 683–684; Smith, *Ibid.*, pp. 125–131; Harry Gilmor, *Four Years in the Saddle* (New York, 1866), pp. 181–183; Polk wife, n.d., SHC/UNC; J. Stoddard Johnston, "Notes of March of Breckinridge's Corps from Lynchburg June 19 to Leesburg July 15," entries June 20, 21, 1864, New York Historical Society (NYHS), New York.

19. Dowdey and Manarin, *Lee's Wartime Papers*, pp. 206–207; Douglas Southall Freeman, *R. E. Lee, A Biography* (New York, 1935), v. 4, pp. 240–241.

20. Telegram, R. E. Lee-Jubal A. Early, June 26, 1864, Folder II, Telegraph Book, R. E. Lee Headquarters papers, p. 241, Virginia Historical Society (hereinafter cited VHS); *ORA*, I, 37, pt. 1, pp. 766-767.

21. Allan, "Reminiscences," p. 22; Polk-wife, June 16, 1864; Bennette diary, June 4, 20, 21, 27, 1864, all SHC/UNC; Vandiver, *Jubal's Raid*, pp. 59–60, Johnston, "Notes," June 22, 1864.

22. Bean, *Stonewall's Man*, pp. 203–205; William C. Davis, *Breckinridge; Statesman, Soldier, Symbol* (Baton Rouge, 1974), p. 443; Gary W. Gallagher, *Stephen Dodson Ramseur; Lee's Gallant General* (Chapel Hill, 1985), p. 124; Susan P. Lee, *Memoirs of William Nelson Pendleton, D. D.* (Philadelphia, 1893), pp. 360–361; Robert E. Park, "Diary," *Southern Historical Society Papers*, v. 1 (1876), p. 375; Douglas, *I Rode with Stonewall*, pp. 291–292; Allan, "Reminiscences," p. 22, SHC/UNC.

23. W.W. Scott, editor. "Diary of Capt. H.W. Wingfield," *Bulletin of the Virginia State Library*, v, 16 (July 1927), p. 42; Richard W. Iobst, *Bloody Sixth; The Sixth North Carolina* (Gaithersburg, Md., 1987), p. 213; John B. Worsham, *One of Jackson's Foot Cavalry* (Wilmington, N.C., 1987 edition), p. 149; *ORA*, I, p. 43, pt. 1, p. 602.

24. In addition to Worsham, Wingfield, and Iobst, *Ibid.*, see Lee, *Pendleton*, pp. 343–361; James I. Robertson, *The Stonewall Brigade* (Baton Rouge, 1963), p. 230; George H. Lester, "War Record of the Tom Cobb Infantry," Georgia Division," *This They Remembered;* in the United Daughters of the Confederacy, (Washington, Ga., 1960), p. 104; G.W. Nichols, *A Soldiers Story of His Regiment* (Gessup, Ga., 1898 edition), pp. 168–169; W.H. Runge, editor, *Four Years in the Confederate Artillery; Diary of Private Henry Robinson Berkeley* (Chapel Hill, 1961), p. 84; also Letter, Richard Colbert-Mrs. E.M. Potts, July 24, 1864; Archives of North Louisiana Historical Association, Centenary College, Shreveport, Louisiana (hereinafter cited NLHA); "Draft Report of Twentieth North Carolina Regiment," July 1, 1864, Thomas F. Toon papers, North Carolina Department of History and Archives, Raleigh (hereinafter cited NCHA).

25. Park, "Diary," p. 374; also "The Twelfth Alabama Infantry, Confederate States Army," *Southern Historical Society Papers*, v. 33 (1905), p. 262; John O. Casler, *Four Years in the Stonewall Brigade* (Dayton, 1971 edition), p. 326; J.E. Green diary, June 17–July 12, 1864, and Stephen D. Ramseur-wife, June 27, 1864, Ramseur papers, both SHC/UNC.

26. Iobst, *The Bloody Sixth*, pp. 214–215.

27. *ORA*, I, 37, pt. 1, p. 763; Allan, "Reminiscences," p. 24, SHC/UNC.

28. Joseph T. Durkin, editor, *Confederate Chaplain; War Journal of Reverend James B. Sheeran* (Milwaukee, 1960), p. 93; Iobst, *The Bloody Sixth*, p. 213; Park, "Diary," p. 375; Runge, Berkeley Diary, p. 85.

29. Vandiver, *Jubal's Raid*, pp. 64–66; Smith, "The General and the Valley," pp. 154–155.

30. Douglas Southall Freeman, *Lee's Lieutenants*, (New York, 1951), v. 3, p. 558; Vandiver, *Ibid.*, pp. 65–66.

31. Alexander Hunter, *Johnny Reb and Billy Yank* (New York, 1905), p. 649; *ORA*, I, pt. 1, p. 766; Vandiver, *Jubal's Raid*, pp. 67–68; Smith, "The General and the Valley," pp. 155–56; Freeman, *Lee's Lieutenant*, III, xv–xv.

32. *ORA*, I, pt. 1, 37, pp. 703–704; Vandiver, *Ibid.*, pp. 69–70.

33. Early, *War Memoirs*, p. 49, and "The Advance on Washington," *Southern Historical Society Papers* (July–August 1881), pp. 301–302. W. H. Taylor and William Allan computations, Folder R, Strength of the Army of Northern Virginia at Various Times, Lee Headquarters Papers, VHS; Davis Breckinridge, p. 143, f.n. 15, citing Field Report of Second Division, Breckinridge's Corps, June 28, 1864, Field Return of the Regiments and Battalions composing the different Brigades of the 1st Division, Breckinridge's Corps, n.d. [June 24–June 26, 1864], Field Return of Troops Commanded by Major General Breckinridge, July 15, 1864, all in James W. Eldridge collection, Huntington Library (HL), San Marino, California; also Smith, "The General and the Valley," pp. 231–232, f.n. 50, and pp. 239–240, f.n. 65; and John G. Barnard, *Defenses of Washington*, p. 121, also pp. 119–120. Given all of Early's postwar statements, it may well have been that even he had but an approximate idea of his actual strength at the time.

34. Iobst, *The Bloody Sixth*, pp. 213–214; Manly, Wellman, *Rebel Boast; First at Bethel—Last at Appomattox* (New York, 1956), pp. 164–165; Scott, "Wingfield Diary," p. 43; "Henry D. Monier Diary," in Napier Bartlett, *Military Reecord of Louisiana* (New Orleans, 1875), pp. 50–51; Zebulon York, Official Report, July 22, 1864, Eldridge collection, Huntington Library (HL).

35. Bennette diary, July 1, 1864 entry, SHC/UNC.

36. *ORA*, I, 51, pt. 2, pp. 1028–1029.

37. Wellman, *Rebel Boast*, pp. 166–167; Park, "Diary," p. 377; Runge, *Berkeley Diary*, p. 85; John G. Young diary, July 4, 1864 entry, NCHA; Lucy Buck quoted in Laura Virginia Hale, *Four Valient Years* (Strasburg, Va., 1968), p. 379; George Wilson Booth, *Personal Reminiscences of a Maryland Soldier* (Baltimore, 1898), p. 121.

38. Early, *War Memoirs*, pp. 382–383.

39. *ORA*, I, 37, pt. 1, 174–177, pt. 2, p. 6; Samuel Clarke Farrar, *The Twenty-Second Pennsylvania Cavalry* (Pittsburgh, 1911), pp. 254–255; T. A. Meysenburg, "Notes on Battle Around Martinsburg, Va.," July 2, 1864 entry, Perkins Library, Duke University (hereinafter cited DU); Virgil Carrington Jones, *Ranger Mosby* (Chapel Hill, 1944), p. 185.

40. Farrar, *Ibid.*, pp. 255–256; Bushong, *Old Jube*, p. 195; Gilmor, *Four Years in the Saddle*, pp. 182–187.

41. *ORA*, I, 37, pt. 1, pp. 174–176; Farrar, *Ibid.*, pp. 257–263; Meysenburg, "Notes," July 3, 1864 entry, DU; Howard K. Beale, editor, *The Diary of Edward Bates.* (New York, 1971 reprint), p. 382.

42. Letter, R.G. Coleman-wife, July 6, 1864, Mary E. Schooler papers, DU; *ORA*, I, 37, pt. 2, p. 591; Johnston, "Notes," July 3, 1864, NYHS.

43. Letter, T.E. Morrow-father, August 2, 1864, original in author's collections, copy, Defenses of Washington files, Fort Ward Museum and Park, Alexandria, Va. (FWP); Wellman, *Rebel Boast*, p. 167; Runge, *Berkeley Diary*, p. 377; *ORA, Ibid.*; Bennette diary, July 5, 1864 entry, SHC/UNC; and Park, "Diary," p. 377.

44. *ORA, Ibid.*, pt. 2, 15; UDC, Ga. Div., *This They Remembered*, p. 105.

Chapter 2

1. Adam Badeau, *Military History of Ulysses S. Grant* (New York, 1885), II, p. 444; Everhard H. Smith, "The General and the Valley; Union Leadership During the Threat to Washington in 1864," unpublished doctoral dissertation, University of North Carolina, Chapel Hill, 1977, pp. 136–142; John Emmet O'Brien, *Telegraphing in Battle: Reminiscences of the Civil War* (Scranton, 1910), pp. 142–150, especially pp. 150–151; William R. Plum, *The Military Telegraph during the Civil War* (Chicago, 1882), I, pp. 137–138; II, pp. 130–132, pp. 260–261; Bruce Catton, *Grant Takes Command* (New York, 1968), p. 314.

2. US War Department, *The War of the Rebellion; A Compilation of the Official Records of Union and Confederate Armies* (Washington, 1880–1901), series I, volume 32, part 2, p. 408; Volume 34, Part 3, Page 333; volume 36, part 2, p. 329 (hereinafter cited *ORA*, with reference to series, volume, part, and page). Also, Howard K. Beale, editor, *Diary of Edward Bates* (New York, 1971), p. 385; Gideon Welles, *Diary* (Boston, 1911), I, 180, p. 373; W.A. Croffut, editor, *Fifty Years in Camp and Field; Diary of Major General Ethan Allen Hitchcock* (New York, 1909), pp. 463–464; Lew Wallace, *Autobiography* (New York, 1906), II, pp. 577–580; Ella Lonn, *Foreigners in the Union Army and Navy* (Baton Rouge, 1951) pp. 179–180.

3. *ORA*, I, 37, pt. 1, p. 657; 40, pt. 2, pp. 269–270.

4. *Ibid.*, I, 37, pt. 1, pp. 694–695; also pp. 644–645, pp. 650–651, pp. 664, 670, 673, 674, 677, 687, 689.

5. *Ibid.*, I, 37, pt. 2, p. 3.

6. *Ibid.*, I, 37, pt. 2, p. 33, also pt. 1, pp. 174– 175.

7. *Ibid.*, I, 37, pt. 2, pp. 16–18.

8. *Ibid.*, I, 37, pt. 1, pp. 697–706; compare these figures with Grant's assembled army group (Meade, Butler) on June 30, 1864 showing 105,337 officers and men "present for duty equipped," with possibly two-thirds actually available for operations, I, 40, pt. 1, p. 177; also Croffut, *Fifty Years in Camp and Field*, pp. 463–464.

9. *ORA*, I, 37, pt. 2, pp. 58–60, pt. 3, pp. 4, 59; E.N. Atkinson, "Report of Evans Brigade," July 22, 1864, James W. Eldridge Collection, Huntington Library (HL), San Marino, Calif.; John B. Gordon, "Report," July 22, 1864, Lee's Headquarters Papers, Virginia Historical Society (VHS), Richmond; J. Stoddard Johnston, "Notes of March of Breckinridge's Corps from Lynchburg June 19 to Leesburg, July 15," entries July 4–7, 1864, New York Historical Society (NYHS), New York.

10. *ORA, Ibid.*, pt. 2, p. 65; Telegram F. N. Haskett (Sandy Hook) to W.C. Quincy, 5:25 p.m., July 5, 1864, Mss. 1860, Maryland Historical Society (MHS), Baltimore.

11. *ORA*, I, 37, pt. 2, pp. 58–60, 50; pt. 3, 4, 6, 18, 32; George C. Agassiz, editor, *Meade's Headquarters, 1863–1865, Letters of Colonel Theodore Lyman from the Wilderness to Appomatox* (Boston, 1922), pp. 184–185.

12. Jubal A. Early, *War Memoirs* (Bloomington, 1960 ed.), p. 385; Edward J. Stackpole, *Sheridan in the Shenandoah* (Harrisburg, 1961), p. 53; *ORA*, I, 37, pt. 1, pp. 174–180, pp. 184–185; George Wilson Booth, *Personal Reminiscences of a Maryland Soldier* (Baltimore, 1907), pp. 126–127; also, Robert E. Lee, *Recollections and Letters of General Robert E. Lee* (Garden City, 1904), pp. 131–132.

13. Early, *Ibid.*, p. 386; see also Douglas Southall Freeman editor, *Lee's Dispatches* (New York, 1915), pp. 269–271; Clifford Dowdey and Louis Manarin, editors, *The Wartime Papers of R.E. Lee* (New York, 1961), pp. 807–808; *ORA, Ibid.*, pp. 766–768; and R. G. Coleman to wife, July 6, 1864, Mary E. Schooler papers, Perkins Library, Duke University (DU).

14. John E. Worsham, *One of Jackson's Foot Cavalry* (Jackson, Tenn., 1964 ed.), pp. 233–234; Henry Kyd Douglas, *I Rode with Stonewall* (Chapel Hill, 1940), p. 293; Robert Park, "Diary," *Southern Historical Society Papers*, I (1876), p. 378; W. H. Runge, editor, *Four Years in the*

Confederate Artillery; Diary of Private Henry Robinson Berkeley (Chapel Hill, 1961), p. 85; John N. Opie, *A Rebel Cavalryman with Lee, Stuart, and Jackson* (Chicago, 1899), pp. 244–245; John G. Young diary, July 6, 1864 entry, North Carolina Department of History and Archives (NCHA); Wilmington, (NC) *Daily Journal,* July 27, 1864.

15. George H. Lester, "War Record of the Tom Cobb Infantry," in UDC Georgia Division, *This They Remembered* (Washington, Ga., 1965), p. 106; Manly Wade Wellman, *Rebel Boast; First at Bethel—Last at Appomattox* (New York, 1956), p. 169; John O. Casler, *Four Years in the Stonewall Brigade* (Dayton, 1971 ed.), p. 227.

16. Millard Bushong, *Old Jube* (Boyce, Va., 1955), p. 197; Coleman-wife, July 6, 1864, DU; *ORA,* I, 37; pt. 2, p. 592; Park, "Diary," p. 377; Young diary, July 4, 1864 entry, NCHA; William Beavens diary, July 4, 5, 1864, Southern Historical Collection/University of North Carolina, Chapel Hill (SHC/UNC); Wellman, *Rebel Boast,* pp. 166–167.

17. J. Thomas Scharf, *History of Western Maryland*(Baltimore, 1968 ed.), pp. 285–286; Early, *War Memoirs,* pp. 384–386.

18. Scharf, *Ibid.,* pp. 286–287; F.Y. Goldsborough, *Early's Great Raid; Battle of the Monocacy,* (n.p. 1898, Frederick 1989 reprint), p. 6.

19. Scharf, *Western Maryland,* p. 287; Middletown *Valley Register,* July, 22, 1864; J. Kelly Bennette diary, July 1–8, 1864, SHC/UNC; "A Brief Sketch of Cole's Independent Maryland Volunteer Cavalry," n.d., pp. 7, 8, MHS; *ORA,* I, pt. 1, p. 1171.

20. Scharf, *Ibid.,* pp. 287–288; *ORA,* I, 37, Pt. 1, pp. 194–195; Bradley T. Johnson, "My Ride Around Baltimore in 1864," *Journal of the United States Cavalry Association,* II (September 1889), p. 252; *ORA, Ibid,* pp. 1170–1171; Goldsborough, *Early's Great Raid,* pp. 6–12.

21. Goldsborough, *Ibid,* p. 11; *ORA,* I, 37, pt. 2, p. 110; 51, pt. 1, pp. 1171–1174; Wallace, *Autobiography,* II, pp. 738–744; Frederick W. Wild, *Memoirs and History of Captain F.W. Alexander's Baltimore Battery* (Baltimore, 1912), p. 120; Johnson, *Ibid,* p. 252; Scharf, *Ibid.,* p. 287; William R. Quinn, editor, *The Diary of Jacob Engelbrecht* (Frederick, 1976), pp. 271–272; Letter, Elihu H. Rockwell to Mrs. E. R. Coleman, July 25, 1864, Frederick County Historical Society (FHS).

22. Bennette diary, July 7, 8, 1864, SHC/UNC; Rufus Woolwine diary, July 7,8, 1864, Virginia Historical Society (VHS); Harry Gilmor, *Four Years in the Saddle* (New York, 1866), pp. 189–190; Glenn H. Worthington, *Fighting For Time* (Frederick, 1932), pp. 69–73, pp. 81–84; Wallace, *Ibid.,* II, pp. 718–730; Goldsborough, *Ibid.,* pp. 12–13; Abner Hard, *History of the Eighth Illinois Cavalry* (Aurora, Ill., 1868) pp. 297-298.

23. Young diary, July 7, 8, 9, 1864, and Thomas F. Toon, "Draft Report on Twentieth [NC] Regiment," July 7, 8, 1864 entries, both NCHA; Joseph McMurrea diary, July 7, 8, 1864, Virginia State Library (VSL); Buckner McGill Randolph diary, July 7, 8, 1864, VHS; Richard W. Waldrop diary, July 7, 8, 1864, SHC/UNC; I.G. Bradwell, "Early's March to Washington in 1864," *Confederate Veteran,* XVIII (May 1920), p. 176, and unpublished typescript of same, chapter 3, MHS; Thomas S. Kenan, compiler, *Sketch of Forty-Third North Carolina* (Raleigh, 1895); Archie P. MacDonald, editor, *Make Me a Map of the Valley; The Civil War Journal of Stonewall Jackson's Topographer* (Dallas, 1973), p. 214; Early, *War Memoirs,* p. 386.

24. *ORA.,* I, 37, pt. 1, pp. 194–195; 51, pt. 1, pp. 1174–1175; Wallace, *Autobiography,* II, pp. 738–744.

25. Wallace, *Ibid.,* pp. 742–743; Scharf, *Western Maryland,* p. 288; Frederick, (Md.) *News* November 28, 1908.

26. Wallace, *Ibid.,* pp. 746–747.

27. Park, "Diary," p. 378; Douglas, *I Rode with Stonewall,* p. 293; Young diary, July 8, 1864, NCHA; Bennette diary, July 8, 1864, SHC/UNC; Johnson, "My Ride Around Baltimore," p. 252; Joseph T. Durkin, editor, *Confederate Chaplain* (Milwaukee, 1960), p. 94.

28. Quinn, *Englebrecht Diary,* pp. 271–272; Worthington, *Fighting For Time,* pp. 282–289.

29. Scharf, *Western Maryland*, pp. 288–289; Edward Delaplaine, "General Early's Levy on Frederick," in Frederick County Civil War Centennial, *To Commemorate the Battle of Monocacy* (Frederick, 1964), pp. 48–54; Quinn, *Ibid.*, p. 274.

30. William Allan journal, pp. 29–30, SHC/UNC.

31. See facsimiles of Frederick corporation replies and tally sheet in Nancy F. Whitmore and Timothy L. Cannon, *Frederick: A Pictorial History* (Norfolk, 1981), pp. 56–57; Scharf, *Western Maryland*, p. 289; Bushong, *Old Jube*, p. 197; Delaplaine, "General Early's Levy," pp. 50–54.

32. Quinn, *Englebrecht Diary*, p. 275; Young diary, p. 38, NCHA; Allan journal, pp. 29–30, SHC/UNC; MacDonald, *Make Me A Map*, p. 215.

33. David J. Lewis, *Frederick War Claim; Evidence and Argument in Support of Bill to Refund Ransom Paid by the Town of Frederick . . .* , 1912, copy, FHS, pp. 3, 4, 18, 19, 20.

Chapter 3

1. Lew Wallace, *Autobiography* (New York, 1906), II, pp. 699-700.

2. Ezra J. Warner, *Generals in Blue* (Baton Rouge, 1964), pp. 535-536; Kenneth P. Williams, *Lincoln Finds A General* (New York, 1952-1959), III, pp. 362, 524; Irving McKee, *"Ben-Hur" Wallace; The Life of General Lew Wallace* (Berkeley, 1947), chapters II-VI.

3. Wallace, *Autobiography*, II, pp. 710-711; for messages and troop movements, see U.S. War Department, *War of the Rebellion; A Compilation of the Official Records of the Union and Confederate Armies* (Washington, 1880-1901), series I, volume 37, part 2, pp. 20-31, hereinafter cited *ORA*.

4. Wallace, *Ibid.*, pp. 712-714, 725, 727.

5. *Ibid.*, pp. 715-721; Frederick W. Wild, *Memoirs and History of Capt. F.W. Alexander's Baltimore Battery* (Baltimore, 1912), p. 118.

6. Wallace, *Ibid.*, p. 728, also pp. 715, 719-727; *ORA*, I, 37, pt. 2, p. 91; Abner Hard, *History of the Eighth Cavalry Regiment, Illinois Volunteers* (Dayton, 1984 reprint), pp. 290-296.

7. Osceola Lewis, *History of the One Hundred and Thirty-Eighth Pennsylvania*, (Norristown, 1866), p. 113; Edwin M. Haynes, *History of the Tenth Vermont* (Rutland, 1894), p. 184; Lemuel A. Abbott, *Personal Recollections and Civil War Diary* (Burlington, 1908), p. 94; George R. Prowell, *History of the Eighty-Seventh Regiment, Pennsylvania Volunteers* (York, 1901), pp. 174-176; Alfred S. Roe, *History of the Ninth New York Heavy Artillery* (Worchester, 1899), pp. 120-121; J. Newton Terrill, *Campaign of the Fourteenth New Jersey Volunteers* (New Brunswick, 1884), p. 74.

8. Wallace, *Autobiography*, II, pp. 735-737; *ORA*, I, 37, pt. 2, pp. 101-102.

9. Glenn H. Worthington, *Fighting for Time* (Frederick, 1932), p. 86; *ORA, Ibid.*, pp. 100-101, 108, 111; Wallace, *Ibid.*, pp. 745-750; J. Thomas Scharf, *History of Western Maryland* (Baltimore, 1968 edition), p. 285.

10. Wallace, *Ibid.*, pp. 751-755.

11. Worthington, *Fighting For Time*, pp. 169, 172, 236; Roe, *Ninth New York Heavy Artillery*, pp. 301-302; T. J. C. Williams, *History and Biographical Record of Frederick County, Maryland*, (Baltimore, 1910), p. 32.

12. Worthington, *Ibid.*, p. 236; Roe, *Ibid.*, pp. 301-302.

13. *ORA*, I, 37, pt. 1, p. 196; Wallace, *Autobiography*, II, p. 756; William H. James, "A Baltimore Volunteer of 1864," *Maryland Historical Magazine*, XXXVI (March 1941), pp. 24–30.

14. Worthington, *Fighting for Time*, pp. 107-111; Wallace, *Ibid.*, pp. 256–262; Abbott, *Personal Recollections*, pp. 98–99.

15. Roe, *Ninth New York Heavy Artillery*, p. 307.

16. Jubal Early, *War Memoirs* (Bloomington, 1961 edition), p. 386.

17. Abbott, *Personal Recollections*, p. 100; Hard, *Eighth Illinois Cavalry*, pp. 298–299; Early, *Ibid.*, p. 386; Worthington, *Fighting For Time*, p. 118; *ORA*, I, 37, pt. 1, p. 220; 51, pt. 1, p. 1175.

18. Wallace, *Autobiography*, II, pp. 757–770; Early, *Ibid.*, p. 387; *ORA*, I, 51, pt. 1, pp. 1175–1176.

19. Worthington, *Fighting for Time*, chapter XIV; Early, *Ibid.*, p. 387. Wallace, *Ibid.*, p. 770, fn. 1.

20. Albert E. Conradis, "The Battle of Monocacy," in Frederick County Civil War Centennial, Inc., *To Commemorate the One Hundredth Anniversary of the Battle of Monocacy* (Frederick, 1964), p. 21; *ORA*, I, 37, pt. 1, pp. 213–219.

21. Benedict, *Tenth Vermont*, pp. 196–199; Worthington, *Fighting for Time*, p. 113.

22. *ORA*, I, 37, pt. 1, pp. 197–198; 51, pt. 1, p. 1177; Wallace, *Autobiography*, II, pp. 773–777.

23. Wallace, *Ibid.*, p. 775; Worthington, *Fighting for Time*, pp. 113–114; Roe, *Ninth New York Heavy Artillery*, p. 128.

24. Abbott, *Personal Recollections*, pp. 100–101; Worthington, *Ibid.*, chapter XVIII; Wallace, *Ibid.*, pp. 778–780.

25. Conradis, "Monocacy," pp. 21–22.

26. *ORA*, I, 37, pt. 1, pp. 348, 350; Early, *War Memoirs*, pp. 387–388; Worthington, *Fighting for Time*, chapter XVIII.

27. John H. Worsham, *One of Jackson's Foot Cavalry* (Jackson, Tenn., 1964 ed.), p. 193; Worthington, *Fighting for Time*, p. 129.

28. John B. Gordon, *Reminiscences of the Civil War* (New York, 1904) pp. 310–311; *ORA*, I, 37, pt. 1, pp. 350–351; Ralph L. Eckert, *John Brown Gordon; Soldier, Southerner, American*, (Ann Arbor, 1984), I, p. 106; Wallace, *Autobiography*, II, pp. 775–776; I. G. Bradwell, "The Shenandoah Valley Campaign of 1864," typescript, 4, 5, Maryland Historical Society (MHS), and published versions, "Early's Demonstration Against Washington in 1864," XXII (October 1914), p. 439 and "Early's March to Washington in 1864," XXVIII (May 1920), p. 177, and "In the Battle of Monocacy, Md.," XXXVI (February 1923), pp. 56–57, all *Confederate Veteran*.

29. *ORA*, I, 37, 2, pp. 138–139; also LI, pt. 1, pp. 1175–1177; Wallace, *Autobiography*, II, pp. 784–789.

30. Wallace, *Ibid.*, pp. 782–783; for the only surviving dispatch to either Halleck or Grant on this date, see Wallace to Halleck after the battle and received in Washington at 11:42 p.m., July 9, 1864, *ORA*, I, 37, pt. 1, p. 145.

31. Gordon, *Reminiscences*, p. 313; Wallace, *Ibid.*, pp. 790–792; Conradis, "Monocacy," p. 25.

32. Bradwell, "Shenandoah Valley," 3, MHS and published versions; T.E. Morrow to father, August 2, 1864, author's collection, copy in Defenses of Washington files, Fort Ward Museum, Alexandria, Va. (FWM); G. W. Nichols, *A Soldiers Story of His Regiment* (Jessup, Ga., 1898), pp. 170–171; Haynes, *Tenth Vermont*, p. 194.

33. Zebulon York to B. B. Wellford, July 18, 1864, Reel One, White-Wellford, Taliaferro-Marshall family papers, Southern Historical Society Collection, University of North Carolina, Chapel Hill (SHC/UNC); also York's report, July 22, 1864, Huntington Library (HL), San Marino, Calif., Bradwell, *Ibid.*, p. 6; Terry L. Jones, *Lee's Tigers* (Baton Rouge, 1987), pp. 211–212; *ORA*, I, 37, pt. 1, p. 351; Prowell, *Eighty-Seventh Pennsylvania*, p. 186.

34. Worsham, *One of Jackson's Foot Cavalry*, pp. 238–239; Gordon, *Reminiscences*, pp. 310–317; Bradwell, *Ibid.*, pp. 4,5; Worthington, *Fighting for Time*, pp. 139, 166, 168; J. Floyd King to J. Stoddard Johnston, July 22, 1864, and E. N. Atkinson, "Report of Evans Brigade," July 22, 1864, both HL.

35. Lewis, *One Hundred and Thirty-Eighth Pennsylvania*, pp. 116–117; Roe, *Ninth New York Heavy Artillery*, pp. 132–133; Lewis H. Clark, *Military History of Wayne County, New York; The County in the Civil War* (Sodus, NY, c. 1881), p. 601.

36. Bradwell, "Battle of the Monocacy, Md.," p. 57; Gordon, *Reminiscences*, pp. 312–313; Worthington, *Fighting for Time*, p. 139.

37. G. C. Benedict, *Vermont in the Civil War* (Burlington, 1888), II, pp. 315–316; Haynes, *Tenth Vermont*, p. 195; U.S. Department of the Army, *The Medal of Honor* (Washington, 1948), p. 164; Bradwell, "Shenandoah Valley," p. 7, MHS; *ORA*, I, 51, pt. 1, p. 1176.

38. Thomas F. Toon, "Draft Report on the Twentieth Regiment, North Carolina State Volunteers, CSA," August 1, 1864, North Carolina Department of History and Archives, (NCHA); V. E. Turner and H. C. Wall "Twenty-Third Regiment," in Walter E. Clark, editor, *Histories of Several Regiments and Battalions from North Carolina* (Raleigh, 1901), II, pp. 245–246; Richard W. Iobst, *The Bloody Sixth; The Sixth North Carolina Regiment* (Gaithersburg, 1987), p. 215; Haynes, *Tenth Vermont*, pp. 196–204; Department of the Army, *Ibid.*, p. 164.

39. James, "A Baltimore Volunteer," p. 29; unidentified clipping, Baltimore *Sun*, c. July 15, 1864, MHS; *ORA*, I, 37, pt. 1, pp. 213–219; Conradis, "Monocacy," p. 27; Samuel C. Farrar, *The Twenty-Second Pennsylvania Cavalry* (Pittsburgh, 1911), p. 267.

40. *ORA*, I, 37, pt. 1, pp. 219–221, 248; Silas D. Wesson diary, July 9, 1864, Wesson papers, Civil War Times Illustrated Collection, U.S. Army Military History Institute, Carlisle Barracks, Pa. (USAMHI); Hard, *Eighth Illinois Cavalry*, pp. 300–301.

41. York to Wellford, July 18, 1864, SHC/UNC; William O. Davis, *Breckinridge, Statesman, Soldier, Symbol* (Baton Rouge, 1974), pp. 445–446; Worthington, *Fighting for Time*, pp. 166–167; Worsham, *One of Jackson's Foot Cavalry*, pp. 239–240; James Hutcheson, "Saved the Day at Monocacy," *Confederate Veteran*, XXIII (February 1915), p. 77; W. H. Runge, editor, *Four Years in the Confederate Artillery; Diary of Private Henry Robinson Berkeley* (Chapel Hill, 1961), p. 86.

42. "Personal Experience of William R. Browning," in George R. Perkins, *A Summer in Maryland and Virginia or Campaigning with the One Hundred and Forty-Ninth Ohio* (Chillicothe, 1911), pp. 51–52; Roe, *Ninth New York Heavy Artillery*, pp. 307–308.

43. Early, *War Memoirs*, p. 389; Gordon, *Reminiscences*, p. 131; Eckert, *Gordon*, p. 108; Conradis, "Monocacy," p. 35; *ORA*, I, 37, pt. 1, p. 204; unidentified Baltimore *Sun* clipping, c. July 15, 1864, MHS.

44. Wesson diary, July 10, 1864, USAMHI; Wallace, *Autobiography*, II, p. 808; *ORA*, I, 37, pt. 1, pp. 199–202.

45. *ORA, Ibid.*, pp. 192, 200.

Chapter 4

1. Reuben T. Prentice to sister, July 8, 1864, Illinois State Historical Library, Springfield (ISHL); J. Cutler Andrews, *The North Reports the Civil War* (Pittsburgh, 1955), p. 591.

2. U.S. War Department, *War of the Rebellion; A Compilation of the Official Records of the Union and Confederate Armies* (Washington, 1880–1901), series I, volume 37, pt. 2, p. 145, also pp. 134–135, 138–139, hereinafter cited *ORA*; Andrews, *Ibid.*, pp. 590–591.

3. U.S. Grant to J. Russell Jones, July 5, 1864, in John Y. Simon, editor, *The Papers of Ulysses S. Grant* (Carbondale and Edwardsville 1967), Volume II, p. 176; *ORA, Ibid.*, pp. 145, 146.

4. *ORA*, I, 37, pt. 2, pp. 79, 80; also 40, pt. 3, pp. 32–33, 34; M.R. Aldrich, "Fort Stevens," *The National Tribune*, September 20, 1900; Daniel W. Shaw, "Fort Stevens," *The National Tribune*, August 22, 1901.

5. *Ibid.*, I, 37, pt. 2, pp. 119–120, also 98; 40, pt. 3, p. 72.

6. Eli Parker to William R. Rowley, July 9, 1864, William R. Rowley papers, Illinois State Historical Library, Springfield (ISHL); C. C. Coffin, *The Boys of '61* (Boston, 1886), p. 386.

7. *ORA*, 1, 37, pt. 2, pp. 133–136; 40, pt. 3, p. 95.

8. Tyler Dennett, *Lincoln and the Civil War in the Diaries and Letters of John Hay* (New York, 1939), pp. 195–208.

9. *ORA*, I, 37, pt. 2, p. 140; A.E.H. Johnson, "When Early Came," The Washington *Star*, October 12, 1895; Gideon Welles, *Diary* (Boston, 1911), II, pp. 69–70; Howard K. Beale, editor, *The Diary of Edward Bates* (New York, 1971 reprint), pp. 383–384.

10. *ORA, Ibid.*, I, 40, pt. 3, p. 121.

11. *Ibid.*, I, 37, pt. 2, pp. 155–157, 191.

12. *Ibid.*, p. 156; 40, pt. 3, pp. 123–128, 144–145, 158–159, 168–169.

13. Dennett, *Hay diaries*, 208; Albert Gallatin Riddle, *Recollections* (New York, 1895); L. E. Chittenden, *Recollections of President Lincoln and His Administration* (New York, 1891), p. 404, and "A Chapter For My Children to Read," courtesy of Dr. Frank Vandiver, College Station, Texas, copy, Defenses of Washington files, Fort Ward Museum (FWM).

14. The Washington *Star*, July 12, 1864 extra edition; Beale, *Bates diary*, pp. 383–384; Welles, *Diary*, p. 70; Frederick W. Seward, *Reminiscences of a War Time Statesman and Diplomat* (New York, 1916), pp. 246–247.

15. Martin D. Hardin, "The Defence of Washington Against Early's Attack in July, 1864," Military Order of the Loyal Legion (MOLLUS), Illinois Commandering, *Military Essays and Recollections*, II, 1894, p. 138; P.J. Staudenraus, editor, "Mr. Lincoln's Washington"; *Selections from the Writings of Noah Brooks, Civil War Correspondent* (New York, 1967), p. 355; Chittenden, *Recollections*, p. 408; John Nicolay, *A Short Life of Abraham Lincoln* (New York, 1902), p. 403; *ORA*, I, 37, pt. 2, pp. 143, 162; and Taylor, quoted in Andrews, *North Reports the Civil War*, pp. 591–592.

16. *ORA*, I, 37, pt. 2, p. 171, and pt. 1, p. 697 for June figures; Seward, *Reminiscences*, p. 248.

17. *ORA*, I, 21, pp. 903–914, especially 904.

18. *ORA*, I, 37, pt. 2, pp. 83–85.

19. On the emergence of emphasis upon defensive tactics and use of field fortifications, see Edward Hagerman, *The American Civil War and the Origins of Modern Warfare* (Bloomington, 1988); and Grady McWhiney and Perry D. Jamieson, *Attack and Die; Civil War Military Tactics and the Southern Heritage* (University, Ala., 1982).

20. *ORA*, I, 37, pt. 2, pp. 140, 148–155, 162, 184–191, 196; Henry E. Alvord, "Early's Attack Upon Washington," MOLLUS, District of Columbia Commandery, *War Papers, #26* (1897), p. 18; Fred Smith, *Samuel Duncan Oliphant* (New York, 1967), pp. 163–164, 166; William E. Doster, *Lincoln and Episodes of the Civil War* (New York, 1915), p. 249.

21. Hardin, "The Defence of Washington," p. 131; *ORA*, I, 37, pt. 2, p. 172; Ezra J. Warner, *Generals in Blue* (Baton Rouge, 1964), p. 12; William V. Cox, "The Defenses of Washington — General Early's Advance on the Capital and the Battle of Fort Stevens, July 11 and 12, 1864," *Records of the Columbia Historical Society*, IV (1901), pp. 735–736, reprinted as pamphlet (Washington, c. 1901–1902), p. 7.

22. Hardin, *Ibid.*, pp. 131–132; *ORA*, I, 37, pt. 1, pp. 231, 236; pt. 2, p. 141; Warner, *Ibid.*, pp. 204–205.

23. *ORA*, I, 37, pt. 2, pp. 162–170; Whitelaw Reid, *Ohio in the War* (New York, 1868), p. 677.

24. John H. Wolff, "Defending the Capital," *The National Tribune*, November 9, 1899; Seward, *Reminiscences*, p. 247; Hardin, "Defence of Washington," pp. 125–126, 131; Edgar S. Dudley, "Reminiscence of Washington and Early's Attack in 1864," MOLLUS, Ohio Commandery, *Sketches of War History* (Cincinnati, 1888), I, pp. 110–115, 121; Cox, *The Defenses of Washington*, p. 9; Calvin Green, "Burning of Blair Mansion," *The National Tribune*, August 16, 1900; Joseph A. Goulden, "Remarks," *The National Tribune*, October 14, 1914; R. I. Smith, "Fort Stevens," *The National Tribune*, January 20, 1916.

25. *ORA*, I, 37, pt. 2, pp. 168–172; also pt. 1, pp. 248–251; William R. Plum, *The Military Telegraph During the Civil War* (Chicago, 1882), II, p. 153; Daniel O. Bowen, "The Fort Stevens Fight," *The National Tribune*, December 29, 1911.

26. Henry Kyd Douglas, *I Rode With Stonewall* (Chapel Hill, 1940), p. 294; J. Stoddard Johnston, "Notes of March of Breckinridge's Corps," June 19– July 15, 1864, entry July 10, 1864, New York Historical Society (NYHS), New York, NY; E. N. Atkinson, "Report of Evan's Brigade," July 22, 1864, Eldridge collection, Huntington Library (HL), San Marino, Calif.

27. George Perkins, *A Summer in Maryland and Virginia or Campaigning with the One Hundred and Forty-Ninth Ohio Volunteer Infantry* (Chillicothe, 1911), p. 52; J. Cutler Andrews, *The South Reports the Civil War* (Princeton, 1970), pp. 408– 409; Sergeant Major John G. Young, diary, North Carolina Division of History and Archives (NCHA), pp. 39–40; W.W. Scott, editor, "Diary of Captain H. W. Wingfield," *Bulletin of the Virginia State Library*, XVI (July 1929), p. 43; Baltimore *Sun*, July 9, 1864.

28. John T. De Sellum, narrative reminiscence, copy, n.d., pp. 46–48 and "Farm Family in County had 1,800 troops as 'Guests'," undated clipping, both Montgomery County Historical Society, Rockville (MCHS); Alexander Hunter *Johnny Reb and Billy Yank* (New York, 1905), p. 650; Perkins, *Ibid.*, pp. 52–53.

29. De Sellum, *Ibid.*, pp. 49–52.

30. Clay Hamilton and Charles T. Jacobs, "Greenbrier Civil War Soldier Buried in Maryland," Lewisburg, West Virginia, *Daily News*, October 11, 1983.

31. Virginia Campbell Moore, "Reminiscences of Life Along the Rockville Pike during the Civil War," *The Montgomery County Story*, XXVII (November 1984), p. 137; Alvord, "Early's Attack," p. 17; *ORA*, I, 37, pt. 2, pp. 155–157, 166–167, 170–190; Virgil Carrington Jones, *Ranger Mosby* (Chapel Hill, 1944), p. 189.

32. *ORA, Ibid.*, pt. 1, pp. 236–254, pt. 2, pp. 203–206, 594; Hunter, *Johnny Reb and Billy Yank*, p. 651; John Claggett Proctor, *Proctor's Washington* (Washington, 1949), p. 348; Milton Evans, "Fort Stevens," *The National Tribune*, March 30, 1916.

33. *ORA, Ibid.*, pt. 1, pp. 202–203, 236, 239–240, 250, 258; pt. 2, p. 199; John G. Barnard, *Report on the Defenses of Washington* (Washington, 1871), p. 1; Edward W. Emerson, *Life and Letters of Charles Russell Lowell* (New York, 1907), pp. 321–322, 405; "Where the Fighting in Defense of Washington Began," Washington *Star*, October 15, 1916; Roger S. Cohen, Jr. "The Defenses of Washington Located in Montgomery County During the Civil War," *The Montgomery County Story*, IV (February 1961), p. 3; C.O. Welch, "Defending Washington," *The National Tribune*, April 12, 1900.

34. See Judith Beck Helm, *Tenleytown, D.C.; County Village into City Neighborhood*, (Washington, 1981), chapter III; Benjamin Franklin Cooling and Walton B. Owen, *Mr. Lincoln's Forts; A Guide to the Civil Defenses of Washington* (Shippensburg, Pa., 1989), pp. 137–147, appendix D; K. Willard Brown, *The Signal Corps, U.S.A. in the War of the Rebellion* (Boston, 1896), Department of Washington chapter.

35. Cooling and Owen, *Ibid.*; Barnard, *Defenses of Washington*, plate 30.

36. Alfred Seelye Roe, *Ninth New York Heavy Artillery* (Worchester, 1899), p. 318; Perkins, *A Summer in Maryland and Virginia*, pp. 52–53; Young diary, NCHA, p. 40.

37. W.H. Farquhar, *Annals of Sandy Spring or Twenty Years of History in a Rural County in Maryland* (Baltimore, 1884), p. 13; Mildred Newbold Getty, "The Silver Spring Area," *The Montgomery County Story*, XII (November 1968), pp. 3–4; John Worsham, *One of Jackson's Foot Cavalry* (Jackson, Tenn., 1964), pp. 141–142; G.W. Nichols, *A Soldiers Story of His Regiment*, (Jessup, Ga.), p. 173.

38. *ORA*, I, 37, pt. 1, pp. 230–231, 236, 246; pt. 2, p. 594; Dudley, "Reminiscence," pp. 122–123; Cox, "The Defenses of Washington," pp. 11–12.

39. James C. Cannon, *Record of Co. K, One Hundred and Fiftieth Ohio Volunteer Infantry, 1864*, (n.p.), 1907), pp. 14–15, 19; A.A. Safford, "Saw Lincoln at Fort Stevens," *The National Tribune*, April 4, 1912..

40. Doster, *Lincoln and Episodes of the Civil War*, p. 252; *ORA*, I, 37, pt. 1, p. 255; pt. 2, pp. 194, 200, 202, 205; John V. Brinton, *Personal Memoirs* (New York, 1914), p. 279; Henry

Ivins diary, July 11, 1864, US Army Military History Institute (USAMHI); "Saving the Capital," undated clipping, Defenses of Washington files, (FWM); Samuel C. Smith, "Detailed from Dismounted Camp," *First Maine Bugle*, XXV (July 1893), p.3; A.G. Jacobs, "Getting There in Time," *The National Tribune*, August 23, 1900; M.B. Aldrich, "Defense of the Capital," *The National Tribune*, September 20, 1900; F. S. Morgan, "At Fort Stevens," *The National Tribune*, August 1, 1912; John H. Wolff, "The Fight at Fort Stevens," *The National Tribune*, January 22, 1914.

41. D. R. B. Nevin, "Fort Stevens," *United Service Journal*, 2 (July 1889), p. 39; *ORA*, I, 37, pt. 1, p. 231; "The Life of Lieutenant Colonel David B. Lang, 62d Virginia Regiment," n.d., typescript, Civil War Times Collection, and *Veterans Advocate*, Concord N.H., June 15, 1886, clipping, both USAMHI.

42. Elbert B. Smith, *Francis Preston Blair* (New York, 1980), pp. 172–173.

43. *Ibid.*, pp. 358–359; Getty, "The Silver Spring Area," pp. 2–3; Farquhar, *Historical Montgomery County Maryland Old Homes and History* (Baltimore, 1952), pp. 285–286; Aldace Freeman Walker letters, 1862–1865, Vermont Historical Society (Vt.HS) recount the relations between Union soldiers stationed in the Silver Spring vicinity and the Blair families.

44. Lang, "Life of," USAMHI; "Memorable Incidents of Old Fort Stevens," unidentified clipping, History files, Rock Creek Nature Center, National Park Service, Washington DC (RCNC); Proctor, *Proctor's Washington*, p. 348.

45. I. G. Bradwell, "On to Washington," *Confederate Veteran*, XXXVI (March 1928), p. 95; Cannon, *Memorial of Company K*, p. 9; Frank B. Wilkeson, *Recollections of a Private Soldier in the Army of the Potomac* (New York, 1898), p. 214; Roe, *Ninth New York Heavy Artillery*, *ORA*, I, 37, pt. 1, pp. 231, 244–245, 348; pt. 2, p. 195; Frank Fuller, "At Fort Stevens," *The National Tribune*, June 1, 1911; James M. Singer, "Lincoln at Fort Stevens," *The National Tribune*, February 8, 1912.

46. Young diary, NCHA, p. 40; Wilkeson, *Ibid.*, p. 214; Bradwell, "Early's Demonstration against Washington in 1864," *Confederate Veteran* (October 1914), p. 438, and "Early's March to Washington in 1864," Confederate Veteran (May 1920), p. 177; *ORA*, I, 37, pt. 1, pp. 231, 238, 241–242; Robert Park, "Diary," *Southern Historical Society Papers*, I (1876), p. 379; Doree G. Holman and Gertrude D. Bradley, *Old Bethesda—Bethesda Not So Old*, (Gaithersburg, Md.), p. 44; *ORA*, XLIII, pt. 1, p. 602; Atkinson, "Evan's Brigade Report" (HL); John C. Clevenger, "At Fort Stevens," *The National Tribune*, June 19, 1900; A. F. Jackson, "Dismounted Cavalry," *The National Tribune*, August 9, 1900.

47. George T. Stevens, *Three Years in the Sixth Corps* (New York, 1867), pp. 372, 375–376; "Veteran, 102d Pa.," "At Fort Stevens," *The National Tribune*, August 2, 1900.

48. *ORA*, I, 37, pt. 1, pp. 270–275; Herbert Mitang, editor, *Noah Brooks, Washington D.C. in Lincoln's Times* (Chicago, 1971), p. 160; Penrose Mark, *Red, White, and Blue Badge* (Harrisburg, 1911), p. 279; Harris H. Beecher, *Record of the One Hundred and Fourteenth Regiment* (NYSV), (Norwich, 1866), pp. 372–376; A. G. Jacobs, "Getting There in Time," *The National Tribune*, August 23, 1900; F. S. Morgan, "At Fort Stevens," *The National Tribune*, August 1, 1912.

49. A. T. Brewer, *History of the Sixty First Regiment* (Pittsburgh, 1911), p. 105; Smith, "Detailed from Dismounted Camp," p. 25; *ORA*, I, 37, pt. 1, pp. 264–265, pt. 2, p. 209; Wilkeson, *Recollections*, pp. 212–213; Charles Burr Todd, *History of the Second District of Columbia Infantry* (New York, 1889), p. 157; Proctor, *Proctor's Washington*, p. 348; Cox, "The Defenses of Washington," pp. 13–14.

50. John B. Gordon, *Reminiscences of the Civil War* (New York, 1904), p. 314; Sylvanus Cadwallader [Benjamin P. Thomas, editor], *Three Years with Grant* (New York, 1955), p. 227.

51. Jubal A. Early, "The Advance on Washington in 1864," *Southern Historical Society Papers*, p. 9 (July, August 1881), p. 306, and *War Memoirs* (Bloomington, 1960 reprint), p. 389.

52. William Allan memoirs, 32, Southern Historical Collection, University of North

Carolina, Chapel Hill (SHC/UNC); Early, *War Memoirs*, p. 390 and "The Advance on Washington," p. 306; Worsham, *One of Jackson's Foot Cavalry*, p. 242; John Opie, *A Rebel Cavalryman with Lee, Stuart, and Jackson* (Chicago, 1899), p. 246; Nichols, *A Soldier's Story*, p. 173; Joseph T. Durkin, editor, *Confederate Chaplain* (Milwaukee, 1960), p. 95; Manley Wade Wellman, *Rebel Boast; First at Bethel—Last at Appomattox* (New York, 1956), p. 172; Gordon, *Ibid.*, pp. 314–315; Edwin French, "The Fight at Fort Stevens," *The National Tribune*, August 11, 1904.

53. George Haven Putnam, *Memories of My Youth, 1844– 1865*, New York, 1914, p. 340; *ORA*, I, 37, pt. 2, p. 199; S.J. Weiler, "Cavalry at Fort Stevens," *The National Tribune*, April 5, 1900; Robert Connelly, "At Fort Stevens," *The National Tribune*, July 19, 1900.

54. *ORA*, I, 37, pt. 1, pp. 275–276; Dudley, "Reminiscence," pp. 122–123.

55. Concerning Lincoln at Fort Stevens on July 10 and 11, see Lucian C. Warner, *The Story of My Life* (New York, 1914), pp. 47–48; Cannon, *Record of Company K* pp. 16, 26, and *Memorial, 150th Ohio, Company K*, (Cleveland, 1907), pp. 8–10; John H. Bierck, "He Saw Lincoln Under Fire," *Liberty Magazine*, XIV (1937), p. 7; Dennett, *Lincoln and the Civil War*, p. 208; Welles, *Diary*, II, p. 72; Seward, *Reminiscences*, p. 248; Frederick C. Hicks, "Lincoln, Wright, and Holmes at Fort Stevens," *Journal of the Illinois State Historical Society*, XXXIX (September 1946), pp. 329–330. Analysis of the conflicting stories about Lincoln at Fort Stevens can be best followed in John H. Cramer, *Lincoln Under Enemy Fire* (Baton Rouge, 1948), chapters 2 and 3 especially; Isaac A. Hawk, "Fort Stevens," *The National Tribune*, September 27, 1900; also John B. Southard to sister, July 16, 1864, Southard Family papers, New York Historical Society (NYHS).

56. *ORA*, I, 37, pt. 1, pp. 231–232, 255, 258, pt. 2, pp. 194, 206–207; Perkins, *Summer in Maryland and Virginia*, p. 54; Roe, *Ninth New York Heavy Artillery*, p. 319.

57. *ORA*, I, 37, pt. 1, p. 259, also p. 232; Capt. A.B. Beamish, "Battle of Fort Stevens near Washington, DC, July 12, 1864, A Little Different Version," *Grand Army Scout and Soldiers Mail* (Philadelphia, July 10, 1886), copy, Defenses of Washington files, FWM; Alvord, "Early's Attack," pp. 17–18.

Chapter 5

1. Aldace F. Walker to father, October 25, 29, 1862, and July 13, 1864 especially, although Walker's correspondence relating to Fort Massachusetts and Stevens spans the period September 1862 to May 1864, with random letters in July 1864, all typescript copies, Vermont Historical Society, Montpelier (Vt. HS); A. C. Fletcher, "At Fort Stevens," *The National Tribune*, September 27, 1900; Charles Carswell, "Lincoln and the Sixth Corps," *The National Tribune*, August 16, 1912.

2. John Claggett Proctor, *Proctor's Washington* (Washington, 1949), pp. 348–350.

3. Horace H. Shaw and Charles J. House, *The First Maine Artillery* (Portland, 1903), chapter IX; Stephen F. Blanding, *In the Defenses of Washington or Sunshine in a Soldier's Life* (Providence, 1889), p. 35; Augustus Woodbury, *The Second Rhode Island: A Narrative of Military Operations* (Providence, 1875), p. 287; James L. Bowen, *History of the Thirty-Seventh Regiment, Massachusetts Volunteers* (Holyoke and New York, 1884), p. 352; G.G. Benedict, *Vermont in the Civil War* (Burlington, 1886), I, pp. 374, 486.

4. See B. Franklin Cooling, *Symbol, Sword, and Shield* (Hamden, Ct., 1975), pp. 68–70; B. Franklin Cooling and Walton Owen, *Mr. Lincoln's Forts; A Guide to the Civil War Defenses of Washington* (Shippenburg, 1989), pp. 150–155 for sources on individual forts; Joseph Grabenstein, "History Is Just a Hike Away," *St. John's Quarterly*, 4 (Autumn, 1983), p. 11.

5. Cooling and Owen, *Ibid.*, pp. 155–167; Woodbury, *Second Rhode Island*, p. 53.

6. Cooling and Owen, *Ibid.*, pp. 167–173; Caroline E. Chamberlin editor, *Letters of George E. Chamberlin*, (Springfield, Ill., 1883), pp. 246–247, 253, 266–268, 271, 296, 304.

7. Shaw and House, *First Maine Heavy Artillery*, chapter IX; A.P. Smith, *History of the Seventy-Sixth New York* (Cortland, 1867), pp. 44–57; Fort Stevens Miscellaneous Documents, Defenses of Washington files, Fort Ward Museum and Park (FWMP), Alexandria, Virginia; Cooling and Owen, *Ibid.*, pp. 156–161.

8. George F. Ward, *History of the Second Pennsylvania Heavy Artillery* (Philadelphia, 1904), p. 25; William Van Zandt Cox, *The Defenses of Washington; General Early's Advance on the Capital and the Battle of Fort Stevens* (Washington, 1907), p. 4 fn; Bernard Kohn, "Restored Civil War Fort Is New Sightseeing Shrine," Washington *Sunday Star*, July 4, 1937.

9. Aldace F. Walker, *The Vermont Brigade in the Shenandoah Valley, 1864* (Burlington, 1869), pp. 28–29; John G. Barnard, *A Report on the Defenses of Washington* (Washington, 1871), appendix.

10. US War Department, *War of the Rebellion; A Compilation of the Official Records of the Union and Confederate Armies* (Washington, 1880–1901), series 1, volume 37, pt. 2, p. 223; 50, pt. 1, p. 1177, hereinafter cited *ORA*; Washington *Evening Star*, July 12, 1864; while the financial situation of the nation was noted by Colonel John McElroy, Grand Army of the Republic local commander in "Fort Stevens as National Park Favored as Tribute to Lincoln," Washington *Star*, June 27, 1923.

11. Jubal A. Early, *War Memoirs* (Bloomington, 1961 reprint), p. 392; Early to Editor, Baltimore *Gazette*, December 14, 1874, copy, Defenses of Washington files (FWMP); Jubal A. Early, "The Advance on Washington," *Southern Historical Society Papers*, 9 (August 1881), p. 309; *ORA*, I, 37, pt. 1, p. 348; John B. Gordon, *Reminiscences of the Civil War* (New York, 1904), pp. 314–315; Henry Kyd Douglas, *I Rode With Stonewall* (Chapel Hill, 1940), pp. 294–295; Cox, *Defenses of Washington*, pp. 15–16.

12. E.N. Atkinson, "Report of Evans Brigade," July 22, 1864, Eldridge collections, Huntington Library (HL), San Marino, Calif.; G.W. Nichols, *A Soldier's Story of His Regiment* (Jessup, Ga., 1890), p. 172.

13. *ORA, Ibid.*, pp. 232, 238, 242, 246, 247; George T. Stevens, *Three Years in The Sixth Corps* (New York, 1870), p. 377; Cox, *Defenses of Washington*, p. 20 fn.

14. *ORA, Ibid.*, pt. 1, 234–235, 240, 250, 255–259, 271–272; pt. 2, 224–225, 229; Henry B. Hibben, *History of the Washington Navy Yard* (Washington, 1890), p. 139; J. Willard Brown, *The Signal Corps in the War of the Rebellion* (Boston, 1896), p. 664.

15. Journal of an Anonymous Crewman, Steamer George Leary, entries July 10, 11, 12, 1864, Manuscript Department, Perkins Library, Duke University (DU); Emil Rosenblatt, editor, *Anti-Rebel, The Civil War Letters of Wilbur Fisk* (Croton-on-Hudson, 1983), p. 236; F.C. Morse to Nellie, July 10, 11, 12, mother and sister, July 11, "My dear bosom companion," July 13, all 1864, all Massachusetts Historical Society (MSHS); Deborah Hamblin, compiler, *Brevet Major General Joseph Eldridge Hamblin* (Boston, 1902), p. 39.

16. W.F. Parish, "Fort Stevens," *The National Tribune*, January 15, 1914; Augustus Buell, *The Cannoneer; Recollections of Service in the Army of the Potomac* (Washington, 1890), pp. 265–269.

17. William E. Doster, *Lincoln and Episodes of the Civil War* (New York, 1915), p. 253; Benedict, *Vermont in the Civil War*, I, pp. 488–489; Alanson A. Haines, *History of the Fifteeneth New Jersey* (New York, 1883), chapter XIV; Woodbury, *Second Rhode Island* (Providence, 1875), pp. 285–287; James L. Bowen, *History of the Thirty-Seventh Massachusetts Volunteers* (Holyoke, 1884), p. 352; Albert G. Riddle, *Recollections of War Time* (New York, 1895), p. 289; Gideon Welles, *Diary* (Boston, 1911), I, p. 75; Lucius Chittenden, "A Chapter for My Children to Read," unpublished manuscript, courtesy of Frank Vandiver, College Station, Texas, copy, Defenses of Washington files (FWMP); also Maine Adjutant General, *Annual Report, 1864* (Augusta, 1865), pp. 228–320.

18. On sources concerning Lincoln at Fort Stevens, see chapter four, fn. 54, in addition to Penrose G. Mark, *Red, White and Blue Badge, History of the Ninety-Third Pennsylvania* (Harrisburg, 1911), p. 280; Frederick D. Bidwell, compiler, *History of the Forty-Ninth New York* (Albany, 1916); and A.B. Beamish, "Battle of Fort Stephens [sic] near Washington, D.C. July 12, 1864, A Little Different Version," *Grand Army Scout and Soldiers Mail* (Philadelphia), Saturday, July 10, 1886; also John Y. Simon, editor, *The Papers of Ulysses S. Grant* (Carbondale), volume 11, p. 222, fn. 1.

19. The fullest account of varying interpretations of the Lincoln-Holmes story can be found in John H. Cramer, *Lincoln Under Enemy Fire* (Baton Rouge, 1948), chapters 2 and 3; also Buell, *The Cannoneer*, p. 271; Albert A. Safford, "Saw Lincoln at Fort Stevens," *The National Tribune*, April 4, 1912.

20. Thomas W. Hyde, *Following the Greek Cross* (Boston, 1895), p. 223; Aldace F. Walker to father, July 13, 1864, Vt. HS; Cramer, *Ibid.*; John B. Southard to sister, July 16, 1864, Southard papers, New York Historical Society (NYHS); Isaac A. Hawk, "Fort Stevens," *The National Tribune*, September 27, 1900; Oliver Edwards, "President Lincoln at Fort Stevens," *The National Tribune*, August 20, 1903.

21. C.H. Enos, "Fort Stevens," *The National Tribune*, March 23, 1916; George E. Farrington, "Sixth Corps at Fort Stevens," *The National Tribune*, July 12, 1912; Lewis Cass White, "President Lincoln at Fort Stevens," *The National Tribune*, March 6, 1913; B.T. Plugh, "Fort Stevens," *The National Tribune*, September 23, 1915.

22. "Lincoln's Order When Under Fire," *The Washington Herald*, May 31, 1908.

23. *ORA*, I, 37, pt. 1, p. 232.

24. Chittenden, "A Chapter for My Children to Read;" Barnard, *Defenses of Washington*, Plate 10; S.A. McDonald, "Fort Stevens Affair, Part 1," *The National Tribune*, April 12, 1894, and "Part 2," April 19, 1894.

25. For various accounts of Bidwell's attack and the afternoon/evening battle, see S.A. McDonald, "Fort Stevens Affair, Part 1" *The National Tribune*, April 12, 1894, and "Part 2," April 19, 1894; Milton Evans, "Fort Stevens," *The National Tribune*, March 30, 1916; John D. Shuman, "War at Fort Stevens," *The National Tribune*, March 7, 1912; Edward H. Fuller, "Fort Stevens," *The National Tribune*, July 22, 1915; Stevens, *Three Years with the Sixth Corps*, p. 378; Mason W. Tyler, *Recollections of the Civil War* (New York, 1912), p. 245; Southard to sister, July 16, 1864, NYHS; *ORA*, I, 37, pt. 1, pp. 232, 242, 244, 246, 247, 276–277, 348–349, and 43, pt. 1, p. 603; Welles, *Diary*, I, p. 75; Riddle, *Recollections*, p. 288; Cox, Defenses of Washington, pp. 16–22 as well as his remarks in James C. Cannon *Record of Co. K, One Hundred and Fiftieth Ohio Volunteer Infantry, 1864*, (n.p., 1907); Mark, *Red, White, and Blue Badge*, p. 280; Bidwell, *Forty-Ninth New York*, pp. 64–65; Haines, *Fifteenth New Jersey*, pp. 226–227; Bowen, *Thirty-Seventh Massachusetts*, pp. 352–353; Stevens, *Three Years in the Sixth Corps*, pp. 377–381; Tyler, *Recollections*, pp. 244–246; State of Maine, Adjutant Generals Office, Report, 1864 (Augusta, 1864), pp. 228, 233, 320.

26. David B. Swinfern, *Ruggles' Regiment; The One Hundred and Twenty-Second New York Volunteers in the American Civil War* (Hanover and London, 1982), pp. 50–51; Daniel H. Bee, "Wounded at Fort Stevens," *The National Tribune*, April 11, 1912; George S. Orr, "Death of Colonel Visscher," *The National Tribune*, June 28, 1894.

27. Atkinson, "Report of Evans Brigade," HL.

28. Swinfern, *Ruggles Regiment*, p. 51; McDonald, "Fort Stevens Affair, Part 2."

29. Douglas, *I Rode with Stonewall*, pp. 295–296; for other Confederate accounts, see John H. Worsham, *One of Jackson's Foot Cavalry* (New York, 1912), p. 242; Manly Wade Wellman, *Rebel Boast* (New York, 1956), pp. 172–173; Joseph T. Durkin, *Confederate Chaplain* (Milwaukee, 1960), p. 95; George Perkins, *A Summer in Maryland and Virginia or Campaigning with the One Hundred and Forty-Ninth Ohio* (Chillicothe, 1911), p. 54; for action in other sectors,

see *ORA*, I, 37, pt. 1, pp. 238, 256, 259; M. B. Aldrich, "Defense of the Capital," *The National Tribune*, September 20, 1900.

30. *ORA, Ibid.*, p. 232; Washington *Star*, May 20, 1934; Lucius Chittenden, *Recollections of President Lincoln and His Administration* (New York, 1891), pp. 420, 421; Cox in Cannon, *Memorial of Company K*, pp. 10–11; Mildred Newbold Getty, *Grace Episcopal Church, 1857–1957* (Silver Spring, 1957), p. 7; "Memorable Incidents of Old Fort Stevens," clipping, files Rock Creek Nature Center, National Park Service, Washington, DC (RCNC); Cooling and Owen, *Mr. Lincoln's Forts*, pp. 162–167; *ORA*, I, 43, pt. 1, p. 603; Atkinson, "Report of Evans Brigade," HL.

31. I.G. Bradwell, "Reminiscences," chapter 3, p. 9, Maryland Historical Society (MHS); "Burning of the Blair House," *Confederate Veteran*, XIX (July 1911), p. 336; Jubal Early to Edmund Jennings Lee, September 26, 1872, Lee papers, DU; William C. Davis, *Breckinridge; Statesman, Soldier, Symbol* (Baton Rouge, 1974), p. 449; Early, "The Advance on Washington in 1864," pp. 310–311; Douglas, *I Rode with Stonewall*, p. 296; Leonidus Lafayette Polk to wife, July 17, 1864, Southern Historical Collection, University of North Carolina, Chapel Hill (SHC/UNC); Robert E. Park, "Diary," *Southern Historical Society Papers*, I (1876), pp. 379–380; V.E. Turner and H.C. Wall, "Twenty-Third Regiment" in volume 2, p. 245 as well as Cyrus B. Watson, "Fifty-Fifth Regiment," in volume 3, p. 55 of Walter E. Clark, *Histories of the Several Regiments and Battalions from North Carolina in the Great War* (Raleigh, 1901) James McMurran diary, July 12, 1864 entry, Virginia State Library and Archives (VSLA); *ORA*, I, 42, pt. 2, 62; and New York *Times*, July 22, 1864; Hudson Strode, *Jefferson Davis: Tragic Hero* (New York, 1964), p. 67; Alvin Green, "Burning of Blair Mansion," *The National Tribune*, August 16, 1900; A. C. Fletcher, "At Fort Stevens," *The National Tribune*, September 27, 1900.

32. Daniel C. Bowen, "The Fort Stevens Fight," *The National Tribune*, December 29, 1911. Morse to "My dear bosom companion, July 13, 1864," MHS; James D. Sorensen, "Letters to Editor," *Smithsonian* (September 1988), p. 18; Tyler, *Recollections*, p. 246; "Memorable Incidents," clipping RCNC; Proctor, *Proctor's Washington*, 350.

33. *ORA*, I, 37, pt. 1, p. 259; George A. Armes, *Ups and Downs of an Army Officer* (Washington, 1900), p. 114; Jacob Schmid memoirs, United States Army Military History Institute (USAMHI); John H. Niebaum, *History of the Pittsburgh Washington Infantry, One Hundred and Second (Old Thirteenth) Regiment* (Pittsburgh, 1931), pp. 116–117; A.T. Brewer, *History of the Sixty-First Regiment* (Pittsburgh, 1911), p. 108; Amanda A. Stearns, *The Lady Nurse of Ward B* (New York, 1909), p. 306; Will Plank, *Banners and Bugles; A Record of Ulster County, New York and the Mid-Hudson Region in the Civil War* (Marlborough, NY, 1963), p. 99; Richard Castle to father, mothers, sister, July 12, 1864, copy, Defenses of Washington files, FWMP; "Son and Daughter of Enemies Tell of Fort Stevens Skirmish," Washington *Star*, July 13, 1934; "The 150th Ohio at Fort Stevens," *The National Tribune*, October 15, 1903.

34. Chittenden, *Recollections*, p. 421.

35. Lucian C. Warner, *The Story of My Life During Seventy Eventful Years, 1841–1911* (New York, 1914), pp. 49–50; Chittenden, *Ibid.*

Chapter 6

1. Jubal A. Early, *War Memoirs* (Bloomington, 1961 ed.), p. 388; Bradley T. Johnson, "My Ride Around Baltimore in Eighteen Hundred Sixty-Four," *Journal of the United States Cavalry Association*, II (September 1889), pp. 251-253.

2. Johnson, *Ibid.*, p. 253; J. Kelly Bennette diary, entry July 9, 1864, Southern Historical Collection, University of North Carolina, Chapel Hill (SHC/UNC); Harry Gilmor, *Four Years in the Saddle* (New York, 1866), pp. 190-191.

3. Gilmor, *Ibid.*; also Carroll *Record*, July 1895, quoted in Frederic Shriver Klein, editor, *Just South of Gettysburg; Carroll County, Maryland in the Civil War* (Westminster, 1973), pp. 216-217.

4. Gilmor, *Ibid.*, p. 191; Johnson, "My Ride," p. 254; Bennette diary, July 10, 1864, SHC UNC.

5. Richard R. Duncan, "Maryland's Reaction to Early's Raid in 1864: A Summer of Bitterness," *Maryland Historical Magazine* 65, (Fall 1969), p. 257; Morgan Dix, compiler, *Memoirs of John A. Dix* (New York, 1883), pp. 23, 25; photocopy of unidentified, Rinehart diary, entry July 11, 1864, Maryland Historical Society, Baltimore (MHS).

6. Duncan, *Ibid*, pp. 258–259; U.S. War Department, *War of the Rebellion; A Compilation of the Official Records of the Union and Confederate Armies* (Washington , 1880–1901), series I, volume 37, part 2, pp. 145–154 (hereinafter cited *ORA*). J. Thomas Scharf, *A History of Baltimore City and County* (Philadelphia, 1881), p. 146; also Union League of Baltimore diary, entries July 10–15, 1864, MHS.

7. Duncan, *Ibid.*, pp. 258–260; William H. James, "Blue and Gray, I, Volunteer of 1864," *Maryland Historical Magazine*, XXXVI (March 1941), p. 31; Richard P. Thomas to brother, July 10, 1864, MHS; copy, Scharf, *Ibid.*, pp. 146–148.

8. Johnson, "My Ride," 254; Gilmor, *Four Years*, pp. 192–193; Gilmor to Booth, July 28, 1864, Gilmor papers, MHS; also for a modern analysis of the Gilmor raid, see Robert E Michel, *Colonel Harry Gilmor's Raid Around Baltimore* (Baltimore, 1976), pp. 6–12.

9. Bennette diary, July 11, 1864, SHC/UNC; Johnson, "My Ride," p. 254; Michel, *Gilmor's Raid*, pp. 13–15; Duncan, "Maryland's Reaction," pp. 266– 267; Governor Augustus Bradford, Executive Journals, entries July 7, 11, 1864, and Governor Bradford's house protection memorandum, folder Bradford to Committee on War Claims, no date, both MHS.

10. Edward R. Rich, *Comrades Four* (New York, 1907), pp. 163–164; George Wilson Booth, *Personal Reminiscences of a Maryland Soldier in the War Between the States* (Baltimore, 1907), p. 124; Henry G. Mettam (Samuel H. Miller, editor); "Civil War Memoirs, First Maryland Cavalry, C.S.A.," *Maryland Historical Magazine*, 157 (June 1963), p. 58; Johnson, "My Ride," pp. 254–255; Bennette diary, *Ibid.*

11. *ORA*, I, 37, pt. 2, pp. 212–216, 253; Bennette diary, July 11, 1864, *Ibid.*

12. *ORA, Ibid.*, pp. 215, 217–219, 552; Duncan, "Maryland's Reaction," pp. 260–264.

13. Gilmor, *Four Years*, pp. 193–196; Michel, *Gilmor's Raid*, pp. 16–17.

14. *Ibid.*

15. *ORA*, I, 37, pt. 1, pp. 225–226, 230.

16. *Ibid.* pp. 224–230; Daniel Toomey, *Civil War in Maryland* (Baltimore, 1983), pp. 127–128; Gilmor, *Four Years*, pp. 194–196; W. Emerson Wilson, "City Prepares to Fight Invaders," Wilmington *Morning News*, July 15, 1964, p. 22; Michel, *Gilmor's Raid*, pp. 14–18.

17. U.S. Department of the Navy, *Official Records of the Union and Confederate Navies in the War of the Rebellion* (Washington, 1894–1927), series I, volume 5, pp. 292–294, 458–471, 547, hereinafter cited *ORN*.

18. Gilmor, *Four Years*, pp. 197–202; Michel, *Gilmor's Ride*, pp. 20–24; Virginia Walcott Beachamp, *A Private War, Letters and Diaries of Madge Preston, 1862–1867* (New Brunswick, 1987), p. 119.

19. *ORA*, I, 37, pt. 2, p. 248; Isobel Davidson, *Real Stories from Baltimore County History* (Hatboro, Pa., 1967), p. 107; Gilmor to Booth, July 28, 1864, MHS; Gilmor, *Four Years*, pp. 201–202; Michel, *Gilmor's Raid*, pp. 24–26.

20. *ORA, Ibid.*, pp. 321–324, 359, 373; Wilson, "A City Prepares to Fight," p. 22.

21. Johnson, "My Ride," 256; *ORA, Ibid.*, pp. 224– 225; Bennette diary, July 12, 1864, SHC/UNC; Mettam, "Memoirs."

22. Duncan, "Maryland's Reaction," pp. 267–268; *ORA, Ibid.*, p. 219.

23. Johnson, "My Ride," p. 257.

24. Douglas S. Freeman, editor, *Lee's Dispatches* (New York, 1915), pp. 269–271; a full discussion of Wood's role appears in Royce G. Shingleton, *John Taylor Wood, Sea Ghost of the Confederacy* (Athens, 1979), pp. 116–118.

25. *ORA*, I, 40, pt. 3, p. 761; II, 7, p. 458; *ORN*, I, 10, pp. 721–722; Edward Crenshaw, "Diary of . . .," *Alabama Historical Quarterly* (1930), pp. 449–450, as cited in Wade Hampton, "The Raid on Point Lookout; A Study in Desperation," unpublished seminar paper, American University, 1970, copy, MHS; James H. Rochelle to Surgeon Conrad, July 17, 1864, Naval Historical Society Collections, New York Historical Society (NYHS), New York.

26. *ORA*, I, 37, pt. 2, p. 295; II, 7, pp. 399– 400; *ORN*, I, 5, pp. 458–459, and pp. 10, 281, 287–289; Johnson, "My Ride," p. 257; Hampton, *Ibid.*, pp. 50, 54–57; Edwin W. Beitzell, *Point Lookout Prison Camp for Confederates* (n.p., 1972), pp. 41, 54, 59, 77.

27. Johnson, *Ibid*; Booth, *Personal Reminiscences*, pp. 124–125.

28. Duncan, "Maryland's Reaction," p. 269; *ORA*, I, v. 37, pt. 2, p. 381; Baltimore *Sun*. July 15, 1864; Scharf, *Baltimore*, p. 148; Richard Cary, "When Gilmor Threatened Baltimore," Baltimore *Sun*, December 1, 1929.

29. Rebecca Davis journal, entry July 16, 1864, MHS.

30. Harry Wright Newman, *Maryland and the Confederacy* (Annapolis, 1976), p. 204; Scharf, *Baltimore*, p. 148; "Mollie" to "Aunt Judie," July 25, 1864, and Davis journal, entries July 16, 30, 1864, both MHS.

Chapter Seven

1. J. Willard Brown, *The Signal Corps, U.S.A. in the War of the Rebellion* (Boston, 1896), p. 664; Colin R. Ballard, *The Military Genius of Abraham Lincoln* (Cleveland, 1952), p. 211; US War Department, *War of the Rebellion: A Compilation of the Official Records of Union and Confederate Armies* (Washington, 1880–1901), series I, volume 37, part 1, pp. 232, 259 (hereinafter cited *ORA*).

2. *ORA*, I, 37, pt. 1, pp. 242, 248, 252–262; D. R. B. Nevin, "Fort Stevens," *United Service Journal*, 2 (July 1889), pp. 39–40; W. H. Farquhar, *Annals of Sandy Spring or Twenty Years History of a Rural County in Maryland* (Baltimore, 1884), p. 14; Joseph P. Farley, *Three Rivers: the James, the Potomac, the Hudson: A Retrospect of Peace and War* (Washington and New York, 1910), p. 149.

3. London *Times*, July 25, 1864; *Frank Leslie's Weekly*, August 6, 1864; Aldace F. Walker to father, July 15, 1864, typescript copy, Vermont Historical Society (Vt.HS); James Commons, "Led Him Out of Danger," *The National Tribune*, November 1, 1900.

4. J. Cutler Andrews, *The North Reports the Civil War.* (Pittsburgh, 1955), pp. 594–595; Meigs quoted in Russell F. Weigley, *Quartermaster General of the Union Army: A Biography of M. C. Meigs* (New York, 1959), p. 352.

5. Tyler Dennett, *Lincoln and the Civil War in the Diaries and Letters of John Hay* (New York, 1939), pp. 209–210; John H. Cramer, *Lincoln Under Enemy Fire* (Baton Rouge, 1948), pp. 63, 66.

6. Dennett, *Ibid.*

7. Edward W. Emerson, *Life and Letters of Charles Russell Lowell* (Boston, 1907), pp. 40–41; Washington *Evening Star*, July 13, 1864; New York *Times*, July 4, 1864.

8. W. W. Goldsborough, *The Maryland Line in the Confederate Army* (Baltimore, 1900), p. 206; Emil Rosenblatt, *Anti-Rebel: The Civil War Letters of Wilbur Fisk* (Croton-on-Hudson, 1983), pp. 240–241; Emerson, *Ibid.*, pp. 40, 41; Bradley Johnson, "My Ride Around Baltimore in Eighteen Hundred and Sixty Four," *Journal of the United States Cavalry Association*, II (September 1889), p. 258; George W. Booth, *Personal Reminiscences of a Maryland Soldier in the War Between the States* (Baltimore, 1907), pp. 125–126; "War Reminiscence," *Montgomery County*

Sentinel, October 10, 1890; J. Kelly Bennette Diary, diary entries July 13, 14, 1864, Southern Historical Collection, University of North Carolina, Chapel Hill (SHC/UNC); Washington *Evening Star*, July 13, 1864.

9. *ORA*, I, 37, pt. 2, pp. 300–301; John Y. Simon, *The Papers of Ulysses S. Grant* (Carbondale and Edwardsville, 1967), v. 11, pp. 225–280 preserves the relevant correspondence illustrating the manifold problems with Union command and control in this period. On Lincoln, see Dennett, *Lincoln and the Civil War*, p. 209.

10. *ORA*, I, 37, pt. 1, pp. 265–266; pt. 2, pp. 284–287; G. G. Benedict, *Vermont in the Civil War* (Burlington, 1886), I, p. 492; Aldace F. Walker, *The Vermont Brigade in the Shenandoah Valley* (Burlington, 1869), p. 97; Aldace F. Walker to father, July 15, 1864, VtHS; Richard B. Irwin, *History of the Nineteenth Army Corps* (New York, 1893), pp. 356–357; Virginia Campbell Moore, "Reminiscences of Life Along the Rockville Pike During the Civil War," *The Montgomery Story*, p. 27 (November 1984), p. 137.

11. Alfred Seelye Roe, *History of the Ninth New York Heavy Artillery* (Worchester, 1899), p. 136; George N. Carpenter, *History of the Eight Regiment Vermont Volunteers* (Boston, 1886), pp. 156–157; Alanson A. Haines, *History of the Fifteenth Regiment New Jersey Volunteers* (New York, 1883), p. 227.

12. Roe, *New York Heavy Artillery* pp. 308–309, 320; William H. Runge, ed, *Four Years in the Confederate Artillery: Diary of Private Henry Robinson Berkeley* (Chapel Hill, 1961), p. 88; Joseph T. Durkin, ed, *Confederate Chaplain, War Journal of Rev. James B. Sheeran* (Milwaukee, 1960), p. 381; William Beavens, diary, entries July 13, 14, 1864, pp. 78–79, SHC/UNC; Robert Parks "Diary," *Southern Historical Society Papers* (SHSP), I (1876), p. 381; Willard Bushong, *Old Jube* (Boyce, Va., 1955), p. 210; J. Kelly Bennette, diary entry July 13, 1864, SHC/UNC; C. S. Hart voucher to A. Dawson, July 14, 1864, owned by Kim Holien, Alexandria, Virginia, copy, Defenses of Washington files, FWMP.

13. G.W. Nichols, *A Soldiers Story of His Regiment* (Jessup, Ga., 1898), p. 175; Bradley Johnson, "My Ride," p. 258; J. Kelly Bennette diary, July 14, 1864, SHC/UNC; I.G. Bradwell unpublished reminiscences, 9, typescript, Maryland Historical Society (MHS).

14. Tyler Dennett, *Lincoln and the Civil War in the Diaries and Letters of John Hay* (New York, 1939), p. 210; *ORA*. I, 37, pt. 1, pp. 266–267; Bradwell, reminiscences, 1945, p. 10; Rosenblatt, *Anti-Rebel*, p. 241; William H. Shaw, Diary (n.p., n.d.), p. 49; Walker, *The Vermont Brigade*, pp. 37–38; Haines, *History of the Fifteenth New Jersey* (New York, 1883), p. 228; Theodore F. Vaill, *History of the Second Connecticut Heavy Artillery* (Winsted, Ct., 1868), p. 84; James L. Bowen, *History of the Thirty-Seventh Massachusetts* (Holyoke, 1884), pp. 353–355.

15. Roe, *Ninth New York Heavy Artillery*, pp. 322–323; Browning in George Perkins, *A Summer in Maryland and Virginia or Campaigning with the One Hundred and Forty-Ninth Ohio Volunteer Infantry* (Chillicothe, 1911), pp. 54–55; Durkin, ed, *Confederate Chaplain*, p. 96; John G. Young diary, July 15, 1864, North Carolina Department of History and Archives (NCHA); Overton Steger to friend, July 21, 1864, Lewis Leigh Collection, USAMHI; John W. Worsham, *One of Jackson's Foot Cavalry* (New York, 1912), pp. 243–244.

16. *ORA*, I, 37, pt. 1, p. 349; Park, "Diary," p. 381; Durkin, *Confederate Chaplain*, p. 96; Worsham, *Ibid.*, pp. 243–244; Archie P. MacDonald, editor, *Make Me A Map of the Valley* (Dallas, 1978), p. 216; W. R. Redding to Wife, July 18, 1864, Redding papers, SHC/UNC; Nichols, *A Soldier's Story*, p. 175.

17. Caleb Linker to Daniel Linker and family, July 17, 1864, CSA Archives, Miscellaneous Officer and Soldiers Letters, Perkins Library, Duke University (DU); Joseph McMurran diary, July 13, 14, 1864, Virginia State Library (VSL); Pfohl quoted in Laura Virginia Hale, *Four Valient Years in the Shenandoah Valley* (Strasburg, Va., 1968), p. 387.

18. *ORA*, I, 37, pt. 1, p. 349; Stephen Ramseur to wife, July 15, 1864, SHC/UNC; on southern news coverage, see J. Cutler Andrews, *The South Reports the Civil War* (Princeton:

Princeton University Press, 1970), pp. 408–409; Zebulon York, report, July 22, 1864, John Page Nicholsen Collection, Huntington Library (HL), San Marino, California.

19. *ORA*, I, 37, pt. 1, p. 346.

20. *ORA*, I, 37, pt. 2, pp. 329–332.

21. Simon, *Grant Papers*, v. 11, pp. 353–354.

22. Aldace F. Walker to father, July 17, 1864, Vt. HS.

23. George E. Pond, *The Shenandoah Valley in 1864* (New York, 1883), pp. 79–81; *ORA*, I, 37, pt. 1, pp. 267–268, 319; pt. 2, pp. 343, 350–351; Aldace F. Walker to father July 17, 1864, Vt. HS.

24. Robert Smith Rodgers, manuscript history of Second Eastern Shore Regiment, Maryland Infantry, unpublished manuscript, DU, p. 5; MacDonald, *Make Me a Map*, p. 216; Samuel Clarke Farrar, *Twenty-Second Pennsylvania Cavalry* (Pittsburgh, 1911), pp. 275–277; Worsham, *One of Jackson's Foot Cavalry*, pp. 243–244; Richard W. Waldrop, diary, July 15, 16, 1864, SHC/UNC; *ORA*, I, 37, pt. 1, pp. 268–269, 320, 337–341, 350–355; John H. Niebaum, *History of the Pittsburgh Washington Infantry* (Pittsburgh, 1931), p. 109; Frederick W. Weld, *Memoirs and History of Captain F.W. Alexander's Baltimore Battery* (Baltimore, 1912), p. 138; Harris N. Beecher, *Record of the One Hundred and Fourteenth New York* (Norwich, NY, 1866), p. 382; John B. Southard to sister, July 16, 1864, New York Historical Society (NYHS).

25. Leonidus L. Polk to wife, July 17, 1864, Polk papers; George Whitaker Wills to sister, July 17, 1864, Wills papers; William Beavans diary, July 16, 1864, Beavans papers; John Parris, diary, July 16, 1864, all SHC/UNC; John G. Young diary, July 16, entry, NCHA; Rufus Woolwine diary, July 16, 1864, VHS; Nichols, *A Soldier's Story*, p. 177; Richard Iobst, *Bloody Sixth: Sixth North Carolina Regiment* (Gaithersburg, 1987), p. 219; Robert Park, "Diary," p. 381.

26. Jeffrey Wert, "The Snicker's Gap War," *Civil War Times Illustrated*, XVII (July 1978), p. 38; Pond, *Shenandoah Valley*, p. 82.

27. *ORA*, I, 37, pt. 2, pp. 328–329, 350.

28. *Ibid.*, pt. 2, pp. 316, 373–374, 400.

29. For a sympathetic portrait of Halleck, see Stephen E. Ambrose, *Halleck: Lincoln's Chief of Staff* (Baton Rouge, 1962), pp. 176–177.

30. *Ibid.*, pp. 384-385.

31. *Ibid.*; see also, Cooling, *Symbol, Sword, and Shield*, chapter 5.

32. *ORA*, I, 37, pt. 2, pp. 408, 412-414; Ulysses S. Grant, *Personal Memoirs* (New York, 1885), II, p. 317.

33. Beavens diary, July 17, 1864, SHC/UNC; Hale, *Four Valient Years*, pp. 382-384; MacDonald, *Make Me a Map*, p. 216.

34. The most thorough study of the Castleman's Ferry fight is the little known study by Peter J. Meany, O.S.B., *The Civil War Engagement at Cool Spring*, July 18, 1864 (Berryville, 1980), chapters 4-8; also Aldace Walker to father, July 19, 1864, Vt. HS; William H. Beech, *The First New York (Lincoln) Cavalry* (New York, 1902), p. 389; Pond, *Shenandoah Valley*, 1864, pp. 82-83; Wert, "Snicker's Gap," p. 39; *ORA*, I, 37, pt. 1, pp. 269, 290-292, 320-321; James M. Gasper diary, July 17, 1864, Civil War Misc. Collec. USAMHI; J. Newton Terrill, *History of the Fourteenth New Jersey* (New Brunswick, 1884), pp. 78-79.

35. *ORA*, I, 37, pt. 1, pp. 287, 291; 43, pt. 1, pp. 603-604.

36. Meaney, *Engagement at Cool Spring*, pp. 43, 54, 55-57; Leonidus Polk to wife, July 22, 1864, SHC/UNC; Rev. James B. Sheeran, "War Journal," pp. 1229-1230, copy, USAMHI; Wert, *Ibid.* pp. 39-40; Pond, *Shenandoah Valley*, 1864, pp. 82-84; *ORA*, I, 37, pt. 1, pp. 292-294, 320-321; Union accounts of the fight include Augustus Woodbury, *History of Second Rhode Island* (Providence, 1875), pp. 287-288; Terrill, *Fourteenth New Jersey*, pp. 78-79; Roe, *History of the Ninth New York Heavy Artillery* (Worchester, 1899), p. 137; Lemuel A. Abbott, *Personal Recollections and Civil War Diary, 1864* (Burlington, 1908), pp. 124-125; Rodgers, "History of Second

Eastern Shore Regiment Maryland Infantry," pp. 5, 6, (DU); Confederate impressions include; Mac Donald, *Make Me A Map*, p. 216; Park "Diary," pp. 381-382; E.A. Osborne, "Fourteenth North Carolina," in Walter E. Clark, ed, *Histories of Several Regiments and Battalions from North Carolina in the Great War* (Raleigh, 1901), I, pp. 259-261; Manly Wade Wellman, *Rebel Boast* (New York, 1956), pp. 175-178; Beavens diary, July 18, 1864; John Paris diary, July 18, 1864, SHC/UNC; Young diary, July 18, 19, 1864 NCHA both; and McMurran diary, July 18, 19, 1864, (VSL); E.N. Atkinson, Report of Evans Brigade, July 22, 1864, Eldridge Collection (HL).

37. *ORA*, I, 37, pt. 1, pp. 269, 287; Wert, "Snicker's Gap War," p. 40; Meaney, *Engagement at Cool Spring*, chapter 9.

38. Elias P. Pillet, *History of the One Hundred and Fourteenth New York* (Norwich, 1866), pp. 247-248; Shaw, Diary, p. 50; Mason Whiting Tyler, *Recollections* (New York, 1912), p. 249; Perkins, *A Summer in Maryland and Virginia*, pp. 25-26; Terrill, *Fourteenth Regiment New Jersey*, p. 79; Beecher, *One Hundred and Fourteenth Regiment New York*, pp. 382-383; Haines, *Fifteenth Regiment New Jersey*, p. 229.

39. Clack to cousin Carrie, July 28, 1864, Clack papers; Ramseur-Ellen, July 23, (2), August 1, 3, 10, 15, 28, 29, 30, 31, and Ramseur to brother, August 20, all 1864, all Ramseur papers; both SCH/UNC; also Gary W. Gallaher, *Stephen Dodson Ramseur* (Chapel Hill, 1985), p. 133; Pond, *Shenandoah Valley*, 1864, pp. 86-88; MacDonald to Hotchiss, *Make Me A Map*, p. 217.

40. *ORA*, I, 37, pt. 1, p. 269; Vaill, *Second Connecticut Heavy Artillery*, pp. 85-86.

41. Aldace F. Walker to father [n.d. circa July 19-26, 1864], Vt. HS; Deborah Hamblin, comp. *Brevet Major General Joseph Eldridge Hamblin* (Boston, 1902), p. 39; Anson Shuey to wife, July 24, 1864, Shuey papers, CW Misc. Collection, also James M. Gasper diary, entries July 16-24, 1864, both USAMHI; Abbott, *Personal Recollections*, pp. 124-126; Haines, *Fifteenth New Jersey*, pp. 232-233; Survivors Association, *History of the Twenty-Third Regiment (Pa.)*, (Philadelphia, 1903), p. 162; Beecher, *One Hundred and Fourteenth New York*, pp. 384-387; Roe, *Ninth New York Heavy Artillery*, pp. 137-138; Perkins, *A Summer in Maryland and Virginia*, p. 26; Tyler, *Recollections*, pp. 249-252; Shaw, Diary, pp. 49-51; George Carpenter, *History of the Eighth Vermont* (Boston, 1886), pp. 158-159.

Chapter 8

1. US War Department, *War of the Rebellion; A Compilation of the Official Records of the Union and Confederate Armies* (Washington, 1880–1901), series I, volume 37, part 2, pp. 408–409, (hereinafter cited *ORA*); John Y. Simon, editor, *The Papers of Ulysses S. Grant* (Carbondale and Edwardsville, 1967–), v 11, p. 300.

2. P. J. Staudenraus, *Mr. Lincoln's Washington; Diary of Noah Brooks* (South Brunswick, 1967), p. 360; Mary Mitchell, *Divided Town* (Barre, Mass., 1968), pp. 161–163; Gideon Welles, *Diary* (Boston, 1911), II, p. 77; L. E. Chittenden, *Recollections of President Lincoln and His Administration* (New York, 1891), p. 421; Fred Smith, *Samuel Duncan Oliphant; the Indomitable Campaigner* (New York, 1967), pp. 163–167; George R. Kimball to I. B. Upham, August 10, 1864, U.S. Army Military History Institute, Carlisle Barracks, Pa. (USAMHI).

3. *Army-Navy Journal*, v. 1, July 1, 1864; London *Times*, July 25, 1864; Samuel P. Heintzelman journal, entry July 13, 1864, Library of Congress, Washington DC (LC); *ORA*, I, 37, pt. 2, pp. 260– 261; Gideon Welles, *Diary* (Boston, 1911), II, p. 80; Howard K. Beale, editor, *The Diary of Edward Bates* (Washington, 1930), p. 384.

4. Transcript of letters regarding Baughman and Ebert familes; Order of Arrest and Release, Isaac Reich and family, 1864; Harriet Pettet Floyd, "Civil War Memoirs," n.d., typescript;

Robert Cornwell to wife, August 3, 1864; Edward S. Delaplaine collection, all Frederick County, Maryland Historical Society (FCHS); William R. Quinn, editor, *The Diary of Jacob Englebrecht* (Frederick, 1976), p. 276; Letters Thomas Gorsuch–Robert Gorsuch, July 19, 1864, Elihu Rockwell–Mrs. E. R. Coleman, July 25, 1864, copies, Maryland Historical Society, Baltimore (MHS); J. Thomas Scharf, *History of Western Maryland* (Pittsburgh, 1882), pp. 295–296.

5. Bayly Ellen Marks and Mark Norton Schatz, editors, *Between North and South: A Maryland Journalist Views the Civil War; The Narrative of William Wilkins Glenn 1861–1869* (Rutherford, N.J. 1976), p. 138; Abner Hard, *History of the Eighth Illinois Cavalry* (Aurora, Ill., 1868), pp. 301–302; Silas D. Wesson diary, July 12, 1864, USAMHI; Scharf, *History of Baltimore City and County* (Philadelphia, 1881), p. 148.

6. James I. Robertson, *The Stonewall Brigade* (Baton Rouge, 1963), p. 233; John O. Cassler, *Four Years in the Stonewall Brigade* (Girard, KS., 1906), pp. 226–229; J. E. Green diary, entries July 18–31, 1864, and Reverend William Gwaltney diary, entries July 22–31, 1864, both Southern Historical Collection, University of North Carolina, Chapel Hills (SHC/UNC); George H. Lester, "War Record of the Tom Cobb Infantry," in United Daughters of the Confederacy, Georgia Division, *This They Remembered* (Washington, Ga., 1965), p. 106; Richard Colbert to Mrs. E. M. Potts, July 24, 1864, Folder 57, North Louisiana Historical Association Archives, Centenary College, Shreveport (NLHA).

7. Douglas Southall Freeman, *R. E. Lee: A Biography* (New York, 1935), pp. 460–461; Jeffrey D. Wert, *From Winchester to Cedar Creek: The Shenandoah Campaign of 1864* (Carlisle, Pa., 1987), p. 9; Stephen D. Ramseur to wife, July 23, 1864 SHC/UNC; Abner Pickering, "Early Raid in 1864, Including the Battle of the Monocacy," unpublished student paper, 39, *US Army War College*, Session 1913–14, Army War College Curricular files, USAMHI.

8. Eugene L. Blackford to mother, July 27, 1864, Lewis Leigh collection, book 33, USAMHI; R. H. Early, *Lieutenant General Jubal Anderson Early CSA* (Philadelphia, 1912), pp. 396–400; *ORA*, I, 37, pt. 1, pp. 290–319, 327–329; pt. 2, p. 423; John Worsham, *One of Jackson's Foot Cavalry* (New York, 1912), chapter XXIX; Archie P. MacDonald, *Make Me A Map of the Valley, The Civil War Journal of Stonewall Jackson's Topographer* (Dallas, 1973), p. 218; and William H. Beech, *The First New York (Lincoln) Cavalry* (New York, 1902), chapter XXXVII; G. W. Nichols, *A Soldiers Story of His Regiment* (Jessup, Ga., 1898), p. 176.

9. Walker quoted in Richard Iobst, *Bloody Sixth; The Sixth North Carolina RFegiment* (Gaithersburg, 1987), p. 221; also John Young diary, entry July 24, 1864, North Carolina Department of History and Archives (NCHA); Worsham, *One of Jackson's Foot Cavalry*, pp. 158–160; Leonidus Lafayette Polk to wife, July 25, 1864, SHC/UNC; T. E. Morrow to father, August 2, 1864, author's collection; Blackford, *Ibid;* and Robert E. Park, "Diary," *Southern Historical Society Papers*, I (1876), p. 384.

10. MacDonald, *Make Me A Map*, pp. 218–219; W. W. Scott, editor, "Diary of H. W. Wingfield," *Bulletin of Virginia State Library*, XVI (July 192–), p. 43; James McMurran diary, entry July 25, 1864, Virginia State Library (VSL); Young diary, entry July 25, 1864, NCHA; Morrow to father, *Ibid;* Colbert to Potts, July 27, 1864, NLHA; Monier journal, July 25 to August 1, 1864, in Napier Bartlett, *Military Record of Louisiana* (Baton Rouge, 1964 reprint); Nichols, *A Soldiers Story*, pp. 176–197; Park, "Diary," pp. 384–385; David Seibert to father, July 22, 1864, Siebert family papers, Harrisburg Civil War Round Table Collection, (CWRT) USAMHI; *ORA*, I, 37, pt. 1, p. 286; pt. 2, p. 423.

11. Anson B. Shuey to wife, August 1, 1864, Civil War Miscellaneous collection, USAMHI; Aldace F. Walker to father, July 26, 28, 29, 1864, typescript copies, Vermont Historical Society, Montpelier (Vt.HS).

12. G. G. Benedict, *Vermont in the Civil War* (Burlington, 1888), I, pp. 494–495; Emil Rosenblatt, *Anti-Rebel; The Civil War Letters of Wilbur Fisk* (Croton-on-Hudson, 1983), pp. 245–246; Walker to father, July 29, 1864, Vt. HS; George W. Carpenter, *History of the Eighth*

Vermont Volunteers (Boston, 1886), p. 159; John H. Niebaum, *History of the Pittsburgh Washington Infantry, One Hundred and Second Pennsylvania* (Pittsburgh, 1931), p. 109; Augusta Woodbury, *The Second Rhode Island* (Providence, 1875), pp. 289–290; J. Newton Terrill, *Campaigns of the Fourteenth New Jersey* (New Brunswick, 1884), pp. 80–81; Alanson A. Haines, *History of the Fifteenth New Jersey* (New York, 1883), pp. 234–237; Alfred Seelye Roe, *History of the Ninth New York Heavy Artillery* (Worchester, 1899), pp. 139–140; Frederick W. Wild, *Memoirs and History of Captain F. W. Alexander's Baltimore Battery* (Baltimore, 1912), pp. 150–154; Edwin M. Haynes, *History of the Tenth Vermont* (Rutland, 1894), pp. 233–234; Lemuel A. Abbott, *Personal Recollections* (Burlington, 1908), pp. 128–129; William H. Shaw, *Diary* (n.p., n.d.), pp. 51–52; Mason W. Tyler, *Recollections* (New York, 1912), pp. 255–259; James Gasper diary, entries July 26–August 1, 1864 and Jacob Seibert to parents, August 1, 1864, both USAMHI; also Cowan, "Pursuit of Early," *The National Tribune*, September 23, 1915.

13. Millard Bushong, *Old Jube* (Boyce, Va., 1955), p. 227; Beach, *First New York Cavalry*, p. 404; Elias P. Pellet, *History of the One Hundred and Fourteenth New York* (Norwich, 1866), pp. 250–251; Abner Hard, *History of the Eight Regiment, Illinois Volunteers* (Aurora, Ill., 1868), p. 307.

14. J. Thomas Scharf, *History of Western Maryland* (Baltimore, 1882), I, pp. 295–296.

15. Bushong, *Old Jube*, chapter 22 discusses this business in some detail; see also *ORA*, I, 37, pt. 2, pp. 366, 374–375; also see Beach, *First New York Cavalry*, pp. 393–395.

16. For the most recent work on the burning of Chambersburg, see Theodore Alexander et al., editors, *Southern Revenge: Civil War History of Chambersburg, Pa.* (Shippensburg, Pa., 1989) ch. 6; *ORA*, I, 37, pt. 1, pp. 129–132, 286, 292–298, 301–302, 322–324, 327–328, also 43, pt. 1, pp. 2–8, 764; Moses Gipson, "Valley Campaign of General Early," Richmond *Times-Dispatch*, August 26, 1906, as printed in *Southern Historical Society Papers*, 34 (1906), p. 214; Harry Gilmor, *Four Years in the Saddle* (New York, 1866), pp. 205–212; Beach, *First New York Cavalry*, chapter XXXVIII; Jubal Early to Edmund Jennings Lee, September 26, 1872, Perkins Library, Duke University (DU); George E. Pond, *The Shenandoah Valley in 1864* (New York, 1883), pp. 96–100.

17. Thomas E. Lewis et al. *The Shenandoah in Flames* (Alexandria, 1977), pp. 91–99; also George Wilson Booth, *Personal Reminiscences of a Maryland Soldier* (Baltimore, 1907), pp. 109–112.

18. *ORA*, I, 37, pt. 1, pp. 330–331; 43, pt. 1, pp. 2–8, 84, 505–506, 551, 734, 994; W.W. Goldsborough, *The Maryland Line in the Confederate Army 1861–1865* (Baltimore, 1900), chapter IX, especially pp. 210–211.

19. Blackford to mother, August 23, 1864, Lewis Leigh collection, Box 33, USAMHI; Edward Bok, *The Americanization of Edward Bok* (New York, 1920), p. 209; A.S. Pendleton to brother, August 8, 1864, Pendleton papers, SHC/UNC; Rebecca Davis journal, entry August 6, 1864, while on Early's Williamsport interview see unidentified clipping, Carey scrapbook, both MHS; J. Thomas Scharf, *History of Baltimore City and County* (Philadelphia, 1881), p. 148.

20. *ORA*, I, 37, pt. 2, pp. 433–434, also 427.

21. *ORA*, I, pt. 2, pp. 444–447, 458–459, 463.

22. *ORA*, I, 43, pt. 1, p. 681; also 37, pt. 2, pp. 558, 559, 573, 582–583; Bruce Catton, *Grant Takes Command* (Boston, 1968), pp. 336–343.

23. *ORA*, 1, 37, pt. 2, p. 582; 42, pt. 2, pp. 38, 48; pt. 1, p. 681; Simon, *Grant papers*, II, p. 379.

24. Robert Cornwall to wife, August 3, 4, 1864, typescript copies, Edward Delaplaine collection, Frederick County Historical Society (FCHS); Walker to father, August 2, 1864, Vt.HS.

25. The critical communiques of this time period may be found nicely concentrated in Simon, *Grant papers*, 11, pp. 376–383.

26. David Seibert-father, August 7, 1864, Seibert family papers, Harrisburg CWRT Collection; USAMHI; Ulysses S. Grant, *Personal Memoirs* (New York, 1886), 11, pp. 319–320; Glen H. Worthington, *Fighting For Time* (Frederick, 1932), pp. 205–207.

Chapter 9

1. Coverage of Sheridan and Early in the valley should be studied in Jeffrey D. Wert, *From Winchester to Cedar Creek: The Shenandoah Campaign of 1864* (Carlisle, 1987); Thomas A. Lewis, *The Shenandoah in Flames, The Valley Campaign of 1864* (Alexandria, 1987); Edward J. Stackpole, *Sheridan in the Shenandoah; Jubal Early's Nemisis* (Harrisburg, 1961), and George E. Pond, *The Shenandoah Valley in 1864* (New York, 1883). While the latest scholarship on Lincoln's reelection is reflected in James M. McPherson, *Battle Cry of Freedom; The Civil War Era* (New York, 1988).

2. On the Washington campaign losses, see Gordon's report, July 22, 1864, Nicholson collection, and Breckinridge's fieled returns, July 15, 1864, Eldridge collection, Huntington Library (HL), San Marino, Calif.

3. Clifford Dowdey and Louis H. Manarin, editors, *The War Time Papers of R. E. Lee* (Boston, 1961), pp. 832–835, 845–850, 852–853; U.S. War Department, *War of the Rebellion: A Compilation of the Official Records of the Union and Confederate Armies* (Washington, 1880–1901), series I, volume 37, pt. 2, p. 599, hereinafter cited *ORA*.

4. Grant and Sheridan's role can be followed best in John Y. Simon, *The Papers of Ulysses S. Grant* (Carbondale and Edwardsville, 1967–), vols. 12 and 13 inter alia.

5. Benjamin Franklin Cooling, *Symbol, Sword and Shield; Defending Washington during the Civil War* (Hamden, Ct., 1975), pp. 217–232; J. Howard Kitching, "More than Conqueror, or Memorials of . . ." (New York, 1874); Kimball papers, U.S. Army Military History Institute, Carlisle Barracks, Pa. (USAMHI); J. Willard Brown, *The Signal Corps, USA* (Boston, 1896), p. 664; William J. Gleason, *Historical Sketch of the One Hundred Fiftieth Regiment Ohio Volunteer Infantry* (Rocky River, Ohio, 1899), p. 16.

6. W. H. Farquhar, *Annals of Sandy Spring or Twenty Years of a Rural County in Maryland* (Baltimore, 1884), pp. I, 14; A.G. Thomas to brother, October 10, 1864, Maryland Historical Society (MHS); unidentified clipping, "Guerrillas Plagued Sand Spring in Late Days of Civil War," August 25, 1960, Montgomery County Historical Society (MCHS).

7. Ezra Warner, *Generals in Gray* (Baton Rouge, 1959), pp. 34–35, 79–80.

8. William C. Davis, *Breckinridge, Statesman, Soldier, Symbol* (Baton Rouge, 1974), pp. 530, 543, 548; Indictments United States vs. Jefferson Davis, United States vs. John C. Breckinridge, District of Columbia Supreme Court, May 26, 1865, both Virginia Historical Society (VHS).

9. Warner, *Generals in Gray*, pp. 80, 83, 111–112, 130, 156–157, 287–288, 302, 331, 347–348; representative reminiscences can be found listed in the bibliography at the end of this work.

10. Warner, *Generals in Blue* (Baton Rouge, 1964), pp. 12–13, 19–20, 176–177, 195–197, 205–206, 294–295, 308–319, 403–404, 447–448, 535–536, 545–546, 575–576; *Generals in Gray*, pp. 197–198; representative reminiscences may be found listed in the bibliography at the end of this work.

11. Jubal A. Early, *A Memoir of the Last Year of the War for Independence* (Lynchburg: C.W. Button, 1867), p. 395, fn.; John G. Barnard, *A Report on the Defenses of Washington* (Washington, 1871), p. 119.

12. Letter, Early to Editor, Lynchburg *Republican*, December 14, 1874, in Richmond *Sentinel*, June 1875, copy, Defending Washington files, Fort Ward Museum and Historic Site (FWMHS) Alexandria, Va.

13. Compare Early, "The Advance on Washington in 1864," *Southern Historical Society*

Papers, 9 (July, August, 1881), pp. 297–312, with Barnard, Defenses of Washington, Appendix A, especially pp. 119–121.

14. John W. Daniel, "General Jubal A. Early," Richmond Va. *Dispatch*, December 14, 1894, in *Southern Historical Society Papers*, XXII (1894), p. 300; Henry Kyd Douglas, *I Rode With Stonewall* (Chapel Hill, 1940), p. 297.

15. John B. Gordon, *Reminiscences of the Civil War* (New York, 1904), pp. 314–319.

16. Alexander Hunter, *Johnny Reb and Billy Yank* (New York and Washington, 1905), pp. 649–652; John N. Opie, *A Rebel Cavalryman with Lee, Stuart, and Jackson* (Chicago, 1899), p. 247.

17. George Wilson Booth, *Personal Reminiscences of a Maryland Soldier* (Baltimore, 1907), pp. 126–128.

18. Lew Wallace, *Autobiography* (New York, 1906), II, pp. 809–811; Ulysses S. Grant, *Personal Memoirs* (New York, 1885), II, pp. 304–306.

19. Warner, *Generals in Blue*; Horace D. Porter, *Campaigning with Grant* (New York, 1906), pp. 235–240.

20. Examples of veteran comments in *The National Tribune* include those of S. A. McDonald, April 12, 19, 1894; Rufus R. Lord, February 22, 1900; R. Guyton, March 29, 1900; J. Fred Loeble, April 26, 1900; J. G. Bridaham, July 19, 1900; A. F. Jackson, August 9, 1900; Charles Porter, September 27, 1900; A. G. Jacobs, August 23, 1900; John H. Wolff, September 27, 1900; also Gleason, *Historical Sketch of the One Hundred and Fiftieth Regiment*, p. 17; and Russell F. Weigley, *Quartermaster General of the Union Army* (New York, 1959), p. 302.

21. See Benjamin Franklin Cooling and Walton B. Owen, *Mr. Lincoln's Forts; A Guide to the Civil War Defenses of Washington* (Shippenburg, Pa., 1988), pp. 164–167, and accompanying research files FWMHS; Frederick *News*, July 9, 1907, November 24, 1908; "Battle of Monocacy," vertical file, Frederick County Historical Society (FCHS); Mildred Newbold Getty, *Grace Episcopal Church, 1857–1957* (Silver Spring, 1957), p. 7.

22. Stuart Abramowitz, "The History of Silver Spring," unpublished paper, n.d.; Montgomery *Journal*, October 21, 1983; Washington Post, May 29, 1955; Maryland *News*, May 27, 1955; Maryland National Capital Park and Planning Commission, "Silver Spring-Sligo Creek Historical Trail," all in files MCHS. Also John Claggett Proctor, "Preservation of Historic Fort Stevens," *Washington Sunday Star*, July 8, 1945; Blair Lee, "The Day Confederates Marched into Montgomery County History," *The Montgomery Sentinel*, June 28, 1989.

23. Judith Beck Helm, *Tenleytown, D.C.; Country Village into City Neighborhood* (Washington, 1981), chapter IV; and George Alred Townsend, *Washington, Outside and Inside* (Hartford, 1873), p. 640.

24. Helm, *Ibid.*, pp. 37–245; Cooling and Walton, *Mr. Lincoln's Forts*, pp. 130–173 in order to visit the area today; and Claudia Levy, "Capitol View Park: A Step Back in Time," Washington *Post*, May 13, 1989.

25. District of Columbia National Guard, Engineer Platoon of the Engineer Corps., *Guide to and Maps of the National Capital and Vicinity, Including the Fortifications* (Washington, 1892), pp. 20–22.

26. U.S. Congress, 57th, 1st Session, Senate Document 433, Fort Stevens Lincoln National Military Park (Washington, 1902), p. 2; District of Columbia Civil War Centennial Commission, Commemorative Ceremony Program One Hundredth Anniversary of the Battle of Fort Stevens, July 11, 1864; J. C. McFerran to M. C. Meigs, March 17, 1870 relating to title, Battleground Cemetery and Accompanying Correspondence, Rock Creek Nature Center, National Park Service, Washington, D.C. (RCNC).

27. Sen. Doc. 433, *Ibid.*, pp. 10–12.

28. Washington *Times*, June 26, 1904; John Claggett Proctor, "Preservation of Historic Fort Stevens," Washington Sunday *Star*, July 8, 1945; other miscellaneous clippings, Fort Stevens files, RCNC.

29. DC Civil War Commission, *Fort Stevens Program*, n.p. 1964; Lewis Cass White, "Fort Stevens and the Lincoln Boulder," in John H. Niebaum, *History of the Pittsburgh Washington Infantry, One Hundred and Second (Old Thirteenth Regiment), Pennsylvania Veteran Volunteeers* (Pittsburgh, 1931), p. 115; Lewis Cass White, "President Lincoln at Fort Stevens," *The National Tribune*, March 6, 1913.

30. DC Civil War Commission, Fort Stevens Program, *Ibid.*; Cooling and Owen, *Mr. Lincoln's Forts*, p. 161.

31. Washington *Star*, February 26, 1925.

32. Washington *Star*, May 16, 1925, October 29, 1927, January 15, 1924; Bernard Kohn, "Restored Civil War Fort Is New Sightseeing Shrine," Washington *Sunday Star*, July 4, 1937; Federal Writers Project, Works Progress Administration, *Washington City and Capital*, (Washington, 1937), pp. 593–594; land acquisition information supplied by Gary Scott, National Capital Parks, NPS, Washington, D.C.

33. Collection of Memorial Day programs, miscellaneous clippings and notes, Fort Stevens file, Defenses of Washington collection, FWMHS; Washington *Star*, December 22, 1912; Washington *Post*, July 5, 1964.

34. "Memorial Park on Monocacy Battlefield," *Confederate Veteran*, XXXVI (February 1928), p. 44.

35. U.S. 70th Congress, 1st Session, House of Representatives, Committee on Military Affairs, *Hearings—National Military Park at Battlefield of Monocacy, Maryland, April 13, 1928* (Washington, 1928), pp. 1–3, 6–14.

36. Miscellaneous clippings and data sheets, Monocacy vertical files, FCHS; Fact Sheets and Visitor Brochures, Monocacy National Battlefield, Monocacy file, Defenses of Washington collection, FWMHS.

37. John B. Southard to sister, July 16, 1864, NYHS.

38. Robert Engelman, "Fellowship of the Rings," The Washington *Post*, June 25, 1989; Edward C. Smith, "When the Confederates Came to the Capital," Washington *Post*, July 9, 1989.

39. Frank Wilkeson, *Recollections of a Private Soldier* (New York, 1898), p. 219; Comrade Peterson, "Fort Stevens," *The National Tribune*, December 2, 1915.

Index